CHINA WATCHER

RICHARD BAUM

CHINA WATCHER

CONFESSIONS *of a* PEKING TOM

A Samuel and Althea Stroum Book

UNIVERSITY OF WASHINGTON PRESS
Seattle & London

*This book is published with the assistance of a grant from
the Samuel and Althea Stroum Endowed Book Fund.*

© 2010 by the University of Washington Press
First paperback edition © 2014 by the University of Washington Press
Printed in the United States of America
Design by Thomas Eykemans
18 17 16 15 14   5 4 3 2 1

UNIVERSITY OF WASHINGTON PRESS
PO Box 50096, Seattle, WA 98145, USA
www.washington.edu/uwpress

LIBRARY OF CONGRESS CATALOGING-IN-PUBLICATION DATA
Baum, Richard, 1940-
China watcher : confessions of a Peking Tom / Richard Baum.
p. cm.
Includes bibliographical references and index.
ISBN 978-0-295-99253-2 (pbk : alk. paper)
1. Baum, Richard, 1940- 2. Sinologists—United States—Biography.
3. College teachers—United States—Biography. 4. China—History—1949-
5. China—Politics and government—1949- I. Title.
DS734.9.B38A3 2010
951.05092—dc22
[B]
2009035336

Unless otherwise noted, all photographs are by Richard Baum.

For my mentors

Robert A. Scalapino

Chalmers Johnson

and

in memoriam

H. Arthur Steiner

Contents

Foreword

THAT THE U.S.-CHINA relationship is the most important of the twenty-first century has become a truism—likewise that the rise of China is, for us, both a challenge and an opportunity. But few understand that the way to deal with the challenge is to take full advantage of the opportunity. Richard Baum's fascinating and refreshingly honest account of his forty years of China watching offers readers in both countries a key ingredient for resolving this riddle: information and insight about the other side.

For Americans, this shows how an experienced, highly trained specialist sees Chinese realities—but in a personal, rather than an academic, mode. For Chinese, it is a candid display, told with goodwill, of how an American China watcher of integrity views their country. Some of Professor Baum's views on China are quite different from my own, but I firmly believe that Americans and Chinese alike should read his book.

China watchers are a unique breed. Fifty years ago, when I was an "insider" in Beijing, I considered their writings on China to be hopelessly superficial and even ludicrous. I had access to classified information—what did they know?

It soon turned out, however, that while I knew the trees better than they did, they knew the forest. They were right about some of the large issues that I, on the inside, couldn't see. Of course, when I say "they," I am referring to serious, unbiased China scholars like the author of this book, not to professional China bashers. Americans who wish to get an accurate, workable understanding of China need to refer to American China scholars as well as to authoritative information from China itself. Arrogant nationalism (often masquerading as patriotism) or simplistic China bashing based on political or ideological agendas can lead us into a swamp of misunderstanding and counterproductive behavior.

I heartily commend Professor Baum's book to thoughtful readers on both sides of the Pacific—or, for that matter, throughout all the Seven Seas.

SIDNEY RITTENBERG
Member, Chinese Communist Party, 1946–78
Author, *The Man Who Stayed Behind*

Preface

SINCE FIRST PEERING into the Chinese looking glass from a Hong Kong hilltop in 1968, during the tumultuous Cultural Revolution, I have spent my academic career puzzling over the ever-changing political landscape of contemporary China. Over that forty-year span I have witnessed the death throes of radical Maoism, the birth contractions of the post-Mao reform era, the emotional upheavals of the Tiananmen Square student demonstrations (and subsequent bloody repression), and the rise—some say peaceful, some not—of a globalized, marketized Chinese economic powerhouse. In an effort to make sense of these momentous changes, I have written several books and made more than three dozen trips to China, traveling to twenty-three of its twenty-seven provinces, lecturing at fourteen of its universities, and speaking with thousands of Chinese people, from senior Politburo leaders to ordinary peasants and workers.

Having been deeply immersed in the study of Chinese politics for such a long time, my reactions to what I have seen and heard have been complex, varied, and sometimes quite intense. By inclination neither a credulous "panda hugger" nor a cynical China basher, I have at times been deeply moved and inspired by what I have witnessed in China; at other times I have been just as deeply dismayed and appalled.

Throughout my career I have struggled to maintain a certain professional distance and detachment from my object of study. Keeping China at arm's length has not been easy. Objectivity is an elusive grail, and facts do not always—or often—speak for themselves. Events like the Cultural Revolution and the Tiananmen massacre strain one's capacity for dispassionate analysis. Personal sentiments and emotions seep in unannounced, subjectively skewing and coloring one's perceptions.

In writing this book, focusing on China's convoluted journey from Maoism to modernity, I have discarded my customary impersonal, scholarly mode of presentation. Gathering together a wide variety of previously undisclosed personal experiences, observations, impressions, and anecdotes, I have endeavored to weave these into an accessible, user-friendly guide to China's post-Mao development. This is China up close and personal, a record of one man's intellectual and emotional odyssey—including a fair number of embarrassing missteps—through the ever-changing, ever-fascinating landscape of a renascent, reinvented Middle Kingdom.

The book is written largely, but not entirely, in the first-person singular. Its point of view shifts periodically from the perspective of the watcher to that of the watched—and back again. And there are only two solitary footnotes in its three hundred pages of text. Unable to shed completely the habits of a lifetime, however, I have appended at the end of the book a set of supplemental notes keyed to the narrative content of each individual chapter. The payoff for this dual sacrifice of clinical detachment and meticulous documentation is, I hope, a gain in the depth, texture, and spontaneity that come from authentic, unsanitized personal reflection and introspection, grounded in a lifetime of observation and experience.

MY INDEBTEDNESS TO colleagues and friends who contributed to shaping this enterprise—some consciously, some not—is enormous. First, to my University of California mentors, Robert A. Scalapino, Chalmers Johnson, and the late H. Arthur Steiner, I owe the inspiration that kindled a lifetime of fascination with Chinese politics. The idea for this particular book grew out of a suggestion by Barbara Pillsbury, who several years ago urged me to record some of my more amusing China-watching adventures. Once I started down that road, I found it hard to stop.

Most of the writing was done during a magical sabbatical year spent in the south of France, *dans l'ambiance enchantée de la Provence*, where I enjoyed the gracious hospitality of Alain and Josette Hontanx. Along the way, several people read portions of the manuscript, providing critical feedback, making timely corrections to my flawed memory of events that transpired long ago, and generally forcing me to write more lively, candid, and compelling prose. Among those who helped to improve the manuscript (though they bear no responsibility for its remaining flaws) are Jan

Berris, Roger Detels, John Dolfin, Irv Drasnin, Steve Fitzgerald, Bruce Gilley, Tom Gold, Merle Goldman, Harry Harding, Joyce Kallgren, Bob Kapp, Perry Link, Barbara Pillsbury, Sidney Rittenberg, Michael Ross, Dorothy Solinger, Kevin Stuart, Fred Teiwes, Anne Thurston, Marc Trachtenberg, Andy Walder, and Chaohua Wang.

My agent and literary maven Theron Raines forced me to trim and tuck—and on occasion slice away completely—pockets of bloated prose and extraneous anecdote. Lorri Hagman, executive editor at the University of Washington Press, lent her considerable talents to elevating the book's authorial tone and improving its narrative flow. Throughout the writing process my head cheerleader, life partner, and muse, Karin Joffe, provided nonstop encouragement and acute editorial feedback, embedded in a steady stream of electronic Post-It notes, gently demanding to know "Where's the beef?" and periodically admonishing me to "Cut the crap!" and "Lose the attitude!" Finally, my colleagues on Chinapol, the global electronic network of China scholars, journalists, and policy analysts, provided a continuous flow of information, insight, and opinion about the latest goings-on inside the Beijing Beltway and beyond. To all of you, my heartfelt thanks.

THERE IS A classical Chinese aphorism, oft quoted by Mao Zedong, that speaks disdainfully of those who, in their everyday lives, are content to "look at flowers from horseback" (*zouma kanhua*), reserving praise for those with the courage to "climb off the horse to see the flowers" (*chuma kanhua*). For much of my academic career I have remained safely on horseback. It is now time to dismount. The reader is cordially invited to join me.

CHINA WATCHER

1

The Occidental Tourist

FOR MORE THAN forty years China has been my drug of choice. From time to time there have been experimental forays into other stimulants, but China has always produced the most reliable high. When you find something that works, that doesn't lose its kick or require stronger doses over time, you stick with it.

As a Jewish American kid growing up in Los Angeles, I had no particular predisposition toward China or the Chinese. My parents were the offspring of Russian and Eastern European immigrants. Before graduating from high school, the closest I ever came to Chinese culture was Charlie Chan, Fu Manchu, and the egg rolls at Madame Wu's Cantonese Garden; the only pearls of ancient Oriental wisdom I encountered were the faux-Confucian platitudes embedded in said Madame Wu's fortune cookies.

After starting at the University of California, Los Angeles, in 1957, I floundered for a while as a pre-law major, taking some constitutional law classes and pitching for the freshman baseball team. In the middle of my sophomore year I realized that law was not for me and switched to political science. I also joined a campus fraternity, but I soon tired of the bloated, beery bravado of the "brothers" and dropped out after one year. By then, chronic bursitis in my left shoulder had put an end to my pitching aspirations. I tried playing first base for a while but just couldn't hit the curve ball. After batting only .167 in half a dozen intrasquad games, the baseball coach, Art Reichle, called me aside and told me I was being cut from the varsity. I was crushed.

For two years at UCLA my grades were mediocre—mostly Bs and Cs.

3

Like so many other students then and now, I was adrift, lacking motivation. But being cut from the baseball team helped focus my attention. At around the same time, the end of my sophomore year, I began dating my future wife, Carolyn Paller—a community college transfer student who carried an intimidating 4.0 grade point average. Her academic success stirred my competitive juices, and in my junior year I began studying in earnest. I took a couple of courses on international relations and found them to my liking. One of my professors, a gentle, grandfatherly Scotsman named Malbone Graham, took me under his wing. I began to blossom, and my grades showed distinct improvement.

But it was not until my senior year that I accidentally stumbled into the course that would ultimately change my life. With baseball practice no longer part of my daily regimen, I had a part-time job as a storeroom clerk at the UCLA Student Health Service. Because of my work schedule, I needed to find a Tuesday-Thursday afternoon class that would count toward my major in political science. As it happened, the only one offered that semester—the spring of 1961—was Poli. Sci. 159, "Government and Politics of China." Such are the banal roots of life-altering events that Chinese politics, far from being a calling, was in the first instance merely a scheduling convenience.

The professor, H. Arthur Steiner, was a crusty old geezer, a former Marine Corps colonel who had displayed no particular interest in China prior to being assigned to the U.S. liaison force that landed at Tianjin, in Northeast China, at the close of World War II. Professor Steiner was a real piece of work. Rigid and demanding, brooking no nonsense from students, he was the closest thing to a drill instructor I ever encountered. But he was a challenging teacher, and his stories about postwar China were fascinating. He definitely got my attention.

The first book we read in Steiner's class was *Red Star over China*, Edgar Snow's engrossing tale of the early years of the Communist revolution, including the first authorized biography of Mao Zedong and a blow-by-blow account of the Red Army's epic 1934–36 Long March. It was utterly captivating—a real-life adventure of derring-do, featuring Mao and his heroic band of Red Army guerrillas repeatedly outwitting and outmaneuvering Chinese Nationalist generalissimo Chiang Kai-shek and his much larger but inept anti-Communist forces.

When I told my father about *Red Star over China*, he was, to say the least, skeptical. A union shop steward in the Hollywood film industry, he was an intense, emotional man, with strong liberal political views and a rabid anti-Communist streak. During World War II his union had fought an attempted takeover by Stalinist agents, and he never outgrew his visceral disdain for anything "made in Moscow." When I tentatively suggested that the Chinese Communists were somehow *different*, he merely scoffed. Affecting the self-assured, dismissive manner of Gertrude Stein, he firmly proclaimed that "A Communist is a Communist is a Communist."

Thus rebuffed in my first full-blown Oedipal offensive, I retreated meekly, immersing myself in my studies. Professor Steiner next assigned us Benjamin Schwartz's compelling history of the Chinese Communist Party (CCP), *Chinese Communism and the Rise of Mao*, along with Harold Isaacs's eye-opening anti-Stalinist exposé, *The Tragedy of the Chinese Revolution*. The Chinese Communists really *were* different, it seemed. Mao had rejected Stalin's self-serving directives in the late 1920s and 1930s, thwarting the Soviet dictator's plans to turn China into a Soviet puppet state. My self-confidence began to grow.

Toward the middle of the semester we read John K. Fairbanks's classic account of chronic American misperceptions of the Chinese revolution, *The United States and China*, along with the as yet unpublished World War II dispatches of John Stewart Service, a career foreign service officer who, as a member of the U.S. government's "Dixie Mission," had liaised with Mao Zedong and Zhou Enlai at their wartime Yan'an headquarters in 1944. These readings portrayed a dynamic Chinese Communist movement possessed of high morale, outstanding military leadership, and the broad support of China's peasant masses.

The more I read, the clearer it seemed that the Chinese Communists had been welcomed as liberators by most of the populace. Mao had confiscated the property of the rapacious landlord-gentry class and distributed it to the impoverished peasants; his outmanned, under-equipped guerrilla forces had fought victoriously against both Chiang Kai-shek's corrupt Nationalists and the brutal Japanese invaders—architects, among other things, of the horrific Rape of Nanking. At this early point in my education I was still quite naïve, but I was definitely hooked. My arguments with my father now became a bit more heated—and a lot more evenly matched.

Then, in the last half of Steiner's course, my Oedipal struggle took a sudden turn. Reading about the new institutions and policies of the post-1949 Communist regime in China, I began to see that by the mid-1950s the CCP had begun implementing policies that, on balance, had done more harm than good. After distributing land to the peasants, the Maoists took it away again. At first, participation in collective farms was voluntary, but after 1955 it became compulsory. Resistance was met with disciplinary "struggle" and even imprisonment. By 1957 a large number of Chinese intellectuals, who at first had generally welcomed the Communist regime, turned against it. In the Hundred Flowers Movement they expressed their dissenting opinions on wall posters—only to suffer persecution as "rightists" in a subsequent rectification campaign. At that point in Steiner's course, a few weeks before the final exam, I stopped arguing quite so vehemently with my father. His general distrust of Communism seemed a bit more reasonable than before—though I continued to insist that Mao's brand of Communism was very different from Stalin's.

Then disaster overtook China. Mao launched his Great Leap Forward in 1958, and in the last few weeks of Steiner's class we pored over the available documents. Steiner would come into class each Tuesday and Thursday afternoon armed with stacks of mimeographed documents, hot off the ditto machine. I devoured them eagerly, searching for clues as to what had gone wrong with Mao's radical experiment in social engineering, and why. By the time the course ended, Steiner had dissected the rise and fall of the Chinese rural people's communes, cornerstones of Mao's utopian vision. The communes—with their ubiquitous backyard steel furnaces, free food distribution scheme, militarized labor organization, and unrealistic procurement quotas—proved to be a man-made calamity of the first magnitude.

Though we did not know it then, Mao's folly ultimately cost the lives of more than thirty million people. But the "Great Helmsman" was too stubborn to acknowledge error, and he purged those, like the outspoken army commander Peng Dehuai, who dared question his judgment. By 1959 the debacle could no longer be hidden, and Mao was forced to retreat from the front line of policy making. Thereafter, the Great Leap was quietly but effectively dismantled by two of Mao's more sensible and pragmatic lieutenants, Liu Shaoqi and Deng Xiaoping.

I found all this quite riveting. I couldn't possibly know it then, but over the next forty years I would spend an inordinate amount of time and energy pondering the impact of these three men—Mao, Liu, and Deng—on the course of modern Chinese history.

To prepare for Steiner's final exam, I pulled several consecutive all-nighters. Coffee, No-Doz, and the occasional Dexamyl upper fueled my orgy of concentrated study. I thoroughly reviewed all the books, articles, documents, and class notes from the course. By the day of the exam I was *primed*. Then the old coot threw me a curve. One of the two most heavily weighted essay questions on his final exam asked for an analysis of a mimeographed CCP document on the organization of the rural people's communes. I drew a complete blank. Somehow I had overlooked this one particular reading assignment. On the verge of panic, I did the only thing I could think of—bait and switch. I wrote a couple of brief paragraphs on the organization of the communes and then, without breaking stride, shifted my focus onto a different issue altogether—the collapse of the Great Leap Forward. Although it was off topic, it was a damned good essay. After the exam I went home and found the missing document, which had somehow gotten shoved under my bed. I waited nervously for the better part of a week to get the exam results, cursing my stupid oversight. When the postcard came in the mail, it contained a short, cryptic note in Steiner's hand: "Nice try!"

I got an A from Steiner—the most treasured grade of my entire college career—and it changed me. First of all, my struggle with my dad ended well. Though neither of us would concede error, he began listening to me more attentively, showing new, if grudging, respect for my opinions. Second, I became a very good student, pulling straight As in my senior year. Third, I made up my mind to go to graduate school. H. Arthur Steiner had lit a fire in my belly.

MAJORING IN POLITICAL science, I entered graduate school at the University of California, Berkeley, in the fall of 1962. My declared field of specialization was international relations (IR). It seemed like a reasonable choice for a kid who was hooked on world politics, and besides, Chinese politics was not a terribly practical career option—the more so since I was still, at that point, a complete stranger to the Chinese language.

It took me about two months to realize that I had made a big mistake. My first course in IR theory at Berkeley was taught by a visiting professor from Oberlin College. We read the "great books" on international politics, written by such eminent scholars as Hans Morgenthau, Ernst Haas, and Kenneth Waltz. By the end of the eighth week of the class I was totally depressed. The big debate in IR theory—over whether interests or ideologies were more important in shaping relations among nations—struck me as basically silly. Whole armies of theorists were arrayed on one side or the other of this epic battle, but I wanted no part of it. It seemed perfectly obvious to me then (and still does now) that both interests *and* ideologies matter, and that the two serve to shape, constrain, and define each other. Perhaps I was missing some of the subtler nuances in the debate, but I didn't care: IR was not for me. (I hasten to add that IR theorists are still fighting this same battle. Although their arguments and methodologies have become more complex and sophisticated in the intervening forty years, the essence of the debate remains unchanged.)

At the end of my first semester of graduate school I wrote to Arthur Steiner, telling him of my quandary and asking for advice. He suggested that I get in touch with a Berkeley political science professor, Robert A. Scalapino, and take a course from him if possible. Scalapino taught East Asian politics and foreign relations, and Steiner held him in high esteem.

My first classroom encounter with Bob Scalapino, though not as random as my initial encounter with Steiner, had an equally profound effect. From the outset, I responded positively to his rich understanding of East Asia, his nondogmatic style of teaching, and his consummate professionalism, both in and out of the classroom. Bob had very mixed feelings about China's emergence as a Communist power, but he never became emotional about the People's Republic of China (PRC), and when asked about the future of U.S.-China relations, he invariably replied that he was cautiously optimistic. Indeed, "cautious optimism" was Bob's signature mantra. I did quite well in his class, and he became my academic adviser as well as my mentor and role model. After finishing his course, I left the field of international relations for good and never looked back.

At the end of my first semester with Scalapino, he urged me to take a course with one of his young colleagues, Chalmers Johnson, who was just beginning his teaching career at Berkeley. I enrolled in Chal Johnson's first seminar on Chinese politics. It was a real eye-opener. A couple of weeks into the course, he was lecturing on the World War II Dixie Mission. About halfway through the lecture a tall, gaunt fellow in the back row, wearing wire-rimmed glasses and appearing quite a bit older than the rest of us, raised his hand. Eventually Johnson called on him. "With all due respect, sir," the man began politely, "there's a part of the story that's missing." Johnson, who did not take kindly to being contradicted by mere students, looked at him with a mixture of contempt and disbelief. "And just who might *you* be?" he demanded. "My name is Service, sir," came the soft-spoken response. A look of slow-dawning recognition crept over Johnson's face. He began to stammer. "Not . . . not *John Stewart* Service?"

he asked. "Yes sir," came the reply. For the first and only time in all the years I have known him, Chal was at a complete loss for words.

Jack Service's frank wartime assessment of debilitating Nationalist corruption and superior CCP leadership had landed him in deep trouble in the early 1950s, as hard-line anti-Communists in the U.S. Congress searched for scapegoats to explain the "loss" of China. For his candor as a member of the 1944 Dixie Mission, and for his postwar connections with the Institute of Pacific Relations, a liberal Wilsonian forum devoted to the analysis of East Asian affairs, Service was hounded out of the foreign service as a "Communist sympathizer" by Senator Joseph McCarthy and his supporters. Subsequently reinstated by order of the U.S. Supreme Court, he came to Berkeley in 1962 to pursue a master's degree in political science. Afterward, he stayed on as library curator and publications editor for the university's Center for Chinese Studies. There he generously shared with me and other graduate students his rich personal experiences and insights about China. Later he would play a small but pivotal role in helping to launch my professional career.

Throughout my Berkeley years, Bob Scalapino and Chal Johnson proved to be superb academic mentors. As different as night and day—Bob was soft-spoken, reflective, and diplomatic, while Chal was opinionated, bombastic, and blunt—they complemented each other nicely. Though our relationship would be tested at times by the severe political storms of the '60s, I benefited enormously from their guidance.

In the late 1950s Berkeley had established the Center for Chinese Studies, funded by a multiyear, million-dollar Ford Foundation grant that was intended to stimulate academic research on Chinese Communism. Happily for me, my fascination with China deepened just as the center began dispensing graduate fellowships. With the applicant pool relatively sparse (few graduate students were specializing in the study of Chinese Communism in those years), Bob and Chal urged me to apply. I survived the screening process, and for the next five years my tuition, fees, and basic living expenses were paid by the Ford Foundation and its administrative successor, the Foreign Area Fellowship Program. In exchange for my stipend I was expected to take a series of Chinese-language classes plus five hours a week of individual and small-group language tutorials.

FOR A BUDDING young Berkeley China junkie, the mid-1960s were the best and the worst of times. China was just beginning to undergo revolutionary turbulence, its people stirred to revolt by their aging idol, Mao Zedong. Now in his seventies, Mao had returned to the front lines of power with a vengeance, riding on the shoulders of his youthful minions, the Red Guard. Teenagers ran wild, waving Mao's "Little Red Book" of quotations, smashing all traditional icons, emblems, and embodiments of rank, status, and authority save one—Überchairman Mao himself. The Cultural Revolution was a living political laboratory, a real-time experiment in the dialectical interplay of utopian fantasies and totalitarian nightmares, poetic omelettes and prosaic eggs. "A revolution is not a dinner party," said Chairman Mao in his characteristically enigmatic, oracular way.

In some ways China's national trauma was a graduate student's dream. Observing the Cultural Revolution at a safe distance from the commanding heights of the Berkeley Bear's Lair, my peers and I sipped coffee and debated the finer points of Mao's "strategic plan." For some of my Berkeley classmates—the left-wing *philosophes sois-disants* and radical acolytes of Herbert Marcuse, Che Guevara, and Frantz Fanon—the Maoist vision of an egalitarian future free from egoism, greed, and the "revisionist" pursuit of material self-interest trumped all considerations of human cost and collateral damage. Berkeley was, after all, the birthplace of the Free Speech Movement (FSM), the Black Panthers, and the Vietnam War resistance, a mélange of disparate liberationist philosophies cavorting together under an existential blanket of pot-blown communal bliss.

For some, however, the high costs of Mao's last revolution could not be wished, washed, smoked, or philosophized away. Untold numbers of Chinese people were reportedly being humiliated, imprisoned, tortured, or driven to suicide in the name of revolutionary virtue. Though the full human toll of the Maoist "decade of destruction" would not be calculated for years to come, enough was known by the mid-'60s to raise serious questions about the relationship between the Maoists' arguably virtuous ends and their palpably brutal means. In their haste to rid China of bourgeois influence, Mao and his radical acolytes, including his notorious wife Jiang Qing and her Shanghai colleagues, later reviled as the Gang of Four, were pushing China to the brink of anarchy. While some saw Red Guard violence as "necessary destruction," others grasped the relevance of Molière's ironic caveat: "More men die of their remedies than of their illnesses."

Berkeley's graduate students were not alone in debating the relative costs and benefits of Mao's last revolution. Our academic mentors were similarly divided. More often than not the faculty's intramural disputes mirrored preexisting ideological and political schisms, sharpened and amplified by the ongoing antiwar and Free Speech movements. The resulting antagonisms were intense and often deeply personal, and more than a few graduate students found their career prospects held perilous hostage to philosophical rifts among and with their faculty advisers. One friend, a teaching assistant, had his academic dreams abruptly shattered when his supervisor fired him for encouraging students to take part in an antiwar boycott.

Not all the career-threatening wounds suffered by grad students in the Berkeley culture wars were inflicted by the faculty. Some were self-inflicted. My best friend Jerry dropped out of school in 1966 to become a self-styled "movement junkie" after being manhandled by police, who dragged him off in handcuffs from a Sproul Hall sit-in led by Joan Baez. Today he still wears Birkenstocks, curses the "pigs," and recites poetry in Berkeley coffeehouses, when he isn't off demonstrating to save the Indonesian rain forest or the baby seals in Newfoundland. I might have gone down that road, too, but when I heard the police were coming into Sproul Hall, I made a quick exit. Comps—the hellish battery of written examinations endured by all pre-doctoral students midway through their graduate studies—were just a few weeks away, and I couldn't afford to spend the night in jail, not even with Joan Baez as a cellmate. And besides, I had family responsibilities now: I had married my college sweetheart, Carolyn, and we had a newborn son, Matthew.

Fortuitously, my own career did not suffer from the intense ideological polarization of the '60s. As a more or less typical Berkeley grad student, I was considerably left of center politically, meaning that I was against the Vietnam War and in favor of the Free Speech Movement. I was also vice president of the Graduate Student Association in Political Science, which actively supported such protest measures as classroom boycotts and teaching assistant strikes. This put me squarely on the opposite side of the barricade from Bob Scalapino and Chal Johnson, both of whom supported the Vietnam War and opposed the FSM. Bob, to his lasting credit, always scrupulously respected the boundary between the political and the professional, never letting the former intrude upon the latter in his dealings with graduate students; Chal was more volatile and unpredictable, and, if provoked, he could also be vindictive.

So it was that when I sat for my Ph.D. oral qualifying examination in the spring of 1966, I had some reason for concern. Being grilled by Chalmers Johnson was worrisome enough, but it was the third member of my examining committee who made me most nervous: H. Franz Schurmann. Schurmann, a brilliant but erratic sociologist, was chairman of the Center for Chinese Studies. Unlike Bob and Chal, he was also viscerally antiwar and pro-FSM. On more than one occasion in the recent past he had publicly—and bitterly—locked horns with Bob and Chal.

As I entered the oral examination room, an ancient aphorism flashed briefly through my mind, purportedly of South Asian origin: "When elephants fight, the grass suffers." I took a deep breath. The exam began. Within the first few minutes my worst fears began to dissipate. In the clash of conflicting egos and ideologies that took place over the next two hours, the grass miraculously escaped unscathed. As the elephants parried and postured and occasionally butted heads, they barely took notice of me, asking few questions and posing no serious challenges. I passed with flying colors.

Having endured four years of Chinese language classes and passed my comps and Ph.D. oral qualifying exam, I was now certified as ready for the next stage of my academic apprenticeship—field research in East Asia, the final run-up to writing my doctoral dissertation. By now I was deeply addicted to China, and I could hardly wait to roam free in the poppy fields of Maoism.

2

A Dissertation Is Not a Dinner Party

BERKELEY IN THE 1960S WAS a magnet for world-class social thinkers, and apart from my addiction to China I had developed an abiding interest in grand sociological theory. Like many of my classmates and teachers I was disposed to favor elegant, abstract concepts over messy, inconvenient facts. I was particularly enamored of the classical European sociologists Max Weber and Emile Durkheim. Seventy years earlier they had predicted the inevitable triumph of secular industrial institutions and values—such as specialized labor, bureaucratic organization, and cost-benefit (i.e., instrumental) calculation—over the traditional, patriarchal institutions and absolute values of premodern agrarian societies and religious communities. By contrast, Mao Zedong was attempting to build a late-twentieth-century society of quasi-religious true believers, one in which "red" zealots held sway over technical and professional "experts," where bureaucracy and hierarchy were denounced as devices for enslaving workers and peasants, and where instrumental calculations of personal cost and benefit were regarded as symptoms of "bourgeois individualism." I was eager to test the practical limits of Mao's utopian experiment against the predictions of grand sociological theory.

There was just one fly in my ointment, albeit a very large one: Mainland China was off limits to American scholars. The U.S. government, in its infinite wisdom, continued to recognize Chiang Kai-shek's Nationalist regime-in-exile on Taiwan, the Republic of China (ROC), as the authentic voice of 600 million Chinese. As the next best thing to doing research in China proper, I devised a plan to spend a year in the British Crown

Colony of Hong Kong, interviewing Chinese refugees and scouring local Chinese newspapers and magazines for evidence to support my principal thesis that Mao's revolutionary, antibureaucratic ideology was profoundly incompatible with the structural requirements of running a modern industrial society.

Unhappily for me, the Wise Men who administered my fellowship funds felt I wasn't quite ready to be turned loose on Hong Kong. They thought my Chinese-language skills needed further refining and polishing, so they stipulated, as a precondition for my Hong Kong research, a preparatory year of full-time immersion language study in the Republic of China. A year in Taiwan: Take it or leave it.

I TOOK IT. Arriving at Taipei's Sung-shan Airport in the summer of 1966 in the wake of a grade-3 typhoon, with wife Carolyn and infant son Matthew in tow, my first reaction was one of dismay. Walking across the tarmac we got soaked to the bone, while all around us people were chattering away in an abrasive, incomprehensible dialect that sounded only vaguely and distantly like anything I'd ever heard before. I went into shock. After four years of intensive classroom language study, including private lessons with a tutor who spoke only the purest of standard Chinese (Mandarin) bell tones, I could not understand a word anyone was saying. Who *were* these people? What language were they speaking?

Articulating slowly and haltingly in my formal classroom Chinese, I managed to communicate with an equally dismayed and uncomprehending taxi driver. I asked him to take us to an inexpensive hotel, whereupon he led us on a long and costly journey through the waterlogged streets of Taipei before depositing us in a seedy-looking neighborhood, in front of a neon sign flashing the Chinese characters *fandian* (飯店), which means "hotel." Negotiating uncertainly with a puzzled-looking desk clerk, I secured a room, where the three of us dried out, bathed, and eventually fell asleep, exhausted by our ordeal. Only much later, when we were awakened in the wee hours of the night by incessant banging, creaking, and groaning through the walls and ceiling of our poorly insulated hotel room, did it slowly dawn on us that we had landed in one of Taipei's notorious "bouncing tatami" hotels—a brothel. I now understood the desk clerk's initial puzzlement. Welcome to Free China!

After a mostly sleepless night, we spent the next day wearily hunting for a place to live. Discouraged by unrelenting rains that left low-lying areas of Taipei under as much as three feet of water, we reluctantly called off our search in mid-afternoon. That evening we dragged ourselves to an orientation session for incoming graduate students and their spouses at the Inter-University Program for Chinese Language Studies (IUP), known informally as the Stanford Center. There I confirmed my painful discovery of the previous day: The standard Chinese dialect I had studied so laboriously in Berkeley did not even remotely resemble the heavily accented Taiwanese regional patois.

The good news was that I was not alone in my dismay. Most of the other incoming students, representing a dozen or more U.S. elite universities and colleges, were equally unable to fathom what the locals were saying. But—mirabile dictu—we could understand one another perfectly well. Speaking in our flat, toneless, grammar school–level Chinese, with thick American accents, we had little difficulty conversing among ourselves. And so, two distinct linguistic clusters quickly formed that night: we students, huddled together nervously in a tight knot for security, speaking *our* Chinese language, and the teachers, laughing and chatting together amiably, speaking *theirs*.

After eventually finding a house to rent (and waiting three days for its typhoon-damaged floors and walls to dry out), I settled down to my language classes. Studying Chinese had never been a particularly enjoyable experience for me, and my ten months at the Stanford Center in Taipei proved no exception. I had a good ear for languages, which came in handy, but I disliked the incessant daily drills. Chinese is a language that must be memorized, slowly and painfully, complex character by complex character. No shortcuts, no alphabet, no prefixes or suffixes, no tenses, and no Latin roots to guide the search for meaning. Just the steady drip, drip, drip of continual repetition and rote memorization. To make matters worse, as a left-hander whose crabbed calligraphy was barely legible even in English, there was no way I could properly use an ink brush to draw traditional Chinese characters, mastery of which was traditionally a major hallmark of the proper Confucian "gentleman." In the old days, teachers would have forced me to hold the brush in my right hand (there were no left-handers in China). But these were modern, enlightened times, so our teachers graciously confined themselves to cluck-clucking about my awkward southpaw calligraphy.

If life in Taipei was stressful for me, it was even harder for my family. Taiwan in the '60s was in many respects a Third World sump hole, with poor sanitation, poor flood drainage, endemic disease, primitive living conditions, and a paranoidal authoritarian political regime. Carolyn hadn't wanted to be there in the first place. When I first informed her that my "grand prize" in the Berkeley fellowship sweepstakes included a year in Taipei, she was less than overjoyed, far less. For one thing, she was not a Sinologist; she had been an English major at UCLA when we met, with Shakespeare as her forte. For another, our son was not yet a year old, and I was far too anxiously self-absorbed in my studies to be much of a helpmate to her. Worse still, within a month of our arrival in Taipei, Matthew developed a chronic, life-threatening intestinal disorder of unknown origin, which sapped his strength and required constant monitoring to prevent potentially fatal dehydration.

Had it not been for the timely intervention of a U.S. Navy doctor encountered by chance during our first week in Taipei, Matt might have died. After our first shell-shocked night in a brothel we splurged the second night, booking a room at the fanciest guesthouse in town—the ostentatious, over-the-top Grand Hotel, owned by Mme. Chiang Kai-shek herself. Jet-lagged and traumatized by our first twenty-four hours in Taipei, we found ourselves pacing the ornate halls of the Grand in the middle of the night, entertaining a suddenly energetic and wide-awake Matt. We were not alone. Also on duty in the hallways that night, walking *his* jet-lagged infant son, was Dr. Roger Detels, an American epidemiologist recently drafted into the U.S. Navy.

After commiserating on the travails of intercontinental travel with small children, Roger and I became friends. A few weeks later he pulled the necessary strings for Matt to be admitted to the U.S. Naval Hospital in Taipei, where, after weeks of debilitating intestinal illness, Matt received life-saving antibiotics and intravenous nourishment. Lab tests revealed that his condition most likely had been brought on by a chemical intolerance for local infant formula. Thereafter, we changed his primary liquid nutrients to apple juice and imported formula. His recovery was rapid and complete.

To help pass the time in Taipei, Carolyn studied Chinese painting and ceramics, while I played basketball with the Stanford Center team. With a total student body of twenty-five, the Stanford Center had three unusually tall, highly skilled athletes, each of whom had played college basketball. Surrounded by a supporting cast of smaller, slower players, myself included, our three talented giants dominated the undersize local univer-

Enjoying a distinct height advantage over local Taiwanese teams, the Stanford Center basketball team compiled a winning record in 1966–67. The author is in the back row, fourth from left. Photo courtesy of Craig Canning.

sity teams, and we remained undefeated through the first five games of our abbreviated seven-game schedule. Toward the end of the year, however, we lost two straight games—one to the ROC national team, in a very close contest, and the other to the U.S. Navy Pacific Command All-Stars, in a brutal forty-point blowout. Although I played sparingly, scored few points, and gasped audibly from a recurrence of childhood asthma triggered by the heavily polluted Taipei air, my distinctive facial adornment, consisting of mustache and goatee, was duly noted by a member of the local media, who dubbed me Dahuzi (The Bearded One).

Throughout our time in Taipei we found ourselves under loose surveillance. Students' phones were periodically—and intrusively—tapped: Sometimes we could hear the sound of breathing; other times the recording machinery whined audibly. Our mail, both incoming and outgoing, was regularly intercepted and clumsily opened; some of it never got delivered at all. And once or twice a week an unmarked car belonging to the security police would show up across the street from my house around dawn, its lone occupant seemingly dozing at the wheel. The entire ROC security system was a study in contradictions: intrusive surveillance coupled with mind-boggling inefficiency. On more than one occasion Carolyn and I received parcels from our parents containing various contraband items, including jars of instant coffee and powdered infant formula. Wrapped inside socks and underwear, the smuggled foodstuffs evaded detection. Once I even received in the mail a forwarded copy of the CCP's flagship newspaper, *People's Daily*, which had inexplicably been ignored by the local postal inspectors.

Life in Taipei was a continuous game of chance. Power outages were routine, mosquitoes bred in foul-smelling open sewers with children playing nearby, and the air itself was thick with coal dust. But most dangerous of all were the taxi drivers. Three-wheeled pedicabs had recently been outlawed in Taipei, and their drivers—mostly retired army veterans—were given free taxicabs, compliments of the Retired Serviceman's Association. Driving lessons were not included in the giveaway, however, and the taxis were piloted with reckless abandon at maximum speed through Taipei's congested streets—onto sidewalks, through traffic lights, and, not infrequently, directly into the path of oncoming traffic. One didn't have to be a passenger to be seriously traumatized by such vehicular anarchy. Pedestrians, bicyclists, and motorcyclists alike were forced to take frequent, sudden evasive actions to escape these motorized kamikazes.

Obtaining the basic necessities of life in Taipei (which in our case included sterile apple juice for Matt and Johnnie Walker Black Label for Mom and Dad) also required skillful negotiation—on the local black market. We often found ourselves getting ripped off by street hustlers who made their living selling hard-to-get imported goods, mostly stolen from the U.S. Navy Post Exchange, to foreign residents. Sometimes the goods we purchased on the black market turned out to be fake. Forced to deal with such annoyances on a daily basis, we quickly mastered the essential vocabulary of everyday life in Taiwan: *meiyou guanxi* (it doesn't matter), *meiyou banfa* (there's nothing for it), *buqingchu* (it isn't clear), *luanqi bazao* (it's all screwed up), and *mama huhu* (whatever).

If *meiyou guanxi* (it doesn't matter) was one of the essential keys to dealing with the daily frustrations of life in Taiwan, an even more vital one was its antonym, *guanxi*. As I soon learned, the cultivation of *guanxi* (literally, "connections") was the single most important key to survival in a Chinese cultural environment. I discovered this the hard way. After our first month in Taipei I received in the mail a bill from the local water and power company. There was no return address on the envelope, so I asked our neighborhood grocer's teenage son if he knew where I could pay the bill. He offered to take me there, and I gratefully accepted the offer. He hopped on the back of my motorcycle, and we drove off to pay the bill. The entire transaction took maybe fifteen minutes, after which I delivered him promptly back to his parents' grocery shop. I thanked him warmly and, as a gratuitous afterthought, told him, in my best idiomatic Chinese, "If there's anything I can do for you, just let me know." (What I actually said was "Ni bang wode mang, wo bang nide mang," or "You scratched my back, so I'll scratch yours.")

Big mistake. Early the next morning we were awakened by a loud banging on our front door. It was the grocer's son. He was carrying a battered leather pouch filled with official-looking documents, which he proceeded to show me, one by one: his birth certificate, school certificate, health certificate, military registration certificate, Taipei residency card, and so on. I stared at him uncomprehendingly. "What's this all about?" I asked. "You get me a job at the American military base," came his response, followed by a repetition of my phrase from the previous day, but with the pronouns reversed: "Wo bang nide mang, ni bang wode mang" (I scratched your back, so you'll scratch mine). Taken aback, I proceeded to tell him that I was just a lowly graduate student, that I had not one iota of *guanxi* with the U.S. military, and that there was absolutely nothing I could do for him. He was devastated. His parents refused to talk to me after that. I felt terrible. But I did learn a valuable lesson: One accepts unsolicited favors or gifts in a Chinese society at one's own peril. Obligation follows generosity, as the night the day.

THROUGHOUT THE YEAR the Nationalist government periodically staged public relations events to impress their American guests. At one point the Stanford Center students were invited as a group to tour the ROC's offshore island stronghold of Quemoy, or Jinmen, as it's known locally. Back in 1949 Quemoy was occupied by the retreating Nationalist forces when they were driven off the Chinese Mainland. Flying across the turbulent waters of the Taiwan Strait in a lumbering old U.S. C-154 cargo plane at an altitude of five hundred feet to avoid detection by Chinese radar, our hotdogging ROC air force pilot showed off for the *guailo* (foreigners). Dipping down sharply to skim the waves below, then pulling out in a rollercoaster-like maneuver, he caused several of us to become airsick. By the time we reached the island, I was green with nausea.

My condition was not helped when, at a welcoming luncheon, the head of the Quemoy Garrison Command insisted on offering repeated toasts to his American visitors, challenging us with a benign, smiling *ganbei* (bottoms up) to down glass after glass of a prized local liquor, *Jinmen gaoliang*, a clear, pungent, sorghum-based brew with the kick of a mule. After lunch several of us—myself included—could barely stand up. One valuable lesson learned from that encounter, albeit the hard way, was that it is perfectly acceptable in Chinese society to merely sip from the glass when responding to a *ganbei* challenge, rather than downing its entire contents in a single gulp.

Our guided tour of the island—a mere two miles offshore from the Mainland Chinese port city of Xiamen, or Amoy—was partially shrouded in an alcoholic haze. We were shown the massive underground military bunkers where the garrison forces had lived since the mid-1950s, when Communist artillery barrages first tested the U.S. government's resolve to defend Taiwan. Aboveground, Quemoy's shell-pocked fields and rolling hills were now virtually deserted. They looked serenely pastoral, belying both the ferocity of the enemy's past bombardment and the vastness of the military complex beneath. The only settlement we saw aboveground was a small town whose civilian occupants had two main sources of employment: production of Jinmen Gaoliang and prostitution. Groups of female sex workers were ferried over from Taiwan on a rotational basis to service the thousands of soldiers living underground.

The soldiers themselves were carefully screened before being assigned to duty on Quemoy. Because of the island's proximity to the Chinese Mainland, the Nationalist government feared that Taiwanese-born military conscripts—many of them resentful of the Nationalists' heavy-handed regime—might defect to the enemy if given half a chance. Consequently, the Quemoy garrison was overwhelmingly composed of Mainland-born soldiers.

The highlight of our daylong visit was an inspection of the fortified artillery emplacements and propaganda facilities at the western tip of the island. There, from a high promontory, using high-powered army field glasses, we could easily see farmers and fishermen on the Chinese Mainland going about their business. We could also hear the Communists' loudspeakers across the water blaring their continuous appeals to "Taiwan compatriots" on Quemoy to defect to the warm embrace of the motherland, promising that they would be richly rewarded and welcomed as heroes. Responding in kind, the Quemoy Garrison Command blasted its own continuous propaganda toward the Mainland. Wholly dependent upon the prevailing winds to carry their respective messages across two miles of open water, the two sides engaged in a high-pitched, high-decibel game of dueling broadcasts. In this bizarre competition the Quemoy garrison enjoyed one clear advantage: Being on a tiny island facing a huge continental landmass, when the winds were from the east, the garrison forces could launch thousands of helium-filled propaganda balloons, laden with leaflets and small packets of household necessities, secure in the knowledge that these would land *somewhere* on the Chinese Mainland. We were told that some of the balloons had been picked up by farmers in Sichuan, more than eight hundred miles to the west.

When the garrison commander, flanked by an official photographer, invited the Stanford Center students to participate in launching propaganda balloons, I begged off, not wanting to be a pawn in a Nationalist propaganda stunt directed against the *Gongfei* (Communist bandits). After all, I was still hoping, however remotely, to get to the Mainland one day. My caution was not unwarranted, as photos of the American students launching balloons were published in several Taiwanese newspapers the next day.

AS THE MONTHS in Taipei passed all too slowly, Carolyn and I began to count the days and weeks until our getaway to Hong Kong. To relieve the water-torture tedium of daily language classes, I spent my spare time in the autumn of 1966 beefing up my dissertation proposal. Riffing on ideas drawn from Benjamin Schwartz's brilliant 1965 treatise on Chinese Communism's stressful encounter with industrial modernity, "Modernisation and the Maoist Vision," I tried to develop a more concise and coherent sociological critique of Mao's program for revolutionary change. On a lark I sent off the resulting essay—which compared Mao's blueprint for radical societal transformation to the premodern mystique of charismatic religious sects—to a U.S. government-funded journal devoted to critical analysis of Communist systems.

Three months went by and I heard nothing, not even an acknowledgment of my submission. Eventually I concluded that the ROC's postal police had probably hijacked my manuscript. I didn't bother resending it but simply shrugged it off with the now all-too-familiar Taiwanese refrain *meiyou banfa* (nothing for it). Then one morning in the winter of 1967, I happened to look out my window just as the fellow in the unmarked car across the street got out of his vehicle and placed a small parcel in my mailbox. I waited a decent interval before retrieving the package. Wrapped in plain brown paper with no external markings, it contained a set of galley proofs and a cover letter. My essay on Maoism as a political religion had been accepted for publication. I eagerly corrected the proofs, rewrapped the parcel, and gave it to a friend who was about to return to the United States, asking him to mail it from his hometown. The guy in the unmarked car continued his episodic vigil across the street, but he never again delivered any mail. My article was published two months later, in the magazine *Problems of Communism*.

As the gloomy Taipei winter turned to spring, my battle against the deadening monotony of language study took a new turn. I began spending each Friday afternoon, after classes were over for the week, in the "dirty books" room of an ROC government think tank, the Institute of International Relations, in downtown Taipei. The reading materials in the room were kept under lock and key, inaccessible to ordinary citizens. The pornography housed there was not sexual in nature, but political—Communist publications from Mainland China. And so I spent my Friday afternoons reading *People's Daily* and *Red Flag* and *Peking Review*, soaking up whatever information I could find about the latest twists and turns of political fortune on the Chinese Mainland. It was the spring of 1967, and Mao's Cultural Revolution was cresting in one of its periodic high tides of violence and destruction.

In the course of my weekly visits to the institute's reading room I befriended a young assistant librarian, David Auw, an overseas Chinese from Indonesia. David spoke good English and moonlighted as an English translator for the ROC Ministry of National Defense. The materials he translated included a fair number of important CCP documents seized by Nationalist commando teams in guerrilla raids on coastal areas of Fujian, the province just across the Taiwan Strait. David's translations were peddled to interested consumers in the West, including the U.S. government.

One Friday afternoon in April, with about a month to go before my scheduled departure for Hong Kong, I entered the dirty books room at the Institute of International Studies as usual, only to encounter an obviously agitated David Auw. Pointing to a stack of soiled, water-damaged documents on his desk, he began to curse the Defense Ministry (Guofangbu). "Those *wangbadan* [turtle eggs] at the Guofangbu need these translated in three weeks," he said, "and I don't have any time." Glancing over at the documents I noticed the word *mimi* (秘密), "secret," stamped on their covers. Not having the slightest idea what was in them, but sensing a rare opportunity to examine classified Chinese Communist materials, I offered to translate the documents for him. It would be good practice for me, I suggested hopefully.

David resisted, saying he couldn't possibly let the documents out of his sight, let alone turn them over to a foreigner. But the impossibility of his predicament led him to have second thoughts, and eventually he relented—though he insisted that I do the actual translation work at a nearby table where he could keep an eye on me. I was not to take any of the materials out of the room at any time, and when I left in the evening, I was to show the security guard the contents of my briefcase. No notes, no carbon copies, no nothing.

With about thirty pages of single-spaced, densely packed Chinese documents to translate, and only a few Friday afternoons remaining before my scheduled departure from Taipei, I began to skip language classes at the Stanford Center. Rationalizing my truancy as a necessary sacrifice that would enable me to sharpen my linguistic skills (wasn't this why I had been sent to Taiwan in the first place?), I spent the next three weeks, five days a week, in the dirty books room, from early morning until evening, leaving only when the doors closed at night. Dutifully I translated the documents, taking no notes and making no carbons. Each night I put the originals back on their proper shelf along with my daily translations, allowing the guard to inspect my briefcase before leaving.

Within the first half hour that the documents were in my possession, I knew—or rather sensed—their importance. There were five in all, the earliest dated May 1963, the latest January 1965. Each bore the imprint of a Central Committee *zhongfa* (the official numbering system used to designate important Communist Party directives). The documents spoke of an intensive Socialist Education Movement (also referred to as the Four Cleanups, or Siqing) that had been under way in rural China since the fall of 1962, in the wake of Mao's catastrophic Great Leap Forward. Each successive document shed new light on the nature, purposes, and techniques of the new movement. Some went into greater detail than others, and there was a good deal of overlap and repetition. All were generously laced with Chairman Mao's quotations and "instructions." But there were also clear, intriguing differences in language and emphasis among them, as if they had been written by different people with very different agendas, priorities, and constituencies in mind.

There were two principal and at times conflicting themes that kept recurring throughout the documents. One was the persistent demand, raised by Mao himself, for intensified class struggle to prevent a "capitalist restoration" in China; the other was a repeated warning about the spreading epidemic of cadre corruption in rural China in the wake of the Great Leap. Some of the documents stressed the need to dispatch Communist Party–led "work teams" to the countryside to investigate and punish corrupt rural officials (the Big Four Cleanups); others emphasized the need to mobilize the poor peasant masses to conduct didactic ideological education and struggle against the "capitalist tendencies" of landlords and rich peasants (the Small Four Cleanups). It soon became clear to me that such differences of emphasis were in fact symptomatic of a deeper rift among China's top leaders.

The last of the five Socialist Education Movement documents confirmed the severity of this fissure. Based on reports delivered at a Central Committee Work Conference in December 1964, the document, known as the "Twenty-Three Articles," contained a startling revelation, attributed to Mao himself. The main goal of the Socialist Education Movement, Mao exhorted, was "*to rectify those people in positions of authority within the Party who take the capitalist road.*" The document went on to allege that certain unnamed top-level Party officials had "lost their class standpoint" and were "opposed to socialism."

By the time I translated these documents in the spring of 1967, it was no longer news that Mao deeply distrusted his top lieutenants, including Liu Shaoqi and Deng Xiaoping. Liu in particular had been obliquely attacked in the summer of 1966 for allegedly "suppressing the masses" in the initial stages of the Cultural Revolution, and both men had been removed from power at a Central Committee Plenum in August of that year. But these initial attacks were enigmatic, their explanation shrouded in mystery. What, *specifically*, had they done to offend Mao so grievously? Here, in the divergent and at times sharply worded texts of five Central Committee directives, was the earliest documented evidence of Mao's rising animus toward his erstwhile comrades.

Specifically, Liu and Deng stood accused of hijacking Mao's plan to rekindle the long-term class struggle between socialism and capitalism. Instinctively distrustful of the worker-peasant masses (and of Mao's preference for radical mass mobilization), the two men diverted Mao's plan for a mass-oriented, "open door" rectification into a more secretive, "closed door" campaign to root out cadre corruption, with the entire movement orchestrated and led by centrally directed work teams. In this manner, Liu and Deng effectively sabotaged Mao's trademark populism, supplanting it with their own brand of bureaucratic elitism. Here was an obvious smoking gun; here, too, was the first clear foreshadowing of the Cultural Revolution purges to come. (Subsequently it was revealed that at the December 1964 Central Committee Work Conference, Mao and Liu had argued heatedly and at length about the nature of the Four Cleanups.)

Working furiously during the last two weeks in May, I finished translating the documents. I hardly slept, knowing that I'd have to turn over all the materials, including my translations, on the last Friday of the month. Just before closing time on the final Thursday, as I polished the next-to-last section of text, I was struck by a sudden, jolting realization: *I cannot relinquish these documents.* As I finished for the evening, I placed my translations back on the library shelf as usual. Then, without considering the possible consequences of my actions, I turned my back to the guard and stuffed the original documents into a sealed inner compartment of my briefcase. Pulse pounding, I walked toward the main door, hastily showing the guard the contents of my briefcase before stepping out into the warm spring night.

Mounting my motorcycle, I headed for the U.S. Navy Hospital on Zhongshan North Street. One of Roger Detels's associates, a Harvard-trained medical historian with whom I had become friendly during Matthew's treatment, was on night duty there, along with a solitary night nurse. Of more immediate importance to me, the hospital had a Verifax dry-copy machine in its now darkened administrative office. The three of us chatted for a while; then they were called to the emergency room to treat an American sailor who had been admitted with some sort of acute seizure. When they had gone, I ducked into the deserted office.

Precursor to the Xerox machine, the Verifax was a much slower, less dependable photocopier, and it took me almost two hours to copy the thirty pages of text. With only the dim light from a nearby utility closet for illumination, I worked in semidarkness, afraid of being discovered. In my nervousness, I overexposed several pages and had to recopy them. Fortunately, the machine itself had few moving parts and was relatively noiseless. I finished around midnight. Neither my doctor friend nor the night nurse was anywhere to be seen, so I left the hospital and drove home, nearly knocking over a pedestrian in my haste. By this time I was running on pure adrenaline.

Notwithstanding its inefficient surveillance system, Taiwan in the 1960s was a rigidly authoritarian anti-Communist dictatorship, ruled with an iron fist under a 1949 martial law decree that suspended such legal niceties as due process of law and habeas corpus. Suspected Communist agents and pro-independence Taiwanese nationalists were ruthlessly suppressed. Political dissidents and critics of Chiang Kai-shek's regime were not infrequently imprisoned without trial, sometimes indefinitely. A fair number of them had simply disappeared. Had I been caught with "Communist bandit" documents in my possession—let alone *top secret, purloined* documents—I would have been in very deep doo-doo. At the moment, however, all such considerations were swamped by the immediate thrill of having gotten away with it.

It was only after returning safely home after midnight that the possible downside of my caper began to dawn on me. Taking a deep swig of black market Scotch to calm the uncontrollable tremor that by now had supplanted my earlier adrenaline rush, I wished the death of a thousand cuts to the *wangbadan* of a black market dealer who had expertly replicated the factory seal on my bottle of Johnnie Walker Black after replacing its original contents with amber-colored tea.

After a sleepless night I returned to the dirty books room one final time on the last Friday morning in May. Entering without incident, I waited until David was busy talking to a colleague before slipping the original documents from my briefcase back onto their proper shelf. My felony undetected, I busied myself polishing the final passages of my translation. At around five o'clock, I handed over the entire stack of materials to a visibly relieved, suitably grateful David Auw. Doing my best to avoid eye contact, I said my good-byes and walked guiltily out the door to begin the next stage of my career.

IF TAIWAN WAS purgatory, Hong Kong was near to heaven. Although the Cultural Revolution was wreaking havoc uncomfortably close to Hong Kong's border with China, there were no open sewers, no sooty air, no constant power outages, no black market rip-offs, and no suffocating police surveillance. After a white-knuckle landing at Hong Kong's hazardous Kai Tak Airport, where two commercial flights had recently overrun the runway and landed in Kowloon Bay, we took a cab to our prearranged, furnished apartment on Beacon Hill, above Lion Rock Tunnel, near the boundary between Kowloon and the New Territories. After settling in, I drove our newest family acquisition—a battered 1959 Volkswagen Beetle, purchased from a departing UC Berkeley scholar—to the Universities Service Centre.

Founded in 1963 with support from foundation grants, the Universities Service Centre was designed to assist Western scholars in conducting research on Communist China. I had reserved working space at the center prior to leaving Taiwan. Located in a rather plain, gated two-story house at 155 Argyle Street, Kowloon, the center maintained a small but extremely useful library of Western books and periodicals on China along with an extensive collection of contemporary Chinese newspapers, magazines, and documentary materials. There were nine or ten small, cramped individual offices scattered throughout the building, mostly occupied by American (with a sprinkling of Canadian, British, and Australian) Ph.D. candidates like myself. In addition to its office and library facilities, the center served as a venue for periodic lectures and informal talks by local and visiting scholars, journalists, and diplomats and as a safe house where émigrés from Mainland China could be interviewed. For China watchers who lacked direct access to the Mainland, the Universities Service Centre was the next best thing to being there; in some ways it was even *better*— and certainly a lot more comfortable—than being there.

Every day around noon the center's resident scholars assembled in the lunchroom for a hot meal. The conversation around the table focused mostly on current events, both in China and abroad. At lunch on my first full day there, in early June 1967, I was asked to introduce myself and say something about my dissertation research. As I briefly outlined my interest in the tensions between Maoism and industrial modernity, one of the center's resident Americans, Fred Teiwes, a Ph.D. candidate from Columbia University, changed the subject. Noting that I had just arrived from Taipei, he asked if I had picked up any rumors or gossip there about some secret CCP directives pertaining to the Four Cleanups. A meticulous researcher, Teiwes had been parsing recent Mainland Chinese press reports and radio broadcasts and had come across a number of enigmatic references to a Maoist critique of Liu Shaoqi purportedly contained in a set of unpublished Central Committee documents. A smile of silent comprehension crossed my face as I reached for my briefcase.

Over the next several months Fred and I worked together along converging tracks of inquiry. I re-translated and analyzed the photocopied documents in my possession, while he scrutinized a mass of collateral Chinese media reports and commentaries. By the fall of 1967 we had put together a one-hundred-page monographic study of the Socialist Education Movement, complete with the fully re-translated texts of my five stolen documents. But we did not stop there. In addition to our monograph, which was quickly accepted for publication by the Center for Chinese Studies at UC Berkeley, Fred and I published four other articles on the Four Cleanups between September 1967 and April 1968. Lost in the glare of this sudden publication bonanza, my dissertation proposal remained on the shelf, gathering dust.

As the publication date for our Berkeley monograph approached, I began to worry about my friend David Auw. What would happen to David when the ROC Defense Ministry twigged to the fact that the classified documents he had been charged with protecting had been surreptitiously copied and smuggled out of the country? I spent several anxious nights trying to work out a plausible story to cover my theft. But then in early February 1968, just two months before the publication of our monograph, there came an unexpected stroke of fortune: The complete set of original Four Cleanups documents was about to be published serially, in the original Chinese, in *Issues & Studies* (Wenti yu yanjiu), the in-house journal of the ROC Institute of International Relations. This meant that the documents were now in the public domain. Out of concern to save David's face (or, rather, to cover his ass), shortly before our monograph went to press I wrote to Jack Service at UC Berkeley's Center for Chinese Studies, asking for his advice. Jack was editing our monograph and had done the final polishing on my translations of the Four Cleanups documents. When I told him of my concern for David's career (and my own reputation), Jack suggested inserting a brief acknowledgment into the front matter of the book, stating that "The authors wish to thank the director and staff of the Institute of International Relations, Republic of China, for making available their collection of original documentary materials on the Socialist Education Movement." Whether this flimsy maneuver actually worked, or whether David's Defense Ministry minders were simply asleep at the wheel, I could not then know. But there were no apparent recriminations. David's career was unaffected by my caper (he later became editor of a prestigious Taiwanese cultural journal), and I remained persona grata (sorta) in Taiwan.

OUR YEAR IN Hong Kong was memorable for other reasons as well. With the Cultural Revolution in full bloom just across the Chinese border, there was an atmosphere of heightened political tension. In the late summer of 1967 columns of British armored personnel carriers could be seen heading north each morning on Waterloo Road, carrying Nepalese Gurkha soldiers—Britain's first line of defense against a possible Chinese attack— up to the border at Lok Ma Chau. A curfew kept people off the streets after 10:00 PM, the result of a string of local bombings and assassination attempts (some successful) on British magistrates, policemen, radio personalities, and ordinary civilians. Some of the bombs had been wrapped in colorful gift paper and placed in local parks, where children discovered them. It was ugly business.

Taking advantage of an unusually severe seasonal drought in Hong Kong in the summer of 1967, the Chinese authorities in July abruptly shut off delivery of contracted supplies of fresh water from neighboring Guangdong. Without the imported water, Hong Kong quickly ran dry. Water rationing was introduced, at first rather mild (daylight hours only), then a bit more bothersome (every other day), gradually becoming more and more stringent. By the time the first rains came in late September, running water was available in Hong Kong only for a four-hour period every fourth day. Toilets went unflushed for days at a time, and the smell of raw sewage, baking in the heat and humidity of the Hong Kong summer, was intense. Hardest hit were the squatter communities in Hong Kong's hillside shantytowns, where thousands of residents were forced to line up early in the morning on water delivery days to fill their permitted limit of one ten-gallon tin, drawn from a single communal tap. Foreigners and affluent Hong Kong Chinese, in contrast, enjoyed the relative luxury of filling their bathtubs and multiple fifty-gallon storage drums in the relative comfort of their own flats.

Hong Kong had an active left-wing movement in the late '60s. The leftists were a society within a society. They ran their own businesses, labor unions, and schools. In the spring of 1966 their leaders had organized a protest against the British governor's decision to raise the first-class fare on the popular Star Ferry from HK$.20 to $.25 (approximately US$.05). When a local magistrate sentenced one young demonstrator to two months in prison merely for carrying a sign that said "No fare hikes," a riot broke out in Kowloon, resulting in numerous injuries and charges of police brutality—and a lot of bad press for the British colonial authorities.

On a balmy day in the early spring of 1968, Carolyn, Matt, and I went on a Sunday outing to Deep Water Bay, on Hong Kong Island. Also picnicking at the beach that day, on a nearby dune, were sixty or so middle-school students from one of the local leftist-run schools. They were enthusiastically waving Mao's "Little Red Book" of quotations and singing revolutionary songs in praise of Mao and the Cultural Revolution. Surprised to hear them singing in standard Chinese dialect rather than in Cantonese, the lingua franca of Hong Kong, I approached one of the adults in charge, a middle-aged woman. She eyed me warily as I worked up the nerve to speak. I asked her who these students were and why they were singing in *putonghua* (literally, "common speech") rather than *Guangdonghua* (Cantonese). "They are Chairman Mao's little red compatriots" (Mao zhuxi de hongxiao tongbao), came her guarded reply. As we chatted in *putonghua*, the woman became more animated and friendly. After a few minutes she took my hand and guided me over to meet the group's leader, a "revolutionary" middle-school teacher who was conducting the student singalong. "Do you know any of our songs?" he asked excitedly. In truth, I did. Like other Universities Service Centre scholars, I had been collecting cassette tapes of Cultural Revolution music. At parties we frequently parodied the stilted contents of the songs, substituting irreverent, off-color lyrics for the original, pious praises of Chairman Mao.

I dared not refuse his invitation. Surrounded by sixty exuberant little red compatriots, I managed to stumble through two off-key stanzas of "Chairman Mao Is the Red Sun in Our Hearts" before nervously attempting to effect a retreat. All around me excited youngsters laughed and clapped. A photographer captured the scene with his camera as the students lined up to walk single file past my family, pinning bright red-and-gold tin Mao badges on our shirts. By the time they finished, we were bedecked with dozens of the shiny metallic icons. We bade our farewells and started home, pleasantly amused, our earlier nervousness all but forgotten.

Our levity was short-lived. I was still half asleep the next morning when I received an agitated phone call from the vice-consul of the U.S. Consulate-General in Hong Kong, Allen Whiting. "Baum," he said impatiently, "what the *bleep* do you think you're doing?" Not having a clue what he was talking about, I was at a loss to reply. "Go out and buy the *Wen Wei Po*," he continued, "then call me back." (*Wen Wei Po* was one of several Communist-run newspapers in Hong Kong.) I threw on some clothes and went out in search of the morning paper. I bought a copy at a

福祝唱齊坊街埗水深的遊郊和，席主毛愛熱友朋國外
○疆無壽萬席主毛

The *Wen Wei Po* article of March 1968 shows the author singing revolutionary
songs with Hong Kong Red Guards. Caption reads, in part: "Foreign friend
warmly loves Chairman Mao . . . and sends blessings to Chairman Mao for
a long life without end."

local newsstand and began flipping through its pages. Not knowing what
I was looking for, I stopped dead at page 5. There, staring back at me, was
a clearly recognizable black-and-white photo of Dahuzi, the Bearded One,
surrounded by a crowd of excited youngsters clapping hands. What really
brought me up short, though, was the photo's caption: "Waiguo pengyou
re'ai Mao zhuxi" (Foreign friend warmly loves Chairman Mao). Beneath
the photo was a heartwarming (and mostly fabricated) story of a chance
encounter between a group of revolutionary middle-school students and a
"French merchant seaman on shore leave with his family." No one at the
picnic had bothered to ask my nationality—which was just as well, given
the hostile state of U.S.-China relations at the time—and I certainly hadn't
volunteered the information. France was the most recent Western country

to establish diplomatic relations with China, and it evidently served the *Wen Wei Po*'s political agenda to identify me as a "French friend."

Newspaper in hand I returned home and sheepishly phoned Whiting to explain the circumstances. A renowned Old China Hand (*Zhongguotong*) in his own right, he chuckled at my story and then, half in jest, suggested that since I had been publicly identified as a "foreign friend," I might try taking the newspaper article over to the offices of the *Ta Kung Po*, another local Communist-front paper, whose English-language editor was known to be relatively friendly to Western scholars. Perhaps, Whiting speculated, I might be able to leverage my new status as a foreign friend into a PRC visa. In those pre-Nixon, pre-normalization days, being labeled a friend of China was the only way a U.S. citizen could hope to visit the Mainland legally. A few years later some resident American scholars from the Universities Service Centre would join the anti–Vietnam War Committee of Concerned Asian Scholars, thereby becoming eligible for China visas. But in 1967 no such organization existed, and the best available visa-facilitating option at the time—membership in the Maoist Revolutionary Communist Party USA (Marxist-Leninist)—seemed a bit extreme. So Whiting's half-serious suggestion seemed like it might just be worth a try.

As luck would have it, I met the *Ta Kung Po* editor, Dr. H. C. Ling, at a social gathering a few weeks later. Newspaper clipping in hand (carefully shorn of all references to my being French), I gave him my sales pitch. Dr. Ling listened politely but impassively, promising to get back to me with an answer. I waited patiently for a few weeks, then worked up the courage to phone him at his office. He told me my visa request had been submitted to his superiors, who unfortunately had found it to be *bufangbian* (inconvenient) at this time. In relaying the bad news, his tone was deeply solicitous and apologetic, and he gave the strong impression that he was personally much distressed by the turndown. Later, when I repeated our conversation to Whiting, he just laughed. "Welcome to the world of Chinese bureaucratic evasion," he said. It was my first personal encounter with China's Great Wall of Inconvenience, but it would hardly be my last. I soon learned that when dealing with Chinese officials, politically incorrect or otherwise controversial requests usually evoke an ultra-polite *bufangbian* response, rather than outright rejection.

ALTHOUGH WE DIDN'T know it at the time, Fred Teiwes and I were not the only ones with a strong interest in the Four Cleanups. The CIA was also conducting its own in-house assessment of Mao's falling-out with Liu Shaoqi and Deng Xiaoping. Our first inkling of this came in the winter of 1967–68, a couple of months before the publication of our Berkeley monograph, when a signed article by Charles Neuhauser, a CIA analyst, appeared in *The China Quarterly*, the bible for academic China watchers. In a long piece dealing with the complex vicissitudes of intra-Party politics in the first half of the 1960s, Neuhauser included a brief analysis of the Four Cleanups documents, which he had evidently procured directly from the ROC Defense Ministry, in the original Chinese. Much to our surprise, however, Neuhauser came to a very different set of conclusions about the nature and significance of the documents and, hence, the origins of Mao's rage at Liu and Deng. Either Fred and I had the story wrong, or the intelligence community had it wrong.

With all the insouciant arrogance of a political naïf, I set about countering—nay, trashing—Neuhauser's argument. In a brash "Comment" addressed to the editor of *The China Quarterly*, I asserted that Neuhauser had made "numerous errors of fact and inference," and that he had "predicated his entire analysis of the formulation and implementation of Party policy during the Socialist Education Campaign on an assumption which is demonstrably false and . . . misleading." And then it got worse, as I none too subtly suggested that Neuhauser had not even read the full set of Four Cleanups documents. Neuhauser responded to my assault in kind, penning a long and equally self-righteous rebuttal. Our missives appeared back to back in *The China Quarterly*.

Without knowing it, I had stirred up a hornet's nest inside the U.S. intelligence community. For more than two years a "two-line struggle" had been simmering within the CIA, ostensibly centering on a dispute over the nature and origins of the Cultural Revolution and Mao's role in the decision-making process. In this contest Neuhauser was pitted against another senior CIA China analyst, Philip Bridgham. To a neophyte outsider like me, the salient issues in this quarrel seemed obscure and arcane; within the intelligence community, however, the battle lines were sharply drawn. Perforce, the publication of my "Comment" in *The China Quarterly* gave an unintended boost to Bridgham's camp, for I soon found myself being congratulated—often by people wholly unknown to me—for helping to take "arrogant Charlie Neuhauser" down a peg.

Though I never met Neuhauser personally, in retrospect I think I may have been too hard on him. I had been right about the Four Cleanups, but the differences between us were really not all that big. I think most of all I resented his—and the CIA's—unwanted intrusion onto my hitherto exclusive turf.

Fortuitously, this incident served to raise my visibility within the academic community. By the spring of 1968 I had achieved a certain notoriety in the China field for having put a senior CIA analyst in his place, and by the time our Berkeley monograph was published in late April, I had in hand tenure-track job offers from two major U.S. universities (Michigan and UCLA) plus expressions of strong interest from two others (UC Berkeley and Columbia).

Before leaving Hong Kong, we drove our aging VW Beetle up to the border separating the British colony from the nearby Chinese farming village of Shumchun. A narrow railroad bridge at the British outpost of Lowu marked the actual boundary line. With Matthew in tow, we climbed a nearby hill on the Hong Kong side of the border at Lok Ma Chau and looked down into China. This was the closest I had yet come to the People's Republic. The scene was verdant, pastoral, and primitive. At the edge of the paddy fields below, a few plain white houses could be seen, but no human activity was evident. The lush green fields that receded into the distance were unbroken by any visible trace of human habitation. Before we walked back to our car, I snapped a photo of the scene, making a mental note that the Cantonese name Shumchun was pronounced differently in standard Chinese. Though I could not possibly know it then, in fewer than twenty years this sleepy rural backwater would be transformed into one of the world's most powerful engines of industrial growth—Shenzhen.

WHEN I LEFT Hong Kong in the summer of 1968—more than two years after taking my oral Ph.D. qualifying exam—I had yet to write a single word of my doctoral dissertation. I had gotten incredible mileage from a set of stolen documents, and I was ready to move on. In August, Carolyn and I packed up and returned to our home base in Los Angeles, where I had accepted a position at my alma mater, UCLA. My mentor, H. Arthur Steiner, had recently announced his decision to retire, and I was to be his replacement.

Once back in Los Angeles, it took me two more years to finish my dissertation. By then I had completely abandoned the idea of formulating a grand unified theory of Maoism's evolutionary maladaptation to the imperatives of modernity. Instead, building on my earlier work on the Socialist Education Movement, I enlarged the scope of my previous research to incorporate new archival materials and fresh Hong Kong interview data. And I further extended my time horizon from 1966 to 1968, which enabled me to include new research on the termination of the Four Cleanups and its replacement by the vastly more destructive Cultural Revolution. My dissertation was filed and approved in the spring of 1970. A year later I was granted tenure at UCLA. Carolyn and I celebrated by buying our first house, in the suburban West San Fernando Valley bedroom community of Woodland Hills. Life was good.

3

Confessions of a Peking Tom

IN THE EARLY 1970s Carolyn and I traded our love beads and Birkenstocks for a home mortgage and a station wagon. After the birth of our second child, Kristen, in 1970, we found ourselves being drawn into the seductive somnolence of the suburban L.A. lifestyle. "Hippie chic" was the fashion du jour, and my Berkeley beard, T-shirt, and jeans gave way to muttonchops, psychedelic shirts, a Nehru jacket, and a full Afro-style 'do. Dahuzi had morphed into Datoufa (Big Hair).

My research in this period focused on the dynamics of the Cultural Revolution, which proved to be a major source of frustration for me. Inside China the political situation remained extraordinarily murky, as the smoldering embers of Mao's last revolution continued to flare up periodically, fueled by a powerful new source of political uncertainty: Chairman Mao's deteriorating health and his approaching "appointment with Marx."

The more I struggled to comprehend the broad political and human impact of the Cultural Revolution, the more I found myself unable to grasp its enormity. Without being able to set foot in China it was impossible to determine the magnitude of the devastation or to verify any of the alleged beneficial side effects of radical mass mobilization claimed by the regime's propagandists and echoed by their left-wing sympathizers in the West. Although there were widespread reports of Red Guard violence and anarchy between 1966 and 1969, there were precious few reliable eyewitness accounts and no credible statistics whatever. Moreover, the most horrific tales of rampant death and destruction generally came either from Chinese Nationalist sources with an obvious axe to grind or from inveterate Western anti-Communist organizations with an abiding interest in exaggerating the chaos on the Chinese Mainland. Making matters even more perplexing, a recent spate of books by European and American leftist scholars had portrayed the Cultural Revolution as a huge success in terms of its putative effect of liberating the masses of Chinese workers and peasants from the tyranny of bureaucrats and elitist intellectuals. Amidst such hugely conflicting interpretations, the big picture remained frustratingly opaque.

In this situation I sometimes found myself waffling in my personal assessment of Mao's revolution. For example, when choosing articles to include in a 1971 anthology, *China in Ferment: Perspectives on the Cultural Revolution*, I selected two recent essays by Marxist scholars praising the egalitarian, selfless ideals of the Maoist program. And in my concluding essay I hedged yet again, suggesting that although Mao had failed to eliminate privatism, self-interest, and elitism from Chinese society, it would be unwise to condemn him for trying. Still, my own waffling was rather mild compared to the ringing endorsements of Mao coming from some of my fellow academics. One colleague of high repute, in a burst of hyperbole that he would later come to regret, famously compared Mao to Thomas Jefferson, Winston Churchill, Charles de Gaulle, and Franklin Roosevelt. Another wrote of Mao, shortly after his death, that "By the example of his struggle, [Mao] communicates the vigor of hope, the vitality of possibility, the vision of justice. . . . Had he lived longer, he probably would have pioneered yet brighter trails on steeper mountains."

Because the Cultural Revolution coincided with a rising popular backlash against U.S. participation in the Vietnam War, there was a tendency in some left-wing academic circles to suspend disbelief and embrace the Maoist model as an alternative to American capitalism. This ideological flirtation with Maoism was amplified and reinforced by Middle America's blossoming love affair with China. In the warm afterglow of President Richard Nixon's February 1972 "opening" to China, ordinary Americans were given a sanitized, rose-tinted view of life inside China, as U.S. television networks aired a steady stream of soft news showing industrious people working hard, families picnicking at the Ming Tombs, consumers shopping at well-stocked department stores, and colorfully dressed moppets playing happily at after-school Children's Palaces. The combination of media fawning and left-wing scholarly attraction to the Cultural Revolution's abstract ideals fueled a brief national infatuation with all things Chinese.

My own ambivalence, including my suspension of disbelief, ended rather abruptly in mid-1972, when I came across a detailed firsthand account of Cultural Revolution upheaval in Fujian. It was a riveting tale, authored by a former Fujian Red Guard leader writing under the pseudonym Ken Ling. Titled *The Revenge of Heaven* (Tian chou), Ling's book painted a lurid picture of Chinese youths running wild, systematically defying authority, assaulting their teachers, betraying their parents, and fighting fierce, pitched battles with rival factions. It further portrayed an economy in disarray, marked by widespread industrial absenteeism and a rising tide of urban and rural beggary. In Ling's book, there were no newly liberated workers and peasants happily celebrating their ascent to socialist paradise.

Translated from the original Chinese by an American academic couple living in Taiwan, Ivan and Miriam London, *The Revenge of Heaven,* for all its page-turning excitement, strained credulity. Its horrifying accounts of Red Guard brutality, together with the author's habit of trumpeting his own central role in the events depicted—first as a zealous crusader for Chairman Mao and then as a conscience-stricken penitent—lent the book an air of exaggerated audacity and egotism. And Ling's eyewitness account of scavengers roaming China's back alleys and railroad stations in search of scraps of food conflicted with much of the received wisdom about China's apparent recovery from the Great Famine of 1959–61. After reading the book, I was deeply doubtful of Ken Ling's authenticity.

To satisfy my many lingering doubts, I wrote a long letter to Ivan and Miriam London, detailing the nature and sources of my skepticism and asking if they (or Ken Ling) could provide documentation or other collateral evidence to verify the many sensational claims made in Ling's book. To my surprise, they responded with an even longer letter—twelve pages, typed, single-spaced—containing a point-by-point response to each of my questions, along with an impressive list of bibliographical references (mostly Chinese sources) documenting in considerable detail many of Ken Ling's assertions. It was a serious, thoughtful response, and it ended with the Londons assuring me that notwithstanding a certain amount of authorial hubris, Ken Ling was for real, the genuine article. I found myself persuaded both by the quality of the Londons' evidence and by the measured tone of their response. The Cultural Revolution, I concluded, really had been an unmitigated national nightmare, without significant side-benefits for China's toiling masses, the long-suffering *laobaixing* (literally, "old hundred names").

The chief architect of that nightmare, Mao Zedong, ultimately proved unable to channel its destructive energies or control its outcome. After half a decade of leftist-inspired chaos, interspersed with periodic attempts to tame unruly Red Guards by subjecting them to military discipline, Mao in the early 1970s turned to his loyal lieutenant and chief troubleshooter, Premier Zhou Enlai, to revive China's paralyzed organs of government, revitalize its stagnant economy, and restore the shattered trust and confidence of the Chinese people. Difficult enough under the best of circumstances, Zhou's Herculean task was rendered even more daunting by Mao's failing health.

As the Chairman neared his eightieth birthday, he began to display characteristic symptoms of amyotrophic lateral sclerosis (ALS), a motor-neuron disorder known as Lou Gehrig's disease. Symptoms included muscular atrophy, loss of motor control, and slurred speech. Further complicated by an episode of congestive heart failure in 1972, Mao's worsening condition created deep concern within Zhongnanhai, the state residential compound in Beijing reserved for China's top Party and government leaders. Not coincidentally, the Chairman's deteriorating health also fueled a sharp increase in factional infighting within the Communist Party, as would-be successors began jostling for position.

Zhou Enlai was by temperament a pragmatist and a political moderate, and his efforts to put Humpty Dumpty together again ran afoul of both Jiang Qing, Mao's firebrand wife, who continued to defend the radical policies and purges of the Cultural Revolution, and Mao's latest designated successor, Defense Minister Lin Biao, who in 1969 officially replaced the disgraced Liu Shaoqi as the Chairman's heir apparent. With Mao's health visibly deteriorating, the three-way political tug-of-war between Zhou, Lin, and Jiang Qing began to heat up.

First to fall in the three-way contest for power was Lin Biao. Accused of conspiring to assassinate Mao and carry out a military coup d'état, Lin died in a plane crash in Mongolia on the night of September 12, 1971, while attempting to flee to the Soviet Union. The shocking story of Lin's treachery, as it gradually unfolded, had all the nail-biting suspense and melodrama of a B-grade soap opera. The characters, too, were straight out of central casting. First there was Lin himself, an unlikely conspirator who, by all accounts, was so heavily addicted to sleeping medication that on the night of the alleged coup attempt he was in a drug-induced stupor and had to be rousted out of bed and helped to flee the family home. Then there was

Lin's politically ambitious wife, the libidinous Ye Qun, a desperate house-wife who, frustrated by her husband's lack of attention, looked for love in all the wrong places. In her lustful pursuit of power, Ye fell into a bitter feud with Jiang Qing, herself no stranger to sexual politics and a woman whose own husband was known to have frequent extramural dalliances. (Mao's personal preference was for young peasant girls, a taste he indulged until his late seventies.) Next was Lin Biao's ruthless son Liguo, an air force officer and alleged master planner of the entire coup plot, who used his father's lofty position to further his own sinister ambitions. And last but not least was Lin Biao's faithful daughter Liheng, the well-meaning, tragic heroine of the piece. She inadvertently sealed her father's fate by informing a trusted family friend of her brother's impending coup, thereby setting off alarm bells in Zhongnanhai and triggering Lin Biao's drug-impaired mid-night dash to an airfield near the coastal resort town of Beidaihe, 170 miles from Beijing. There a British Trident jet was forcibly commandeered for an emergency flight that ultimately ended in disaster for Lin, his wife, and several members of the People's Liberation Army (PLA) high command.

As details of the drama leaked out, drop by delicious, voyeuristic drop, the story proved spellbinding—notwithstanding its many internal gaps and contradictions. Most intriguing of all were the glaring inconsistencies between the official Chinese version of Lin Biao's fatal flight and an on-scene investigation by a team of Russian and Mongolian forensic patholo-gists, who were the first to visit the crash site. According to their report, details of which appeared in the Soviet press, Lin's airplane could not have crashed because it ran out of fuel (which was the official Chinese explana-tion), since there had evidently been a struggle on board, involving gun-fire, followed by an explosion and an intense fire at the point of impact, with the plane and its human cargo severely charred as a result. Moreover, the badly burned corpse of the pilot, recovered from the wreckage, bore clear evidence of bullet wounds, further contradicting the official Chinese claim that the airplane's occupants had all perished in the crash.

As implausible as the official story seemed, more implausible still was the campaign of character assassination cooked up by CCP propagandists after the fact to explain Lin Biao's alleged treachery. Among other political high crimes and misdemeanors, Lin was posthumously (and rather incon-gruously) accused of being "a hidden son of the landlord class," "a secret admirer of Confucius," a "swindler like Liu Shaoqi," and a pro-Soviet "revisionist and traitor" who wanted "to practice the fascist dictatorship of the bourgeoisie." All extant photos of Lin were then withdrawn from circulation, and his published works were banned. Even the second edition of Mao's all-time best-selling "Little Red Book"—with more than 500 million copies in print—was quietly removed from Chinese bookstores and libraries: Its preface had been inscribed personally by Lin Biao.

The charge that Lin was a Soviet mole was an especially curious one. Although he had earned a pro-Stalin reputation early in his career (he spent time recuperating in the Soviet Union during World War II), Lin later became an outspoken critic of Soviet "revisionism." When Nikita Krushchev began to pursue détente with the United States in the late 1950s, Lin joined Chairman Mao in vigorously denouncing Krushchev's apostasy. Thereafter, he was unwavering in his public support for Mao's inflammatory anti-Soviet rhetoric.

Mao's claim, during his historic February 1972 meeting with Richard Nixon, that Lin had been the leader of "a reactionary group which is opposed to our contact with you" further compounded the confusion over Lin's true intentions.

Why was Lin Biao *really* killed? The most plausible answer lies in Mao's deepening paranoia, as revealed in the Chairman's well-known (and almost certainly unfounded) suspicion that Lin was preparing to usurp his power by reviving and occupying the long vacant post of President of the Republic, a position last held by the unfortunate Liu Shaoqi. Suffering from the plotter's instinctive fear of being plotted against, Mao assuaged his inner demons, as he had done before, by turning against his top lieutenant. Fully aware of Mao's track record, Lin's son Liguo anticipated Mao's betrayal and launched a preemptive counter-coup. In a classic self-fulfilling prophecy, Mao thus provoked the very thing he feared most.

THE LIN BIAO affair was by no means the only piece of baroque political theater to be acted out in China in the early 1970s. As Mao's health continued to deteriorate, new and increasingly bizarre reports of palace intrigue and conspiracy emerged. In 1973 Mao brought the experienced administrator Deng Xiaoping back from Cultural Revolution exile to help steady China's wobbling ship of state. With Deng's rehabilitation, alarm bells sounded for Jiang Qing and the other members of the Gang of Four, who viewed the pragmatic Deng as a natural ally of Zhou Enlai and a major impediment to their own political ambitions, now that Lin Biao had been removed from contention.

In a series of political maneuvers that can only be described as byzantine, Jiang and her leftist allies set about methodically trying to undermine the Zhou-Deng axis. First they went after Zhou himself, publishing a series of oblique historical allegories in the leftist-controlled press, suggesting that a popular folk hero of three thousand years ago, the Duke of Zhou, had betrayed his king and sold out his country in order to advance his own career. Though the sharp denunciation of an ancient feudal lord was puzzling on its face, to veteran observers there could be little doubt that the accusations of opportunism and treason constituted a thinly veiled attack on the Duke of Zhou's contemporary namesake, the highly popular Zhou Enlai. There is clear evidence, moreover, that Mao himself, in one of his many curious, mercurial mood changes, had authorized the attack. The Chairman was said to be resentful of all the international attention focused upon Zhou, crediting him for China's recent opening to the United States. In Mao's view, Zhou had become a bit too cozy with Henry Kissinger, and the Chairman reminded him, pointedly, that "When joining hands with the bourgeoisie, one tends to forget struggle." Zhou was forced to make a humble "self-criticism" (*ziwo piping*) at the end of 1973. Having been sternly reminded just who was boss, Zhou was spared further criticism. Mao needed him to pilot China's lurching ship of state.

With Zhou Enlai now effectively shielded from further criticism, Jiang Qing and her gang shifted the brunt of their political criticism from Zhou to Deng Xiaoping. Launching a series of media campaigns in 1974 and 1975, they defended the leftist policies of the Cultural Revolution and leveled oblique attacks against a certain "unrepentant capitalist roader" who allegedly sought to dismantle China's socialist economy and weaken the Communist Party's proletarian class dictatorship. While no names were named, there was little doubt that Deng was the principal target, since it was he, in collaboration with Liu Shaoqi, who had dismantled Mao's Great Leap in the early 1960s and blunted the Chairman's subsequent drive to rekindle class struggle in the Four Cleanups. Though the leftists had succeeded—with Mao's blessing—in toppling both Liu and Deng in 1966, Deng was now on the rebound, with the present-day "Duke of Zhou" as his principal patron and protector.

The use of veiled, oblique criticism was necessary because Party rules strictly prohibited direct attacks on named officials without prior Central Committee authorization. Moreover, since Mao had personally signed off on Deng Xiaoping's rehabilitation, openly labeling Deng as an "unrepentant capitalist roader" at this point would cast doubt on Mao's judgment. Not surprisingly, the resulting indirection made the job of China watchers considerably more hazardous and uncertain.

Further compounding the problem of interpreting these events were Mao's frequent, unexplained absences from the public arena. Since the early stages of the Cultural Revolution, Mao had periodically disappeared from view for varying lengths of time, giving rise to a great deal of foreign media speculation, conjecture, and sheer rumor concerning his whereabouts and the state of his health. One of the most bizarre instances occurred early in the Cultural Revolution, in an episode that might be termed, with apologies to Sir Arthur Conan Doyle, "The Strange Case of the Chairman's Meandering Mole."

From November 1965 until July 1966, Mao Zedong did not appear in public. During his long absence, the Hong Kong media buzzed with unconfirmed reports that a Swiss doctor specializing in the treatment of central nervous system disorders had flown secretly to Beijing to treat an unnamed high official. Speculation mounted that Mao was critically ill. So persistent were the rumors of Mao's imminent demise that when the Chairman finally reappeared in public for his famous Yangzi River swim in mid-July 1966, some Western experts ventured the opinion that this was a stand-in, a doppelgänger posing as Mao. Such conjecture was lent added credence when a classified U.S. intelligence report suggested that the post-Yangzi Mao might not be the Chairman at all—his body movements were uncharacteristic and his celebrated mole was not in precisely the correct place on his chin. Such rumors were only put to rest weeks later, when an obviously living and breathing Mao convened a Central Committee meeting in early August. Subsequently, it was confirmed that Mao's mole had not in fact migrated, and that a bloated, overweight Chairman Mao had indeed swum—or, rather, floated downstream like a bobbing cork—in the polluted waters of the Yangzi.

Mao's public appearances became even more infrequent in the early 1970s. In February 1972, when he famously met with Richard Nixon and Henry Kissinger in Beijing during "the week that changed the world," his health was so poor that it almost caused his personal physician to cancel the historic meeting. Unbeknownst to the visiting U.S. president, the room adjacent to Mao's study, where the Mao-Nixon meeting took place, had been outfitted as an emergency medical center, complete with operating theater, with a retinue of doctors and nurses standing by in the event that

Mao required immediate attention. Making matters worse was Mao's distrust of Western medicine, which led him to stubbornly ignore the advice of his personal physician, Dr. Li Zhisui, who had received professional training at a U.S.-run medical college in South China during World War II.

As Mao's physical condition deteriorated, the number of unsolved mysteries swirling around the corridors of Zhongnanhai increased. One of the most puzzling of these concerned the spectacular 1973 ascent of a previously unknown factory security officer, thirty-six-year-old Wang Hongwen, to the exalted post of CCP vice-chairman, making him the number three man in the Communist Party hierarchy, ranking behind only Mao and Zhou Enlai. Just who was Wang Hongwen, and how did he rise so high, so quickly, in a country known for its closed leadership circle of elderly gerontocrats?

Speculation was intense. Some China watchers regarded Wang's rise as a clear-cut victory for the leftist faction under Jiang Qing, since it apparently gave them an additional seat on the all-important Politburo; others regarded it as a tacit victory for Zhou Enlai's moderate faction, since the leftists presumably would have preferred to have one of their senior leaders—such as Shanghai party chief Zhang Chunqiao or even Jiang Qing herself—occupy the important number three spot. Yet a third conjecture, at odds with the others, held that Wang Hongwen was Mao's hitherto unidentified son-in-law, the husband of Mao's only surviving biological daughter, Li Na. The credibility of such speculation was rendered problematic, however, when Australian prime minister Gough Whitlam was granted a rare personal interview with Mao in early November 1973. Unexpectedly, Wang Hongwen was also present at this meeting. Taking advantage of Wang's presence, Whitlam asked the visibly frail, slow-speaking Mao about Wang's background: "He must be very talented. Where did you find him?" Waiting for Whitlam's words to be translated, Mao, who early in the interview acknowledged that his body was "riddled with disease" and that he had "an appointment with God," slowly turned his head, fixing his gaze on Wang. He replied cryptically: "I don't know" (wo buzhidao).

With the internal dynamics of Beijing's factional conflicts and shifting political fortunes carefully hidden from even the most experienced outside observers, the black box of Chinese politics remained, in many crucial respects, a Churchillian "riddle wrapped in a mystery inside an enigma." As fresh rumors of palace intrigue swept through Beijing in the mid-1970s, fueled by reports of Mao's approaching death, I was reminded of yet another Churchillian metaphor. The late British statesman had once famously likened politics in the Kremlin to "bulldogs fighting under a rug. An outsider hears only the growling, and when he sees the bones fly out from beneath it is obvious who won." Outsiders like me could hear plenty of growling under the Chinese rug in the mid-1970s, but in the absence of flying bones, there was no way to tell for sure who was winning, who was losing, or who was doing what to whom. It was all very frustrating.

Political tensions, already high, ratcheted sharply upward again in the first half of 1976. In early January, Zhou Enlai died of bladder cancer. Though his disease was first diagnosed in 1972, Mao's deep distrust of Western medicine led him to impose a curtain of silence, banning additional diagnostic testing and refusing permission for Zhou to undergo surgery. By the time Zhou was finally hospitalized in 1974, the cancer had metastasized.

Immediately after Zhou's death, the Gang of Four, fearful of an antileftist backlash, put out a notice banning all public displays of grief or mourning. Bitterly resentful, Zhou's many supporters bided their time. Three months later their opportunity came. In early April 1976, on the occasion of the annual Qing Ming Festival, a day set aside for sweeping and decorating ancestral graves, hundreds of mourners defied the ban on public grieving, placing funeral wreaths in Zhou's honor at the foot of the Heroes' Monument in the center of Tiananmen Square.

Alarmed, Jiang Qing and her associates ordered the wreaths removed under cover of darkness. When thousands of angry Beijingers showed up the next day to protest removal of the wreaths, the Gang of Four called in teams of leftist "worker militias" to forcibly disperse the protesters. In the ensuing melée, dozens of people were beaten and hundreds more arrested.

Sensing an opportunity to turn an unanticipated mini-crisis to their political advantage, the leftists sought, and were granted, an audience with Mao. By this time Mao, his condition deteriorating visibly, was living in virtual seclusion in his private villa inside Zhongnanhai. At their late-night audience with the Chairman, the leftists put forward their own highly skewed version of the events of the previous thirty-six hours, describing the laying of wreaths in Tiananmen Square, and the subsequent mass protest over their removal, as a "counterrevolutionary incident," and they accused Deng Xiaoping of deliberately manipulating the entire episode in an effort to discredit the Cultural Revolution. This time, a severely enfeebled Chairman Mao accepted their version of events and personally ordered Deng to be struck down yet again. Jiang Qing was jubilant.

When Mao finally expired in early September 1976, the bones began to fly out from under the rug. Jiang Qing had been the moon to Mao's sun, and when his light went out, her reflected luminosity suddenly dimmed. Widely despised for her role in spreading terror and anarchy during the Cultural Revolution, Jiang quickly found herself politically isolated and vulnerable, without powerful patrons or protectors. Four weeks after Mao's death, a coalition of senior military and political leaders, some of them survivors of Cultural Revolution attacks, placed her under arrest along with the other members of her erstwhile gang, including Shanghai Party chief Zhang Chunqiao and the unfortunate, high-flying Wang Hongwen. The most serious charge leveled against Jiang at this point was that she had contrived to seize power by tampering with her late husband's handwritten directives, including both his last testament and his personal choice of a little-known provincial outsider, Hua Guofeng, to succeed him as Party chairman.

The specific allegations leveled at Jiang were enigmatic and ambiguous at best. For example, she was officially accused of forging a brief marginal notation, in Mao's handwriting, on a Central Committee document. "Act according to principles laid down" was the phrase she purportedly inserted. According to the official media, this was clear evidence of Jiang's scheme to succeed Chairman Mao by portraying herself as the most loyal and steadfast defender of the Maoist faith. Along with many other China watchers, I could only scratch my head and wonder what it all *really* meant.

The sudden eruption of previously submerged factional antagonisms caught many people by surprise, including some who ought to have known better. The night Mao died, I was invited to participate in a ninety-minute Public Broadcasting Service (PBS) news special, broadcast live on national television. One of the other participants was my UCLA colleague, historian Philip Huang. To say that Phil and I did not see eye to eye on things Chinese was an understatement. Phil could be arrogant and imperious at times, and he had bought into the Maoist mythology of human liberation through class struggle. His rosy, see-no-evil view of Chinese communism rubbed me the wrong way. (Phil had once argued, for example, that the PLA's 1950 invasion and occupation of Tibet had been entirely peaceful and was welcomed by the local populace.) For his part, Phil had long suspected me of being a covert employee of the CIA. Up to this point, however, our mutual disdain had been kept pretty much under wraps.

The wrapping came off toward the end of the PBS news special, when we began to argue on camera. The question before us was "What's next for China?" Phil boldly proclaimed that there were no significant factional differences dividing China's top leaders, and he confidently predicted a smooth, trouble-free political transition to the post-Mao era. I responded with a somewhat exaggerated display of disbelief, pointing out (among other things) that Jiang Qing and her associates were widely despised in China, and that it probably wouldn't be long before they found themselves under attack. Phil interrupted me repeatedly, and I responded with rising intensity. For the remainder of the broadcast we went at each other with dripping sarcasm and barely disguised mutual contempt, pausing only long enough for our obviously flustered host and moderator, the veteran newscaster Clete Roberts, to sign off the air. Then, with our microphones off and the credits rolling, Phil and I resumed our shouting match. We didn't stop until the stage lights were turned off. My son Matt, who was eleven at the time, was in the studio, and he was deeply embarrassed by my tantrum. "What happened to you, Dad?" he asked as we drove home. I did not have an adequate response. "I just lost it," I said sheepishly. When I got home, Carolyn, who had watched the whole mess on TV, looked at me quizzically, then did her best to reassure me that I hadn't been quite so out of control as I had feared. I have a videotape of the entire PBS blowup but have never had the stomach to replay it. Perhaps I'll show it at my retirement party. (Memo to self: Be sure to invite Phil Huang.)

The man whom Mao Zedong ultimately chose to succeed him, Hua Guofeng, was a former Party secretary in Mao's native Hunan. With a reputation for intelligence and hard work, Hua had gained Mao's confidence during the Chairman's final years by remaining personally loyal and refusing to align himself with any of Beijing's feuding political factions. Now, with Mao dead and Jiang Qing under arrest, Hua set about trying to stabilize his own power and authority. In so doing, however, he found himself facing a mounting challenge from Deng Xiaoping. In the aftermath of the Gang of Four's arrest, Deng's supporters lobbied hard to remove the "counterrevolutionary" label Mao had recently affixed to him at Jiang Qing's behest. It was all very byzantine. The official account of these events had a strangely surreal quality, testing even the most seasoned observer's capacity to suspend disbelief.

As I parsed, pondered, and puzzled over the known facts (and a lot of unknown ones as well), trying to assemble the various pieces into a plausible picture of the dogfight under the rug, my frustration mounted. It occurred to me that the entire murky situation lent itself nicely to satire. Assuming a pseudonymous literary persona, I composed a lighthearted piece of political doggerel with the title "Ode to Jiang Qing." On a lark, I submitted it to an academic journal, *Contemporary China*, under the nom de plume Lim Rick. Since *Contemporary China* was a serious publication devoted to scholarly analysis of Chinese society and politics, I did not expect the editor, Columbia University sociologist Edwin Winckler, to accept it. Much to my surprise, however, the poem appeared in the December 1976 issue:

> *They say that Mao's widow, Jiang Qing,*
> *Did the most terrible thing*
> *As Mao lay deathly ill*
> *She rewrote his Last Will*
> *And scandalized all of Beijing*
>
> *A malevolent influence, she*
> *Conspired to drive Mao up a tree*
> *She squelched his last breath*
> *And nagged him to death*
> *In order Chairwoman to be*
>
> *Upon hearing the news, Hua Guofeng*
> *Whose virtues 'til then were unsung*
> *Confronted Ms. Jiang*
> *Bringing armed guards along*
> *To silence her very sharp tongue*
>
> *As head of the rad "gang of four"*
> *Madame Mao Deng Xiaoping did abhor*
> *To hasten his purge*
> *Her pals she did urge*
> *To falsely accuse him once more*
>
> *Alas, her plans all went awry*
> *Though she gave it the old college try*
> *Poor Deng was dismissed*
> *But his comrades were pissed*
> *So they stuck it to her by and by*

Her scheme having failed to succeed
Madame Mao for her life had to plead
But the masses were rude
For they knew they'd been screwed
By a woman corrupted by greed

Now that this story's been told
The moral appears rather bold:
Those who want to be King
Should remember one thing:
Best wait till the body is cold.

AFTER THE POEM was published, a number of my China-watching colleagues wrote or phoned to ask if I was the mysterious "Mr. Rick," as the editor obliquely identified me. For the record, I neither confirmed nor denied their suspicions. Interestingly, however, no one questioned my professional judgment in making light of such a serious subject as the succession to Mao Zedong; they, too, had been badly wrong-footed by the unexpected events of 1976.

Thus encouraged, I subsequently penned a second piece of waggish Lim Rickery, in a short-lived (and ultimately futile) one-man rebellion against China's recent adoption of *pinyin* (literally, "combined sounds") as the official romanization system for the Chinese language. With its many seemingly illogical, tongue-tying spelling conventions, *pinyin* proved extremely difficult to master, for foreigners and Chinese alike. For example, *pinyin* takes the English sound "she" and renders it as "xi," the sound "ching" (as in "cha-ching") is spelled "qing," and "joe" comes out as "zhou." It is all very confusing and counterintuitive. My one-stanza protest was published in *Contemporary China* in 1979:

I cannot pronounce Deng Xiaoping
Zhang Chunqiao, Qin Shihuang or Jiang Qing.
Though I qerish pinyin
With a xit-eating grin,
I zhust cannot grasp the damned thing.

Sad to say, *Contemporary China* expired in 1980 after an all-too-brief four-year run. I like to think that it folded despite, rather than because of, its louche, over-the-top poetry.

BY FAR MY most fateful—and ultimately unfortunate—venture into the world of satiric verse came toward the end of 1975, when I sent a personal note, also in limerick form, to my friend and colleague Michel Oksenberg at the University of Michigan. Mike Oksenberg was a couple of years my senior. With a Ph.D. from Columbia University, he was possessed of a keen intellect, boundless energy and ambition, and an abundance of boyish charm. By the mid-1970s he was also the fastest-rising star in the field of Chinese politics. Later in the decade he would play a key role in the normalization of U.S.-China relations.

In the fall of 1975, while I was still pondering how to connect the enigmatic pieces of the Chinese political puzzle, Mike gave an interview to *Newsweek* magazine. In it he put forth a bold, definitive interpretation of the conspiracy and death of Lin Biao and a comprehensive explanation of the current factional alignments, ideological disputes, and policy agendas of all the key players at Mao's court. It was, on the face of it, an impressive piece of detective work. But given the extreme murkiness that enveloped Beijing's palace politics in this period, I found Mike's analysis too definitive, clear-cut, and self-assured by half. He had conveniently ignored certain facts while exaggerating others. So I proceeded to tell him so—tweaking him mischievously in a poem titled "For a Peking Tom":

They say that Mao crossed up his heir
Refusing to vacate his Chair
He dumped his successor
(Who always said "yessir")
By knocking him off in mid-air.

This story, you may well concede,
Was invented simply to mislead
Do we really know
Why Lin Biao had to go?
Was he truly undone by his greed?

And what of our friend Deng Xiaoping
Who did the most terrible thing:
With sanzi and yibao[1]
He enraged Chairman Mao
Yet now he's on top in Beijing.

So I say to you, friend Michel O,
With so many things we don't know
It really takes cheek
To claim in Newsweek
That you can tell Mao's friend from foe.

When you state to which factions belong
Chairman Mao, Premier Zhou and Ms. Jiang
It compounds my confusion
So I draw the conclusion
That you are quite probably wrong.

These quibbles aren't wholly gratuitous
Your claims have stirred up a great hue and fuss
But your statements of fact
Make my colon contract
Where'd you get all that bullshit you threw at us?

Mike was not amused. What had started off as good-natured (albeit barbed) satire was taken as a deep personal insult. He responded by sending back my original poem, which he had marked up line by line, criticizing its rhyme, meter, and content. With a series of slashes and cryptic comments penned in black ink, Mike dismissed my poem with a grade of C+. I wrote back, saying I thought it deserved at least an A–. Sadly, this episode touched off a quarrel that was to last for two decades. It was also my last attempt at dabbling in doggerel.

MY RELATIONSHIP WITH Mike Oksenberg had begun innocuously enough. We first met in the late 1960s, at the Universities Service Centre in

[1] *Sanzi yibao* refers to Deng's attempt to restore small-scale family farming in the aftermath of the Great Leap Forward.

Hong Kong. In the early 1970s we attended a number of professional meetings and conferences together, and it was at one of those conferences, held in the Canadian resort town of Banff in August 1970, that a bond of sorts developed between us. The conference theme was "Elites in the People's Republic of China," and it was chaired by Bob Scalapino. Most of the thirty or so participants were, like me, freshly minted young Ph.D.s; also like me, the majority had undertaken their dissertation research at the Universities Service Centre in Hong Kong. The overall youthfulness of the group was offset by the presence of a few eminent senior scholars, including Bob, A. Doak Barnett, John Lindbeck, and Donald Klein.

Multiday academic conferences tend to exhibit distinctive group biorhythms. They usually begin with a burst of enthusiasm, as participants display high initial energy, efficiency, and seriousness of purpose. Depending on how many sessions, panels, and papers are packed into each day's proceedings, the energy level gradually diminishes. Toward the end of the second day, fatigue sets in and a letdown ensues. If participants have come from afar, jet lag may exacerbate this downturn. In any event, the third day of a conference is generally its lowest point. Attention drifts; discussions lose focus. If evening sessions are held, participants may doze off. Typically on the final day there is a fresh burst of energy, or second wind, as participants approach the finish line.

At the Banff conference, multiple sessions were held each day. The work ethic was strong. Participants presented and discussed papers one after another. It was all quite intense. Toward the end of the second day we found ourselves falling behind schedule and decided to add an evening session. It was late, and we were starting to lose focus. It must have been the mixture of exhaustion, jet lag, and alcohol. How else to explain what happened next?

During a break in the evening's proceedings, four of us—Doak Barnett, Don Klein, Mike Oksenberg, and I—were sitting at the hotel bar, chatting. We were feeling fatigued and a little giddy. The paper under discussion at the moment concerned the impact of the Cultural Revolution on China's ethnic minorities. Someone in the group of four suggested that, in consideration of the lateness of the hour and the waning energy and enthusiasm of the participants, perhaps we should try to liven things up a bit. Doak smiled and said, "Why don't we discuss the 'Kunming incident'?" For a brief moment Don looked puzzled. "What's that?" he asked credulously, whereupon Doak winked at him. Don immediately twigged, and Mike and

I exchanged glances. The newly constituted "gang of four" shared a brief, conspiratorial grin before getting up to rejoin our unsuspecting colleagues at the conference table. The fix was in.

A few minutes later the meeting reconvened. Halfway into the group discussion of June Dreyer's paper on minority nationalities, Doak raised his hand. "There's a lesson to be learned here from the Kunming incident," he suggested earnestly. He then proceeded to spin a wholly fabricated, extemporized yarn about an Islamic general, Ma Dapu, who had rebelled against the Maoists during the Cultural Revolution. As if on cue, Don (who was a well-known biographer of Chinese Communist leaders) interrupted with a reassuring, "Yeah, that's the guy," thereby reinforcing Doak's account of the Kunming incident. The hook was now baited.

Next, Mike picked up the thread of the story, adding an entirely new wrinkle: a supposed intra-family quarrel between General Ma Dapu and his (equally fictitious) half brother, Ma Dafu. Mike proceeded to analyze the origins of the dispute between the Ma brothers, tracing it back to their different pre-1949 PLA field army affiliations. When Mike's narrative began to falter, I jumped in to pick up the slack, spinning the yarn still further. Around the room, people were paying close attention. Most looked vaguely puzzled, as if they *should know* what we were talking about; a few nodded vigorously, affecting total comprehension of the Kunming incident and its Ma family protagonists. None of the thirty or so participants displayed even the slightest hint of incredulity. June Dreyer, whose paper we had hijacked, looked stunned. Neither she nor anyone else in the room thought to challenge the supreme *truthiness* of this tale of fratricidal rivalry and rebellion.

I continued to embellish the story, shifting my focus onto the nature of factional cleavages among Chinese Muslims. Riffing on a typographical error in one of the conference papers (the word "economic" had been misspelled), I made the point that while some roots of ethnic conflict in China were obviously *exonomic* in nature, others were clearly *endonomic*. Still, no one twigged to the hoax. All remained silent, listening attentively. So I continued to confabulate, finding it harder and harder to keep a straight face as I spun grand, nonsensical theories to explain the imaginary split between nonexistent Islamic militarists. My grad school training in sociological abstraction was finally paying off. I even fooled my own mentor!

As I spoke, I glanced discreetly in Mike's direction, then at Doak and Don, all of whom were struggling to maintain their composure. At that point I lost control and burst into laughter, followed immediately my three coconspirators, who howled with delight. Around the room people stared uncomprehendingly at the four of us, then at one another, not knowing what to make of it all. As the realization dawned that they had been victims of a prank, they, too, began to laugh—except for June Dreyer. She was far too upset to find our little joke amusing. Afterward, June remained angry at me for the better part of a decade. Happily, the ice melted in the 1980s, and we have been friends ever since—though neither of us has ever mentioned the Kunming incident.

That incident cemented my bond with Mike. From then on we shared a semi-bantering, semi-affectionate, semi-rivalrous relationship, reminiscent of same-sex siblings. As his intelligence, drive, and ambition subsequently propelled him to the front ranks of the profession in the mid-'70s, and thence into national politics as the resident China expert on the National Security Council (NSC) staff during Jimmy Carter's presidency, I experienced clear twinges of envy. I suspect this helps to explain my plunge into poetic parody following Mike's 1975 *Newsweek* interview. In any event, by the time Mike went to Washington, D.C., in 1977, the competitive undertones in our relationship were clearly evident.

While Mike's star rose rapidly in the mid-1970s, my own career trajectory began to level off. A turning point occurred late in 1975, when I was nominated for a prestigious International Affairs Fellowship, awarded to scholars under thirty-five years of age by the Council on Foreign Relations (CFR) in New York. I eventually made the short list, and after a number of notes and phone calls between the CFR staff and myself, it was proposed that I should spend my fellowship tenure in residence at the State Department's Bureau of Intelligence and Research in Washington, D.C. I was deeply flattered, but I was also deeply ambivalent. A position in the U.S. government would mean moving my family again, for at least one year and more likely two. This presented problems. Carolyn was preparing to go back to school to begin training as a psychiatric social worker, and Matthew was about to enter junior high school, a difficult transition under the best of circumstances. And to top it off, our daughter Kristen, age six, was just entering kindergarten. Moving would clearly be disruptive. Still experiencing periodic pangs of guilt for having put Carolyn and Matthew through two stress-filled years in Taiwan and Hong Kong, I felt an obligation to redress the imbalance between career needs and family values. Carolyn had put her own career on hold for me;

now it was time for me to reciprocate: *Ni bang wode mang, wo bang nide mang.*

After a good bit of agonizing, I turned down the CFR fellowship. Though I strongly supported Carolyn's resumption of her long-delayed professional training, and though I tried hard to accept the notion that turning down the fellowship was the right thing to do, I never quite succeeded in convincing myself. No matter what story I told myself, when all was said and done it *felt* like a major sacrifice. And besides, Mike Oksenberg was moving to Washington, D.C. Didn't *his* family have needs, too?

The contrast between my own highly conflicted concession to family responsibility and Mike's unambivalent, full-bore pursuit of personal ambition served to amplify the tension between us. On one occasion, a couple of years later, we almost came to blows. We were chatting with a group of colleagues during a break in a China conference when Mike proudly boasted that his wife Lois always packed his bags for him before he went on a business trip. I quipped that it probably wouldn't hurt him to pack his own bags. There followed a sharply worded exchange, with the subject quickly shifting from packing suitcases to women's liberation. Mike said something unkind about the feminist movement, and I called him a chauvinist. Tempers flared, and our colleagues had to step in to restrain us. Without my being aware of it, my envy of Mike—he being the older, and more celebrated sibling—had morphed into full-blown resentment.

MIKE'S GOVERNMENT SERVICE coincided with the full normalization of U.S.-China relations. Working under Jimmy Carter's National Security adviser Zbigniew Brzezinski, Mike was very active in the negotiations leading up to the final agreement of December 15, 1978. In May of that year he accompanied Brzezinski on a trip to China, in the course of which a significant diplomatic breakthrough occurred. With Mike advising him, Brzezinski offered the Chinese the one thing they most wanted from the United States (other than Taiwan on a silver platter): a common front against the aggressive Soviet polar bear to the north.

"Hegemonism" was the Chinese code word for Soviet global expansion. And it was Mike who originally suggested that Brzezinski could warm the hearts of his Chinese interlocutors by criticizing Moscow's hegemonic ambitions in world politics. (Previously, in the interest of maintaining U.S. evenhandedness in the escalating Sino-Soviet dispute, the Nixon and Ford administrations had carefully refrained from publicly using the H word.)

Brzezinski waited for his opening, then seized it. While on a sightseeing excursion to the Great Wall with his Chinese Foreign Ministry hosts, Brzezinski played the Russia card. Pointing to the long, steeply inclined stairway leading to the top of the Wall, he proposed an unusual sporting wager: "Last one to the top fights the Russians in Ethiopia!" He then led his Chinese hosts in an impromptu footrace. He won, then stopped to chat with a group of Chinese sailors who asked to have their picture taken with him. "Do you know you are posing with an imperialist?" he joked. Not so, said one of the navy men. "We are having our photograph taken with the polar-bear tamer."

One can only imagine the excitement that reverberated behind the walls of Zhongnanhai that evening. The following night, at an official banquet, Brzezinski underscored the change in U.S. attitude by proposing a toast in which, for the first time, he specifically acknowledged a common Chinese-American security interest in opposing hegemonism. And he went on to state that the United States had "made up its mind" to normalize relations with China. Though he did not mention the Soviet Union by name, the intended target of his remarks was clear.

Shortly thereafter, negotiations on the full normalization of U.S.-China relations moved into high gear. The talks proceeded smoothly and rapidly. In July a high-level U.S. government delegation, led by President Carter's science adviser Dr. Frank Press, arrived in Beijing to discuss the initiation of Sino-American cooperation in science and technology. Although no major breakthroughs were announced at the time, a significant anti-Soviet initiative was discussed at this meeting: a proposed arrangement under which the United States would install a sophisticated, top-secret CIA electronic listening post deep inside Xinjiang, in Northwest China, to monitor Soviet missile tests and military communications. The U.S. government was growing deeply concerned about rising political instability in Iran and was looking to relocate its northern Iranian electronic surveillance facilities. Under the proposed arrangement, the CIA would share with China all "comint"—communications intelligence—gleaned from the operation of this new listening post. Mike was deeply involved in these early discussions, which reached fruition a year later.

When the final U.S.-China normalization agreement was announced in mid-December 1978, it was a milestone for China's new leader, Deng Xiaoping. Having recently triumphed over Hua Guofeng in a tortuous two-year contest of wills, Deng relished his new role as China's "paramount leader."

In a triumphal tour of the United States in January 1979, Deng donned a ten-gallon hat, attended the Grand Ole Opry in Nashville, rode a stage-coach at a Texas rodeo, test-piloted a NASA flight simulator—and promised to punish Vietnam for its recent, Soviet-backed invasion of Cambodia.

A man of his word, when Deng returned to Beijing he promptly launched a large-scale "punitive counterattack" against Vietnam. Though the State Department verbally protested China's behavior, the U.S. government basically sat on its hands, taking no concrete action. Brzezinski's sporting wager thus passed its first major operational test: China and the United States had become tacit strategic allies against the Soviet polar bear and its client states.

Notwithstanding China's short, nasty war with Vietnam and a sharp Congressional backlash against President Carter's willingness to pay a heavy price for normalization with China in terms of the abrupt termination of formal U.S. diplomatic and military relations with Taiwan, Mike Oksenberg could barely hide his personal satisfaction. A longtime champion of closer U.S.-China ties, he basked in the warm afterglow of normalization. If he was bothered by China's Vietnam invasion, or by anti-American demonstrations in Taipei, or by the deepening schism between his boss, Zbigniew Brzezinski, and Secretary of State Cyrus Vance, he didn't show it. Vance had been a proponent of strict evenhandedness in U.S. relations with China and the Soviet Union, and he had argued strongly against Brzezinski's anti-hegemonic partnership with the People's Republic. When Brzezinski won over the Chinese leaders with his bear-baiting tactics, Vance found himself, and his top Asia policy adviser, Assistant Secretary of State Richard Holbrooke, frozen out of the U.S.-China policy loop throughout the final stages of the normalization process. Mike, on the other hand, was in like Flynn. The animosity between the two became so thick that when Mike maneuvered to exclude Holbrooke from a key meeting with Deng Xiaoping, Holbrooke had to be physically restrained from assaulting him.

For the remainder of his term at the NSC, Mike was the most prominent China expert in the Carter administration. He seemed to relish the intense, partisan milieu of Washington politics, and he clearly enjoyed his ascendancy over Holbrooke. On those few occasions when I visited him in his office at the Old Executive Office Building, near the West Wing of the White House, we chatted with superficial amiability, sometimes sharing a laugh about our Banff conference hoax, but there was also a hint of condescension and a patronizing undertone in Mike's voice. He was clearly at the top of his game.

TOWARD THE END of Jimmy Carter's presidential term in 1980, Mike left the government to resume his teaching career in Ann Arbor. Evidently he also resumed nursing old wounds. To mark his initial post-NSC reappearance on the national academic scene in the spring of 1981, he chose the annual meeting of the Association for Asian Studies (AAS), held that year in Toronto. He accepted an invitation to serve as commentator on one of the many scholarly papers being presented there. The AAS usually reserves one or two of its most spacious meeting rooms, seating several hundred people, for plenary sessions involving a current hot topic or an appearance by a notable personage. Within the Asian studies community, Mike was now a very notable personage indeed. As expected, his appearance drew a large crowd, and he obviously relished being in the limelight. Coincidentally or not—I still do not know for certain—the paper he had agreed to critique was mine.

In the months preceding the 1981 AAS meeting, I had been in residence at the Research Policy Institute of the University of Lund, Sweden. At the invitation of the institute's director, Jon Sigurdsson, I had prepared a lengthy study of China's traditional approach to scientific knowledge, research, and experimentation and its implications for China's post-Mao efforts to catch up with the advanced science of the West. It was a complex research project that dug deep into China's ancient past to explore the philosophical and cultural antecedents of the contemporary Chinese fixation on "scientism" as a panacea for China's ills.

When I presented my paper at the Toronto AAS meeting, I began with a rather dense and complex theoretical exposition, which contained a fair amount of Berkeley-style sociological jargon. Here is how I framed my main argument:

> Chinese science has been, and continues to be, fettered by a series
> of endemic cognitive constraints that have their origins not in
> any particular pattern of formal administrative relations, organi-
> zational structures, or incentive systems, but rather in the more
> abstract and elusive realm of human culture. Specifically, the insti-
> tutionalization of the ethos of modern scientific inquiry in China
> has been significantly impeded by the persistence of a number of

atavistic cultural traits that have survived the passing of China's traditional Confucian order. The strength and durability of these traits is a function of their high degree of congruence with the ideology and political ethos of Chinese communism.

In all, my presentation took almost forty minutes and was laced with references to such premodern Chinese cultural traits as number mysticism, associative thinking, and cognitive formalism. When I finished, I took my seat. Across the stage, Mike walked slowly to the podium. Grinning his boyish grin, he looked out at the five hundred people in the packed auditorium. Pausing a moment for effect, he proceeded to rip my paper—and me—to shreds. His voice heavy with sarcasm, he first congratulated me on my sophisticated polysyllabic vocabulary and on my somewhat belated discovery of the nature of traditional Chinese culture. Then came feigned admiration for my "brilliant observation" that present behavior often has its roots in the past. He went on in that vein for about fifteen minutes, heaping scorn upon ridicule upon abuse. The audience sat in stunned silence; I went into deep shock as *my* bones flew out from under the rug.

When Mike finished, I rose unsteadily to respond but couldn't think of anything to say. I was dumbfounded. After a pause that seemed like hours (but was probably only moments), I decided it would be futile to rebut ridicule with reason. I had to fight fire with fire. So I returned his sarcasm in kind, suggesting that the next time he agreed to comment on a paper he might consider reading it first. If necessary, I continued, I'd be happy to explain the "big words" to him. And I went on to inquire solicitously whether he had experienced a sudden loss of cabin pressure on his flight to Toronto, causing a temporary oxygen deficit to his brain. Feeble, to be sure, but it was the best I could do on short notice.

The corridors were already buzzing as I made my escape from the conference hall to the nearest restroom, wishing I could become invisible. "Did you hear *that*?" I overheard one person say. "It was *brutal*," replied a second. "What's got into Mike?" asked a third. "How could he *do* that?" Only then did it dawn on me that, like Chinese science, Mike's verbal assault was also rooted in ancient history—in this case, *our* history:

> *. . . your statements of fact*
> *Make my colon contract*
> *Where'd you get all that bullshit you threw at us?*

In the aftermath of my verbal mugging in Toronto, friends and colleagues were generally very supportive, offering their sympathies and expressing amazement at Mike's intemperate outburst. But that was small comfort, and I felt like crawling into a small hole.

IT HAS BEEN rightly observed that academics as a breed tend to be intensely competitive and egoistic. We can be savagely territorial when it comes to defending our intellectual turf. As Henry Kissinger once famously quipped, academic disputes tend to be nastier than real-world battles precisely because the stakes are so low. And it is thus not unusual for scholars in the same field to trade cleverly veiled (or not so veiled) barbs at academic meetings and in the pages of learned journals. In the course of my own career, aside from my long-running feuds with Mike Oksenberg and Phil Huang (and my brief exchange of unpleasantries with Charlie Neuhauser), I have generally avoided quarreling with colleagues in public. And even with Mike and Phil, the underlying hostility remained buried most of the time, only occasionally erupting into open animosity.

Over the years I have generally prided myself on not taking myself—or my career—so seriously that I couldn't laugh at my own foibles. That quality, sorely tested after my PBS shouting match with Phil and my disastrous Toronto mauling by Mike, has enabled me, for the most part, to maintain a reasonably balanced perspective on matters both personal and professional. In the end, I even managed to take away something of value from my otherwise intensely painful AAS encounter with Mike: Never again did I lard my professional writings with dense patches of theoretical jargon. They say old habits die hard; well, this one died abruptly. I guess I should be grateful to Mike after all.

4

Through the Looking Glass

MY MAIDEN VISIT to China in 1975 involved a rather long and complex odyssey. It began in April 1971 when, at Mao Zedong's initiative, Zhou Enlai unexpectedly sent a message to a U.S. table tennis team then on tour in Japan, inviting them to stop over in Beijing for "friendly competition." The table tennis itself was no contest. Ranked number one in the world, the Chinese players toyed with their twenty-eighth-ranked U.S. counterparts, deliberately (and conspicuously) throwing a few matches in order to avoid humiliating their guests. But an important connection was nonetheless established, and the initial round of Ping-Pong Diplomacy was followed in July 1971 by Henry Kissinger's secret trip to Beijing, setting the stage for Richard Nixon's "week that changed the world."

The Shanghai Communiqué, signed by Nixon and Zhou on February 28, 1972, cleared the way for the gradual growth of informal relations of trade, technology transfer, and scientific and cultural exchange. Shortly after the Nixon visit, the members of a Chinese ping-pong team became the first PRC citizens to venture onto American soil. The two countries set up unofficial diplomatic missions, known as liaison offices, and U.S. companies began scurrying to get a foot in the door of the new, untapped China market. Boeing Aircraft quickly cemented a deal to sell ten of its state-of-the-art 707 passenger jets to China's Civil Aviation Administration, while a consortium from the Pullman-Kellogg companies consummated a deal to set up a string of chemical fertilizer plants in China. A U.S. college all-star basketball team toured China in 1973, handily routing all opposition and thereby avenging the defeat suffered earlier by the U.S.

ping-pong team. American scientific delegations also began to visit China in growing numbers, representing such fields as seismology, solid-state physics, paleoanthropology, and medical and life sciences.

Within China, Zhou Enlai's opening to the United States proved highly contentious. Lin Biao and Jiang Qing strongly opposed "sleeping with the enemy." Although Lin's sudden death in September 1971 cleared a path for Zhou's diplomatic breakthrough, soon afterward Jiang Qing began pseudonymously publishing her accusations of betrayal and treason by the "Duke of Zhou."

One early indication of leftist obstruction of the normalization process occurred in January 1972, when Jiang Qing and her Shanghai cronies attempted to sabotage the visit of an advance team of U.S. government officials, led by Deputy National Security Adviser Alexander Haig, who had been sent to China to prepare for Nixon's arrival. As members of Haig's team arrived at the famously scenic West Lake district of Hangzhou, to assess its suitability as a presidential sightseeing venue, a boat ride was arranged for them. Normally, tour boats used to entertain visiting dignitaries in China are well heated and lavishly stocked with food and drink. On this occasion, however—a bitterly cold, blustery day—the boat was unheated and there was no food or drink aboard. A Chinese interpreter assigned to escort the Americans, Zhang Hanzhi, was astonished by the lack of amenities, and she hastily put through a phone call to Premier Zhou's office in Beijing. Zhou, in turn, contacted Chairman Mao, who reportedly expressed indignation over the discourtesy shown to the American guests. Since in China nothing is left to chance when it comes to relations with foreign countries, and in particular important foreign visitors, it was simply inconceivable that such a diplomatic slight could have occurred accidentally. Someone high up had sent a clear signal of defiance—a conclusion later confirmed by Zhang Hanzhi, the interpreter, who revealed that the order for a bare-bones boat ride for the Americans had come directly from the Shanghai Revolutionary Committee, the Gang of Four's operational headquarters.

Signs of left-wing defiance became even stronger as the political infighting in China heated up in 1974–75. By that time, with Mao's blessing, cultural exchanges between China and the United States were a regular occurrence. In addition to ping-pong and basketball teams, the United States had sent a variety of delegations, including a symphony orchestra, university presidents, secondary educators, world affairs specialists, and swimming and diving teams; China had reciprocated with acrobats, martial arts specialists, and ping-pong and basketball teams. Two Chinese pandas, Ling Ling and Xing Xing, were donated to the National Zoo in Washington, D.C. In exchange, the U.S. side sent two rare white musk oxen to Beijing. Unfortunately, these latter ambassadors of goodwill failed to flourish in the confines of the Beijing Zoo. Suffering from a debilitating skin disease, the two oxen—Matilda and Milton—soon lost their hair.

Since there were as yet no official government-to-government relations between the two countries, all bilateral exchanges between 1972 and 1978 had to be arranged informally by nongovernmental organizations (NGOs). On the American side, there were two facilitating bodies: the Committee on Scholarly Communication with the PRC (CSCPRC), an offshoot of the U.S. National Academy of Sciences, set up to coordinate scientific and technical exchanges, and the National Committee on U.S.-China Relations, which handled cultural exchanges. The National Committee was a nonprofit NGO established in 1966 to educate U.S. opinion leaders about China. Bob Scalapino was its first president, and he invited me to join the organization's board of directors in the early 1970s. By mutual agreement, all cultural exchanges were to be entirely apolitical in nature: no propaganda, no political content, and no political controversy.

Despite the Nixon-Zhou opening, after 1972 a near-total ban on independent travel to China remained in effect for U.S. scholars, journalists, and diplomats. Fortuitously, the cultural and scientific exchange formats provided an opportunity to bypass this long-standing prohibition, and it soon became standard practice for both the CSCPRC and the National Committee to pad their delegation lists with a few extra, ancillary personnel. By 1973 each outbound U.S. delegation routinely included a few supplementary "escorts," generally including a China scholar, a diplomat, a journalist, and one or two staff administrators. For their part, the Chinese did the same thing. As a member of the National Committee's board of directors, I was eligible to be a scholar-escort, but as a relative newcomer to the board, I was nowhere near the top of the pecking order.

My number came up unexpectedly in the spring of 1975, when I received a phone call from the National Committee inviting me to accompany a delegation of U.S. municipal mayors who were scheduled to visit China in September of that year. I was ecstatic. I renewed my passport, read John Lewis's book *The City in Communist China*, and hired a tutor to help polish my spoken Chinese, badly neglected since my 1968 departure from Hong Kong.

All too soon my ecstasy turned to agony. In late March 1975, Jiang Qing struck again. Violating the ban on political content, the Chinese side at the last minute informed the National Committee that it intended to change the scheduled repertory of a Chinese performing arts troupe on its upcoming U.S. tour. A new choral piece was being inserted into the program in place of an innocuous folk song. The new song, "Taiwan Compatriots, Our Own Brothers" (Taiwan tongbao, wo gurou xiongdi), contained the inflammatory lyric "We shall certainly liberate Taiwan!" (Women yiding yao jiefang Taiwan!). After hastily conferring with the State Department, the National Committee informed the Chinese side that the proposed program change violated the "no politics" rule and was therefore unacceptable. The Chinese responded by canceling the tour. I panicked. September was close at hand. Would there be further repercussions? Retaliation? Would my mayoral delegation be scratched? Not surprisingly, when I asked Bob Scalapino for his appraisal of the situation, he replied that he was "cautiously optimistic." But I was not reassured. I picked up the phone and called Jan Berris, the National Committee's senior administrator in New York. "What's the next delegation headed for China?" I asked urgently. "In two months," came the reply, "the AAU [Amateur Athletic Union] national track and field team." Without a moment's hesitation, I offered to swap my mayors in the bush for Jan's jocks in the hand.

As it turned out, my hunch was correct: In mid-September the Chinese side, in a retaliatory display of solidarity with a small but vocal Puerto Rican independence movement (who knew?), refused permission to include the "colonialist" mayor of San Juan, Puerto Rico, in the U.S. mayors' delegation. The National Committee responded by canceling the visit. Encouraged by this disruption, Jiang Qing redoubled her efforts to sabotage the U.S.-China relationship.

Her efforts peaked in February 1976, when Richard Nixon—by now in deep disgrace in his own country—paid a second visit to China on the fourth anniversary of his 1972 triumph. Mme. Mao invited him and his wife, Pat, to an evening of musical entertainment in Beijing's Great Hall of the People. At one point during the performance, Jiang Qing suddenly jumped to her feet, loudly applauding a young tenor's bravura solo number. Emulating their hostess, the Nixons rose up from their seats to clap, only to be sharply but tactfully restrained by an alert U.S. government official, who had recognized the title of the tenor's song, "Taiwan Compatriots, Our Own Brothers," with its inflammatory lyric, "We shall certainly liberate Taiwan!" The Nixons quickly sat down in their seats, refraining from joining in the ovation. Thus did Jiang Qing narrowly fail in her attempt to sandbag the former U.S. president into openly cheering for Taiwan's liberation.

AND SO IT came about that, alarmed by Jiang Qing's proven capacity for disruptive mischief, in May 1975 I approached the Friendship Bridge at Hong Kong's Lowu border crossing for the second time, accompanied by ninety-five of the world's fastest, strongest athletes. Unlike my previous visit to the Hong Kong–China frontier seven years earlier, when I had wistfully gazed at the Lowu crossing from a nearby hillside, this time *I was on the through train to China.*

Well, not quite the through train. In those days, the Kowloon-Canton Railway had its terminus at the tip of the Kowloon Peninsula in Tsim Sha Tsui, across from the Peninsula Hotel, near the clock tower where the Hong Kong Cultural Center now stands. Belying its name, the train did not actually cross into China. It stopped at Lowu, where passengers were off-loaded and required to cross the railroad bridge on foot. At the far side of the bridge, PLA border guards carefully inspected our travel documents. After a brief delay, we boarded a Chinese train for the trip to Guangzhou (Canton), sixty miles to the northwest. Passing by Shumchun, the train slowed. The day was warm and humid. I leaned out the window to take a photo of a barefoot young child of two or three, standing in the shade of a protective parasol on a path leading to an austere, tile-roofed farmhouse. No one else was in sight; time seemed to be standing still. There was still no hint of Shenzhen's staggering metamorphosis to come.

Stepping off the train onto the station platform in Guangzhou, I was exhilarated—a kid in a candy store. For more than a decade I had been watching China from afar, at second hand, from Taiwan and Hong Kong, in print and on film, unable to experience the elusive Middle Kingdom directly. Viewed at a distance, China seemed enigmatic and inscrutable, a fantasyland of surreal political stereotypes and extreme ideological clichés, but lacking in living, breathing human beings. Until that day, my most vivid image of contemporary China was the all-too-familiar celluloid scene of frenzied Red Guards waving Mao's "Little Red Book." As I walked through the railroad station, I found myself scrutinizing the people around me. The mass insanity of the Cultural Revolution seemed light years removed from this very quotidian scene. Observing a group of middle-school students on an outing, I wondered idly if their older brothers and sisters had participated in beating up teachers or informing on parents.

Up close, the Chinese people seemed so . . . *normal*. With some surprise, I noted the ordinariness of their appearance, their clothes, and their mannerisms. What do they talk about at dinner? I wondered. How do they react when they see an American? Feeling conspicuous and self-conscious, I was oblique and indirect in my gaze, reluctant to initiate eye contact. The objects of my attention were not nearly so discreet, however. They stared right at me, boldly, without the slightest hint of shame or embarrassment. On one occasion a passing bicyclist stared at me so intently he crashed into a light post. I found this combination of curiosity and brazenness off-putting at first, but endearing later on, as my Chinese friends and acquaintances exhibited no qualms whatever about grilling me as to the cost of my clothes, or the amount of my monthly income, or whether I had a Chinese girlfriend. I recalled from my Berkeley language training that the concept of privacy was not translatable into Chinese. One Chinese dictionary had defined it as "a Westerner's liking for loneliness."

The Guangzhou train station was crowded. Hundreds of people were in motion, though few seemed to be hurrying. Many were simply waiting—for what? I wondered. Several squatted on their haunches, a posture few Westerners can comfortably sustain. Others clustered in small groups, smoking and chatting among themselves. Most of them—men and women alike—wore plain, unisex cotton pants and shirts in three basic colors: gray, blue, and olive drab. There was a smattering of white shirts in the crowd. Women wore their hair in either short pigtails or simple pageboy cuts; there was no jewelry and no makeup, depressing evidence of Jiang Qing's lingering influence as chief arbiter of cultural taste and fashion.

Mme. Mao's austerity was said to reflect, in part, her deep resentment toward the more refined and elegant Mme. Liu Shaoqi. Shortly before Liu's 1966 purge, his wife, the glamorous Wang Guangmei, had appeared in press photos wearing an elegant Chinese evening gown while accompanying her husband on a state visit to Indonesia. On that occasion Wang had worn an expensive string of pearls with matching earrings, a stylish hairdo, and bright red lipstick. When Liu Shaoqi was brought down in the Cultural Revolution, Wang was forced to submit to public humiliation at Beijing's Tsinghua University, where she, wearing a harlot's gown, a strand of ping-pong balls painted like pearls, and a grotesque, smeared-on stain of scarlet lipstick, was paraded before a hostile mob of students. Wang's own daughters, Pingping and Tingting, stood at the rally with their fists raised, shouting "Down with Wang Guangmei." Thereafter, no Chinese woman dared to appear publicly in colorful, stylish clothing, jewelry, or cosmetics of any kind.

Presiding over this austere sartorial regime was Mme. Mao herself. In the privacy of her own sumptuous villa, however, Jiang—a former Shanghai movie actress who once played Nora in Ibsen's *A Doll's House*—acted out her own decadent fantasies, collecting ancient imperial regalia, affecting modern Western dress and jewelry, and screening old Greta Garbo movies. At the time of her arrest after Mao's death in 1976, some of the most telling caricatures to appear on wall posters in Beijing viciously lampooned Jiang's hypocritical habits of lavish self-indulgence and private preening.

On our first evening in Guangzhou I went out for dinner with the two National Committee staff members, Arne de Keijzer and Peggy Blumenthal, along with our State Department escort, Neal Donnelly. We went to what was, by reputation, one of Guangzhou's finest restaurants, the Beiyuan. I later wrote in my trip notes: "Restaurant lavish and decadent. Built as large rectangular courtyard house (*siheyuan*). A dozen banquet rooms on four sides, surrounding traditional Chinese garden. Stained glass panels in each room, richly hued in deep blues and reds. Exquisite wooden furniture, hand carved. Excellent food; incredible service."

The meal cost ¥54 for five of us, approximately $6 apiece at the current exchange rate, or roughly two weeks' salary for an average Chinese worker. Small wonder most of the patrons were Westerners, in town for the recently concluded annual Canton Trade Fair. This was most definitely a *haut bourgeois* dining experience, far removed from the egalitarian hype of Maoist publicity.

What happened *after* dinner left an even deeper impression. I had often heard that Chinese went to extraordinary lengths to return personal items that had been misplaced, or deliberately discarded, by foreign guests. To test this, at the end of our meal at the Beiyuan I attached a small AAU lapel pin to a pack of Chinese cigarettes and left it in a darkened corner of our banquet room. We then took a cab back to the hotel, where I began writing up my notes on the day's activities. An hour or so later the hotel's floor attendant walked in without knocking, completely oblivious to my obvious annoyance. (One quickly learns to give up one's expectations of

A 1977 cartoon caricatures Jiang Qing's decadent, hypocritical lifestyle. The caption at right quotes a line from one of Jiang's poems: "From time to time, the craggy face of the mountain may be glimpsed [through the fog]."

personal privacy in Mao's China.) His eyes bright with triumph, the attendant proudly displayed my cigarette pack in his hand, the lapel pin still attached. It was an impressive piece of detective work. We had not made an advance booking at the restaurant, we had not given anyone our names, and after dinner we had hailed our own taxi, some distance away from the restaurant. How did they find us so quickly? Somewhere in this experience lay a cautionary tale: Big Brother is watching!

Guangzhou's taxi fleet was something to behold. The majority of taxis were exact copies of 1946 De Soto–Plymouth four-door sedans. When I asked how this curious situation came about, I was told that at some point in the past China had purchased the entire tool-and-die works from an obsolescent Chrysler Corporation assembly line in Detroit. Whatever their source, these thirty-year-old behemoths were amazing to behold. Considering their age, their bodies were in reasonably good shape, but the engines were something else again.

A mechanical breakdown en route to our hotel gave me the opportunity to peek under the hood of one of these beasts. As our driver labored with his tool kit to nurse the wheezing, sputtering engine back to life, I looked over his shoulder. What I saw was startling. Lacking spare engine parts, the cab had been kept in running order through ad hoc patches and engineering improvisations. A bulky, jerry-built replacement carburetor, distributor, and starter motor had long ago replaced the original factory equipment, and a profusion of homemade belts, bolts, and cables now protruded at odd angles from the engine block, fastened together with a considerable amount of baling wire and electrical tape. The overall effect was that of a homemade Rube Goldberg device. I had to admire the considerable ingenuity that went into keeping the aging Guangzhou taxi fleet in service.

THE U.S. TRACK and Field delegation spent three days in Guangzhou, three in Shanghai, and four in Beijing. In each city a two-day track meet was held, matching the American athletes—who included several past and present world champions—against seriously outmanned Chinese provincial teams. Considering that track and field was in its infancy in China, the crowds were impressive, ranging from thirty thousand in Guangzhou to more than seventy thousand in Beijing. Though most in attendance had clearly never seen a track meet before, the spectators were generally polite and attentive, dutifully applauding winning performances. Fortunately for all concerned, our delegation's visit had been organized under the slogan "friendship first, competition second" (*youyi diyi, bisai di'er*). It was fortunate because the track meets themselves were anything but competitive, and the results were anything but pretty, at least from a Chinese perspective. With thirty individual events held in each city, including both men's and women's competition, a total of ninety first-place medals were awarded. The U.S. athletes captured eighty-nine of them. Then, in one of the final events on the final day of the final meet in Beijing, a Chinese runner in the women's 1500-meter event caught—and passed—the lead American runner with less than 400 meters to go. Suddenly the previously inert crowd came alive. "Jia you! Jia you!" they began to chant in unison—"Pour it on! Pour it on!" When the Chinese runner built an insurmountable lead

Opening ceremony of the track and field competition between the U.S. AAU national team and a Guangdong provincial team, Guangzhou, May 1975. Banner in background reads: "Long live the friendship between the people and athletes of China and the world."

with less than 200 meters remaining, the chanting turned to screaming: "*Jia you! Jia you!*" The crowd pumped out more pure adrenaline during that brief outburst than had been displayed in the previous five full days of athletic competition. Notwithstanding the debilitating traumas of the Cultural Revolution and other Maoist excesses, Chinese national pride and patriotism were evidently still alive and well, lying dormant, awaiting only a superb performance by a gutsy Chinese athlete to be reawakened.

Several years later I discovered that the ubiquitous "friendship first" motif, displayed so prominently throughout our three-city track and field tour, did not long outlive the death of Mao and the advent of Deng Xiaoping's market reform and opening-up policies. During a Chinese intra-league basketball game in Shanghai in the early 1980s, I was both startled and slightly amused to discover that local fans, apparently emulating their counterparts in the United States, delighted in heaping abuse upon visiting players, chanting "*yang-wei*" (can't get it up) whenever an opponent missed a shot, and "*xiong-qi*" (erection) whenever the home team scored. I took such trash talk as tangible evidence of the two-edged nature of China's opening up.

Toward the end of our trip, on a sightseeing visit to the Great Wall north of Beijing, I got into a rather heated discussion about photography with one of our local guides, a Ms. Li. I was an avid amateur photographer and had been taking quite a few pictures from the window of our bus, mostly focusing on peasants working in the fields, balancing heavy loads on shoulder poles, sleeping by the side of the road, or riding on horse-drawn wooden carts. After a while Ms. Li tapped me on the shoulder. "You must like old carts," she said. "Why don't you take pictures of our modern buildings?" I responded that in America we have lots of modern buildings, but not so many horse carts or shoulder poles. Obviously annoyed, she proceeded to deliver an impromptu lecture on the dangers of "lying with your camera." I asked her what she meant. She told me that the Italian film-maker Michelangelo Antonioni had made a film in China two years earlier that lied about China. "He filmed only poor rural villages, old houses, and shabbily dressed peasants," she scolded. "He lied with his camera, just as you are doing now." I protested that Antonioni merely filmed what he saw, and that what he saw was real. Dissatisfied, but not wishing to offend a for-eign guest, she abruptly terminated the conversation. "We have a different viewpoint than you do," she said dismissively. A few years later, after Jiang Qing was toppled, the Chinese government apologized to Antonioni and invited him back.

There were other surprising encounters as well. One of the more mem-orable of these occurred during an evening stroll along the famous Bund in Shanghai. Situated on a quay alongside the Huangpu River, near the mouth of the Yangzi, the Bund (the Urdu word for "embankment") was built by Europeans shortly after the turn of the twentieth century. With its monumental mix of Romanesque, Gothic, and Baroque architecture, the thirty or so massive concrete buildings along the Bund formed the finan-cial and diplomatic hub of Shanghai's pre–World War II international set-tlement, its famous skyline a trope signifying the city's modern history of Western domination.

I was walking along the northern bank of the Bund with Neal Don-nelly when we heard whispers coming from a nearby, darkened bridge. It was a moonless night, and there was no illumination on this particular stretch of riverbank, where the Huangpu joins the Suzhou Creek. Strolling onto the darkened bridge, we could make out shadowy forms lining the railings on either side. As our eyes adjusted to the darkness, we saw dozens of young couples, crowded together along the bridge railings, in various stages of sexual intimacy. All were more or less fully clothed, and all were standing upright. But there was clearly a good deal of body heat being generated.

At one point two young men approached us, speaking to each other, weighing the costs and benefits of confrontation. One said, "Let's hassle the foreigners a bit." The other replied, "Are you crazy? We'll be shot on sight." Self-preservation prevailed over bravado, and the youths retreated without incident. In point of fact, the penalty for crimes committed against foreigners in those days was extremely harsh; for physical assault, the penalty was death. We felt very safe on China's streets. On the other hand, we now had clear evidence that despite decades of puritanical moral education and a constant stream of Communist Party propaganda claiming that China's young people routinely sublimated their sexual urges to higher ideological principles, hanky-panky was very much alive and well in Shanghai—albeit only in a few designated sanctuaries. (Public parks were another favored venue for youthful heavy breathing.)

Earlier that same evening Neal and I had visited the Foreign Seamen's Club on the Bund. I had been told by one of our Chinese guides that duty-free goods were available there for merchant sailors at rock-bottom prices. We decided to check it out for ourselves. Inside the front entrance, a clerk in the anteroom asked for the name of our ship and pushed a register in front of us. I signed the book in English, nervously scrawling "Dick Deadeye, HMS Lollipop." The clerk looked at the signature, shrugged, and motioned us inside. There we saw three or four large display cases filled with foreign cigarettes, perfume, and liquor of every description—including half a dozen top-quality brands of single malt Scotch, various exotic brandies, and nine or ten Russian and East European vodkas. I pointed to a one-liter bottle of Johnnie Walker Black Label and asked the clerk, "How much?" (*duoshaoqian?*). "Thirteen yuan" (*shisankuai*), came the response. I bought two bottles. At $7 apiece, this was less than half the usual retail price. Later that night, savoring my first smooth sip of the clear amber liquid, the flavor of authentic Highland malt dispelled any lingering memories of Taipei's adulterated black-market Scotch. From then on, until the Foreign Seamen's Club moved to new headquarters under a tightened security regime in the early 1980s, each time the Good Ship Lollipop dropped anchor in

Shanghai, Able Seaman Dick Deadeye would show up to claim his two bottles of Black Label.

One of the U.S. male track athletes had a rather chilling encounter with the local public security police in Shanghai. On the first day of our two-day track meet there, after winning his event he got caught up in the spirit of "friendship first" and ran up into the grandstand waving a small Chinese flag and shaking hands with a number of enthusiastic spectators. It was a spontaneous display of intercultural goodwill. Later that evening, as I was dressing for dinner, he knocked on my door. He told me that during his jaunt into the stands that afternoon a Chinese spectator had discreetly shoved a note into his hand. After glancing uncomprehendingly at the Chinese characters, he put the note in the pocket of his warm-up jacket and soon forgot about it. Some time later, two plainclothes Chinese security police visited him in his hotel room, inquiring about the note and its author. Did he still have the note? Did he recall who handed it to him? His suspicions aroused, he told them he had thrown the note away and couldn't remember who gave it to him. After his visitors left, he waited a half an hour or so, then knocked on my door. He handed me the note and asked me to translate it. "Long live the friendship of the Chinese and American people," it said, in hastily scrawled characters. He asked me what he should do if the police came back again. I told him that if he wanted to keep the note as a souvenir, he should stuff it in the toe of one of his shoes inside his duffel bag and then make a mental note of where things were positioned in his room and in his bag before he went out for the evening. Later that night, after dinner, he knocked on my door once again. His room had been searched, and a few personal items were now out of place. But they hadn't found the note. It was another small but sobering reminder that China remained firmly in the grip of xenophobic autocrats.

ON OUR LAST full day in Shanghai we were taken on a tour of a Chinese factory, the Shanghai Turbine Plant, one of the largest and most modern in China. The plant produced the giant turbine engines used to generate hydroelectric power. In the reception room, the plant's public relations director gave us the standard, obligatory Brief Introduction to the factory and its history. Before the Cultural Revolution, he told us, the plant's managers and engineers had oppressed the workers, forcing them to comply with hundreds of detailed rules and docking their pay if they violated any regulations. Managers had also shown favoritism to better-educated workers, looking down on the uneducated and the unskilled. Consequently, plant morale had suffered and productivity had lagged badly. After the Cultural Revolution began in 1966, he said, things changed. The workers became "masters of the house" as the plant introduced participatory management. The old managers, along with administrative staff, engineers, and technicians, were criticized for their arrogant, bourgeois attitudes and work styles and were forced to scrub toilets and do menial work on the factory floor. As a result, morale improved greatly, and the plant registered outstanding improvements in both the quantity and the quality of turbine production. It was a typical Cultural Revolution morality tale—stereotyped, melodramatic, and almost certainly untrue.

This particular vignette bears repeating only because some three years later, in the summer of 1978, after the overthrow of the Gang of Four and at the outset of Deng Xiaoping's second political comeback, as chance would have it I returned to the Shanghai Turbine Plant. By this time the worm had turned, and many of the revolutionary virtues celebrated during the Cultural Revolution were being decried as "ultra-leftist poison" spread by the Gang of Four. Not surprisingly, this new morality was incorporated into a revised Brief Introduction at the turbine plant. Curiously, the narrative on this occasion was given by the very same public relations flack who had addressed the U.S. track and field athletes three years earlier. But this time his story line was quite different. During the Cultural Revolution, he said, agents of the Gang of Four had sabotaged production in the plant. Overthrowing the management, they spread anarchy on the factory floor. Workers played cards during working hours, while managers were ruthlessly "struggled." Engineers and technicians stayed home, unwilling to risk criticism as "bourgeois authorities" if they dared to display initiative in solving technical problems. Consequently, the quantity and quality of output suffered badly. More than 70 percent of all the turbine engines produced at the plant between 1967 and 1976 were rejected as substandard. However, in the past two years, he continued, things had begun to turn around. The workers came to understand that their thoughts had been poisoned by the Gang of Four, and managers, engineers, and technicians were rehabilitated and permitted to do their jobs. The factory introduced piece rates, along with monthly bonuses for overfulfillment of quotas, and production consequently rebounded. They were now well on their way to breaking previous records for productivity, innovation, and quality. It was an inspiring story. At the end of his spiel he looked around the room and asked for questions. I raised my hand.

"Three years ago," I reminded him, "you stood in this same room and gave a very different Brief Introduction to another group of foreign guests." I then highlighted the contrasting elements in his past and present narratives, asking him how he could reconcile such strikingly different stories. He stammered and sputtered for a moment before blurting out the only possible explanation under the circumstances: "My thinking was poisoned by the Gang of Four." This anodyne phrase became China's unique and ubiquitous national mantra in the late 1970s, as 800 million people struggled to reconcile their recent "revolutionary" words and deeds with the new, more pragmatic requirements of political correctness in the age of Deng Xiaoping. The ability to turn on an ideological dime, rationalizing one's previous attitudes and behavior in order to minimize personal culpability, shame, and opprobrium, had become an essential survival skill.

The widespread use of the "thought poisoning" rationale as a one-size-fits-all excuse for bad behavior was striking. On one occasion in the fall of 1978 I was taking an early morning constitutional through one of Beijing's older urban neighborhoods, a rabbit warren of narrow *hutongs*, or alleyways, when an elderly man with a weather-beaten face and tattered clothes, a cigarette dangling from his lips, invited me into his home. I was surprised by the spontaneity of his gesture, since ordinary Chinese, the *laobaixing*, were normally not permitted to socialize with foreigners without explicit authorization. Eagerly accepting his unexpected invitation, I entered the front gate of his residence and found myself in a small courtyard. I followed my host into his bedroom, a tiny, windowless cubicle barely large enough for a small bed and a folding stool. As I sat on the edge of his bed, he offered me a cigarette. We had barely begun to converse when an obviously agitated, gray-haired woman in her fifties burst into the room. Wearing a red armband that signified her status as a member of the neighborhood residents' committee, she began angrily berating the old man. "You cannot behave like this," she scolded. "You are not allowed to bring a *laowai* [foreigner] into your home."

Unofficial guardians of social order and public morality, China's infamous "granny police" were on the job. I stepped in to defend my host. "It was my fault," I pleaded in Chinese. "I invited myself in. This old comrade (*lao tongzhi*) was just being polite to a foreign guest." Unmoved by my explanation, the woman continued to browbeat the elderly gentleman. By then—no more than five minutes after I first stepped through the front gate—a crowd had formed in the courtyard, spilling over into the street, and the entire neighborhood was abuzz. A uniformed local gendarme soon came on the scene. He listened patiently to my explanation, then interviewed the other participants. The gray-haired committeewoman finally calmed down a bit. Satisfied that the entire dust-up had stemmed from a misunderstanding, the policeman eventually shooed away the onlookers and politely invited me to continue on my way.

Later that morning I related the details of the incident to my local guide from the Ministry of Education, asking him as a personal favor to check up on the old man to make sure he hadn't gotten into any further trouble after my departure. The next evening the guide reported back to me. The ill-tempered granny had undergone "criticism and self-criticism" for having scolded the old man in the presence of a foreigner. In explaining her behavior, she invoked the now familiar exculpatory formula: Her thinking was "poisoned by the Gang of Four."

ON OUR FINAL evening in China, after the track and field team had finished its last day of competition in Beijing, a lavish farewell banquet was laid on for us at Beijing's International Club. The event was organized by the U.S. Liaison Office, whose *chef de mission*, Ambassador George H. W. Bush, and his wife, Barbara, served as hosts for the evening. Approximately two hundred people were there, including, in addition to our delegation, a number of Chinese government officials, leading members of the All-China Sports Federation, and various other VIPs. The American athletes had been in training for two full weeks, on a strict dietary and recreational regimen that excluded alcohol, drugs, and late-night revelry. They were young, they were energetic, and they had been tightly wound. Now, with the rigors of competition at an end, they were ready to break loose. At each table, small glasses of Maotai, a potent Chinese barley liquor closely related to Gaoliang, were refilled at frequent intervals during the banquet, as were larger glasses of sweet red Shaoxing rice wine. Glasses of lukewarm beer were also constantly refreshed throughout the evening. Three or four courses into the meal, the decibel level in the banquet hall rose noticeably as the athletes' inhibitions began to melt away. By the fifth or sixth course, raucous laughter echoed through the room. By the time soup was served after the eighth course, my well-trained Berkeley olfactory senses detected a familiar, sticky sweet scent wafting through the room.

As waiters cleared the dishes prior to serving dessert, Ambassador Bush stood up to speak, and the ambient noise level in the room dropped a bit. After making a few introductory remarks, Bush raised his wine glass in the direction of the Chinese officials sitting at the head table, intending to propose a toast. Before he could say "Ganbei," however, a commotion broke out at the back of the banquet hall. I looked up in time to see a tall, lanky pole-vaulter from Texas lurching drunkenly up the center aisle, heading toward Ambassador Bush, calling out, "I'm gonna kill that sonofabitch." Just before he reached Bush, a heavily muscled American shot-putter jumped up and tackled him. It was no contest. The pole-vaulter was quickly subdued and carried bodily out of the banquet hall, whereupon Mr. Bush, seemingly unfazed, resumed his toast. Later, I was told that the offending athlete had been drinking and smoking pot since late that afternoon. Evidently, Maotai was the coup de grâce that sent him over the edge. After being carried from the hall, he was taken to the team bus, where a couple of his teammates sobered him up.

On the afternoon preceding that final bacchanalian banquet, I sat next to a dour Chinese government official in the VIP section of Beijing's seventy-thousand-seat Workers' Stadium. He had arrived late. The track meet was already under way, and we introduced ourselves hastily. I didn't quite catch his name, but it didn't sound familiar. (I have always had a poor memory for Chinese names.) I recall feeling vaguely disappointed, as I had been hoping to meet someone *really important*. In the course of the day's competition, I made several attempts to draw the fellow into conversation, but he wasn't interested in chatting. Nor did he seem to be enjoying the track meet. Clearly he wished he were somewhere else. After a while I stopped making any effort to engage him.

Fast-forward eight months to January 1976. The international China-watching community was abuzz with rumors about the succession to Premier Zhou Enlai, who had succumbed to bladder cancer on January 8. Although First Deputy Premier Deng Xiaoping was next in line to succeed Zhou, there had been no formal announcement. Rumor had it that the Party Politburo was deadlocked between Deng Xiaoping and Jiang Qing's preferred candidate, Zhang Chunqiao. Then, on January 28, the Chinese press agency Xinhua issued an otherwise routine report about the arrival in Beijing of West German chancellor Helmut Schmidt. Accompanying the report was a photo of the airport reception for the visiting German leader, with the following caption: "Acting Premier Hua Guofeng greets

Chancellor Helmut Schmidt." Immediately, China watchers everywhere picked up their telephones and started calling each other: "Hua Guo*who*?" we asked. A frantic search of *Who's Who in Communist China* yielded the information that Hua Guofeng was a provincial party secretary from Hunan (Mao's native province) who had been brought to Beijing late in 1971 to serve on the commission of inquiry investigating Lin Biao's conspiracy and death. Hua had evidently impressed Mao with his performance on the commission, for in 1974 he was promoted to the important post of Minister of Public Security—China's top cop. Looking at the Xinhua photo, I thought that Hua Guofeng looked vaguely familiar. Though I didn't recognize the name, I felt sure I had seen the face before.

On a hunch, I began sifting through the hundreds of photographs and other memorabilia from my visit to China the previous May. It didn't take long to find what I was looking for. There, in grainy black and white, was China's mystery man, Hua Guofeng, sitting next to yours truly at Beijing's Workers' Stadium. I could have kicked myself. Why hadn't I recognized his name? Why hadn't I persisted in trying to chat him up at the track meet? For years afterward I kept that photo, now badly faded, pinned to a bulletin board in my UCLA office as a memento of my close encounter, and a reminder to work harder on my retention of Chinese names. With the exception of two brief viewings of Mao's embalmed corpse, a National Committee luncheon with Deng Xiaoping, and a five-minute photo op with Jiang Zemin, that was as close as I ever got to a Chinese Communist supremo.

Hua Guofeng's moment in the sun proved to be short-lived. By mid-1978 it had become clear that Hua would most likely be a transitional figure, and that Deng Xiaoping was likely to eclipse him. Hua did not go quietly, however. In 1977 he and his supporters ginned up a full-blown propaganda campaign designed to create a personality cult around him. Newspapers and magazines ran stories glorifying his proletarian virtues and celebrating his deep affection for the *laobaixing*. Dozens of new songs and dances in praise of Chairman Hua were commissioned and performed at every festival and holiday occasion. Portraits of Hua's benign visage were routinely hung in public places and private homes, alongside Chairman Mao's. Hua's handlers also worked on his physical image. In 1977 he began appearing in public and in photos wearing Mao's trademark loose-fitting PLA uniform, though he had never been a soldier. He also grew his hair long, abandoning his traditional close-cropped crew cut in favor

The author, with Hua Guofeng at a Beijing track meet, May 1975.
Less than a year later, Hua was chosen to succeed Mao Zedong
as chairman of the CCP Central Committee.

of slicked-back hair combed away from his sloping forehead, à la Chairman Mao. He even altered his calligraphy to make it resemble that of his illustrious predecessor. The pièce de résistance, however, was a nationwide campaign to saturate Chinese cities and towns with billboard-size posters depicting the now-famous "anointment scene," showing Hua sitting with Mao in April 1976, receiving the moribund Chairman's last bequest: "With you in charge, I'm at ease" (*Ni ban shi, wo fang xin*).

This was Hua's indisputable ace in the hole: Mao had personally selected him as his successor. Not even Mao's own wife had been able to overcome such a potent trump card. But Deng Xiaoping had an ace up his own sleeve, and he played it masterfully: Hua Guofeng had been complicit in the Gang of Four's attempt to frame Deng on the charge of fomenting a "counterrevolutionary incident" at Tiananmen Square in April 1976, leading to Deng's second purge. Not long after the four were arrested, the fabricated nature of the charge against Deng was exposed, along with Hua's role in helping to silence Deng and his supporters. Hua was now a marked

你办事 我放心

An artist's romanticized rendering depicts a gravely ill Mao Zedong anointing Hua Guofeng as his chosen successor, April 1976. The caption reads: "With you in charge, I'm at ease (*Ni ban shi, wo fang xin*). Photo courtesy of Stefan Landsberger.

man. By mid-1977 the irrepressible Deng had been reinstated; a year later he was exonerated of all charges of wrongdoing. At the same time, Deng's supporters began to undermine Hua's credibility.

One thing that contributed mightily to Hua Guofeng's undoing was his blind obeisance to Chairman Mao's every word and deed. Given the destructiveness of the Cultural Revolution, such absolute fealty proved to be a distinct liability. When Hua proclaimed that it was impermissible to question "whatever Chairman Mao instructed or approved," Deng's boosters countered by quoting a pragmatic aphorism plucked from the repertory of Mao's own early writings: "Practice is the sole criterion of truth." Not content with merely refuting Hua's injunction mandating unconditional loyalty to whatever Chairman Mao said or did, they further saddled Hua and his supporters with a sarcastic epithet, labeling them the "whatever faction" (*fanshi pai*).

My first indication that Hua was in serious trouble came in the summer of 1978. I was taking a leisurely stroll along Beijing's main thoroughfare, Chang'an Boulevard, east of Tiananmen Square, when I saw a sizable knot of thirty to forty people gathered near the base of a large billboard. Everyone was looking up at three workmen who were slowly changing the billboard's display, pasting one panel at a time over the freshly whitewashed surface. By the time the second vertical panel was unfurled and pasted down, it was evident that the new poster was an artist's rendering of the now-famous scene of Hua Guofeng receiving Mao's deathbed benediction.

I watched quietly for several minutes. As the workmen prepared to paste the fifth and final panel in place on the billboard, the first five characters of the legend at the bottom were visible: Ni ban shi, wo fang. . . . Just then, a young man standing immediately in front of me turned to his equally youthful companions and, in a voice loud enough for everyone in the crowd to hear, completed the phrase by substituting a new sixth character, giving the statement an entirely different meaning. "Ni ban shi, wo fang pi," he said, with evident sarcasm in his voice: "With you in charge, I fart." There was an immediate ripple of laughter in the crowd.

Now, such a spontaneous youthful descent into bathroom humor might not have been remarkable in many other settings, but in early post-Mao China it was surprising, to say the least. During the Cultural Revolution people had been "struggled"—or even beaten and imprisoned—for far more innocuous offenses against the Supreme Leader, such as wrapping fresh produce in a newspaper containing Chairman Mao's photo or drawing a cartoon featuring Maoist slogans. The idea that such an unflattering joke could now be cracked publicly at the new Maximum Leader's expense—and that others would openly laugh—suggested that Hua's attempt to build a personality cult to replace Mao's had gained little traction. At that moment it struck me that Hua's reign was likely to prove transitory, and that Chairman Mao's big shoes would remain unfilled for a while longer.

5

Democracy Deferred

WHILE HUA GUOFENG struggled for his political survival, others in China were struggling for the return of human decency and dignity. In the fall of 1978 I visited China's University of Science and Technology, once the crown jewel of the Chinese Academy of Science. During the Cultural Revolution the university had fallen on hard times. Convinced that its eminent faculty—many of whom were Western educated—constituted a dangerous hotbed of "revisionist" thinking, Jiang Qing and her leftist allies banished the entire university from Beijing to a primitive site on the outskirts of Hefei, capital of poverty-ridden Anhui. Touring the Hefei campus, I was shocked by its run-down appearance—dilapidated buildings, peeling paint, broken laboratory equipment, poor classroom lighting, and a near total absence of temperature and humidity controls. Most depressing of all was the visibly poor health and low morale of the faculty, who had been cut off from outside contact for almost a decade.

My visit to Hefei, with a small group of American computer scientists, had been arranged by the CSCPRC. We were the first Westerners to visit the transplanted campus, and our arrival produced strong emotions among the older Chinese scientists, several of whom were visibly moved to see us. Some fought back tears; a few wept openly. The senior scientists we met were shabbily dressed and frail looking; most appeared older than they actually were. Several suffered from respiratory diseases, and the flow of our conversation was frequently punctuated by staccato coughing and wheezing. Their decade of banishment had clearly taken its toll.

At a reception that evening I met Professor Fang Lizhi, a distinguished, soft-spoken forty-two-year-old astrophysicist who had first run afoul of the Maoists in 1957 and then, during the Cultural Revolution, suffered harsh personal attacks for his efforts to popularize modern cosmological theory, including the theories of relativity and the Big Bang. Professor Fang was very gracious and said he hoped he would soon be able to resume his career in scientific research and teaching. One of his senior colleagues at the reception—an elderly professor of engineering who held a pre-1949 graduate degree from Brooklyn College—told us that he had not dared to speak English in public since 1957, when he was labeled a "rightist" in the crackdown that followed Mao's short-lived Hundred Flowers experiment. In February of that year Mao had invited China's intellectuals to speak their minds freely ("Let a hundred flowers blossom; let a hundred schools of thought contend," said the Chairman), only to turn angrily against them a few months later when their criticism of the Party's policies and practices became bitter and intense. Ironically, Mao had placed Deng Xiaoping in charge of implementing the anti-rightist campaign, in the course of which tens of thousands of intellectuals were cruelly struggled against and sent down for reeducation through labor.

The elderly engineering professor's voice quivered with emotion as he gave an impromptu recital of Abraham Lincoln's Gettysburg Address—in English, from memory. By the time he finished his slow, soft-spoken recitation, several of the Americans present, including me, were fighting back tears.

Shortly after our visit to Hefei, I learned from a friend in Beijing that the Chinese Academy of Science had allocated substantial funds to build a new, modern campus for the University of Science and Technology in Hefei, and that its faculty members would soon enjoy greatly improved living and working conditions. According to my friend, China's new leaders had decided that Chinese science (and scientists) were long overdue for a substantial boost in funding and respect after two decades of politically induced repression and maltreatment. This came as very good news.

Other signs of welcome change were in the air. After returning to Beijing from Hefei, I took a Sunday afternoon excursion to the Old Summer Palace, Yuanmingyuan, the fabled Garden of Perfect Brightness. Located in a northwestern suburb of Beijing, near the university district, Yuanmingyuan had been the summer home of the ruling Manchu emperors from the early eighteenth century until it was sacked and burned as an object lesson by a joint British-French expeditionary force during the second Opium War, in 1860. With its exquisite, man-made network of scenic lakes, mountain vistas, and meandering, tree-lined garden paths interspersed with more than a hundred magnificent palaces, pavilions, pagodas, temples, and bridges, Yuanmingyuan had been a symbol of China's imperial splendor. Now it stood in ruins, a painful reminder of China's nineteenth-century national humiliation.

I visited Yuanmingyuan in the company of Lynn Pascoe, a diplomat at the U.S. Liaison Office in Beijing. Lynn and I had been fellow language students at Taipei's Stanford Center in 1966–67, and we had hooked up again when I returned to Beijing. It was he who suggested an outing to the Old Summer Palace.

For all its historical significance, Yuanmingyuan proved surprisingly hard to find. Although it was as large in area as the Forbidden City—almost eight hundred acres—the Old Summer Palace did not appear on any of Beijing's official tourist maps or travel guides. Instead, visitors were routinely directed to the New Summer Palace at Yiheyuan, a short distance away. With its colorful, carefully restored Qing dynasty pavilions, its artificial lake, and its famous Marble Boat, commissioned by the notorious Dowager Empress Ci Xi in the 1880s, Yiheyuan was a major tourist attraction, surpassed only by the Great Wall and the Forbidden City among Beijing's most celebrated architectural wonders. By contrast, Yuanmingyuan did not even have a well-paved access road, and our driver, who was totally unfamiliar with the location, had to stop several times en route to ask directions.

When we finally found it, unmarked and accessible only on foot through an overgrown field, I could barely contain my astonishment. In the intervening 118 years since they were laid waste, the European-style palaces and courtyards of Yuanmingyuan had remained in a spectacular state of undisturbed decay, a surreal baroque apparition lying smack in the middle of a neglected, overgrown field near Peking University. Strewn across the landscape, like so many discarded papier-mâché movie props, were massive marble archways, enormous stone tablets, and Romanesque columns. Interspersed with these, dozens of intricately carved classical stone animals—turtles, lions, and bulls, each weighing well over a ton—lay scattered about, covered in weeds. No one was in sight. Yuanmingyuan was deserted.

Or so it seemed. After walking around the abandoned ruins for a few minutes, I heard voices coming from a nearby stone outcropping. Walking toward the source of the sound, I received my second major surprise of the day. There, standing near a cluster of massive stone animals, a handful of young Chinese men was reciting poetry. Fifty meters or so farther on, a second group of young men had set up easels on a large eighteenth-century stone slab and were painting watercolor landscapes of the surrounding ruins. A third group, standing off to one side near a grove of trees, was gathered around a young man who strummed a battered old guitar. Without speaking a word, I visited the three groups in turn. The poetry was modern, edgy, and rich in irony, which I found rather surprising, given the fact that China's post-Mao reforms had not yet gotten off the ground. I listened to one young poet but could not comprehend his imagery, so I asked if I could look at his poem. Its subject—the first blush of spring, with melting snows, blossoming buds, and the lilting birdsongs that follow a long, cold winter—though surprisingly romantic, was readily identifiable as a metaphor for China's emergence from the deep chill of revolutionary Maoism.

After spending a few minutes observing the landscape painters, I strolled over to the knot of young men surrounding the guitar player and listened for a while. They were trying to sing, in English, a Bob Dylan song, "Blowin' in the Wind," but they were not succeeding. The guitar was out of tune, the guitarist strummed the wrong chords, and the singers were articulating poorly and singing off key. I had been playing folk guitar since high school, and I knew much of the Dylan repertory by heart. When I began to sing along with them, they responded warmly, inviting me to join the group and asking me to help them with the proper English phrasing, pronunciation, and guitar chording. And so I spent the next two hours playing and singing the musical works of Dylan, Joan Baez, and Judy Collins. Lynn snapped a few pictures, and when it was time to leave, I exchanged names and addresses with the eager young men, none of whom had telephones. It was a hopeful encounter. At long last, spring was coming to China.

I STUMBLED UPON yet another piece of welcome news in the course of my autumn 1978 travels with the computer science delegation. Months earlier, PRC leaders had quietly begun planning for the initiation of direct academic exchanges with American universities. I first heard of these plans quite by accident during our delegation's visit to Nanjing University (Nanda). The main purpose of our visit there was to assess the current state of university-based research and training in the emerging field of computer

"Blowing in the Wind": An impromptu September 1978 hootenanny at Yuan-mingyuan symbolized the dawning of a new era of personal freedom in China. The toddler in the foreground is the son of Lynn Pascoe, a foreign service officer assigned to the U.S. Liaison Office in Beijing.

science. While members of our group held technical discussions with their Nanda counterparts, I requested a tour of the university's library, reputed to be one of the best in China. Accompanied by a local professor of history, I first visited the foreign languages collection. There, among other curiosities, I found an aged, moth-eaten English-language edition of Adam Smith's classic, *The Wealth of Nations*. Curious as to who would have dared to read such heretical material in Maoist China, I opened the back cover to examine the library slip. The previous user, name unknown, had checked out the book almost twenty years earlier, in April 1957, just before Mao cracked down on "rightist" intellectuals. I wondered to myself when—and if—the book would ever be checked out again.

As we continued our tour, I was impressed by the library's vast collection of original historical materials. On a whim I asked my host if I or my UCLA colleagues might be permitted to access the archives on a regular basis. He hesitated for a moment, then asked me to repeat the name of my university. I replied, "Jiazhou Daxue Losanji" (UCLA), whereupon he shook his head discouragingly. "That won't be possible," he said. "I'm afraid only University of Wisconsin scholars will be allowed to use our library. UCLA professors will have to go to Zhongda [Zhongshan University] in Guangzhou."

Taken aback by his response, I asked for clarification. He told me that in the spring of 1978 a National Education Conference had been held in Beijing. At that meeting, plans had been drawn up, under Deng Xiaoping's guidance, to establish a set of sister university relationships between China's ten leading institutions of higher learning and their American counterparts. Since this was the first that I, or any other American, had heard of such a plan (it had not been made public), I pressed my host for details. He proceeded to lay out the full list of ten proposed pairings, which included the following institutional links: Peking University with Harvard; Tsinghua University with MIT; Fudan University with UC Berkeley; Nanjing University with Wisconsin; and Zhongshan University with UCLA. There was a clear logic to the pairings, which matched institutions with similar academic profiles. The list had clearly been prepared by people with extensive academic experience in America.

As soon as our visit to Nanda ended, I telephoned John Thomson, the U.S. Information Agency rep at the U.S. Liaison Office in Beijing, and recounted my recent conversation. He took down the information and promptly alerted his State Department principals that a major Chinese educational initiative was in the offing. It was a real coup, and I was excited about the possibilities that lay ahead.

Upon returning to Los Angeles in mid-October 1978, I alerted my faculty colleagues and UCLA administrators, and together we began to plan for the inauguration of academic exchanges. A few weeks later, in early November, the anticipated opening came when Dr. Paul Lin, a Chinese Canadian professor who served as an informal conduit between the PRC and North American scholars, phoned my UCLA colleague, Barry Richman, a fellow Canadian, informing him that UCLA could expect to receive an "important invitation" very soon.

When the invitation came from Zhongshan University in mid-November, we were primed and ready, and when the normalization of U.S.-China relations was announced one month later, on December 15—removing the last hurdle in the path of direct university-to-university exchanges—we had our airline tickets in hand.

THE DELEGATION OF ten UCLA faculty members and administrators who touched down at Guangzhou's International Airport on January 5, 1979, represented the first American university since 1949 to enter into an institutional exchange with a Chinese counterpart. In a series of cordial meetings with the president and two vice presidents of Zhongda, the UCLA team agreed in principle to fund an annual exchange of a small number of faculty and graduate student researchers, and we proposed to set up an English-language training institute in Guangzhou, staffed by personnel from UCLA's Department of Teaching of English as a Foreign Language (TOEFL) under the leadership of Professor Russell Campbell, who was a member of our delegation. Having reached preliminary agreement, we flew off to Beijing to finalize the deal with the Ministry of Education. We were ill prepared for what we encountered next.

In the late autumn of 1978 the political atmosphere in Beijing was crackling with the electricity of anticipated change. In November the erstwhile "counterrevolutionary" Tiananmen incident of April 1976 was declared "fully revolutionary," vindicating Deng Xiaoping and casting a deep shadow over the political future of Hua Guofeng. Welcoming Deng's return to political prominence, groups of Chinese citizens pasted up a number of *dazibao*, or handwritten "big-character posters," on a two-hundred-yard stretch of city wall along Beijing's Chang'an Boulevard at Xidan, west of Tiananmen Square. Dubbed "Democracy Wall" (Minzhuqiang), the edifice at Xidan soon became the focal point for a remarkable display of unfettered public political discourse.

Wall posters had long served as pressure valves for the release of political tension and as informal conduits for disseminating inside information and opinion in China. In the spring of 1978, the people's right to post *dazibao* had been enshrined in the new PRC constitution, along with the rights to "big debates," "big blooming," and "big contending," as part of the so-called four big freedoms. The idea, redolent of the 1957 Hundred Flowers campaign, was to allow the masses to express themselves more freely and openly and thereby relieve their pent-up frustrations. But much like that earlier movement, which saw China's intellectuals unleash a torrent of criticism at the Communist Party, the masses soon exceeded the boundaries of permissible discourse.

The president and vice president of Zhongshan University are greeted at UCLA by faculty and staff in 1979, inaugurating a bilateral educational exchange program.

Among the various opinions expressed in posters at the Xidan wall in the fall of 1978, two themes stood out from the rest: intensified criticism directed at Hua Guofeng's key supporters, who, in addition to being dubbed the "whatever faction," were now derisively referred to as a Little Gang of Four, and questions about Mao's own political judgment, in particular his relations with the Cultural Revolution leftists. As one anonymous poster writer put it: "Ask yourself: How could Lin Biao reach power without the support of Mao? Ask yourself: Did Mao not know that Jiang Qing . . . [and] Zhang Chunqiao [were] traitors? Ask yourself: Without the consent of Mao, would it have been possible for the Gang of Four to launch the campaign against Deng Xiaoping? Ask yourself: Without the consent of Mao, would it have been possible to label the Tiananmen episode a counterrevolutionary incident?"

By late November such "big blooming" and "big contending" had attracted considerable attention. Individually and in small groups, citizens of Beijing gathered at the Xidan wall to read the latest political broadsides and participate in an unprecedented public discussion of pressing national issues. The vast majority of participants were young workers, clerks, and unemployed middle-school graduates in their twenties and thirties. Although most had the equivalent of a high school education, few university students or higher intellectuals played an active role.

At first, party leaders, including Deng Xiaoping himself, were ambivalent about the new epidemic of wall posters. Although Deng was a beneficiary of the anti-Hua, anti–Gang of Four discourse at the Xidan wall, he harbored reservations about the libertarian potential of the burgeoning mass movement. In an interview with a group of visiting Japanese politicians in late November, Deng guardedly endorsed free speech, calling it "a good thing," but with one important caveat: Mao Zedong must not be criticized. Word of Deng's conditional approval spread rapidly through the city, and the crowds at Xidan and other poster sites in and around Tiananmen Square quickly swelled. Within a relatively short time, what had begun as a small fringe movement of disaffected workers, educated youths, and former Red Guards was transformed from guerrilla theater for the few into participatory democracy for the many.

Meeting in November and December of 1978, the Eleventh CCP Central Committee, at its third plenary session, approved Deng Xiaoping's pioneering proposals for sweeping economic reforms and opening up to the outside world. It was a major watershed in China's modern history, marking the end of the Maoist era. As the Central Committee chiseled away at Hua Guofeng's power and prestige, Deng Xiaoping could afford to affect a benign, patronizing attitude toward Democracy Wall. The *laobaixing* had embraced him. In a silent tribute to Deng's return to power, thousands of "small bottles" (*xiaopingzi*), a play on Deng's given name, were strung from lampposts and fences along Beijing's city streets in the fall of 1978. Up to that point, most of the *dazibao* at the Xidan wall were strongly supportive of both Deng and the spirit of economic and political reform, and many were openly hostile to Hua's "whatever faction." (Years later, after martial law was declared in Beijing in May of 1989, the Beijing *laobaixing* would smash thousands of small bottles in the streets in a symbolic display of anger at their former hero.) Yet within the burgeoning poster movement there were signs of a deeper, more fundamental antagonism toward the core political institutions and values of Chinese Communism.

Spurred on by Deng's conditional expression of support for free speech, Xidan activists became bolder and more outspoken. At the end of November an anonymous sixty-six-page wall poster appeared on Mao's Memorial

Beijing residents congregate to read and debate wall posters at Democracy Wall, January 1979. Some posters contain demands for political reform and openness; others relate personal tales of Cultural Revolution persecution. Three months later the municipal government banned the placement of leaflets and wall posters in public places.

Hall at the southern end of Tiananmen Square, calling on the Chinese people to rise up and "settle accounts" with all dictators, "no matter who they are." It also demanded—in violation of Deng's explicit prohibition—a reassessment of Mao's contributions and shortcomings. In a somewhat less combative mode, in early December participants in an open forum at the Heroes' Monument in Tiananmen Square urged greater freedom and democracy for China. Some speakers criticized Mao's economic strategy; others urged party leaders to study the positive aspects of American-style democracy, including its system of constitutional checks and balances and its two-party system.

By early December, as the poster campaign spread from Beijing to Shanghai, Wuhan, Guangzhou, and other major cities, a unifying theme began to emerge from among the disparate groups participating in the new movement: the call for political democratization and respect for human rights as prerequisites of successful economic modernization. As one Xidan poster put it: "China's system of government is modeled on the Russian system [which] produces bureaucracy and a privileged stratum. Without changes in this system, the Four Modernizations will stop halfway . . . , as in Russia where the state is strong and the people are poor . . . . We need a state where all delegates are elected and responsible to the people."

Visibly perturbed over the increasing radicalism of posters at the Xidan wall, Deng stepped up his warnings against direct criticism of Mao and of the Chinese political system. Undeterred, a few bold activists responded by openly chastising Deng himself. One poster admonished: "Vice-Premier Deng, you are wrong, completely wrong. . . . There is no doubt that, a long time ago, the Chinese people took note of Chairman Mao's mistakes. Those who hate the Gang of Four cannot fail to have grievances against Chairman Mao." Another particularly harsh assessment came from a twenty-eight-year-old electrician-turned-activist named Wei Jingsheng, whose lengthy wall poster, "Democracy—The Fifth Modernization," appeared in Beijing on December 5. The poster began by noting that the hopes and aspirations of the Chinese people had been greatly elevated following the arrest of the Gang of Four and the return to power of Deng Xiaoping, but these expectations had been severely dampened when the new leaders turned out to be nearly as rigid and undemocratic as the old ones:

> [When] Vice-Premier Deng finally returned to his leading post
> . . . how excited people were, how inspired. . . . When Deng Xiaoping raised the slogan of "getting down to business" . . . the people
> wanted to "seek truth from facts," to investigate the past. . . . But
> "some people" warned us: . . . Chairman Mao is the great savior of
> the Chinese people. . . . If you don't agree with this, you will come
> to no good end! . . . Regrettably, the old political system so hated
> by the people was not changed, the democracy and freedom they
> hoped for could not even be mentioned. . . . When people ask for
> democracy, they are only asking for something they rightfully
> own. . . . [Under such circumstances] are not the people justified in
> seizing power from the overlords?

The UCLA delegation arrived amid mounting political tension in the Chinese capital, on Monday, January 9, 1979. As we drove in from the airport, I could sense an atmosphere of palpable excitement. Beijing was coming alive. The country was poised on the knife edge of change.

As soon as we checked into our rooms at the Beijing Hotel, I set out on foot with two colleagues, Perry Link and Phil Huang. We headed straight for Tiananmen Square. Despite the bone-chilling cold, the square was alive with activity. Clusters of people had gathered around the base of the Heroes' Monument, which was festooned with wall posters and floral wreaths commemorating the third anniversary of Zhou Enlai's death. Other posters welcomed the news that several prominent former Communist Party leaders, disgraced during the Cultural Revolution, had recently been rehabilitated. On a temporary plywood construction wall along the eastern edge of the square, a huge poster, made up of a dozen or more three-by-five-foot panels, had been put up, containing excerpts from Thomas Paine's classic American revolutionary broadside "The Rights of Man." The poster exhorted Chinese citizens to demand democratic reform and human rights. Using red and black markers, eager readers had underscored many key passages on the panels. It was an incredibly vibrant scene, as scores of people engaged in passionate (but civil) discussion about China's past and future. Caught up in the excitement, I became separated from my UCLA colleagues. When one group of ardent young debaters discovered a Chinese-speaking foreigner in their midst—an American at that—they began peppering me with questions about American democracy, human rights, and President Jimmy Carter. Perhaps naively, I sensed a rare historical moment at hand—people longing to reclaim their own destiny from leaders who had abused their trust.

Eventually making my getaway, I continued my journey westward, past Tiananmen Square to the Xidan wall. There I saw hundreds of hastily scrawled notices (*xiaozibao*, or "small-character posters"), many addressed to individual Chinese leaders, containing detailed descriptions of horrendous persecution and suffering endured by Chinese citizens during the Cultural Revolution. In some cases the authors named their tormentors, appealing to the authorities for long-overdue justice. Other entreaties were posted by educated urban youths, sent down to the countryside during the "rustication" (*xiaxiang*) campaign at the end of the Cultural Revolution, who were now flocking back—illegally—to Beijing and other large cities in hopes of having their cases reviewed and their urban "household registration permits" (*hukou*) restored.

Most of the petitioners were poor; many were in dire straits. Some had traveled long distances on foot, carrying their possessions in knotted bundles; others had hitched rides into the city on freight trains or trucks. Gathering in clusters near railroad stations and around the city center, petitioners took to begging for food or peddling small household items while waiting for their cases to be reopened. One foreign journalist described a group of petitioners, living in squalor at a temporary encampment, as having come "straight out of a Goya painting ... sick, on crutches, dressed in rags and tatters, wretchedly poverty-stricken."

Taking all this in, I was overwhelmed with the sheer pathos of it. The deep, silent scars of a long-suffering people were being exposed to the light. Old wounds were being torn open, old antagonisms aired. A national catharsis was in progress. It was painful, yet fascinating, to watch.

As I prepared to return to my hotel, one *xiaozibao* caught my eye. Scrawled hastily in black ink on a pink background, under the heading "public announcement" (*gong gao*), it called on all Chinese who had "suffered persecution at the hands of the Gang of Four" to assemble in Tiananmen Square for a protest demonstration at 1:00 PM the following Sunday, January 14. The poster bore the name of the demonstration's principal organizer, Fu Yuehua. Fu, a thirty-two-year-old female construction worker, had been fired from her job after reporting that she was raped by the Party secretary in her work unit. Unable to gain a fair hearing, Fu soon became impoverished and suffered a nervous breakdown. Later she organized rural petitioners and sent-down youth in Beijing to demand an end to hunger and oppression in China. On January 8, 1979, the third anniversary of Zhou Enlai's death, she led the first organized protest march in post-Mao China. I made a mental note of the date of the next scheduled demonstration—January 14.

Over the next several days we were kept busy with exchange-related meetings and officially escorted visits to various universities, research institutes, and cultural sites, followed by a succession of evening banquets. There were few opportunities to return to the Xidan wall or Tiananmen Square. Phil Huang, however, suggested that he, Perry Link, and I slip away from our Ministry of Education hosts long enough to meet with two famous longtime Western residents of Beijing—Rewi Alley and Sidney Rittenberg. Alley, a New Zealander, had first come to China in 1927, when he helped to found the Chinese industrial cooperative movement during the anti-Japanese War. After the war he worked as a teacher, writer, and poet, traveling the length and breadth of China, popularizing his experiences in a series of books and magazine articles intended for English-speaking audiences throughout the world. He was rewarded for his long-standing service to China (and to the Chinese Communist Party) with a spacious apartment in central Beijing, a retinue of personal servants, and a handsome stipend. Along with such other longtime "foreign friends" as Israel Epstein, Dr. George Hatem, Sidney Rittenberg, Sidney Shapiro, Agnes Smedley, Edgar Snow, Anna Louise Strong, and William Hinton, Alley personified the CCP's "united front" strategy of co-opting and pampering influential non-Communist foreign intellectuals and cultural elites.

It should be said that for all his contributions to China's wartime co-op movement, Alley's poetry, though spirited in style, was banal and simplistic. In any event, when we met him in his lavishly appointed flat in January 1979, Alley was eighty-one years old and quite frail. At that point, his reputed homosexual predations (which evidently had included sexual liaisons with several of his teenage male students in the 1940s) had not yet been exposed; indeed his preference for young boys was carefully covered up for four decades by an outwardly puritanical (though inwardly promiscuous) CCP leadership—much as Mao's legendary appetite for young rural female playmates had also been hushed up. While Alley regaled us with reminiscences of his World War II adventures with his close friend and fellow Sinophile Dr. George Hatem (aka Ma Haide), his servants lavished attention on him. As we finished our tea and prepared to take our leave, Hatem himself turned up, and we exchanged pleasantries. Upon leaving, we each received an autographed copy of Alley's latest book of poems. Somehow, the iconic Rewi Alley seemed a good deal smaller in life than in legend.

Sidney Rittenberg was another story entirely. Rittenberg had come to China with the U.S. Army near the end of World War II; when the war ended, he stayed on to work with the United Nations Relief and Rehabilitation Administration (UNRRA). In Yan'an after the war, he translated radio broadcasts for Chinese Communist leaders and trained Chinese journalists in the art of English translation. Like Alley, Rittenberg stayed in China after the revolution, only to be arrested in 1949 as an American spy. After he was released from solitary confinement in 1955, his friendship with Zhou Enlai, dating from the Yan'an days, provided him with an entrée into elite Communist Party circles, and he became the first American citizen admitted into the CCP. Working for the international section of Radio Peking, Rittenberg became radicalized during the Cultural Revolution, playing a leading role in a leftist "rebel" group that participated in the 1967 public humiliation of Wang Guangmei. Subsequently denounced by Jiang Qing and her allies as an anti-Party element, Rittenberg was arrested again early in 1968. He spent the next ten years in solitary confinement, finally gaining his release more than a year after the downfall of the Gang of Four.

When we met Rittenberg he was fifty-nine years old and had only recently been released from prison. For a man who had spent more than half the previous thirty years in solitary confinement on a variety of serious political charges, he was remarkably calm, idealistic, and optimistic about China's future. Most surprising of all, he bore no visible animus toward the regime that had treated him so badly. His wife, Yulin, who had also been imprisoned during the Cultural Revolution, displayed similar equanimity. Phil, Perry, and I listened in rapt silence as he recounted the story of his Cultural Revolution activism, captivity, and ultimate release. I had difficulty understanding then—as I do now—such apparently benign idealism and forgiveness. As "foreign friends" of China go, Sid Rittenberg was far more interesting than Rewi Alley.

On our last full day in Beijing, Sunday, January 14, our delegation had scheduled a final, all-day negotiating session with the Ministry of Education. The meeting took place in a conference room on one of the upper floors of the Peking Hotel. As the day wore on, we were getting close to a final agreement on academic exchanges. At one point, Perry, getting up to stretch his legs, strolled over to a nearby window. After a couple of minutes he came back to the table. As he passed my chair, he whispered, "Take a look outside, in the street." Sauntering casually over to the window, I looked down. There, several floors below, marching slowly in uneven columns along Chang'an Boulevard toward Tiananmen Square to the west, were several hundred demonstrators, carrying banners reading "End hunger" and "Human rights and democracy." At the head of the procession was a woman whom I assumed to be Fu Yuehua. I watched for a few minutes, fascinated. Such a demonstration would have drawn barely any attention in Berkeley, where protest marches were almost a daily occurrence. But in Beijing? In broad daylight? Along the most famous thoroughfare in the country—China's Champs Elysées? It was hard to wrap my mind around what I was seeing.

Over the next twenty minutes or so, my UCLA colleagues and I took turns getting up from the table to stretch our legs. By now the demonstrators were receding into the distance, having reached Tiananmen Square a

Sid Rittenberg, with Mao Zedong, 1964. Rittenberg spent fifteen years in solitary
confinement in China as an American spy and "bourgeois revisionist" during the
Mao era, before being released in 1977. Photo courtesy of Sidney Rittenberg.

half mile west of the hotel. I kept looking at my watch, wanting the meeting to end. My pulse was pounding. I wondered if our Chinese hosts had
any inkling of what was going on outside—or if they even cared.

Just before dusk we reached a final agreement with our ministry hosts.
The appropriate documents were signed, and there were smiles and hand-
shakes all around. As soon as people began packing up their briefcases
and heading for the elevators, I dashed out to the nearest stairwell, literally bounding down half a dozen flights of stairs. By the time I hit the
street, twilight was closing in and no demonstrators were in sight. It was
bitterly cold, with a chill wind blowing in from the northwest. I turned
up my collar and jogged as fast as I could toward Tiananmen but could
see no unusual activity in the square. Continuing on, I spotted a flurry
of movement on the road ahead. By the time I reached the well-guarded
front entrance to Zhongnanhai, a half mile farther on, it was getting dark.
A minor traffic jam was causing confusion. Winded from my exertion, I
could make out the silhouettes of perhaps 150 people sitting down in the

street, still carrying their banners. They shouted no slogans but merely sat, quietly but defiantly, in front of the CCP leaders' residential compound, blocking traffic on Beijing's busiest thoroughfare. The armed guards in front of Zhongnanhai stood rigidly at attention, unblinking. At the edge of the crowd I watched, fascinated, wishing I had brought my camera. After about fifteen more minutes of this silent vigil, someone in the group passed the word and people began to stand up and disperse, in groups of three or four. Fu Yuehua was one of the last to leave. By now it was almost totally dark. I tried to approach Fu, but two of her associates nudged me aside, fearful of having her photographed by police in the company of a Westerner.

Fu Yuehua's triumph in organizing a large-scale, peaceful display of civil disobedience was short-lived. Four days later, on January 18, the Beijing municipal police, alarmed by the rising boldness of the petitioners' movement, arrested Fu, making her the first known political casualty of the new Chinese Democracy Movement. Shortly thereafter, plainclothes police were observed tape-recording conversations at the Xidan wall and copying down license numbers of bicyclists who stopped to participate in political discussions. By this time, however, we had returned to Los Angeles, where we could only read with alarm the news of mounting police harassment of pro-democracy activists.

Behind the scenes in Beijing, the rival conservative and liberal reform wings of the CCP were engaged in an intense political debate. Deng himself was caught in the middle, not wanting to use force to curtail free speech but annoyed at the growing impudence of the regime's critics. Testing the limits of Deng's tolerance, Wei Jingsheng, author of the provocative "Democracy—The Fifth Modernization" wall poster and editor of the underground journal *Explorations*, published a biting critique of Deng at the end of March 1979, "Do We Want a Democracy or a New Dictatorship?" In it, Wei accused Deng of shedding his mask as protector of democracy, betraying the people's trust, and metamorphosing into a "dictatorial fascist" in the mold of the recently deposed ultra-leftists.

A few days later, the Beijing municipal government announced strict new regulations governing mass meetings and demonstrations. Henceforth, petitioners and protesters would not be permitted to block traffic, interfere with the work of public offices, or instigate the masses to "cause trouble," and the placement of leaflets and wall posters on all streets, public places, or buildings outside of "specially designated areas" was now prohibited.

Early in April, Wei Jingsheng, who had vigorously protested against Fu Yuehua's arrest, was himself detained. Held without charges for more than six months, Wei was quietly tried in mid-October and sentenced to fifteen years in prison for engaging in "counterrevolutionary incitement" and conveying "official secrets" to a foreign journalist. At the end of November, precisely one year after Deng Xiaoping first publicly endorsed the use of wall posters, Xidan was placed off limits to poster writers, and Democracy Wall was moved, on orders from the Beijing municipal government, to a quiet, out-of-the-way location some two miles distant. A few weeks later Fu Yuehua was tried, convicted, and sentenced to two years in prison for "violating public order." By the end of the year, the newborn Chinese Democracy Movement had been effectively silenced. The anticipatory political excitement, so palpable a year earlier, soon dissipated as Deng Xiaoping now sought to redirect the attention and energy of the Chinese people away from political reform and onto the more immediate lure of economic prosperity. China was about to embark on the uncharted path of market reform and opening up to the outside world. Seven more years would elapse before the next pro-democracy demonstration would be held in Tiananmen Square.

6

Capitalism with Chinese Characteristics

IN JULY 1962, with China just beginning to recover from the catastrophic Great Leap Forward, Deng Xiaoping deeply offended Mao by arguing that economic performance was more important than ideological principle. As Deng famously put it, "It doesn't matter if the cat is white or black, so long as it catches mice." Now, twenty years later, Mao was dead, his economic theories had collapsed, and Deng's willingness to experiment with new economic forms was everywhere in evidence. One of the most important was his experiment with small-scale urban self-employment.

Until the early 1980s self-employment was strictly prohibited in China. But with as many as ten million sent-down youths now flooding back into Chinese cities from their post–Cultural Revolution rural exile, large numbers of young people had little or nothing to do. In this situation, government leaders decided that small-scale self-employment could help relieve the pressure of burgeoning unemployment. Thus were born the *getihu* (individual households).

"PAI NI ZHAOPIAN MA?" asked the two young men hopefully: "Take your picture?" It was the summer of 1983. I was on a morning walk through Tiananmen Square, hoping to get in line outside Mao's Memorial Hall early enough to view the Chairman's embalmed body without waiting for hours in the hot sun. I had first visited the Memorial Hall back in the fall of 1978 and been keenly disappointed by the shriveled, greenish-tinged corpse on display in the refrigerated underground viewing room. It seemed to me that the Chairman had been embalmed badly, and in some haste. Little of his legendary potency or charisma could be extrapolated from those shrunken, slack-jawed remains. But in the intervening four years, a few friends and colleagues had visited the crypt and commented on how plump, rosy-cheeked, and serene Mao looked. I wanted to confirm this magical transformation for myself. I was contemplating this when my reverie was interrupted. "Pai ni zhaopian?" the two youths repeated, having positioned themselves directly in my path. Mao's corpse could wait. I was about to have my first encounter with China's *getihu.*

The two shabbily dressed sent-down youths who intercepted me had, they said in response to my questions, pooled their resources to purchase a secondhand reflex camera. Setting up a small pushcart in the northwestern corner of Tiananmen Square, near the Great Hall of the People, with a large umbrella for shade and a sign advertising their services, the young men were offering to take photos of visitors anywhere on the square, either individually or in groups, for the modest price of three poses for ¥0.5—about $.26 at the current exchange rate—including same-day pickup of the finished prints. Under the disinterested gaze of a policeman patrolling nearby, they were doing a rather brisk business among early-bird tourists. After I paid to have three photos taken, one of the young men volunteered that they had grossed ¥14 ($7.10) on the previous day, almost half of which (¥6) was profit.

As I resumed my walk toward the Memorial Hall, I passed a second photo stand a few hundred meters farther on, near the Heroes' Monument. It was also equipped with a reflex camera and an umbrella, and the two employees were offering to photograph visitors against the backdrop of Mao's famous portrait above the Gate of Heavenly Peace. But they were charging ¥0.3 for a single pose—almost twice as much per print as the *getihu*—and they were not offering same-day pickup. My curiosity piqued, I asked them why they didn't lower their price or improve their service to meet the competition. They just shrugged and pointed to the small print on their neatly lettered sign: "Beijing Municipal Service Bureau." *They were state employees.* They resumed their conversation, ignoring me completely. Not a single customer had appeared since I first approached them. I made a mental note to come back after viewing Mao's corpse.

After waiting in line for more than an hour, I got my second glimpse of Chairman Mao in repose. This time he really was plump, pink-cheeked, and firm-jawed. Either my memory had played tricks or someone had done a hell of a good repair job on his formaldehyde-fixed remains. It was truly puzzling. Only many years later did Mao's personal physician, Dr. Li Zhisui, reveal that a life-size double had been fashioned out of wax before Mao died, just in case something went wrong with the embalming process. Dr. Li further revealed that Mao's body had initially been pumped so full of formaldehyde by nervous morticians that it swelled up to the point of grotesqueness. Here is Dr. Li's description, taken from his 1994 book *The Private Life of Chairman Mao*: "We injected a total of twenty-two litres. The results were shocking. Mao's face was bloated, as round as a ball, and his neck was now the width of his head. His skin was shiny, and the formaldehyde oozed from his pores like perspiration. His ears were swollen too, sticking out from his head at right angles. The corpse was grotesque."

Other, unconfirmed reports claimed that Mao's left ear had come off as a result of the botched embalming, requiring surgical reattachment. The Mao I saw in 1983 (and on one other occasion since) thus might well have been a wax dummy, a stand-in. If so, then what had become of the real, shriveled-up Mao? Unfortunately, Dr. Li died before this mystery could be cleared up. Today it remains unsolved—one of the Mao era's many secrets.

Filing out of the Memorial Hall, I retraced my steps back toward the state-owned photo booth. I circled for a while, at a distance. Not a single prospective customer was in sight. The two young state employees chatted lazily the entire time, sitting on their stools, not bothering to try to drum up business. Looking toward the northwest, I could see a knot of people clustered around the *getihu* booth. Business was still booming there.

In and of itself, this tale of two photo kiosks may not seem particularly significant, yet it carried profound implications for China's future. Under socialist ownership, the prices of all goods and services in the economy were set by the monopolistic state; customers could take it or leave it. Sales-clerks were state employees: Their jobs, wages, and benefits were guaranteed for life under the regime's "iron rice bowl" policy. Their enterprises needn't turn a profit or provide high-quality goods and services. And since all sales revenues were remitted to the state, there was no incentive for enterprise managers to improve the quality of their products or their services. Staff employees didn't care, because they didn't have to. They just put in their time and picked up their paychecks. Ditto their managers.

That, in a nutshell, was the story of China's centrally planned economy as it played out daily in hundreds of thousands of state-owned enterprises. But now the *getihu* had begun to expose the endemic weaknesses of the command economy, and it did not take long for enterprising young men

Self-employed *getihu* youths compete for customers at photo kiosks in Guangzhou, 1985. Small-scale businesses like these represented the first blooming of an emerging private sector in post-Mao China.

and women to begin frontally challenging state monopolies throughout the service sector, from photography and fast food to haircutting and taxicabs.

Wherever private challengers arose, either to contest existing state monopolies or to fill visible gaps in the service sector, consumers were the big winners. Between 1982 and 1986, the quality of food available in many of Beijing's restaurants improved noticeably, as enterprising *getihu* began setting up small food stands and sidewalk cafés around the city, weaning customers away from established state restaurants by offering better food with better service at competitive prices. By the middle of the decade, state enterprises that were losing out in competition with the new, self-employed providers were put on notice that the state would no longer automatically bail them out. If they couldn't turn a profit, they would have to go out of business. Quality slowly began to improve, and state service staff began paying attention to customer satisfaction. As a crude barometer of improved food quality, the famous three-course Peking duck dinner served by the chain of state-owned duck restaurants in Beijing (known locally—not for nothing—as Old Duck, Sick Duck, and Big Duck) went from being incredibly tasteless and greasy in the early 1980s to being rather good—crisp, fragrant, and fresh—by the early 1990s. Though they have never regained the legendary culinary excellence achieved in the declining days of the Manchu dynasty (the restaurant chain dates back to the 1860s), the food today is quite decent.

Two years later, in the summer of 1985, I went back to Tiananmen Square. The photo stand operated by the Municipal Service Bureau was nowhere to be seen, but the two young *getihu* photographers were still there. No longer shabbily dressed, they appeared to be thriving. They had expanded their operation in the intervening two years, purchasing a second reflex camera along with a used Polaroid for those patrons who preferred instant gratification. They had also added a second location in the square, hiring a young man to staff it and a young woman to do all their photo processing in-house. Moreover, they now provided an array of glitzy costumes (including PLA officers' uniforms and ersatz imperial court regalia) and elaborate props (such as a cardboard cutout of a Hongqi limousine, an ornate sedan chair, and a wooden two-humped camel) to satisfy their clients' whims. They proudly told me that they now cleared almost ¥24 ($11) a day in net profit, roughly three times their 1983 take. As success breeds imitation, there were now two other private photo operators competing with them for customers in Tiananmen Square.

After thirty years of heavy-handed state socialism, Adam Smith's "invisible hand" had finally come to China. I couldn't help wondering about the long-neglected copy of Smith's classic *Wealth of Nations* that I had stumbled upon in the Nanjing University library six years earlier. Was it back in circulation? Although I did not have occasion to revisit that particular library, I have since seen many copies of the book in bookstores and university libraries throughout China, where it has become, in Chinese translation, a required text in countless university economics courses.

DESPITE THE REFORMS' clear benefit to consumers, the very concept of individual entrepreneurship remained ideologically suspect. And before Deng Xiaoping could fully establish the legitimacy of China's new mixed economy, with its emphasis on market competition, he had to deal with a troublesome skeleton rattling around in the national closet—the unquiet ghost of Mao Zedong.

Early in 1980, under Deng's overall direction, the CCP Central Committee appointed a small working group to undertake an official assessment of Mao's role in modern Chinese history. Prospective appointees were carefully screened to include both older and younger members, progressive reformers as well as traditionalists. From the outset, Deng insisted that the final document should reflect a consensus view that Mao's contributions were paramount (70 percent) and his shortcomings secondary (30 percent). Nevertheless, the group's deliberations were marked by sharp, recurrent disagreements over the extent and seriousness of Mao's "mistakes" and the relative weight to be assigned them in relation to his "outstanding achievements."

After more than a year of sometimes rancorous debate and multiple drafts, Deng signed off on the finished document in June 1981. Awkwardly titled "Resolution on Certain Questions in the History of Our Party since the Founding of the People's Republic of China," the document was a curious patchwork of strangely worded—and partially contradictory—compromises between those who blamed Mao for a string of horrible man-made catastrophes and those who revered him as a great revolutionary genius.

The resolution's sharpest criticisms dealt with Mao's behavior in the years after 1956, when he allegedly became "arrogant" and "divorced from the masses." He was cited for "unjustly persecuting" large numbers of intellectuals in the crackdown that followed the Hundred Flowers campaign of 1956–57. He was scored for becoming "smug with success" and "impatient for quick results" during the Great Leap Forward, when he recklessly "overestimated the role of man's subjective will," thereby causing untold suffering. And in the 1960s he made an "entirely erroneous" appraisal of the severity of class struggle in China, leading him to "confuse the people with the enemy." Specifically named as innocent victims of Mao's extreme fixation on class struggle were Liu Shaoqi and Deng Xiaoping. For Liu, the exoneration came too late: He had died under horrific circumstances twelve years earlier, in 1969. Suffering from diabetes and pneumonia contracted during his long Cultural Revolution incarceration, Liu had been left alone, naked, in the middle of winter, on a surgical gurney in a bare, unheated room in a prison hospital in Kaifeng. He died of medical neglect.

Although Mao's errors were acknowledged to have caused considerable damage to the Party and to the people, they were nonetheless said to be the mistakes of "a great proletarian revolutionary" who "paid constant attention to overcoming shortcomings," and the dominant tone of the document was, as Deng had instructed, generally positive.

If Mao's mistakes thus received rather lenient treatment at the hands of Deng Xiaoping, the same could not be said for the crimes of the Gang of Four. Held in prison without habeas corpus since October 1976, the four leftists were brought to trial early in 1980, on capital charges. Specifically, the government's indictment alleged that Jiang Qing and her three cronies had been indirectly responsible for the deaths of 34,800 people, including Liu Shaoqi, and the torture or severe maltreatment of 726,000 others in the decade between 1966 and 1976.

At the trial, Jiang Qing was unrepentant to the very end. Acting as her own defense attorney, she steadfastly denied her guilt and denounced prosecution witnesses as traitors. Throughout the trial she repeatedly derided the court and challenged the legitimacy of the government. On two occasions Jiang was ejected from the courtroom after engaging in shouting matches with witnesses, judges, and prosecutors.

For all her dramatic gestures, including the claim that she had acted entirely at Mao's behest—"I was Chairman Mao's lapdog. Whenever Chairman Mao asked me to bite, I bit," she said—the outcome of the trial was never seriously in doubt. The only real question concerned the severity of the sentences. After a post-trial delay of several weeks, Jiang Qing and her principal codefendant, Shanghai Party boss Zhang Chunqiao, were given suspended death sentences, reviewable after two years in the event of "sincere repentance," a fairly standard disposition in Chinese capital cases. The two remaining members of Jiang's clique, Wang Hongwen and Yao Wenyuan, were sentenced to terms of life and twenty years in prison, respectively.

Aside from the sensational trial of the Gang of Four, the year 1980 also witnessed the quiet rehabilitation of many of their high-ranking victims, including both Liu Shaoqi and his wife, Wang Guangmei. Liu was posthumously vindicated by the Party Central Committee in February 1980, and Wang, who had been freed from prison a year earlier and had testified as a prosecution witness at the trials of the four, was fully exonerated and appointed honorary vice president of the Chinese Academy of Social Science.

I first learned of Wang Guangmei's rehabilitation in the spring of 1980, while browsing through a backlog of recent issues of *People's Daily*. On a whim, I decided to send her a copy of my 1975 book on the Four Cleanups,

Prelude to Revolution: Mao, the Party and the Peasant Question, 1962–66.
The book contained a good deal of exculpatory material about the role she
and her husband had played in the Four Cleanups movement. On the flyleaf I inscribed, in my ever-awkward left-handed Chinese calligraphy, a
personal note of condolence to Wang on the loss of her husband. And I
carefully bookmarked those chapters and sections dealing with Liu's and
Wang's Four Cleanups experiences.

More than a year later, in the summer of 1981, I received a phone call
out of the blue from Professor Immanuel Hsü, a distinguished senior
Chinese American historian at the University of California, Santa Barbara. Immanuel told me he had been granted a private audience with
Wang Guangmei a week earlier, and that Wang had entrusted him with
a small parcel for delivery to me. He had no idea what was in it, but he
agreed to send it to me. When I received the package a few days later,
I opened it eagerly and saw my Chinese name, Bao Ruijia (包瑞嘉),
inscribed in a firm hand on the inner wrapper. Carefully removing the
wrapper, I extracted a bound copy of "Resolution on Certain Questions
on the History of Our Party since the Founding of the People's Republic
of China." Inside the front cover was a handwritten personal note from
Wang Guangmei, thanking me for the concern I had shown for her and
her late husband.

WITH MAO ZEDONG'S ghost laid gingerly to rest and the Gang of Four
safely behind bars, reformers were free to introduce a number of economic
innovations. In addition to permitting small-scale private commerce, the
fiscal system was now decentralized, encouraging provinces and localities
to display greater entrepreneurial initiative by permitting them to retain a
significant share of the profits therefrom. In rural areas, the people's communes—cornerstone of Mao's radical agrarian policies—were dissolved,
land was decollectivized and contracted to individual families, and free
markets were reopened. In China's cities, the "iron rice bowl" was subject
to further erosion, as principles of market competition and profit maximi-
zation were officially sanctioned. Deng gave these various experiments a
modicum of ideological legitimacy and respectability by cleverly labeling
his reforms "Socialism with Chinese characteristics."

To provide added incentive for people to work hard and earn more
money, production of luxury consumer goods was ginned up. Television
sets, refrigerators, and motorbikes became the new status symbols, espe-

cially those bearing foreign brand names. Urban women wore makeup, jewelry, and fashionable clothing for the first time in fifteen years.

Gradually, a new culture of personal consumption began to take root, first in China's coastal cities and then spreading to the interior. The reformers' oft-repeated mantra, "Liberate the productive forces," was used to justify the gradual dismantling of China's centrally planned economy. "It's all right for some people to get rich before others," was Deng Xiaoping's new market-friendly clarion call. In some provinces local authorities carried the new ethos even further. Public billboards in Sichuan and Shanxi unabashedly promoted the pursuit of private wealth, proclaiming that "To get rich is glorious!" (*zhifu guangrong!*) Though this latter slogan was not officially sanctioned by Deng or the Party center, it accurately captured the prevailing spirit of the new age.

While the introduction of market forces spawned entrepreneurship and competition, Deng's new "open policy" facilitated growing trade and investment ties with the outside world, in particular the West. Reversing two decades of austere Maoist insularity, the central government opened Special Economic Zones in four coastal counties in Guangdong and Fujian in the early 1980s, designed to attract foreign capital, technology, and management skills. Tourism also expanded rapidly, and English quickly became the foreign language of choice for millions of young Chinese looking to position themselves favorably in the marketplace in anticipation of the next big thing. Along the Guangdong–Hong Kong border, the sleepy rural town of Shumchun morphed into the nascent industrial powerhouse, Shenzhen.

IN AUGUST OF 1980, the telephone operator at Shanghai's stately old Peace Hotel (which catered mainly to foreign businessmen) delivered my wakeup call each morning at 6:00 AM with a freshly memorized sentence from her English textbook. One day it was "Good morning, sir. Would you like your eggs scrambled or over easy?"—a hollow invitation, since the hotel restaurant served only boiled eggs. The next day it was "Good morning, sir. Our city has many famous historical landmarks." And on the third day, "Good morning, sir. We study English for the revolution." That one definitely caught my attention, so I asked her, in English, what that sentence meant. A long silence ensued, so I repeated the question in Chinese. She replied that she "wasn't sure" (*wo buqingchu*) what it meant, but that she had copied it out of her English textbook to practice on hotel guests.

By 1980 English had become a virtual national obsession in China. Tourist hotels, public parks, and recreational venues catering to foreigners were now linguistic magnets, attracting swarms of eager young Chinese looking to practice their English conversation skills. Since Chinese generally were not permitted to enter hotels catering to foreign tourists without written authorization, they would often hover just outside the front gates, waiting patiently for unsuspecting *laowai* to venture out. "Speak English?" was their mantra. They could be very persistent, and I often found myself being trailed by a small phalanx of aspiring Anglophones when I left my hotel.

I took up jogging in the early 1980s, shortly after breaking a twenty-year smoking habit. In China I developed a routine of jogging two or three miles a day, usually at dawn. It was a perfect time to view a city and its inhabitants in their natural, unrehearsed state, and air pollution—already a major problem in many Chinese cities, whose residents burned highly sulfurous coal for household heating and cooking—was minimal in the early morning hours. In any event, it didn't take long for the enterprising young men who habitually clustered outside my hotel to adjust to my daily jogging routine. They began showing up at the crack of dawn, in shorts and sneakers. Matching my pace as I headed out the front gate, they would conduct their conversations with me on the fly. As a newly reformed ex-smoker and lifelong asthmatic, however, I panted audibly when I ran, making coherent speech in any language all but impossible. After a few frustrating days of trying to converse with a gasping, out-of-breath American, most of my young running mates gave up the pursuit, returning to the hotel to lie in wait for more promising quarry.

One young fellow at a guesthouse in Xi'an proved particularly persistent, however. He continued running with me day after day, chatting away long after the others had given up the chase. When I finally pleaded with him to stop pursuing me, he agreed—but only after inviting me to his home for lunch. When I demurred, he said that his twenty-year-old *jiejie*, or big sister, would be gravely disappointed if I failed to show up. "She really wants to meet you," he said earnestly, extracting a photo from his shirt. *Jiejie* was stunning, a lithe, long-legged Chinese beauty. A silent alarm went off in my head. Was I being set up? Was this a honey trap? Or merely the familiar *guanxi* gambit of offering consideration "in kind" in exchange for a favor granted? I never found out. I shook my head, bade him good-bye, and jogged back to the hotel for a long, cool shower.

AS CHINA SHIFTED toward a more open, competitive, and outward-looking economy and society in the 1980s, growing pains were inevitable. Although overall economic growth increased dramatically throughout the decade, averaging around 9 percent annually, an uneven patchwork quilt of partial reforms and halfway institutional innovations generated a series of new societal stress patterns and fault lines. With disparate elements of the old (centrally planned) and the new (market-oriented) economies coexisting in an uneasy—and often mutually friction-filled—relationship, levels of income inequality rose significantly and opportunities for upward social mobility were skewed. Compounding this problem was the persistence of a two-tiered (sometimes three-tiered) pricing system that created strong incentives and ready opportunities for Communist Party and government officials and their families to capture windfall profits by engaging in illicit commodity speculation and commercial arbitrage. For example, in the mid-1980s the wholesale price of coal sold by the state to industrial enterprises was fixed at the old, artificially low, subsidized rate, while the retail price charged to urban consumers (who used coal to heat their homes and cook their meals) was allowed to float upward to a substantially higher market price. Under these circumstances, many factory managers found they could earn large windfall profits simply by selling their allotment of cheap, state-subsidized coal directly to urban consumers at a "gray market" price rather than burning it in their power plants. Caught between the sharp upward drift of retail consumer prices, the quest for windfall profits, and the limited availability of opportunities for upward economic mobility, many urban Chinese experienced a rising sense of frustration.

By the mid-'80s a significant income gap had also opened between semiskilled, self-employed *getihu*, who were free to charge market prices for their services, and skilled professionals living on the low fixed incomes they earned in the state sector. Members of the white-collar and professional classes manifested their resentment in a series of cynical aphorisms that made the rounds in Chinese cities. In the summer of 1986, for example, I heard the following complaints on the streets of Nanjing: "Those who make atomic bombs earn less than those who sell tea-eggs" (*gao yuanzidande buru mai chajidande*) and "He who operates on your brain earns less than he who cuts your hair" (*kaidaode buru lifade*).

The term "red-eye disease" (*hongyanbing*) was used to describe the envy that stemmed from growing income inequality. It was not so much a problem of "some people getting rich before others," as Deng had anticipated. It was rather that those who were getting rich first (known as *wanyuanhu*, or "¥10,000 households") often did so not through their own particular talent or virtue but because they happened to be either self-employed at a time of mounting inflation or (in the case of many administrative cadres) well positioned to extract under-the-table fees for the preferential allocation of scarce state resources, such as business licenses, building and zoning permits, foreign exchange certificates, and other regulatory instruments that controlled market access in the new Chinese economy.

Before the onset of economic reform, the ratio of average incomes earned by people in the top and bottom 20 percent of the Chinese population was only about 2.5:1. By the late 1980s the ratio had more than doubled, to around 6:1, a figure that did not include the substantial illicit gains from corruption enjoyed by many on the upper rungs of the income ladder. In the same period, China's Gini coefficient—a measure of relative income inequality in which 0 equals perfect equality (everyone has the same income) and 1 equals perfect inequality (one person earns all the money)—rose dramatically, from .180 (one of the lowest in the world) to .382 (the highest of any self-styled socialist economy).

Because the early stages of market-driven economic growth are generally accompanied by a significant increase in income disparities, economists disagree on the implications of a rising Gini coefficient. Some actually regard a rising Gini as a sign of economic health and dynamism. But when the coefficient nears .400, as China's did by the end of the 1980s, many economists regard this as a danger sign, portending social discontent. Today, the world's highest Gini coefficients—those above .550—are generally found in South America (Brazil .580, Colombia .586, Bolivia .601) and southern Africa (South Africa .578, Botswana .605, Swaziland .609, Namibia .743). In 2006 the U.S. Gini coefficient stood at .470.

In the mid-1980s Chinese opinion polls began to register a decline in the public's enthusiasm for market reform, reflecting growing unease over rising income inequality. One poll conducted early in 1986 revealed that only 29 percent of urban residents surveyed felt that the reforms were providing equal opportunity for all. By November of the same year, three-fourths of all urban respondents expressed dissatisfaction with higher prices. At the same time, opinion polls revealed a changing youth culture, one that was becoming significantly more materialistic and hedonistic—and considerably less idealistic—than that of preceding generations.

Another sign of changing times in the mid '80s was the dramatic improvement in tourist facilities throughout China. Shiny new hotels—usually developed as joint ventures with Hong Kong or Western partners—sprouted up in city after city. New trains with air-conditioned first-class coaches and "soft" sleeping compartments supplemented existing railroad stock, and large fleets of air-conditioned Japanese tour buses and taxicabs were put in service. Guangzhou's aged fleet of 1946 DeSoto taxis was quietly retired. One thing that didn't change very quickly, however, was the quality of public toilets in China. They were appalling—filthy, fetid, and famously user-unfriendly.

EACH SUMMER FROM 1984 until the late 1990s, I spent two relaxing weeks giving guest lectures aboard a posh commercial cruise ship, *Pearl of Scandinavia* (later rechristened *Ocean Pearl*), plying the coastal waters off China. Qinhuangdao, on the Bohai Gulf in Northeast China, was one frequent port of call. There the ship's four hundred or so passengers would be off-loaded onto a caravan of buses for the three-hour trip to Beijing. The road was pretty crude, at least in the early years, and the buses made a routine comfort stop about halfway to Beijing. In truth, it was less a comfort stop than a pit stop, for what awaited the tourists as they piled out of their luxurious air-conditioned coaches was a primitive earthen outhouse containing two sets of "his" (男) and "hers" (女) holes in the ground. As the passengers approached these primitive, smelly latrines, the looks on their faces generally turned from casual contemplation and mild amusement to varying degrees of shock and horror. Many gasped and groaned audibly, holding their noses as they waited in line; some refused to go anywhere near the fly-infested outhouse; and a few directed colorful epithets at members of the ship's crew, who were along as escorts. Year after year, in the interest of good taste, I resisted the urge to photograph this scene, which repeated itself like clockwork on each trip.

The local residents were not nearly so polite or self-restrained. Evidently the cruise line's buses arrived on a predictable schedule, because each time our caravan pulled up to the outhouse, dozens of local farmers, children in tow, would be there waiting, taking a break from their labor in nearby fields. They would gather directly across the road from the latrines, gawking and grinning and occasionally guffawing with laughter as they observed the bizarre bathroom behavior of the barbarians. Talk about culture shock!

This classic piece of privy pageantry passed into history in the early 1990s, when a brand-new multilane expressway replaced the old two-lane road, and a shiny new full-service convenience center—complete with tiled bathrooms, self-flushing toilets, mini-market, gift shop, and gas station—replaced the old two-hole latrines. Thereafter, the bus ride from Qinhuangdao to Beijing, though much faster, wasn't nearly so much fun.

As the spirit of economic competition and individual enrichment spread throughout China in the 1980s, new cultural role models emerged to replace the stoic, self-sacrificing Maoist-era model of peasants, workers, and soldiers. In Mao's time, the virtues of selfless devotion and "serving the people"—apotheosized by the martyred PLA conscript Lei Feng, who died aspiring to be a "rust-proof screw of the revolution"—were held up for universal emulation by the masses. Now China required more up-to-date role models, people who embodied the "modern" virtues of individual ambition, entrepreneurship, and achievement. The results were sometimes a bit odd. For example, in the summer of 1984, under the headline "Prosperous Girls Attract Husbands," a leading Shanghai newspaper publicized the story of a group of unmarried women from a poor farming village who suddenly became objects of intense matrimonial desire to young men from a nearby factory after the women became prosperous by shifting from collective agriculture to private farming. The moral was clear: To snag a mate, one must be commercially successful.

Enterprising individuals in various walks of life were now given favorable media exposure, from short-order cooks and freelance photographers to young girls who had taken jobs as personal maids and nannies. And the mass media began to celebrate the achievements of trail-blazing entrepreneurs such as the director of a shirt factory in Zhejiang, who composed new lyrics to a popular Cultural Revolution song celebrating the selfless revolutionary spirit of Red Guards. The new lyrics spoke not of proletarian virtues but of variable piece rates, individualized bonuses, and other productivity-raising incentives; its refrain was a rousing call for workers to rededicate themselves, not to revolutionary struggle, but to making life beautiful:

Work hard, hard, hard.
We are the glorious shirtmakers!
With good workmanship and novel designs,
We dedicate our youth
To making life beautiful.

Never one to encourage others to pursue *la belle vie*, Chairman Mao would not have been amused by such bourgeois motivational devices.

PRIOR TO THE mid-1980s, whenever I would ask Chinese youngsters what they wanted to do when they grew up, there was but one standard, universal response: "Whatever the state requires" (*anzhao guojiade xuyao*). Now, when I asked the same question randomly in various parts of China, I received a wide range of highly individuated responses, ranging from astronaut to opera singer, from primary teacher to basketball star, from taxi driver to tycoon. Clearly, young Chinese were privatizing their personal ambitions as they raised their hopes for a "beautiful life."

Further reflective of China's new mood of individualism, permissiveness, and consumer consciousness was the reappearance, with official approval, of high-fashion Western-style clothing, including short, slit skirts and see-through blouses for women and motorcycle jackets and aviator sunglasses for young men. In the winter of 1983–84 both Hu Yaobang and Zhao Ziyang—the two highest-ranking officials in the Chinese Communist Party after Deng Xiaoping—appeared in public wearing Western-style suits and ties for the first time, and in 1984 Hu Yaobang openly endorsed the use of Western eating utensils rather than traditional Chinese chopsticks, for hygienic reasons.

In the initial rush of globalization fever that spread in the mid-1980s, various Western intellectual icons—from free-market guru Milton Friedman to "futurologist" Alvin Toffler and political scientist Samuel Huntington—undertook highly publicized lecture tours in China, drawing standing-room-only crowds at major universities. The mid-'80s also witnessed a proliferation of various avant-garde art forms that, a few years earlier, would have been condemned for their "bourgeois decadence." The glossy magazine *Beijing Review*, for example, published a series of photos of seminude female sculptures in 1984. In the same year, visitors to the newly remodeled international terminal of the Beijing Airport were treated to a recently commissioned wall-length mural depicting ethnic minority women frolicking bare-breasted in their native habitat. In the high tide of economic and cultural experimentation and openness that swept through urban China in the 1980s, such things were possible.

As the ideological forbidden zones of Maoist China were thus breached one after another, conservative Marxists waged a rearguard struggle to uphold the sanctity of traditional institutions and values. In one of its more florid manifestations, this backlash took the form of a crusade against "spiritual pollution" (*jingshen wuran*) in the realm of popular culture. In 1983, under guidelines promulgated by CCP propaganda organs, neighborhood watch groups, recruited from local residents' committees, began to harass residents whose hair was unusually long or who wore flared trousers. The local "granny police" organized house-to-house inspections, and industrial workers were organized to search for pornographic books and videos in factory dormitories. In the city of Lanzhou, local gendarmes were mobilized to "read good books and sing revolutionary songs" as an antidote to such putative evils as "wearing mustaches and whiskers, singing unhealthy songs, being undisciplined, and not keeping one's mind on work." The Beijing Municipal Party Committee posted a notice on the front gate of its headquarters denying admittance to "persons with hair too long, skirts too short, slacks too tight, or face powdered and rouged." After just a few weeks on public display, the bare-breasted females in the new mural at the international terminal of the Beijing Airport were primly covered with strategically placed screens.

In addition to waging periodic guerrilla attacks against spiritual pollutants, both real and imagined, CCP conservatives also, and more ominously, sought to roll back Deng Xiaoping's economic reforms. Although Deng and his fellow reformers had studiously avoided using the word "capitalism," preferring less controversial terms such as "economic mechanism," "socialist commodity economy," "mixed economy," and—most famously—"socialism with Chinese characteristics," orthodox Marxists were not mollified by such circumlocutions. And they took advantage of mounting urban distress—over growing income inequality, inflation, corruption, a rising crime rate, and an *enrichissez-vous* mentality that placed the pursuit of profit ahead of all other social obligations and values—to launch an ideological counterattack on capitalism's corrosive effects.

The C word became a cudgel wielded by self-styled guardians of the socialist faith. Capitalist forces were accused of "seeking to corrupt and harm our country." Attacking Deng's key premise that it was perfectly acceptable for some people to get rich before others, conservatives countered that under socialism people would all get rich together. In an angry rebuff to those who eagerly embraced Western ideas and institutions, one CCP elder statesman complained that "for those who worship bourgeois liberalization . . . it seems that even the moon in the capitalist world is brighter than the sun in our socialist society."

The debate over the dangers of "bourgeois liberalization" was punctuated in mid-decade by an epidemic of small-scale social disturbances. On the surface, these disturbances appeared random, spontaneous, and almost wholly unrelated. In May 1985, a riot occurred at a Beijing soccer stadium when a team of Hong Kong footballers unexpectedly defeated the local club. Shortly thereafter, a group of three hundred sent-down youths staged a sit-in at the headquarters of the Beijing municipal government, demanding the right to return to their homes in the Chinese capital. In Tianjin, a race riot erupted on a local college campus on Sino-African Friendship Day. And in Tiananmen Square, more than one thousand students demonstrated in September 1985 to protest Japanese prime minister Yasuhiro Nakasone's visit to Yasukuni Shrine in Tokyo, a Shinto memorial honoring, among others, the militarists who had launched World War II. It was China's largest protest demonstration since Fu Yuehua's petitioners' march in January 1979. Urban stress levels were clearly rising, and China's college students—long a barometer of societal tensions—were growing increasingly restive.

Specific student complaints were varied and diverse, ranging from dissatisfaction with unhealthy dormitory conditions, inadequate stipends, and rampant inflation to the flagrant corruption of school administrators and the dangers of Japanese economic "neocolonialism." There was little overall coherence or clear direction to their grievances, however, until the autumn of 1986, when campus discontent began to coalesce around a single common denominator: student empowerment.

The lightning rod for this coalescence was Professor Fang Lizhi, who had risen since my initial encounter with him in Hefei in 1978 to become vice president of the University of Science and Technology. Professor Fang gave voice to the feelings of powerlessness and frustration experienced by large numbers of Chinese students. In a series of campus lectures in November and December 1986, he derided corrupt politicians and heaped scorn upon those autocrats who denied people their constitutional right to free expression. Challenging China's students to "break all barriers" to open intellectual inquiry and creativity, he urged young people to boldly take their future into their own hands. Democracy cannot be bestowed paternalistically from above, he exhorted; it must be grasped firmly from below. Wherever Fang Lizhi spoke, he drew crowds of young admirers.

In the wake of his speeches at half a dozen college campuses in Hefei, Shanghai, and Beijing, tens of thousands of students moved from their classrooms and dormitories out into the streets. Altogether, as many as seventy-five thousand students from 150 colleges in seventeen Chinese cities took part in pro-democracy demonstrations in December 1986.

Predictably, Party leaders were divided over how to view these events. Pro-reform politicians generally took them with a grain of salt. Tianjin's progressive mayor Li Ruihuan, for example, urged the people in his city not to be unduly alarmed by the student demonstrations. "There is nothing extraordinary about such incidents," he said. "There is no reason for us to lose our composure." Party general secretary Hu Yaobang—a liberal protégé of Deng Xiaoping—was similarly disinclined to get tough with the students. Others were less tolerant, however, including Beijing's conservative municipal leadership. When several thousand Beijing students turned out for a pro-democracy rally in Tiananmen Square on New Year's day, the official newspaper of the Beijing Municipal Party Committee, the *Beijing Daily*, responded with an editorial questioning the students' patriotism. In defiance, the students built a bonfire and burned several hundred copies of the offending newspaper.

After the students had briefly occupied Tiananmen Square, police began making arrests. Not wanting to confront the authorities, the students decided to leave the square. They had made their point. And besides, the weather had turned bitterly cold, and classes had resumed. With the exception of a few scattered arrests and some bruised feelings, little permanent damage had been done.

Behind the scenes, however, CCP hard-liners were fuming. The students had impudently thumbed their noses at authority and had gotten away with it. Even Deng Xiaoping was angry. Blaming Fang Lizhi for inflaming the students' passions, he demanded Fang's expulsion from the CCP. But hard-line conservatives weren't content to stop there. Calling the recent student demonstrations an outgrowth of the long-term, poisonous trend of "bourgeois liberalization," they demanded the removal of Deng's permissive protégé, CCP general secretary Hu Yaobang. Deng capitulated, and Hu was sacked in January 1987. The empire had struck back.

7

The Road to Tiananmen

I WAS WORKING in the backyard of my home in the leafy Los Angeles suburb of Woodland Hills when the phone rang. It was President's Day weekend, February 1989. Both kids were away at school—Matthew working on an M.A. in international relations at Johns Hopkins and Kristen, our youngest, studying music at Berkeley. Carolyn answered the phone. "It's the White House," she said uncertainly. "Yeah, right," I responded.

Twenty-four hours later I was en route to Camp David, Maryland. The newly inaugurated forty-first president of the United States, George H. W. Bush, was preparing to fly to Japan on his first official foreign mission as president, to attend the state funeral of the Emperor Hirohito. He was also scheduled to stop over in Beijing for a get-acquainted visit with Deng Xiaoping, whom he had briefly met once before, during his term as U.S. Liaison Office *chef de mission* in 1975. To help him prepare for his second encounter with Deng, four American China scholars were being flown in to brief the president and top members of his administration on recent developments in China. A similar set of briefings by a group of Japan experts had been held at Camp David the previous day.

On Monday morning, February 20, President's Day, the invited scholars mustered at the Southwest Gate of the White House, where we were joined by Secretary of State James Baker, Presidential Press Secretary Marlin Fitzwater, and National Security Council staffer Karl Jackson, whom I knew from my graduate student days at Berkeley. While waiting for the limousine to ferry us across the Potomac River to Arlington, from where we would be helicoptered to Camp David, we talked among ourselves. As we chatted, two White House Marine Corps guards searched our over-night bags, which we had been instructed to bring with us. Secretary Baker was saying something about unfair Japanese trade practices when I happened to glance over his shoulder at one of the Marine guards, who was going through the contents of my carry-on bag. As I watched, the Marine lifted out my leather shaving kit, unzipped it, poked around inside, and pulled out—what was that? *Ohmygod!* My heart froze. It was a marijuana joint! That long-forgotten, hand-rolled cigarette had been there for ages, probably years, hidden inside an inner seam of my shaving kit. But now it was a live, ticking time bomb. My knees wobbled as I envisioned the headline: "Scholar Busted Bringing Dope to White House." Time passed with infinite slowness as the Marine guard held the crudely fashioned joint up to the light and gently rolled it between his fingers. He glanced over at us—I could swear he was smiling—and then, after what seemed an eternity, put the cigarette back into my kit and zipped it up. I managed to breathe again, barely regaining my composure in time to answer Secretary Baker's question about the yen-dollar exchange rate.

The other academics in the group were Harry Harding (George Washington University), Larry Krause (University of California, San Diego)—and Mike Oksenberg. At that point, some eight years after our disastrous encounter at the AAS meeting in Toronto, Mike and I were on speaking terms again, though just barely. In our periodic professional encounters we remained cool and guarded. While the limousine sped us to Arlington, the four of us discussed the division of labor for our briefing. It was agreed that Larry would bring the president up to date on recent developments in the Chinese economy; Mike would cover Chinese foreign policy; Harry would discuss domestic Chinese politics; and I would handle U.S.-China relations.

The helicopter ride was uneventful, and the day was cold and brisk as we stepped out onto the landing pad at Camp David. President Bush came out of the main lodge to greet us, wearing a casual gray windbreaker emblazoned with the presidential seal. It was my first encounter with Bush since he had narrowly escaped being tackled by a drunken pole-vaulter in Beijing fourteen years earlier. The president escorted us into the lodge, where we were introduced to Mrs. Bush along with key members of the new administration, including Vice President Dan Quayle and his wife, Marilyn; National Security Advisor Brent Scowcroft; CIA director Robert Gates; Undersecretary of State Lawrence Eagleburger; and the newly designated U.S. ambassador to China, James Lilley.

A photo opportunity with President George H. W. Bush followed a briefing
session at Camp David, Maryland, February 20, 1989. From left: Robert Gates,
Michel Oksenberg, Lawrence Krause, President Bush, the author, Harry Harding,
James Lilley, Karl Jackson. Photo courtesy of the White House.

The first part of the briefing went smoothly enough, with Larry Krause
and Harry Harding making a number of salient points and expertly field-
ing questions from the president and his foreign policy team. After a two-
hour morning session, we broke for lunch and had an escorted golf-cart
tour of the Camp David compound, including a visit to the presidential
bowling alley, theater, and gymnasium (where we unexpectedly encountered the late president John F. Kennedy's niece, Maria Shriver, working
out). At the souvenir store, I purchased a deck of playing cards and some
stationery embossed with the Camp David logo.

When we resumed our briefing after lunch, it was my turn to take the
lead. I sketched out major developments in U.S.-China relations in the
decade since Deng had returned to power in 1979, noting that the relationship was relatively stable and quiescent at the moment, and that the
Chinese side had not, of late, been pushing for any substantial new U.S.

concessions on the Taiwan question. "If it ain't broke, don't fix it," was the general thrust of my assessment.

This led into a discussion of human rights in China, one of the more sensitive issues in U.S.-China relations. At that point James Baker, the secretary of state, asked me how the president should approach this issue in his upcoming encounter with Deng Xiaoping. I suggested that the president continue to take a firm, clear stand on the importance of improving human rights in China, as Jimmy Carter and Ronald Reagan had done before him. But I urged caution and restraint when it came to expressing solidarity with individual Chinese dissidents and human rights activists. For example, I said, it would probably be counterproductive for President Bush to single out Professor Fang Lizhi for special praise, as Fang had recently incurred Deng Xiaoping's wrath by fomenting student unrest, accusing Deng's eldest son of engaging in corrupt business dealings, and publicly calling on Deng to release all Chinese political prisoners. It was at Deng's insistence, moreover, that Fang had been booted out of the CCP in 1987. While Fang Lizhi was obviously someone the United States wanted to nurture and support, I argued, raising his case with Deng Xiaoping on the occasion of their first official meeting would not be an effective way to cement a good working relationship.

We broke for coffee after my presentation. I was chatting with Harry and Mike on an outdoor patio when Ambassador-designate Jim Lilley approached. "Rick," he said, shaking his head, "it's too late. Fang Lizhi's been invited to the presidential banquet in Beijing next Sunday." I gave him a look somewhere between incomprehension and horror, muttering under my breath, "Oh shit." I said that was a really, *really* bad idea, since it would inevitably be interpreted by the Chinese as a deliberate attempt to rub Deng's nose in his human rights problems. "It's a done deal," Jim shrugged.

We resumed our briefing, finishing late in the afternoon. After the obligatory group photo-op with the president, we were helicoptered from Camp David directly back to Dulles International Airport.

The Fang Lizhi banquet invitation continued to gnaw at me. I was disturbed enough about its implications to make a phone call from Dulles Airport before boarding my flight back to Los Angeles. The call was to an old friend, *Los Angeles Times* correspondent Jim Mann. Jim had been the *Times'* Beijing bureau chief a few years earlier, and we had spent a fair amount of time together trying to unravel the mysteries of Chinese politics. I told him I wanted to talk off the record. He agreed, and I told him about the presidential invitation to Fang Lizhi. I said it would be a diplomatic disaster for Fang to attend the dinner, and I wondered out loud how such an impolitic invitation could have been vetted by State Department and NSC staffers, who are paid to (among other things) alert the White House to potential diplomatic blunders. Before saying good-bye, I repeated to Jim that our conversation was off the record, and he confirmed that he would not print anything I had told him. I left Washington not quite sure what I expected Jim to do, but hopeful that he would make some discreet inquiries.

I got back to Los Angeles very late that night. The next morning I was lounging in bed, sipping coffee, feeling rather pleased with myself, when I picked up the newspaper. This headline, "Bush, on China Trip, to See Dissident, Sources Say," on the front page of the *Los Angeles Times* grabbed my attention. The article, under Jim's byline, read:

> President Bush is making plans to meet Fang Lizhi, China's most prominent human rights activist and an outspoken critic of the Chinese Communist Party, during his visit to Beijing this weekend, according to sources familiar with the White House planning. The meeting would mark the first time on any White House trip to Beijing that a President has met with a Chinese dissident. . . .
>
> According to the sources, Fang has been invited to a reception that Bush will attend Sunday at the American Embassy in Beijing. . . .
>
> Asked what his government's reaction would be to a Bush meeting with Fang, a spokesman for the Chinese Embassy in Washington replied late Monday: "We are not aware of this suggestion." He had no further comment.

When the initial shock subsided, I picked up the phone and called Jim in Washington. "What have you done?" I demanded, reminding him of his promise. "I didn't use you as my source," came the reply. "I got the story from someone else who was at the briefing." Skeptical, I asked to whom he had spoken. "Sorry, can't tell you," he responded, continuing to insist that a second source had confirmed everything. I slammed down the phone, furious at Jim but also mentally kicking myself for having spoken to him in the first place. I was reminded of something the critic Janet Malcolm once wrote in *The New Yorker* concerning the nature of the relationship between a reporter and her informants: When you confide in a friendly journalist, she said, you're no longer a *friend*; you're merely a *source*. It was a perfect description of what had transpired.

I was still cursing—at Jim's duplicity and my own stupidity—when the phone rang. It was Mike Oksenberg. "Did you talk to Jim Mann about Fang Lizhi?" he asked accusingly. I paused briefly, considering my options. There weren't any good ones. "Yup," I confessed. "Well," he said (did I detect a note of triumph in his voice?), "the White House is furious." He went on to tell me that Marlin Fitzwater, the president's press secretary, had asked him to find the source of the leak, presumed to be one of the four academic participants. He also said that once the source had been identified, Fitzwater wanted a personal letter of apology sent to President Bush, with copies to the National Security Council staff and the other three academic participants. By this point there could be no doubting Mike's triumphal tone.

My humiliation was now complete. I had not only pissed off the president of the United States, but the message was being delivered by my very own personal bête noir, who was only too happy to instruct me in the appropriate technique for falling on my sword. One of the best days of my life had suddenly turned into one of the worst. I spent the remainder of a very distressed morning composing my apology:

Dear President Bush:

I am writing personally to apologize for having spoken "out of school" concerning your forthcoming Asian trip following our recent briefing session at Camp David. Speaking to a member of the press was certainly an error in judgment on my part; and though it was done without malice and without intent to embarrass any of the participants, in particular the President of the United States, I understand that actions have consequences; and I therefore wish to apologize to you and to all the other participants for my indiscretion, and for any embarrassment it may have caused you.

In a bizarre twist, twenty-four hours after performing this symbolic act of hara-kiri, I received in the mail a signed picture from my photo-op with President Bush, along with a personal note written in the president's own hand. "Dear Rick," it said, "Thanks for winging cross country to come to

Camp David. The session was extremely helpful to me. . . . " What a difference a day makes!

Notwithstanding my painful humiliation, I was right about one thing: The presidential invitation to Fang Lizhi did indeed turn into a diplomatic fiasco. On the evening of the banquet, February 26, someone at the U.S. Embassy in Beijing, eager to avoid an embarrassing diplomatic dustup, at the last minute switched Fang's place card to an inconspicuous table at the very back of the banquet hall, where—it was hoped—he would not be noticed by the high-level Chinese officials in attendance. The officials might have saved themselves the trouble, however. An hour or so before the banquet was scheduled to begin, the car carrying Dr. Fang, his wife, Li Shuxian, and their "safety shield," my UCLA colleague Perry Link, was intercepted and forced off the road by Chinese security police, thus preventing them from attending the presidential dinner. The following day, February 27, the *New York Times* reported the story in an article by Nicholas D. Kristof, headlined "Beijing Stops Key Dissident from Meeting with Bush":

> In a harsh rebuke to the growing enthusiasm here for more democracy, China on Sunday prevented the country's best-known dissident, Fang Lizhi, from attending a banquet to which he had been invited by President Bush.
>
> Earlier in the day, China's top leaders told President Bush in the bluntest terms that the United States should not raise human rights issues in China. Their comments and the police action against Mr. Fang were not only an embarrassment for Mr. Bush, but a clear sign of the Communist Party's alarm at the growing calls for democracy. . . .
>
> Mr. Fang, a 53-year-old astrophysicist who was expelled from the Communist Party two years ago because of his criticisms of Marxism and calls for democracy, was first stopped by the police several blocks from the Great Wall Sheraton Hotel, where Mr. Bush was hosting a Texas-style banquet for about 500 people. Mr. Fang was with his wife, Li Shuxian, a Communist Party member who is a bitter critic of the Government, and Perry Link, a prominent American scholar of Chinese language and literature, as well as Mr. Link's wife.
>
> Mr. Link's driver was accused by the police of a traffic violation,

and so they decided to walk the short distance to the hotel. Mr. Fang said the police there refused to allow them to enter the hotel, and told them they were not on the guest list. When they tried to take a taxi to the American Embassy, the taxi was immediately pulled over for a traffic violation as well. . . .

Mr. Bush and the guests were unaware that Mr. Fang had been turned away. The White House spokesman, Marlin Fitzwater, had earlier said that Mr. Bush probably would not meet with Mr. Fang at the banquet. . . .

Under the circumstances, I took precious little comfort from the knowledge that I had been right to warn the president about the repercussions of reaching out publicly to embrace China's most famous dissident. The damage had already been done. Fang Lizhi was a marked man.

But the fallout from the debacle did not end there. Shortly after the February 26 incident, a bureaucratic donnybrook broke out between the White House and the State Department over just who had been responsible for inviting Fang Lizhi to the presidential banquet in the first place. On March 3, the *New York Times* carried the story, reported by R. W. Apple Jr., under the headline "'Blunder' at Beijing Dinner: U.S. Chides Embassy":

A senior White House official said today that inviting a prominent Chinese dissident to a dinner in Beijing last week honoring the country's leaders had not been President Bush's idea, and he suggested that the resulting contretemps was the fault of the American Embassy there. . . .

The dissident, Fang Lizhi, an astrophysicist and human-rights campaigner, was physically prevented by the Chinese police from attending the dinner given by Mr. Bush at the Great Wall Sheraton Hotel on Sunday. . . .

"Some things they are extraordinarily sensitive to," the White House official said. "Others they let go by without saying a word. . . . [I]t turned out that they were extraordinarily sensitive to this particular individual."

The official, who accompanied Mr. Bush on his five-day Asian swing, said the embassy . . . had sent a proposed guest list to Washington some time ago. He said neither the embassy nor the State Department had "flagged" Mr. Fang's name to suggest that a dinner invitation might stir a controversy.

Selig S. Harrison of the Carnegie Endowment, a longtime China watcher, described . . . the whole notion of asking Mr. Fang to the hotel as "a terrible, incompetent, very clumsy blunder."

The full story emerged slowly, in bits and pieces. A declassified cable sent to the White House on February 18 by Winston Lord, the outgoing U.S. Ambassador to Beijing, revealed that Lord had specifically proposed Fang Lizhi's name for inclusion on the guest list. The list was then submitted to the NSC, the State Department, and the Pentagon for final clearance; however, no one alerted the president to the disruptive potential of Fang's invitation. Thus, by the time I raised the question during the Camp David briefing a few days later, the invitation was a fait accompli. When the whole incident blew up in the president's face, the White House (in the person of NSC director Scowcroft, the "senior White House official" quoted in Apple's story) was quick to lay the blame on Ambassador Lord, who emerged from the incident red-faced and bitter. But by then I was too busy picking shrapnel out of my own wounds to feel much sympathy for Lord.

Already a major irritant to Deng Xiaoping, Fang Lizhi had now become a public enemy. Three months later, when massive student demonstrations in Beijing were brutally suppressed by armored units of the PLA, Fang's name appeared at the top of Beijing's list of most wanted counterrevolutionary criminals. Fearing for his safety, Fang and his wife sought, and were granted, sanctuary in the U.S. Embassy in Beijing, where they remained for twelve months as house guests of the new U.S. Ambassador, Jim Lilley—the same Jim Lilley who had informed me with a shrug at Camp David that it was too late to prevent Fang from being invited to the president's banquet.

In the autumn of 1986, Fang Lizhi's stirring rhetoric had catalyzed the tensions and frustrations experienced by China's college students, giving rise to the first large-scale protest demonstrations of the post-Mao era. Now, more than two years later, in the spring of 1989, those same tensions and frustrations remained largely unrelieved. If anything, they were getting worse. Caught between spiraling consumer prices, burgeoning corruption, and the skewed, limited availability of opportunities for upward mobility, increasing numbers of urban Chinese were experiencing a heightened sense of malaise. And it was increasingly apparent that the malaise could not be easily resolved by a Communist Party leadership that was itself deeply divided over the pace and direction of reform as well as its political and spiritual implications.

My first clear inkling that serious trouble lay ahead came in the fall of 1988, while I was on a visit to Peking University, known locally as Beida. There I was introduced to a young assistant professor of international relations, Jia Qingguo, who had just returned to China after completing his Ph.D. degree at Cornell University. When he was first offered the Beida appointment, Professor Jia had been promised a comfortable new faculty apartment, among other benefits. However, when he arrived at the university, he was informed that his new apartment had been rented to a private bidder outside the campus community. So he would have to live, for the time being, in a graduate student dormitory. When I met him a few months later, Jia was still living in the overcrowded dorm, his books still packed in crates. He was furious over the prevalence of corrupt back-door transactions such as the one that had deprived him of his apartment, and he predicted—memorably—that if this type of corruption wasn't stemmed soon, "There's going to be a rebellion."

The rebellion wasn't long in coming. It began in mid-April 1989 when China's foremost advocate of liberal political reform, Hu Yaobang, died suddenly of a heart attack. Hu had been removed from CCP leadership two years earlier, at the behest of elderly conservatives who blamed him for aiding and abetting the forces of "bourgeois liberalization." When he died on April 15, tens of thousands of Beijing college students marched to Tiananmen Square, demanding that Hu's good name and reputation be restored. When the government refused to acknowledge the students' demands, the demonstrations spread. Concerned about China's fragile political unity and stability, Deng Xiaoping cautioned the students that they were being manipulated by "unpatriotic elements" and that their protests were creating "turmoil" (*dongluan*). Far from calming the situation, Deng's warning, published in a *People's Daily* editorial on April 26, served to catalyze even larger, more widespread urban protests. In the second week of May, a student-led hunger strike was initiated in Tiananmen Square, capturing the attention (and sympathy) of the world's media on the eve of the first official visit to China by Soviet Party chief Mikhail Gorbachev. Deng was humiliated. Things were moving rapidly in the direction of a confrontation. Although the student demonstrations were political in nature, much of the unhappiness fueling them stemmed from the increasingly stressful socioeconomic circumstances of the times.

BY SHEER COINCIDENCE, I was in China at the height of the 1989 student protests, attending an academic conference in the lower Yangzi Valley city of Ma'anshan, about fifty miles upriver from Nanjing. Watching the extraordinary events in Beijing unfold on nightly television news, the conference participants—mostly middle-aged Chinese scholars and policy analysts from the Shanghai Institute of International Studies and their American counterparts from UC Berkeley—overwhelmingly sympathized with the Beijing students. The authorities' hard-line stance and categorical refusal to negotiate with the hunger strikers was, the scholars generally agreed, a sign of governmental arrogance and insensitivity. But one event in particular served to greatly astonish—and deeply disturb—the Chinese scholars present. On the morning of May 18, Premier Li Peng and a small delegation of high-level government officials met with leaders of the student hunger strike in a last-ditch effort to resolve the conflict peacefully. As we sat, spellbound, watching a delayed evening telecast of that meeting, we could see that things had gotten off to a very bad start. Student leaders Wang Dan and Wu'er Kaixi (who was wheeled dramatically into the meeting wearing pajamas, an intravenous drip tube attached to his wheelchair) began by brashly refusing to accept Premier Li's patronizing display of concern for the welfare of the hunger strikers:

> *Li Peng*: Today we will discuss one issue: How to relieve the hunger strikers of their present plight. The party and government are most concerned about the health of the students. You are all young, the oldest among you is only twenty-two or twenty-three, younger than my youngest child....

> *Wu'er Kaixi*: Excuse me for interrupting you, Premier Li, but time is running short. We are sitting here comfortably while students outside are suffering from hunger. You just said that we should discuss only one issue. [Wu'er points his index finger at Premier Li] But the truth is, it was not you who invited us to talk, but we, all of us on Tiananmen Square, who invited you to talk. So we should be the ones to name the issues to be discussed....

When Wu'er Kaixi pointed his finger disdainfully at Li Peng, the Chinese scholars around me let out a simultaneous, audible gasp. They were horrified at the sight of a twenty-year-old college student contemptuously lecturing China's top government official. Sitting on the edge of their seats, they watched in disbelief as the drama unfolded:

Wang Dan: . . . For the students to leave the Square and call off the hunger strike, our conditions must be met in full. . . . First, a positive affirmation of the current student movement as a democratic and patriotic movement, not a "turmoil." Second, a dialogue to be held as soon as possible. . . .

Li Peng: . . . The fact is, social disorder has occurred in Beijing and is spreading to the whole country. The current situation . . . is out of control. . . . Anarchy has reigned in Beijing for the past several days. . . . The government of the People's Republic of China . . . cannot disregard such phenomena. . . .

Wu'er Kaixi: . . . I want to repeat what I have just said: We don't want to be bogged down in discussions. Give an immediate response to our conditions, because the students in the Square are starving. If this is overruled, and we remain bogged down on this one question, then we will conclude that the government is not at all sincere in solving this problem. Then there will be no need for us representatives to stay here any longer.

When the meeting adjourned with Wu'er Kaixi refusing to shake hands with a visibly shaken Li Peng, the premier gritted his teeth in a forced smile, maintaining his composure for the TV cameras. As the film clip ended, the Chinese scholars around me fidgeted nervously, and one of them muttered under his breath, "Nothing good can come of this" (*meiyou shenma hao jieguo*).

He was right. On the following evening, May 19, Li Peng declared martial law in Beijing. Then something remarkable happened. As thousands of uniformed PLA troops poured into the city in truck convoys to enforce Li's decree, they found their path blocked by tens of thousands of citizens, students and nonstudents alike, jamming Beijing's major thoroughfares. The people would not budge. The convoys were stopped in their tracks. A stalemate ensued.

Our conference concluded, we departed from Ma'anshan by bus on May 20, the day martial law troops were blocked in Beijing. We headed for

Shanghai on a chartered bus via Nanjing. En route we stopped off at a couple of small towns, where the local populace seemed largely uninterested in the ongoing political drama in Beijing. When I asked an unscientific sample of townsfolk how they felt about the hunger strike in Tiananmen Square, my queries generally produced blank stares. For these rural dwellers there were evidently more important things to attend to than the antics of a few thousand noisy, self-indulgent college kids in far-off Beijing.

This was clearly not the case in Nanjing, our next stop, where a massive antigovernment rally was in progress in the main public square. Tens of thousands of people of all ages and walks of life were crowded into the city center at the Drum Tower, unified in their support for the Beijing students and their open contempt for Li Peng. Large posters were draped on walls and fences bordering the square, lampooning Li, caricaturing his nerdy appearance, and calling on him to "step down" (*xiatai*). Some banners called for Deng Xiaoping to retire as well, but they were relatively few in number. Many posters demanded the exposure and punishment of corrupt, profiteering high-level officials and their families. A number of young men, toting massive boom boxes, had perched in the branches of trees around the perimeter of the square and were defiantly playing Voice of America broadcasts from Beijing at full volume, describing the latest protest activities in and around Tiananmen Square.

By this time Li Peng had become a ubiquitous target of public derision. It was the first time I had ever witnessed such a massive, spontaneous display of disdain for a Chinese leader. True, Red Guards had publicly humiliated leading party officials, including Liu Shaoqi and his wife, during the Cultural Revolution, but they had been goaded and manipulated by the Gang of Four. And a handful of insouciant teenagers had poked fun at Hua Guofeng's pretentious cult of personality in 1978. But never were Liu, Hua, or any other top-ranking PRC leaders so widely or openly despised as Li Peng.

After our stopover in Nanjing we continued on to Shanghai, where I hastened to book the first available train ticket to Beijing. Forced to wait twenty-four hours for a hard coach seat, I spent the day in Shanghai walking around People's Park and the Bund, where tens of thousands of citizens had gathered in a show of solidarity with the Beijing students. Once again the spirit of open contempt and defiance of the central government was in full blossom. People were publicly mocking Li Peng, calling for his resignation and for Deng Xiaoping's retirement. How, I wondered, could any government—even a self-selected, autocratic Leninist government—possibly survive such a sudden, massive loss of popular support, such a humiliating display of public scorn? I recalled the abortive uprisings in Budapest (1956) and Prague (1968), when liberal reformers had led widely popular but short-lived rebellions against their Stalinist masters, only to have their protests crushed by Russian tanks. But those cases were different. Then it had been the *Soviet* Army that forcibly suppressed popular resistance; surely the Chinese People's Liberation Army would not turn its weapons on its own people!

By the time I retired to my hotel, the city was abuzz with rumors to the effect that martial law would shortly be declared in Shanghai, and that the PLA "will be here soon" (*henkuai jiulai*). People were out in the streets in the early evening, walking around, chatting with strangers, wondering what to expect and how to respond. I went to bed around ten PM with several unanswered questions rattling around in my head. Soon afterward I was awakened by the sound of a loudspeaker blaring on the street below: "Citizens of Shanghai: Do not panic. Martial law will not be declared. No Liberation Army forces will enter the city." It was Shanghai's popular mayor, Zhu Rongji, calling for calm. Evidently his appeal—repeated frequently throughout the night—had the intended effect, for when I left the hotel for the train station early the next morning, the streets were empty. Shanghai remained calm.

Despite the Chinese government's attempt to completely block all unauthorized reportage of events in Beijing, my Shanghai hotel, the Jinjiang, continued to receive both live and taped television transmissions of the unfolding events in Tiananmen Square, via a mysteriously functioning satellite uplink. Just before I sleepily left the Jinjiang at dawn on May 22, I saw a thick knot of uniformed hotel employees clustered around a TV set in an unoccupied guest room, watching CNN's live international video feed from Beijing.

An all-day train ride left me with less than twenty-four hours in Beijing before my scheduled flight back to Los Angeles. Shortly before I arrived in the Chinese capital, the PLA's top leadership ordered the army's immobilized troop convoys, still surrounded by a human sea of civilian protesters, to pull back to the outskirts of the city. By the time I reached Tiananmen Square on the evening of May 22, the celebration had begun. The atmosphere of public jubilation was palpable. The people had won a huge victory. In ordering the army's withdrawal, the government had tacitly conceded

Beijing students demonstrate for political freedom in a mass march to Tiananmen Square, May 1989. The banner's English translation suggests that students were playing to Western media, which had converged on Beijing for the visit of Mikhail Gorbachev. Photo courtesy of Steve Futterman.

defeat. Or so it seemed. The street demonstrations in and around Tiananmen that day and the next were the biggest—and most enthusiastic—to date, with more than one million people participating.

Notwithstanding the general jubilation, however, the sober-minded leader of the newborn Beijing Autonomous Workers Federation, Han Dongfang, sounded a cautionary note. Han, a soft-spoken railway electrician, had set up his federation's headquarters in Tiananmen Square, seeking to build a durable alliance between workers and students. When I met him on the morning of May 23, he spoke softly but eloquently about the precarious balance of power that prevailed in Beijing. He was plainly worried, and he cautioned that the government would not surrender its authority meekly. But his was a minority voice, and few among the assembled throng seemed to be paying attention.

When I flew back to Los Angeles later that day, I was in a state of near euphoria. I had seen history in the making. Never before had a Communist regime been forced to back down in the face of massive, peaceful civil disobedience. In a handful of media interviews over the next few days, I confidently suggested that Li Peng's days were numbered, predicting that his government, lacking even minimal popular support, would most likely fall within a week.

I was hardly alone in my naive, incautious optimism. Although some Chinese had predicted a violent denouement, very few Western experts anticipated the government's use of overwhelming, deadly force. What followed thus came as a real shock. On Friday evening, June 2 (mid-afternoon Saturday, June 3, in Beijing), I was doing a live CNN interview in Los Angeles when the studio in Atlanta broke in with a report that Chinese army units were using tear gas against a surging crowd of demonstrators in Beijing. Soon afterward the station aired a crude video clip showing angry citizens harassing a company of several hundred young, unarmed PLA soldiers as the latter jogged, double-time, toward the center of Beijing. A few hours after that, CNN reported that an army jeep had run over three civilians near Tiananmen Square, killing them. Now there could be no question of a peaceful abdication. It was a humbling moment for me as I realized that twenty-five years of accumulated experience as a China watcher had failed to prepare me for what was about to happen. The deluge had begun.

THE PLA'S DEADLY drive to recapture Tiananmen Square from student demonstrators commenced shortly after dark on June 3. From several outlying muster points, armored military columns slowly converged on the center of the city. Their instructions were to clear the square by dawn's early light, using all necessary force. The order was given by Deng Xiaoping himself, chief architect of the very reforms that had inspired China's students to question Communist Party dogma. It was a surreal moment, calling to mind Berthold Brecht's famous quip about the suppression of workers' protests in East Berlin in 1953: "The people having lost the confidence of the government, the government finds it necessary to dissolve the people and appoint a new one."

The horror that followed was equally surreal. Scratchy news film showed tracer bullets flying overhead as PLA soldiers fired in the direction of massive crowds blocking their advance on Chang'an Boulevard. Pedicarts hauled the civilian dead and wounded to city hospitals, as armored personnel carriers ran amok, scattering crowds before them while being attacked from the rear by angry citizens wielding iron rods, stones, and makeshift Molotov cocktails. Hundreds of buses and trucks were set ablaze. In the confusion, a few dozen unfortunate PLA soldiers became separated from their units, only to be set upon by enraged mobs. Some of the soldiers were beaten to death; others were disemboweled; still others were lynched or set afire, or both.

When the dust settled at dawn, Tiananmen Square had been physically "liberated," but at dreadful cost. Hundreds of civilians were killed and thousands wounded; the real totals may never be known. Forty soldiers also died and a thousand others were injured. But the damage to China's national psyche—and international prestige—was greater still. As Deng Xiaoping himself reportedly commented shortly after June 4, "We restored order, but lost the hearts of the people" (*women huifule zhixu, er shiqule minxin*). The image of a lone young man in civilian clothes, a sport coat slung casually over his shoulder, blocking a column of tanks near Tiananmen Square remains frozen in memory, a timeless trope capturing the entire universe of June 4 (*liusi*) in a single grain of sand.

Before the Chinese government could effectively "appoint a new people," it was necessary to cleanse their existing ranks. A most-wanted list of "counterrevolutionary criminals" was quickly and widely circulated, with prominent intellectual, student, and labor activists topping the list. Wang Dan was arrested after a few weeks in hiding; Wu'er Kaixi escaped to Hong Kong; Han Dongfang walked into a Beijing police station and turned himself in; Fang Lizhi was granted asylum in the U.S. Embassy. Throughout the country thousands of alleged rioters were rounded up, while dozens of "thugs" and "hooligans," mostly unemployed youths and migrant laborers, were hastily tried, sentenced, and summarily executed. Television stations around the country covered these events in solemn, sobering detail—a graphic warning of the dire consequences of active rebellion.

As I watched bits and pieces of the June 4 carnage and its aftermath from Los Angeles, it occurred to me that this must be an incredibly difficult moment to be a PRC diplomat abroad, tasked with defending the brutal actions of the country's leaders. China was under global siege, as foreign governments and the international media directed a cascading chorus of condemnation against the "Butchers of Beijing." Thousands of Chinese students in the United States, Australia, and Western Europe demonstrated nightly in front of local Chinese embassies and consulates. A handful of Chinese diplomats abroad defected; the widely esteemed minister of culture, Wang Meng, resigned in protest; and at least one senior government official, the respected deputy foreign minister Zhang Wenjin, committed suicide, despondent over the brutal suppression of the student movement. Educational and cultural exchanges were abruptly cancelled. Foreign governments, including the United States, imposed punitive sanctions. China had become an international pariah.

At the end of June, I received a small parcel in the mail from the Chinese consulate-general in Los Angeles. It contained a crudely made one-hour composite videotape showing dozens of PLA tanks, armored personnel carriers, and trucks being attacked, their occupants beaten and, in two cases, burned to death by angry rioters wielding iron rods, rocks, and firebombs. The tape, compiled from raw footage captured by closed-circuit security cameras located at various downtown Beijing intersections, had been hastily edited. The narration was out of sync with the video itself, and the tape was filled with anachronisms. The time stamps on the video frames were out of sequence, and the visual images frequently contradicted the narrative voiceover—so much so that it almost seemed as if the editors had deliberately, but subtly, set out to sabotage the government's claim that the army had acted entirely in self-defense. It was puzzling, to say the least.

MORE THAN A year later, in the summer of 1990, I received a phone call from the Chinese consulate, inviting me to an informal dinner with the consul-general, Ambassador Ma Yuzhen, and a small group of diplomats and China scholars. Ambassador Ma's principal concern was with the starkly negative images and attitudes toward China that had been propagated in the American media since June 4. "Tell us what we can do to improve our image," he asked the scholars present. After a few tentative suggestions had been raised by others, I cut to the chase. "You might start," I suggested, "by withdrawing the official characterization of the student demonstrations of April and May as 'counterrevolutionary turmoil' and their leaders as 'unpatriotic.'" Speaking in a mixture of Chinese and English, I ventured the opinion that until the Chinese government had the courage to acknowledge making serious mistakes in the run-up to June 4, there could be no final healing of China's national wound. This was not exactly what Ambassador Ma wanted to hear. Around the table, conversation suddenly stopped. An awkward silence ensued, with the Chinese diplomats averting their eyes and looking down uncomfortably at the food on their plates. Nothing further was said on this subject, and though we eventually bade our hosts a cordial farewell, several years would elapse before I was invited to dine again at the Chinese consulate.

In retrospect it appears that, although the Chinese government, and Deng Xiaoping in particular, bore full responsibility for provocatively labeling student demonstrations as "turmoil" and for later sanctioning the use of deadly force to disperse them, there was plenty of blame to go around in the escalating moral theatrics that led to the bloody endgame of June 3–4. In mid-May, for example, in the early days of the student hunger strike, some hard-line confrontationists among the student leaders, filled with righteous indignation and apparently relishing the star power conferred on them by adoring crowds and international media, had brashly rejected the entreaties of well-meaning government emissaries sent by Party general secretary Zhao Ziyang. The emissaries, including respected Party liberals Yan Mingfu and Dai Qing, had urged the students to compromise with the government in order to avert a potentially catastrophic confrontation. They solemnly promised that there would be good-faith negotiations once the students called off their hunger strike and left Tiananmen Square. Their pleas were rejected out of hand. Shortly thereafter, in the midst of a sharply escalating face-off between government and students, the image of a self-righteous Wu'er Kaixi dismissively lecturing a seething Premier Li Peng was seen by hundreds of millions of Chinese television viewers, pouring fresh salt into an already gaping wound and helping to seal the tragic outcome.

LOOKING BACK ON the events of spring 1989 with the benefit of hindsight, it is apparent that both sides made mistakes and that there were precious few moral triumphs to be savored in the aftermath of the carnage. Most tragic of all, in my view, was the trampling underfoot of the youthful idealism of China's college students, who believed, naively, that by throwing themselves under the wheels of a corrupt, autocratic political machine, they could force the machine to stop, or at least to change direction.

The high cost of their valor was brought home to me in a recent conversation with one of the Beijing student leaders of 1989, Wang Chaohua. Wang escaped from China shortly after her name appeared on the government's post-Tiananmen most-wanted list. In May of 1989 she had tried to mediate between CCP moderates, representing Zhao Ziyang, and student leaders in Tiananmen Square. Her efforts to arrange a negotiated settlement were blocked, she said, by the intransigence of hard-line hunger strikers. After the events of June 3–4, Wang began to experience deep feelings of guilt, along with a crushing sense of remorse for having been unable to prevent the ensuing bloodbath. Today, some twenty years after the fact, she continues to be haunted by recurrent nightmares in which she hears the screams of Chinese students. Where, she asked me, does the responsibility of an arrogant, imperious government end and that of immature, self-righteous students begin? Where indeed?!

8

After the Deluge

SYSTEMATIC REPRESSION OF political dissidents continued throughout June and July 1989, and I returned to China at the end of August at the request of John Hawkins, UCLA's dean of international studies. The repression had raised concerns about the future viability of the university's educational and research exchanges with China, and Dean Hawkins asked me to undertake a firsthand assessment of the situation there and make a recommendation to the UCLA administration. Many leading American educational, research, and administrative institutions, including the Fulbright Scholars Program, the Rand Corporation, the University of Wisconsin, and the City of New York, among others, had elected to break off all relations with China after the Tiananmen debacle. What should we do?

I spent ten days in China between August 24 and September 4, dividing my time evenly between Beijing and Shanghai. In Beijing especially, the situation in the late summer of 1989 remained extremely tense. Tiananmen Square was closed to pedestrian traffic. Soldiers armed with AK-47s, stationed in pairs, patrolled the perimeter of the square as well as major intersections and bridges throughout the city, and armed guards were posted at the entrances to Peking University and the Chinese Academy of Social Science, among other sites of erstwhile political activism. When I tried to take pictures of soldiers patrolling Tiananmen Square (from a slow-moving bicycle on the perimeter), a soldier confronted me and ordered me to expose the film in my camera. I complied meekly, as he seemed in no mood to bargain. Chinese friends later told me that sporadic outbursts of violence by angry citizens against PLA martial law troops had continued throughout the summer, including occasional sniper attacks and at least one attempt by a Beijing resident to kill troops by offering them poisoned drinking water.

In Beijing, post-Tiananmen stress disorder was everywhere in evidence. The atmosphere of heightened political intimidation and surveillance was palpable. One telltale symptom of the disorder was that my friends and acquaintances were unwilling to speak candidly indoors or on the telephone, for fear their conversations would be reported to the authorities. We talked outdoors only, on the street, in public parks, or riding in private cars. When meetings did take place indoors, conversation tended to be strained and oblique, punctuated by darting glances, nervous body language, and carefully chosen euphemisms. On two occasions, when scholars at the Chinese Academy of Social Science discussed with me the highly sensitive subject of civilian deaths in Beijing on the night and early morning of June 3–4, their comments were sanitized and couched in a critique of exaggerated Western media reports of mass slaughter. Such were the Orwellian effects of post-Tiananmen stress disorder that only through such dissembled circumlocution could controversial political topics be broached.

Although my friends were under extreme pressure to toe the Party line—which held that the Tiananmen bloodshed had been provoked by violent nonstudent "hooligans" hell-bent on causing trouble, and that the ferocity of the government's armed response had been blown out of proportion by the Western media—few made any effort to persuade me of the government's righteousness. Instead they pleaded for their American friends not to forsake them in their hour of greatest need. Cutting off exchanges between U.S. and Chinese scientists, scholars, and students would, they argued, benefit only China's anti-Western hard-liners. The people who would suffer most would be liberal reformers and progressive intellectuals, people like themselves. It was a poignant, heartfelt message, and one that I would hear again and again in the days to come.

From two acquaintances who worked for the National People's Congress in Beijing I learned of a developing campaign to defame Zhao Ziyang. Zhao had been peremptorily dismissed from his post as CCP general secretary on May 19, the day martial law was declared in Beijing. He now stood accused of the serious offense of "splitting the Party" because of the excessive tolerance he showed toward student demonstrators and his indiscreet revelation to Mikhail Gorbachev that Deng was still China's supreme political decision maker. Ironically, the charge of being soft on student protest was the same charge that had got Hu Yaobang, Zhao's immediate predecessor as general secretary, fired from the same job in 1987.

CCP conservatives now made the case that it was Zhao's indecisiveness in economic policy that had led China into such dire straits in the late 1980s. Zhao was accused, for example, of failing to give clear and consistent guidance on several key economic policy initiatives, including price and enterprise reforms. Consequently, China had staggered indecisively from policy to policy, like a directionless man seeking to "cross a river by groping for stones" (*mozhe shitou guohe*). It is more than a little ironic that this same extended "river and stones" metaphor, used pejoratively in 1989 to discredit Zhao Ziyang's erratic, indecisive leadership, was later resurrected and turned inside out to explain China's great success in avoiding the type of catastrophic collapse suffered by many European Communist regimes during the "Great Leninist Meltdown" of 1989–91. By 1993 it had become fashionable among Chinese and Western economists alike to claim that the very gradualism and piecemeal, pragmatic experimentalism of China's economic reforms in the 1980s had been the perfect antidote to the disastrous "big bang" and "shock therapy" policies adopted by the Soviet Union and various Eastern European countries. By that time, however, Zhao was in no position to enjoy his belated international recognition as a wise economic strategist, as he had been under house arrest for four years.

My contacts at the National People's Congress also told me that a new four-anti campaign was under way in the nation's capital. The four antis were "political anti-pluralization" (*zhengzhi shang fan duoyuanhua*), "ideological anti-liberalization" (*sixiang shang fan ziyouhua*), "economic anti-privatization" (*jingji shang fan siyouhua*), and "moral anti-individualization" (*daode shang fan gerenhua*). On the face of it, Deng's reforms themselves seemed to be in for a serious challenge, as Party hard-liners stepped up their Thermidorian Reaction against the "turmoil" of the spring of 1989.

Another well-connected Chinese acquaintance told me of a new CCP "reregistration" campaign being launched by Party committees and branches throughout the country. In the course of the campaign all Party members and cadres were ordered to provide detailed accounts of their actions—and those of their coworkers—during the entire period of the spring 1989 disorders. As part of the self-examination process, all cadres were required to reveal their "original thinking" (*yuanshi sixiang*) upon first hearing the news that shots had been fired on the evening of June 3.

In informal meetings with research scholars and staff at Peking University and the Chinese Academy of Social Science, I learned that the conservatives' efforts to identify and punish active supporters of the student movement were being impeded by two major obstacles. For one thing, so many Party members and cadres had displayed open sympathy toward the students in April and May that it was proving extremely difficult to isolate and weed out the most ardent pro-democracy activists. As one old friend put it, "If they arrest me they are going to have to arrest hundreds of thousands of others as well." As a practical matter, he didn't believe the government could do that.

A tacit conspiracy of silence among leading cadres and their deputies in many administrative offices and work units was further frustrating the regime's effort to weed out hard-core activists. Under considerable pressure from higher levels to collect the names of cadres and staff members who had participated in protest-related activities, work-unit leaders responded to the new rectification drive with pro forma compliance, refusing to implicate others and thereby diminishing the impact of the probe. In some cases, I was told, unit heads—up to and including the leaders of some central Party and government departments—had publicly denounced the student disturbances while working quietly behind the scenes to protect their most vulnerable colleagues and subordinates. I left these meetings with the strong impression that most Chinese scholars believed there was safety in numbers, and that it would be highly impractical for the authorities to try to identify, isolate, and punish them all.

Evidently their reasoning was correct. When the final results of the CCP's post-Tiananmen reregistration campaign were officially announced three years later, at the Fourteenth National Party Congress in October 1992, the number of disciplinary cases reported was remarkably low. Nationwide, a total of only 13,254 cadres had been required to undergo "party discipline" for various political transgressions; of this total, only 1,179 cadres (out of more than 800,000 Party members and cadres who had acknowledged supporting the student demonstrations) were punished for their role in the disturbances.

Some friends from the Social Science Academy invited me to lunch at the revolving restaurant atop Beijing's luxurious new International Hotel on East Chang'an Boulevard. There I was shown several bullet holes in the restaurant's thick, shatterproof glass windows, at which soldiers had fired indiscriminately from the street below on June 4 and 5. At the height of the Monday lunch hour, the restaurant was eerily empty—only three of its fifty or so tables were occupied, while teams of bored waiters and busboys stood by with nothing to do. When I remarked on the restaurant's lack of customers, I was told that the occupancy rate at major tourist hotels and restaurants in Beijing had fallen to around 10 percent since early June. So severe was the shortage of tourists that the iconic Great Wall Sheraton, which a few months earlier had charged $130 for a standard double room, had slashed its rate to less than $50.

Later, at Peking University, I met separately with two leading faculty advocates of closer Sino-American ties, political science professors Zhao Baoxu and Yuan Ming. Yuan Ming, who was associate director of the Beida Institute of International Relations, seemed unusually poised and self-confident, unlike most other Chinese scholars I had spoken with during the week, who generally appeared anxious and insecure. Someone suggested to me—plausibly—that Yuan's self-assurance may have stemmed from the fact that she had been in the Soviet Union in late May and early June and had thus fortuitously kept out of harm's way at the peak of the crisis. She was also said to be well connected politically. I found this latter conjecture all the more convincing after Yuan confidently informed me that Americans could "rest assured" that Deng Xiaoping was in good health, thus contradicting earlier rumors emanating (as usual) from the Hong Kong press, to the effect that the Paramount Leader was gravely ill with prostate cancer. And she further intimated that Deng would certainly outlive his elderly conservative comrades on the Party's Central Advisory Committee. (The prophecy turned out to be accurate; Deng lived for nine more years.) Most intriguingly of all, Yuan Ming suggested that Deng had "learned from the government's mistakes," committed during the spring upheaval, though she pointedly failed to specify the nature of those mistakes. As a result, she said, China's handling of its internal political problems was likely to be "more enlightened" in the future. When we parted, she offered a bit of sincere advice: "Tell your American friends to wish Deng Xiaoping a long, long life." Her subtext was clear: Americans should think twice before condemning Deng Xiaoping. Dark forces were gathering strength in China, and Deng remained China's last, best hope for continued reform and peaceful engagement with the West. She was probably right.

When I met with Professor Zhao Baoxu, widely acknowledged as the dean of Chinese political scientists, he asked for my impressions of the current political and intellectual situation in Beijing. I told him that I had mixed feelings and that I thought it would take a long time to restore the shattered confidence and morale of China's young people and intellectuals. Then Professor Zhao said something quite interesting. "You know," he remarked, "any time a government ignores the people, it does so at its own peril." The implication was clear. Along with many of the other intellectuals and scholars I met during my week in Beijing, Zhao felt the government had lost touch with its own citizenry in April and May, thereby contributing to the debacle of early June. He further expressed the view that China's intellectuals, despite their recent silence and sobriety, hadn't really changed. "We have a lot of experience riding out political storms," he said. "We take a long view of things." As we parted, he asked me to convey this point to his many American friends and colleagues.

In a meeting with the Ford Foundation's resident Beijing director, Peter Geithner, I was surprised to hear him issue a rather spirited defense of the Chinese government's actions on June 3–4. Peter spoke of the need to set the record straight concerning the many hyperbolic Western media reports that, he said, had severely inflated the civilian death toll and falsely depicted a massacre of innocent students sitting peacefully in Tiananmen Square. He spent the better part of an hour telling me how such reports had been willfully distorted—how no one had been shot in the square itself, how the civilian shooting victims east and west of the square had been mainly nonstudents, and how there had been serious, repeated provocations before the soldiers opened fire. He also claimed that Chinese students generally had a very narrow, elitist understanding of democracy and that they distrusted the ability of the broad masses, the *laobaixing,* to govern themselves. While I did not dispute most of his individual facts, I had the uncomfortable feeling that Peter was bending over just a bit too far in his effort to rationalize the government's excessive use of force. Of course the students had not been entirely blameless, but I nonetheless found his sangfroid a bit too clinical and detached for own my liking and found myself wondering if he was speaking for himself or for the Ford Foundation.

On the other hand, Peter's claim that China wasn't ready for democracy received unexpected support from a number of my Chinese friends and acquaintances in Beijing. For many of them, the violent outcome of the student protests of April and May served as a sobering reminder of just how close China had come to the brink of chaos and anarchy. Having peered over the edge of the bloody abyss in early June, few were spoiling for a second showdown with the government anytime soon. Even the most ardent pro-democracy activists among them were now more or less resigned to several more years of conservative political dominance, to be followed—they hoped—by a gradual, evolutionary process of political liberalization and pluralism. For the moment, though, democracy had ceased being an immediate, burning issue, and most of my academic friends and acquaintances had grudgingly accepted as valid the incessant, monotonous drumbeat of the government's post–June 4 propaganda message— that the only thing standing between China and total chaos was a unified Communist Party. Nor was fear of chaos merely a convenient rationale for continued autocratic rule, invented by a self-serving Communist Party elite; it also reflected (and resonated strongly with) the very real anxieties of a populace only recently risen from the ruins of a century of debilitating foreign aggression, civil war, and Cultural Revolution madness.

On my last morning in Beijing, accompanied by David Holley, the Beijing bureau chief of the *Los Angeles Times*, I paid a visit to the Chinese Museum of Military History near Muxidi, where a remarkable public exhibit of artifacts from the May–June turmoil was in progress. Arrayed in a double row in front of the museum, like some surreal, larger-than-life Andy Warhol installation, were eight or ten charred, burned-out PLA tanks, armored personnel carriers, and trucks that had been set ablaze the night of June 3. Inside the museum, more than a thousand people were viewing assorted artifacts of the violence, including dozens of crudely fashioned homemade weapons that allegedly had been used by "thugs" and "hooligans" to assault soldiers, as well as numerous display cases filled with student documents, leaflets, printing and broadcasting equipment, and hand-lettered headbands seized from demonstrators in Tiananmen Square. Though the exhibition rooms were plastered with signs prohibiting the taking of photographs, I managed to snap a few surreptitious shots before a military guard confronted me and demanded that I open my camera. This time I played dumb, shrugging innocently to indicate my ignorance of the Chinese language and of the rule against taking photos, all the while holding my Olympus SLR tightly. Not wanting to risk an embarrassing incident with a Western guest, the guard finally gave up and let me go, camera and film intact.

Most interesting of all was a documentary film about the protests and government response that ran continuously in the museum's auditorium. The professionally made, forty-five-minute film was surprisingly straightforward and objective, much more so than the crude, homemade video I had received from the Chinese consulate in Los Angeles two months earlier. The film covered key events from the April 15 death of Hu Yaobang through the bloody climax of June 3–4. If one tuned out the pro-government bias of the narration, and concentrated only on the visual images, one could get a pretty good idea of what actually had happened. The film traced the origins and early development of the student movement, devoting a great deal of footage to peaceful demonstrations in which students and other civilian protesters marched under pro-democracy banners and slogans. Notwithstanding the stilted, propagandistic voice-over, which sought to paint these events in a sinister light, zeroing in on certain student leaders whose motives were questioned and whose loyalty was challenged, the visual aspect of the documentary was on the whole rather fair and balanced.

Audience reaction to the film was quite revealing. When Beida student leader Wu'er Kaixi was shown addressing a crowd in Tiananmen Square, an act the narrator described as "counterrevolutionary agitation," many in the audience—which numbered around two hundred or three hundred civilians and as many as a hundred off-duty uniformed soldiers—tittered uncomfortably. And there were more nervous giggles when Zhao Ziyang was shown arriving at the square before dawn on the morning of May 20, where he apologized to the students for his inability to protect them. The film showed Zhao's entire tear-filled address, delivered via a hand-held amplifier. It was a very intense, emotional scene. I was deeply moved, and I think many in the audience were similarly affected. Far from being derisive, their nervous laughter seemed to convey an underlying, shared sense of compassion.

As soon as graphic scenes of the June 3–4 military crackdown appeared on the screen (stripped of any visual evidence of soldiers shooting civilians), thirty or forty people quietly got up and left the screening room. During the earlier, expository part of the film, the audience sat very still, obviously enthralled by what they saw. When the film's violent climax came, however, a lot of people clearly didn't have the stomach to watch. My impression was that regardless of the government's original intent in mounting this exhibition, both the film and many of the artifacts on display in the museum subtly served to raise (rather than put to rest) doubts about the veracity of the government's one-sided, self-justifying account of the May–June mayhem.

Later that afternoon I had an appointment with Ambassador Jim Lilley, our first face-to-face contact since our fateful encounter at Camp David six months earlier. We talked mainly about the political situation in Beijing, which Jim characterized as extremely complex. The top leadership was divided, he said, and friction within the army was ongoing and serious. He was also closely watching the economic situation in Guangdong, because provincial leaders had recently resisted Beijing's efforts to curb excessive spending, investment, and foreign exchange transactions. The center had been trying to bring Guangdong to heel, and the province had replied, in effect, "Screw you." Jim thought this situation would be a good test of whether the central government retained the necessary clout to impose its will on certain freewheeling, free-spending provincial leaders who had become increasingly bold in their defiance of Beijing's austerity measures.

Our conversation next turned to China's post-Tiananmen leadership. We talked about the fate of various erstwhile "liberals" within Deng's ruling coalition, such as Li Ruihuan and Tian Jiyun, two of the more open-minded, plainspoken members of the Politburo. Jim was not very sanguine about their future leadership prospects. He felt that given the near-death experience suffered by the CCP when Zhao Ziyang departed from Deng's hard-line policy toward student demonstrators, China's leaders would be forced to close ranks around a conservative "law and order" agenda for years to come, leaving little room for liberal political initiatives or leadership. As it turned out, he was correct.

Though we spoke for more than an hour, not a single word was said about the February incident at Camp David or about Professor Fang Lizhi, who by that time had been Jim's houseguest at the U.S. Embassy for almost two months (and who would remain there for another ten months, until June 1990, when the Chinese government agreed to let him emigrate to the United Kingdom). With such a large elephant in the room, our meeting had a rather strained, uncomfortable edge to it.

AFTER FIVE DAYS in Beijing I flew to Shanghai on August 31. Sitting next to me on the airplane was a young computer technician who was on his way to Shanghai to give technical advice on an industrial automation project. Like most ordinary Beijingers I had met during the previous week, he confirmed that people were still angry and upset about what had happened in early June. Although he himself had kept his nose clean during the demonstrations, some people in his work unit, who had participated in the demonstrations, had been subjected to intensive political study and "self-examination" sessions, in which they were thoroughly questioned. He said he had been able to avoid political study because he had stayed away from the protests except for one or two visits to the square, where he was just a fringe spectator. He said he hadn't wanted to jeopardize his career, so he decided to stay clear of active involvement. I could only smile as I recalled my own calculated decision, a quarter century earlier, to make my strategic exit from a Sproul Hall sit-in before the police arrived to make arrests.

An official from the Shanghai Academy of Social Science, who had been designated as my local host, met me upon my arrival. In my room at the Jinjiang Hotel, he gave me the standard pro-government account of the events of the previous spring. Throughout his monologue he fidgeted nervously, which I attributed to the high probability that my room was bugged. After he left, I had the rest of the day free, so I walked the two miles or so from the hotel down to the Bund. I had a solitary dinner in the eighth-floor restaurant at the Peace Hotel, a familiar Shanghai waterfront landmark with a wonderful view of the Huangpu River. Involuntarily, I found myself looking in the direction of the old Foreign Seamen's Club, by now long gone.

In an elevator on the way up to the restaurant, I met two American economists who worked for the World Bank. After dinner I joined them for coffee, and we chatted about the political climate in China. They were very upbeat, saying that everything was back to normal, and that foreigners should be encouraged to return ASAP. I said, well, yes, but what about all the anger and tension roiling just beneath the surface? I used the Chinese phrase *neijin, waisong*, which designates a situation of outer calm but inner stress. They responded, "Oh no, there's very little tension here." It occurred to me then that from the high-rise, glass-enclosed vantage point of the World Bank, little of China's smoldering grass-roots political angst was visible. There was nothing more to be said, so I excused myself.

After dinner, as I walked along the Bund, a young man sidled up to me and asked, sotto voce, as dozens of other young Chinese men had done in recent years, "Change money?" With the official exchange rate pegged artificially low against the U.S. dollar, a significantly higher rate could be had on China's flourishing gray market. Like "Speak English?" the more furtive proposition "Change money?" had become a popular mantra among hawkers trolling for foreigners outside China's major tourist hotels and sightseeing venues. This particular young man's offer to change money had a surprising tag line, however. After I declined his initial proposal, he then said, in heavily accented English, "Hashish?"

I did a double take. In more than a dozen previous trips to China, no one on the street had ever offered to sell me drugs. I turned to look at the author of this surprising proposition. He was dark-complexioned, swarthier than most Chinese. At first I took him to be of Central Asian descent—perhaps Afghan or Pakistani—but he spoke decent *putonghua*, and it soon dawned on me that he was a Uighur from Xinjiang, an ethnic minority with a reputation as freewheeling traders who would deal in virtually anything. In response to his offer of hashish, I shook my head "no." He then started quoting me prices per kilo, which he quickly lowered as I continued to shake my head. He obviously wanted to make a sale. I had been told by some American friends in Beijing about the rising use of pot and hash by college students there, and had even shared a joint on one occasion, and I was aware of a reported dramatic increase in opium addiction in Yunnan, near Southeast Asia's notorious Golden Triangle. But this was my first direct encounter with a Chinese drug dealer, operating openly (if discreetly) in China's biggest city.

Though this was my maiden encounter with illicit commodity commerce in post-Mao China (excluding gray-market money exchanges), it was by no means my last. Indeed, it was not even the last of the day. When I returned to the Jinjiang at the end of a long evening, I received a phone call in my room from two giggling young Chinese women who said, in broken English, that they wanted to talk to me. They clearly didn't have a clue who I was, and they refused to identify themselves. They nonetheless seemed unusually bold, albeit rather nervous, as they told me (in halting, mangled English) that I could "take them to a party" if I wanted to. Naively thinking they had dialed a wrong number, I disengaged from the conversation without giving it much further thought. The next day, however, I was browsing through a magazine in my hotel room when I came across an article describing the recent rise of organized prostitution rings in Shanghai. According to the article, one of the hookers' favorite tactics was to pay hotel bellboys and elevator operators to act as lookouts, alerting them when unaccompanied foreign guests returned to their rooms. The circumstances of my late-night phone call certainly fit this profile, yet the two women's nervous, adolescent giggles made it seem more likely that they were inexperienced novices rather than seasoned professionals. In any event, this was just the first of many similar solicitations I would receive—with increasing frequency and audacity—over the next dozen years, as prostitution began to flourish openly in and around urban tourist hotels, karaoke bars, and massage parlors.

WHILE IN SHANGHAI I met with two high-ranking Communist Party elder statesmen, former mayor Wang Daohan and former Fudan University president and CCP Central Committee member Mme. Xie Xide. My session with Mayor Wang began with his asking for my personal account of reactions in America to the events of spring 1989, including my assessment of the different responses of Congress, the President, and the public. I told him quite candidly of the widespread moral outrage most Americans experienced in response to the events of June 3 and 4. I also told him how the American public had been captivated by video footage of the solitary young Chinese civilian, later dubbed "Tank Man," who had single-handedly stared down a PLA armored column near Tiananmen Square.

After I had spoken for perhaps twenty minutes, Wang Daohan launched into his own lengthy monologue. He stressed two main points: First, no one had been killed in Tiananmen Square on the night of June 3 (which may have been technically correct, insofar as the vast majority of fatalities occurred outside the square), and second, the PLA soldiers were the real heroes of the "June 4 incident." Mayor Wang spoke nonstop for over an hour, giving me the Chinese government's official view of the events in question. He began by quoting two classical Chinese aphorisms. One was "When people stand at a high enough summit, they do not fear being harmed by moving clouds." The other was "When you stand on Mount Lu, you cannot see it." His meaning was clear: Proximity clouds vision; to properly understand Tiananmen, one must take the long view.

Unexpectedly, Mayor Wang next launched into a bitter attack on Fang Lizhi. He argued that it had been a handful of "careerists" and "bad elements" like Fang who had caused major damage in April and May by manipulating the legitimate grievances of students and other urban residents to serve their own "sinister" purposes. This had made the use of military force inevitable, he said. He conceded that there were "many problems and contradictions" in the government's own work, including widespread inflation, corruption, and nepotism, that had contributed to rising urban frustration and disaffection, thereby strengthening public support for student protests in April and May.

According to Wang Daohan, the hunger strikers in Tiananmen Square had been cynically manipulated by careerists with ulterior motives. Originally, the strikers had been told that their fast would last for only thirty hours. Later, in the middle of this thirty-hour period, they were instructed to continue fasting indefinitely. The students were thus induced to start the hunger strike under false pretenses. According to Mayor Wang, the leaders of the strike (who themselves allegedly continued to accept food and drink) had hoped that the strike would not end until some students had died of malnutrition or dehydration, whereupon strike leaders could use the martyrdom of these "innocent victims" as a rallying point for the masses to "bring down the Chinese government." This, according to Wang Daohan, was the sinister aim of the careerists: The death of a few hunger strikers would force the government to accept the dissidents' demands.

The Chinese government intervened, however, and "would not permit the students to die." The government sent ambulances to the square, but student leaders would not permit the ambulances to go near the hunger strikers. Medical workers were told that the students would accept treatment only from Red Cross personnel and not from government medics, whom they distrusted. Thereupon, the government doctors simply put on Red Cross armbands and were allowed to treat the students. In Mayor Wang's telling of it, this humanitarian maneuver was responsible for saving many students' lives. In his view, the careerists didn't want the hunger strike to be interrupted or the students rescued.

According to Wang Daohan, three commands had been given to martial law troops entering Beijing on June 3: (1) don't respond to verbal abuse, (2) don't counterattack if assaulted physically, and (3) don't lock and load your rifles. Under such conditions, the soldiers were placed in a very difficult situation, he said. Eventually, they were "compelled" by the repeated harassment and assaults of the "mob" to load their weapons in self-defense. Wang said that in such a situation, soldiers, students, hooligans, and innocent bystanders alike inevitably suffered casualties.

The mayor went on to recount a number of stories of alleged heroism on the part of Chinese tank and armored personnel carrier crews, which had come under attack on the night of June 3. He told of one tank commander who, when his vehicle was surrounded by an angry mob, refused to move the tank out of danger for fear of running over demonstrators. Instead, he ordered two of his crew members to leave the tank while he stayed inside, refusing to fire at or run over any students. Ultimately, the crowd chased down and beat his two crew members, who were still in the hospital. The tank commander himself burned to death when his tank was set on fire. Such actions clearly showed, Mayor Wang said, that the army was not the enemy of the people. He also had a very different interpretation of the infamous Tank Man episode. In Wang's telling of it, the real hero was the commander of the tank column who refused to be provoked into harming the young man. Thus, when Tank Man repeatedly positioned himself directly in front of the lead vehicle, the commander first swerved to avoid hitting him and then stopped completely. When the young man climbed up onto the tank and began pounding on the turret's hatch, the commander still refused to respond with force. And when Tank Man was finally led away from harm by concerned bystanders, the commander let him go without incident. "This shows," my host said, "that the PLA truly cherishes the people."

Wang Daohan's spirited defense of the June crackdown was a thing of rhetorical beauty, and it took me by surprise, since he was widely reputed to be something of a political liberal. If so, he certainly hid it well this day. I strongly suspect that our conversation was being bugged and that he may well have been covering his ass. If so, it was a chilling commentary on the power of the CCP to enforce strict discipline on its members. Indeed, the very vigor of Wang's defense of the crackdown suggested to me that his own loyalties were quite likely under suspicion after June 4. Mao used to test the loyalty of his lieutenants by requiring them to endorse policies publicly that they privately opposed. In any event, in the face of Wang Daohan's self-righteous, moralistic exegesis of the events in question, I could not bring myself to argue with him—to comment, for example, on the incendiary nature of Deng Xiaoping's labeling of student protests as "unpatriotic" and "counterrevolutionary turmoil," or about the actions of PLA troops who had fired live ammunition into crowds of nonviolent demonstrators and into the windows of apartment houses, office buildings, and at least one revolving restaurant.

The next evening, I had dinner with a group of scholars from the Center for American Studies at Shanghai's Fudan University. The dinner was hosted by Xie Xide, the center's elderly, American-educated director and former president of Fudan. After dinner she held court on the subject of the student disturbances. Like Wang Daohan, Xie was a cagey veteran of China's political and bureaucratic wars. And like Wang, she presented a

lengthy, impassioned monologue—for the benefit of unseen listeners?—
defending the government's crackdown of June 3–4. By the time she finished, I had given up on the idea of trying to engage her in meaningful
dialogue. When she told me that the Chinese government had done "all it
could" to resolve the Tiananmen crisis peacefully, I simply nodded, listening in silence as she predictably concluded that the use of force had been
brought on by the students themselves. Interestingly, some of the other
Fudan scholars in attendance displayed in their facial expressions and
body language some evident discomfort at Xie's monochromatic characterization of the events of the spring of 1989.

Later, when I asked a friend at the Social Science Academy why I had
been granted such extensive face time with elite-level politicians like Wang
Daohan and Xie Xide so soon after the June 4 incident, he told me that I
had been vetted by China's top "America watchers" and found to be relatively "objective" (keguande) in my approach to China. I was neither a
sycophantic "foreign friend" (a revelation that made me smile, recalling
my ill-fated, halfhearted attempt to join that particular fraternity in 1968)
nor a hostile "enemy of China." It was gratifying to confirm that one could
be critical of China—at times even sharply critical—without necessarily
forfeiting one's welcome.

According to a Chinese diplomat who defected after the Tiananmen
crackdown, five categories of friendship and enmity were officially recognized in China. A first-category "friend" was someone who "agreed with
us on everything. . . . These people were so friendly that they would agree
with our policies [even] in the Cultural Revolution." Such sycophants
were useful for propaganda purposes and were often quoted in the official media. A second-category "friendly personage" (youhao renshi) was
someone "whom we often relied on but did not trust very much. . . . Many
of these people . . . were probably doing business with China. . . . Although
they had their own views about communism and the social system, they
had to smile and pretend to be friends." Such persons were objects of diplomatic cajolery, but Chinese officials were instructed, when talking to them,
to "steer the conversation away from ideology." The third category com-
prised "those who really love China but know all the vices of Chinese communism." Such people were "not easily fooled. . . . There was no point in
trying to brainwash them." (This was the category to which I had been officially consigned.) The fourth category was made up of "those people who
love China but hate Chinese communism." These people "belonged to the

category of 'enemies'. . . . What we tried to do was discredit them [either by] spreading rumors or suggesting that . . . they were paid by the Nationalists in Taiwan." The fifth category was a residual, reserved for those who either "didn't know or didn't care much about China." Such people were "useful to the propagandists because we could always invite them to a free film or to a showing of a cultural event, in order to get them to say, 'Oh, it's wonderful. It's marvelous.'"

The day following my dinner with Xie Xide, at the invitation of Professor Wang Xi of the Fudan Center for American Studies, I met with a group of younger Chinese America watchers. Prominent among them were Professors Zhou Mingwei, Wang Huning, and Ni Shixiong of Fudan University. This was easily the most candid and forthright group discussion I had participated in during my entire trip. Unlike my earlier Beijing meetings at Beida and the Chinese Academy of Social Science, where sensitive issues were discussed only obliquely, with considerable circumlocution and distressed body language, post-Tiananmen stress disorder seemed much less intense here. The Fudan scholars were more relaxed than their Beijing counterparts, displaying little physical discomfort or verbal anxiety when we conversed. We talked rather openly about the events of June 3–4, about the public's reaction in the United States, and about the professors' own hopes and fears. To a person, they had initially supported the Beijing students' protests, and they exhibited genuine anguish over the trauma suffered by the civilian populace of Beijing. They were satisfied neither with their government's labeling of the student demonstrations as unpatriotic nor with the various steps taken by the government since early June to crack down on dissident leaders and protest organizers. They did, however, share one thing in common with their Beijing counterparts, as well as their Shanghai Party elders, Wang Daohan and Xie Xide: They fervently wanted American universities to resume, expand, and deepen existing research and exchange programs with China. China's one great hope for recapturing the lost momentum of modernization and reform, they believed, was to step up the exchange of personnel, ideas, and information between China and the West. For these scholars, the link to the West was a vital lifeline.

RETURNING HOME ON September 4, 1989—three months to the day after the bloody crackdown in Beijing—I reviewed my notes and summarized my impressions. First, the Chinese Communist Party was obsessed

with the need to present a unified facade of moral righteousness in justi-
fying its behavior from mid-April to early June. With even such erstwhile
"liberal" politicians as Wang Daohan and Xie Xide loyally toeing the
official line, at least in public, there seemed little likelihood of an early
CCP retreat or reversal of verdicts on either the Tiananmen tragedy or
the Party's harsh condemnation of Zhao Ziyang. Second, although public sentiment in China's major cities remained strongly, if silently, sympathetic with the Beijing students, the sheer strength and ferocity of the
government's politico-military crackdown had left all but the most radical, die-hard proponents of democratic change sobered and resigned to
several more years of conservative authoritarian rule. Among the people
I encountered, most of whom were intellectuals, the vast majority were
clearly gun-shy and chaos-averse; none savored the prospect of renewed
confrontation with the regime in power. Third, although the Beijing
Spring of 1989 deeply affected China's urban population, particularly in
major cities along the eastern seaboard, rural dwellers—who constituted
a sizable majority of the total population—by and large appeared to be
ignorant of, and apathetic toward, events in Beijing. For most rural Chinese, the struggle to put food on the table seemed more immediate and
vital than the struggle to secure vague and only dimly perceived political
rights. A huge urban-rural divide continued to exist in China, one that
would conceivably take many decades to bridge. And finally, while a continuing atmosphere of political intimidation and repression pervaded
the intellectual community of Beijing and (to a lesser extent) Shanghai,
there was an overwhelming, passionate desire within this community
to maintain and strengthen existing ties with counterpart organizations
and individuals in the West. Most felt that it would be disastrous—for
them and for their country—if Westerners turned their backs on China
at this critical juncture. Throughout my visit many Chinese friends and
acquaintances had expressed a strong desire to go overseas as soon as
possible, and I carried back with me several applications for graduate
study and visiting scholar status in the United States.

In my final report to Dean Hawkins at UCLA, I recounted the hopes
and fears of these vulnerable Chinese intellectuals and strongly endorsed
their plea for continued academic contact. I was gratified when the dean
fully endorsed my recommendations. Consequently, UCLA continued
to develop and strengthen its institutional ties with China. At the same
time, nothing I saw during my ten-day sojourn in August–September 1989

served to alter my strong conviction that the Chinese government would eventually have to face up to its own ill-advised provocations and overreactions of spring 1989 before post-Tiananmen stress disorder could finally be healed and long-term political stability effectively ensured.

9

China Rising

MY RETURN TO Peking University in the fall of 1993 was a real eye-opener. On my previous visit, three years earlier, the Beida campus had been swathed in a volatile mix of grief, anger, and resignation. In the interval, massive changes had taken place in the world—and in China. A dozen Communist regimes in Eastern and Central Europe had collapsed in the Velvet Revolution of 1989, throwing a deep fright into Beijing's leaders, who responded by circling their political and ideological wagons ever tighter. And when the Soviet Union itself imploded in 1991, Chinese conservatives were quick to accuse Mikhail Gorbachev of being a "degenerate Marxist" whose seduction by the forces of "bourgeois liberalism" and "peaceful evolution" (*heping yanbian*) had brought disaster to the socialist cause.

More alarming still, China's reactionaries used the Soviet meltdown as a pretext for openly attacking Deng Xiaoping's economic reforms and open policy, which they publicly condemned as "capitalistic." As one particularly blunt *People's Daily* commentary of October 1991 put it, "If we fail to wage a resolute struggle against liberalization or capitalistic reform and opening up, our socialist cause will be ruined. . . . 'Reform and opening up' is a banner for peaceful evolution in China."

As an antidote to such alleged ideological poisons, Communist Party conservatives sought to induce a nationwide revival of Mao Zedong Thought and a new round of class struggle. Even Jiang Zemin, the middle-of-the-road technocrat who replaced Zhao Ziyang as CCP general secretary in 1989, now wavered in his support for Deng's reforms.

Sensing that his program was in serious trouble, Deng fought back.

Throwing caution to the winds, in January 1992 he undertook a month-long "southern tour" (*nanxun*) to China's flourishing southeastern coastal cities and special economic zones. Though ill and infirm—his hearing was severely impaired and he could not walk unaided—the eighty-seven-year-old Deng passionately defended his reforms at every stop. Denying that stepped-up foreign investment and a mixed state-private economy represented the return of Western capitalism and imperialism to China, he chided his conservative critics, many of whom were also in their eighties, for being like "old women with bound feet," a cleverly chosen metaphor once favored by Chairman Mao himself. And he pointedly reminded them that advanced age tends to make people stubborn and intolerant. It was vitally important, insisted Deng, to expand and accelerate the economic reforms and open policy, rather than slow them down or roll them back. If his comrades couldn't be more flexible in their thinking, he admonished, they would be well advised to get out of the way.

Deng and his critics were playing high-stakes poker. With the post-Tiananmen Politburo divided more or less evenly between reformists and atavists, the outcome was anything but certain. Fortunately for Deng (and ultimately for China), the opposition blinked first. Lacking the necessary votes to repeal Deng's reforms, and sensing a shift in the prevailing political winds as a result of Deng's dynamic southern tour, the conservatives grudgingly backed off. When Jiang Zemin belatedly endorsed Deng's call for accelerated economic liberalization in May 1992, the game was over.

A period of frantic, breakneck economic expansion ensued, as provincial and local governments throughout China raced to open their economies to new sources of investment and trade, both foreign and domestic. After three years of post-Tiananmen "wait and see" caution, multinational firms now rushed in to take advantage of China's hot economy. Bank loans, most of them unsecured, rose dramatically, and credit became widely available for commercial development. An unprecedented construction boom followed, accompanied by real estate and stock market surges that drew speculators into the market, driving property and share prices sharply upward. Finally, hundreds of thousands of government and Party officials and their families "jumped into the sea of commerce" (*xiahai*) to set up profit-making firms at the ill-defined boundary between public and private ownership. The roaring '90s had begun. By the end of the decade, the words "China" and "rising economic powerhouse" would be used interchangeably.

MY RETURN TO Beida as a visiting scholar in the fall of 1993 came at the height of the new economic boom. By then, the spirit of *xiahai* had visibly infected the campus. Students were no longer either in mourning or quietly seething, nor were they passively resisting the new economic bargain that Deng was offering them. Indeed, they were eagerly *embracing* it. In 1989 Beida had felt a lot like Berkeley in the '60s. In 1993 it felt more like Harvard Business School. The students had traded their political ideals for tickets to a better future. Fang Lizhi would not have recognized them. The dark, depressive cloud of post-Tiananmen stress disorder had seemingly dissipated.

Alongside the emerging ethos of personal ambition and pursuit of profit, Beida students also displayed a surprising degree of newfound patriotic pride. After being shunned by the international community in the wake of the Tiananmen crackdown, China was making a global comeback. In the summer of 1993, Beijing was selected as a finalist in the competition to host the 2000 Summer Olympic Games. Olympics fever soon swept the Beida campus. After delivering the first of three invited lectures to Beida undergraduates in a class on international communications, I asked the students in the class how they felt about the idea of Beijing hosting the Olympics so soon after the 1989 disturbances. I expected a mixed response. Instead, with only one exception—a student from impoverished Guangxi who objected to paying a mandatory national "panda tax" so that Beijing could spend ¥500 million on urban beautification to impress visiting members of the International Olympic Committee—the students were unambivalently proud that their city had made it to the final round of competition. They were feeling patriotic, and they didn't mind the price tag. Taking all this in, I puzzled over the rapidity with which the anger of 1989 had seemingly dissipated. Was post-Tiananmen stress disorder truly a thing of the past?

On a balmy October night in Beijing, the winning bid in the Olympics sweepstakes was announced in far-off Monaco. At Beida, a crowd of about ten thousand students had gathered at 2:00 AM to watch the televised ceremony on a giant outdoor projection screen, erected for the occasion at the campus triangle. As the moment of decision drew near, the atmosphere was lighthearted and festive. Most students expected Beijing to win, and they were in a mood to celebrate. But when Sydney, Australia, was declared the surprise winner, the mood changed abruptly. Where before there had been warmth and jocularity, now I could sense palpable hostility. Near me, a group of students grumbled that the Europeans and Americans on the selection committee had conspired secretly to swing their support to Sydney to prevent China from winning. Then one of the undergraduate students from the international communications class recognized me in the crowd and approached me. "Why do you Americans want us to fail?" he asked. One of his classmates said, "It's just like the *Yinhe*. America doesn't trust China." I had no good answer for them, so I bit my tongue and refrained from commenting.

The *Yinhe* was a Chinese merchant ship suspected by the CIA of transporting chemical warfare components from North Korea to the Persian Gulf in the summer of 1993. The Chinese government vehemently denied the allegation, whereupon the U.S. Navy pursued the *Yinhe* all the way to the Gulf, where the Saudi Arabian Navy, at the behest of the United States, boarded the ship and searched its cargo holds. No contraband items were found, chemical or otherwise. The incident proved highly embarrassing to the new Clinton administration and highly insulting to the Chinese government and people. China was experiencing the first stirrings of a reawakened nationalism.

I got a further taste of this renaissance a few weeks later in the city of Yichang, on the middle reaches of the Yangzi River in Hubei. I had arrived in Yichang after a three-day downstream cruise from Chongqing. The highlight of the cruise was its passage through China's legendary Three Gorges (Sanxia), immortalized in traditional Chinese poems and landscape paintings. The gorges themselves were breathtaking—mile after mile of rugged canyon walls rising steeply above the banks of the narrow, winding river. But my timing was off. Dense fog and a heavily polluted inversion layer enveloped the Yangzi along major portions of the cruise route, literally throwing a wet blanket over the entire journey.

After three days and nights of near-zero visibility, I left the cruise ship feeling hugely disappointed, with only a handful of murky gray-tinged photographs to show for my adventure. After checking into a hotel in Yichang, I spent half a day walking around the town, where I grudgingly purchased a set of color postcards showing the Three Gorges in all their spectacular, sun-drenched splendor. By late afternoon my energy was flagging, so I hailed a passing pedicab and asked the driver to take me back to the hotel. That's when the trouble started. About five minutes into the ride, a middle-aged man wearing a sweaty T-shirt and rolled-up blue work pants jumped directly into the path of the pedicab, forcing it to stop. Addressing the driver in Chinese, he shouted, "Where are you going?" When the startled driver didn't answer, the man admonished him, "You shouldn't be pedaling the foreign devil [*yanggui*]; the foreign devil should be pedaling you!" Taken aback, the driver just nodded. When the man finally left, the driver turned around and, looking sheepish, apologized for the interruption. Then he started pedaling again. But almost immediately he changed course, and I soon noticed that we were heading away from my hotel rather than toward it. When I pointed this out, the driver assured me that he was taking a shortcut. Though I knew this wasn't true, I didn't argue with him: He had lost enough face for one day. A few minutes later he deposited me on a shadowy street corner in the seediest section of Yichang. Pointing to the mouth of a narrow, unfriendly-looking alley in which a handful of scruffy, apparently unemployed youths were loitering around an outdoor pool table, the driver told me that my hotel was "just over there." I paid him and watched him pedal off, satisfied in his knowledge that he had bested the foreigner and regained lost face. I beat a hasty retreat and eventually flagged a taxi back to my hotel, making a mental note never again to hire a pedicab in China.

These two incidents—the post-Olympics *Yinhe* rant and the Yichang pedicab insult—occurring within weeks of each other, were my first direct encounters with growing anti-Americanism on the streets of China. They would not be my last. In the mid-'90s a series of controversial initiatives by pro-independence Taiwanese president Lee Teng-hui further fueled Chinese suspicions of hostile American motives and intentions. When Lee was permitted to make a pro-independence speech on the campus of Cornell University in the summer of 1995 (after first having been denied a U.S. visa), the Chinese government reacted angrily, holding military exercises, including missile tests, in the Taiwan Strait and threatening to resolve the Taiwan problem by military means if the people of Taiwan should be so foolish as to elect a pro-independence candidate in their upcoming presidential contest. Responding to China's "coercive diplomacy," the United States rattled a few sabers of its own, sending two aircraft carrier groups into the vicinity of the Taiwan Strait.

In the immediate aftermath of these frictional events a best-selling nonfiction book appeared in China with the provocative title *China Can Say No* (Zhongguo keyi shuo bu). Its message (like that of a similarly titled Japanese best seller published back in 1989) was one of defiance: The United States should not take China's goodwill for granted. Citing the examples of the *Yinhe* incident, Beijing's failed Olympics bid, and the U.S. aircraft carrier intrusions near the Taiwan Strait, the authors argued that America was out to "contain" China. They further alleged that some Chinese intellectuals had become "totally Westernized" to the point of turning their backs on their own national heritage and culture. Tellingly, they singled out Fang Lizhi for his "slavish devotion" to everything Western.

The dustup in the Taiwan Strait fueled growing distrust on both sides of the Pacific. In the aftermath of the 1996 U.S. presidential election, Republicans in the U.S. Congress charged the Clinton and Gore reelection campaigns with accepting illegal contributions from a variety of Chinese special interests, including a PRC aerospace company represented by the daughter of a former PLA chief of staff. Shortly thereafter, in 1998, a Taiwanese American nuclear scientist at the Los Alamos National Laboratory, Dr. Wen Ho Lee, was dismissed from his job amid allegations (later dropped) that he had provided Beijing with the designs and codes for the United States' latest nuclear warheads. Several months later, a congressional investigative committee, the Cox Commission, issued a report alleging that China had engaged in a systematic program of nuclear espionage against the United States, resulting in the theft of top secret design information on U.S. warheads, radiation weapons, delivery systems, and reentry vehicles. Predictably, Beijing bristled at these allegations; equally important, the *laobaixing*, long a repository of warm feelings toward the United States, were now turning distinctly negative.

In the United States, too, the atmosphere soured noticeably as a spate of provocative anti-China books appeared in U.S. bookstores with such breathless titles as *The China Threat: How the People's Republic Targets America*, *The Coming Conflict with China*, *Red Dragon Rising: Communist China's Military Threat to America*, and *Year of the Rat: How Bill Clinton Compromised American Security for Chinese Money*. Not even two rather cozy, cordial presidential summits between Bill Clinton and Jiang Zemin in 1997 and 1998 could stem the rising tide of mutual suspicion between Chinese and Americans. On both sides of the Pacific, public opinion polls showed declining trust and goodwill.

Things went from bad to worse in May 1999 when a U.S. stealth aircraft, flying under the NATO flag in the Kosovo conflict in Yugoslavia, accidentally bombed the PRC embassy in Belgrade, killing three Chinese journalists and wounding twenty embassy staffers. The official explanation

Anti-American street demonstrations in Beijing and other Chinese cities followed the accidental U.S. bombing of the Chinese embassy in Belgrade, Serbia,
May 1999. Sign reads: "Resolutely oppose American-NATO Criminal Aggression
against China."

for the mishap—that U.S. intelligence officials planning the mission had
used outdated maps that identified the building as a Yugoslavian military
intelligence facility—was indignantly rejected by the Chinese government,
which termed the attack "barbarous."

By this time, the end of the 1990s, the World Wide Web had become a
significant part of the changing media landscape in China. In the aftermath
of the Belgrade embassy bombing, Chinese Internet chat rooms and electronic bulletin boards—favored hangouts of young male netizens—came
alive with denunciations of U.S. imperialism and demands for repayment
of the "blood debt" incurred by America's "NATO Nazis."

In this atmosphere of deteriorating civility, I had two fresh encounters
with growing Chinese nationalism. In the summer of 1999 I traveled with
a Chinese friend to the Yellow Mountain (Huang shan) in Anhui, a Buddhist mountain retreat famed for its breathtaking vistas and scenic hiking trails. As we strolled through the town at the foot of the mountain, a
visibly distressed elderly woman accosted us on the street. I was wearing

a T-shirt with the University of California logo on it. Jabbing her finger squarely into my chest, the woman angrily admonished me: "You Americans think you can bully us. Just wait till we're stronger. We'll show you!"

Later that same week I was watching the championship round of the Women's World Cup soccer competition in the bar of a Shanghai hotel. The match pitted the reigning U.S. world champions, led by superstars Mia Hamm and Michelle Akers, against a rising Chinese side led by the dynamic striker Sun Wen. After ninety scoreless minutes, the game went into overtime and was eventually decided in America's favor on penalty kicks, 4–3. But slow-motion replays of the decisive Chinese penalty kick, which was dramatically blocked by U.S. goalkeeper Brianna Scurry, showed that Scurry had moved off her line prematurely, a technical violation that should have resulted in a re-kick. But the officials missed it, and the game was over. Walking back to my room, I heard a by now familiar refrain coming from two young, trendily dressed Chinese passersby: "The American turtle eggs cheat; they can't play fair." A few days later, an excursion to several bookstores along Shanghai's bustling upscale retail district on Nanjing Road yielded a number of prominent new anti-American paperbacks, with titles like *America's Sinister Schemes* (Meiguo yinmo), *China Can't Be Intimidated* (Zhongguo buke ru), and *China Can Still Say No* (Zhongguo haishi keyi shuo bu). As I browsed through these (and other) chauvinistic screeds, I experienced an intensifying sense of distress.

A VOLATILE BLEND of patriotic pride and repressed anti-foreign resentment, Chinese nationalism was also on display in the run-up to Hong Kong's long-awaited 1997 retrocession to China. In the early 1980s Deng Xiaoping had made clear to British prime minister Margaret Thatcher that Britain's ninety-nine-year lease on the New Territories—largest and most heavily populated of the three parcels of South China coastal real estate that together made up the Crown Colony of Hong Kong—would not be renewed when it expired at midnight on June 30, 1997. Calculating that the remaining two parcels (Hong Kong island and the Kowloon Peninsula) would not be viable without the people or industrial and agricultural resources of the New Territories, the British negotiated with China for the return of the entire package. The Joint Declaration, a preliminary agreement signed in 1984, called for the incorporation of Hong Kong as a Special Administrative Region (SAR) of China with a "high degree of autonomy." Hong Kong would be allowed to retain its own economic, administrative, and legal institutions, and China pledged noninterference in the SAR's internal affairs for a period of fifty years. A 1990 Basic Law incorporated these principles into a mini-constitution for post-1997 Hong Kong.

The early 1990s were a period of diminishing mutual trust and confidence in Sino-British relations. The Tiananmen crackdown had proved particularly unsettling to Hong Kong's largely immigrant population. Huge crowds of up to one million people, almost 20 percent of the colony's total population, had turned out in the late spring of 1989 to protest the Chinese government's harsh treatment of student demonstrators in Beijing. Although the British authorities wanted a smooth, trouble-free transition, and had accepted in principle a Chinese proposal to freeze all existing political institutions until after the handover (an arrangement known as the "through train"), a substantial number of Hong Kong Chinese began to agitate for the British government to introduce democratic reforms before 1997, to protect them against possible Chinese repression and reprisal.

Under Hong Kong's last and most outspoken British governor, Chris Patten, appointed in 1992, a number of democratic reform measures were adopted, designed to mollify Hong Kong's political activists but which, by the same token, deeply angered the Beijing government. The most highly controversial of these was Patten's 1995 decision to unilaterally expand the number of democratically elected seats on Hong Kong's Legislative Council (Legco), from eighteen to thirty. Labeling Patten's plan a wanton violation of the "through train" principle, the Chinese side threatened to dissolve Legco immediately after the handover should the governor go ahead with his planned reform.

Governor Patten appeared to relish his confrontation with Beijing. At a luncheon for him organized by the Asia Society in the summer of 1995, I pointedly asked him if he was prepared to go ahead with the his controversial Legco reorganization plan in the face of China's promise to annul it. "That's their problem," he said defiantly, "not mine." When I suggested that it might soon become the Hong Kong people's problem, he adroitly steered the conversation onto another subject. A few months later the disputed election was held, and Hong Kong's democrats won a clear victory.

As the large, specially constructed Countdown Clock in Beijing's Tiananmen Square ticked down toward midnight on June 30, 1997, emotions on both sides grew more heated. With Western journalists lamenting the "Death of Hong Kong" and Beijing hurling colorful epithets at Patten, such as "whore of the East" and "the criminal condemned for a thousand generations," many observers foresaw a troubled transition.

Fascinated by all this, and having long had a love affair with Hong Kong, I devised a plan to be on hand for the big event. I proposed that the University of California's Education Abroad Program (EAP) establish a special, one-off Hong Kong Transition Program in 1997. My plan was to bring an elite group of sixteen University of California undergraduates to Hong Kong in January 1997 for a semester of intensive coursework on the history, culture, economy, and politics of Hong Kong, to be followed by summer internships for the students in politically sensitive local organizations such as human rights groups, political parties, religious groups, the mass media, nongovernmental organizations, and leading multinational firms. Though I didn't say as much in the program's promotional brochure, my intention was to place the students in situations where they could, in effect, serve as human seismographs, registering the magnitude and intensity of any transitional shocks that might accompany Hong Kong's transfer of sovereignty. Nor was I alone in anticipating possible turbulence: Some six thousand foreign journalists had descended on Hong Kong to record the historic event.

Everything went according to plan right up to the moment of transition. Starting in January 1997, I put my sixteen hand-picked students through a rigorous set of academic courses at the Chinese University of Hong Kong (CUHK), where I had been appointed a visiting professor. When classes ended in May, the students took up their prearranged internship posts, working for such high-profile organizations as Human Rights Watch, Friends of the Earth, CNN, ABC-TV, the Hong Kong Christian Institute, Morgan Stanley, and the Roper Starch Polling Organization. I even managed to secure a strategic vantage point for myself as a guest commentator for the BBC World Service in the brand-new Hong Kong Convention Center, where the handover ceremony was scheduled to take place at midnight on June 30.

As the witching hour drew near, Hong Kong became a magnet for international scholars and journalists. Hotel rooms had been booked months in advance, and people flocked to witness history in the making. I took advantage of the opportunity to organize a reunion dinner for scholars who had done their dissertation research at the Universities Service Centre in the late 1960s and early 1970s. More than thirty people turned up, including Fred Teiwes (my Four Cleanups coauthor) and Mike Oksenberg.

A thirty-year reunion of Universities Service Centre alumni and staff, Hong Kong, July 1997. The author appears near the center of the middle row, flanked by Fred Teiwes (with beard, left) and Mike Oksenberg.

As the handover approached, there was a certain electricity in the air. A massive pro-democracy street demonstration and candlelight vigil, drawing tens of thousands of Hong Kong people, was held on June 4, commemorating the eighth anniversary of the Beijing massacre. Pro-democracy politicians warned of a serious erosion of civil rights and liberties under Chinese sovereignty. And then a funny thing happened. The handover went off smoothly, without a hitch—no jack-booted PLA troops pouring across the border or goose-stepping into Hong Kong Central, no mass arrest of pro-democracy demonstrators in front of the Legislative Council building, not a single whiff of totalitarian tear gas or heavy-handed political repression. When daylight broke on July 1, 1997, everything was pretty much as it had been the day before, except that Governor Chris Patten, accompanied by Britain's Prince Charles, had set sail from Hong Kong aboard the royal yacht HMS *Britannia*, and the Union Jack had been lowered—forever—to be replaced by the five-starred national flag of the People's Republic of China. Emblematic of the prevailing upbeat, business-as-usual atmosphere, July 1—part of an extended three-day local holiday—was the biggest retail shopping day ever recorded in Hong Kong. The anticipated big bang had turned out to be something of a fizzle: historic, to be sure, but ultimately a political and journalistic bore. By July 3, most of the six thousand foreign media observers had quietly departed, having failed to record any dramatic stories of conflict or confrontation. Personally, I wavered between feelings of relief and disappointment. So much preparation and anticipation—so little excitement to show for it.

But beneath the smooth, uneventful surface of the Hong Kong handover—dubbed the "Great Chinese Takeaway" by one local media wag—there were clear indications of political stress. First, the new government of Hong Kong's Beijing-backed chief executive, Tung Chee-hwa, followed through on its pledge to roll back Patten's controversial legislative reforms. In one of his first acts after taking office, Tung voided the September 1995 Legco elections, dissolving the pro-democratic legislature and appointing in its place a Provisional Legislative Council populated mainly by pro-China politicians.

Soon, a group of these Beijing-oriented politicos began agitating for a new curriculum to be introduced into Hong Kong's public schools. Centered on "patriotic education," the proposed curriculum change was designed to instill a "deep love of the Motherland" in Hong Kong's children, thereby counteracting the "brainwashing" that had occurred under British colonial auspices. One particularly outspoken advocate of the change was local real estate tycoon, playboy, and pro-China politician David Chu Yu-lin, who, in addition to being a member of the Provisional Legislative Council, penned a periodic column in Hong Kong's leading English-language newspaper, *South China Morning Post*.

In several of his columns in the early summer of 1997, Chu had railed against Hong Kong's British-based educational system, repeating his call for a new emphasis on Chinese pride and patriotism. In mid-July, after reading two or three of his inflammatory *Post* columns, I wrote a letter to the newspaper's editor in which I suggested that the last thing Hong Kong's children needed was a heavy dose of über-nationalist Chinese propaganda:

Since arriving in Hong Kong I have followed with some amusement columnist/legislator David Chu's pompous postings. However, his latest polemic on the subject of patriotism has pushed me over the edge. In the Post on July 10 the irrepressible Mr. Chu calls on Hong Kong educators to instill greater patriotic pride in the young people of the SAR. Mr. Chu asserts "lessons on history, public affairs, and culture, while free from ideology must be taught objectively but with a distinct object in mind: that of instilling in our next generation patriotism, cultural pride, personal integrity and the ability to judge for themselves."

I can only shake my head in wonderment at Mr. Chu's blissful attempt to conjoin in one sentence such patently antithetical concepts as patriotism and objectivity, cultural pride and freedom from ideology. More irritating still is his attempt to justify rewriting Hong Kong's textbooks from a patriotic perspective. . . . When "patriotic" PRC textbooks are free to assess and criticize Mainland government actions, then such textbooks should rightly be applauded as "objective" and "free from ideology."

I felt better for having unburdened myself of my annoyance with David Chu. But that was not the end of the matter. Two weeks later, at the end of July, the chairman of the International Studies Programme at the Chinese University of Hong Kong showed me a confidential fax he had just received from Chu. In it, Chu challenged my qualifications as a university professor, suggesting that my "colonial arrogance" rendered me "unfit to be a guest in Hong Kong at public expense."

I was not amused. *He was trying to get me fired.* I promptly drafted a second letter to the editor of the *Post*, revealing the contents of Chu's fax and accusing him of "using his public office to pressure university officials into silencing a critic." The *Post* published my letter on August 4, then put the story on its front page, above the fold, under the attention-grabbing headline "Legislator Tried to Get Me Sacked—Don." From the *Post*'s story, I learned that Chu had sent a similar, defamatory fax to the vice-chancellor of Hong Kong's Baptist University, challenging the academic credentials of another expatriate professor, Timothy Hamlett, who had also dared to publicly challenge Chu's views on so-called patriotic education. Asked by the *Post*'s staff writer for a comment on these allegations of impropriety, Chu responded, "If they are afraid of this, they have no basis being in a free society. Maybe they should go to North Korea." And he went on to state that "Professor Baum [is] not qualified to lecture Chinese people on patriotism."

As soon as the *Post* story hit the street, my phone began ringing off the hook. To avoid the developing media maelstrom, I packed myself and my two houseguests off to Hong Kong's Ocean Park for the day. When we returned in the early evening, the phone was still ringing. A *Post* staff writer called to tell me that Chu was going to phone me with an apology and wanted to take me to dinner at the Foreign Correspondents Club. "Will you accept the invitation?" he asked. "That will depend on Mr. Chu's apology," I replied.

A little while later Chu called to tell me that he was sorry for "being rude." I replied that it wasn't his rudeness that bothered me so much as his attempt to have me sacked. "Well," he responded, changing the subject, "Professor Hamlett has already accepted my apology and is having dinner with me. Will you join us?" I thought about it for a moment and then declined the invitation, wondering why he had bothered making such a casual, wrong-footed apology.

On August 6 the *Post* ran a follow-on article about the incident, written by Gren Manuel and titled "I'm Sorry, I'm Sorry, I'm Sorry, Chu Tells Academics," which included a more elaborate apology from Chu:

> The provisional legislator who sparked a row over academic freedom offered surprise apologies last night to the two professors he had previously blasted as unfit to receive public funding.
>
> "I just got too engrossed in the arguments," David Chu Yu-lin said. . . .
>
> "He is very, very senior," Mr. Chu said [of Professor Baum]. "We may not agree with him but we should be courteous. He is a visitor, he is an eminent scholar and I was quite rude to him". . . .
>
> Mr. Chu said his conduct was not in keeping with the Chinese tradition of respect.

WHY HAD HE backed down so quickly and so publicly? I wondered. The answer came a few days later, when I ran into a journalist friend at a local watering hole in Lan Kwai Fong, the entertainment district favored by members of Hong Kong's expat community. According to my friend's sources in China, Beijing had sharply reprimanded Chu after the first *Post* article appeared in print, blistering him for recklessly stirring up anti-China feelings at a time when the Chinese government was trying to avoid ruffling feathers in Hong Kong.

Whatever the reason, Chu and other local pro-China politicians immediately ceased campaigning for the inclusion of patriotic education in

Hong Kong's public schools. Since then, the Chinese government has carefully avoided the appearance of violating its pledge of noninterference in
Hong Kong's internal affairs. As for Chu, he gave up his Legislative Council seat in 2004 after reportedly being urged to withdraw from his reelection bid by leaders of his own party, the pro-China Hong Kong Progressive
Alliance, who evidently deemed him unelectable.

Although Chris Patten lost his battle to democratize Hong Kong's
Legislative Council, his legacy nonetheless proved enduring. For one
thing, pro-democratic parties won a resounding victory in the first post-
handover Legco elections, held in May 1998, winning two-thirds of the
contested seats. Equally important, Patten helped to instill in the people of
Hong Kong a new sense of civic activism. This was vividly demonstrated
in July 2003, when a massive protest march by half a million Hong Kong
people forced the government of Chief Executive Tung Chee-hwa to post-
pone indefinitely the adoption of a draconian new antisubversion law. The
proposed law would have given the government broad authority to ban
any group that advocated independence for Taiwan or Tibet, or that maintained contact with any foreign political organization. Six months later,
in a second major show of popular defiance against Mr. Tung, 100,000
Hong Kong people demonstrated in support of an accelerated timetable
for introducing full universal suffrage in the selection of both Legco and
the chief executive. With Tung's popularity at an all-time low, Beijing pressured him in 2005 to resign from office. His nondemocratically selected
successor, former chief administrative secretary Donald Tsang, promised
to introduce full universal suffrage no later than 2017. Patten may have lost
the battle, but arguably he won the larger war.

Before leaving Hong Kong at the end of August 1997, I had the good
fortune to reconnect with Han Dongfang, the Beijing labor organizer, at a
social gathering. Han had spent two years in prison since our first meeting
in Tiananmen Square in May 1989. While detained, he contracted tuber-
culosis and had a lung surgically removed. In 1991 he was given a medical
parole and permitted to go the United States for additional treatment. A
few years later, following an unsuccessful attempt to reenter China (he was
turned back at the border), Han settled in Hong Kong, where he founded
the China Labour Bulletin, an NGO dedicated to promoting the rights of
Mainland Chinese industrial workers. He also hosted a weekly radio show
on labor relations for Radio Free Asia, reaching an estimated audience of
forty million people in South China. In the course of our conversation,

I was impressed by Han's strength of character—his gentle manner, his quiet dignity, and his selfless determination to improve the lot of China's workers. I made a mental note to stay in touch with this charismatic young man. In a different sort of China, he would be a natural leader.

LEGEND HAS IT that the emperor Napoleon once said of China, "There lies a sleeping giant. Let it sleep, for when it wakes it will shake the world." As the 1990s came to an end, the slumbering giant's first significant stirrings were being felt across the globe. On the other side of the Pacific, in Washington, D.C., an awakening China was causing some politicians and strategic analysts to question the benign implications of China's rapid rise. And in the run-up to the U.S. presidential election of 2000, the foreign policy brain trust of the Republican Party candidate, George W. Bush, appeared to veer sharply away from the traditional U.S. policy of "constructive engagement" toward a more confrontational approach that specifically identified China as a "strategic competitor." Coming on the heels of China's angry reaction to the Belgrade embassy bombing, such a clear rhetorical shift appeared to augur poorly for the future tranquility of U.S.-China relations.

10

God in the Machine

IN ADDITION TO fueling a rising tide of nationalism, China's accelerated economic growth in the 1990s also ushered in the new Information
Age. At the beginning of the decade there had been fewer than 7 million
private, fixed-line telephone subscribers in all of China, with an additional
200,000 mobile phone users. By decade's end, those numbers had jumped
to 145 million and 78 million, respectively. By the same token, at the time
of Deng's southern tour in 1992, China had only six electronic mail systems, each with a maximum capacity of 3,000 e-mailboxes and no online
data services. By 2000 the number of Internet users in China had jumped
from a few thousand to more than 10 million.

The first major breakthrough in China's information revolution came
with the arrival of telephone-based facsimile machines in the early 1980s.
By the time student protests broke out in Beijing in the spring of 1989,
fax machines had been installed at most university campuses and research
institutes and were being used by media-savvy young dissidents in China
and abroad to circumvent government censorship of the conventional
media. Western journalists referred to this phenomenon as "seeking truth
from fax"—a mocking wordplay on the popular slogan "seek truth from
facts" (*shishi qiushi*), originally authored by Mao Zedong and later appropriated by Deng Xiaoping.

But it was not until the late 1990s that the immense power of the new
electronic media to mobilize and amplify the vox populi became apparent
in China. Two incidents occurring a month apart in the spring of 1999
clearly demonstrated that power. In April mobile phones and Internet

bulletin boards (BBS) were used to rally upwards of ten thousand supporters of the quasi-religious organization Falun Gong for a massive sit-in at Zhongnanhai, protesting the Chinese government's labeling of the group as a "fraudulent cult." Visibly shaken by the sudden appearance of so many dissenting citizens, the government soon launched an intensive crackdown on the Falun Gong. A short time later, in the aftermath of the May 1999 Belgrade embassy bombing, youthful Chinese netizens, using chat rooms and electronic message boards as well as cell phones, mobilized tens of thousands of anti-American demonstrators in Beijing and elsewhere. After initially encouraging the highly emotional demonstrations, the government ended up calling for restraint in order to prevent an ugly situation from getting out of hand. Since those two incidents, the Chinese government has devoted a substantial amount of money and manpower to monitoring and regulating the content of the new electronic media. The results have been mixed: On at least three occasions since 2002, techno-geeks affiliated with the outlawed Falun Gong have thumbed their noses at the Chinese authorities, using radio signals to successfully hijack satellite-TV transmissions beamed into China.

MY INITIAL EXPOSURE to the world of Chinese information technology came in 1978, when I escorted the first U.S. National Academy of Engineering delegation on a visit to China. At that time, China's computer industry was in its infancy. The very first homegrown Chinese data-processing machines were bulky vacuum-tube models, copied from Soviet prototypes procured in the 1950s. They were slow and cumbersome, generating paper-tape output. At several research facilities I visited in 1978, these massive, clattering mainframe machines were still in service, programmed to greet visitors with an electronic rendition of "The East is Red," China's national anthem. It was rather amusing to be serenaded by a room-size automaton, but it wasn't clear at that point just what other, more practical uses these superannuated behemoths were being put to.

In the late '70s the technological leap from vacuum tubes to transistors, and thence to integrated circuits, stimulated the development of smaller, faster, more powerful computers. By the early 1980s a microcomputer boom was under way in China, coinciding with the introduction of Deng's economic reforms and open policy. By the end of 1983 there were an estimated ten thousand computers in use throughout the country, mainly for data processing and for controlling programmable precision machine tools in the defense industry. Over the next three years China's computer inventory jumped tenfold, largely as a result of a $200 million loan from the World Bank, which financed the import of tens of thousands of desktop personal computers from the West and Japan. By that time, China's domestic research-and-development institutions had mastered the art of reverse engineering, and the country was producing large numbers of low-cost knock-offs of the imported PCs. The most popular Chinese-made PC in the early 1980s was a clone of the 8-bit Apple II; by the mid-'80s the Apple had been replaced by the 16-bit IBM-PC as the Chinese technology pirate's design of choice.

The vast majority of Chinese computers in the 1980s were stand-alone machines that could not be networked with other computers. The very first LANs (local area networks), involving a dozen or more hardwired computer terminals, were approved for use in China's national airline reservation system in 1985. By 1987 multi-terminal LANs had been installed in a few tourist hotels in Beijing, to process room reservations, guest registration, and billing. By the end of the '80s, several universities had installed multiuser LANs for instructional purposes in specially equipped computer laboratories. However, when I visited the computer labs at Tsinghua and Beida in 1988, most of the locally networked machines were being used by male undergraduates to play computer games such as Space Invaders and Flight Simulator, rather than for data analysis.

The primitive state of Chinese telecommunication services was one important factor contributing to the slow growth of computer networking in the 1980s. In 1985 China had fewer than one fixed-line telephone for every two hundred people. The paucity of residential phone lines was compounded by poor public telecom facilities and low-quality telephone circuitry, which greatly reduced the ability of computers to "speak" to one another and thus restricted the use of modems in electronic data transfers. In the absence of reliable modem connections, the physical transport of data from one computer to another, via hand-carried floppy disks, remained the networker's technology of choice throughout the 1980s.

By the mid-'80s I had become an enthusiastic convert to the new religion of personal computing, and I was eager to explore the research possibilities of this electronic deus ex machina. Although the Internet was still in its infancy and telephone modem connections remained painfully slow, with data transfer speeds only slightly faster than the average office typist, the commercial availability of electronic databases such as Dialog and

Lexis/Nexis made it possible, at least in theory, to access an entire universe of information from the comfort of one's home or office. Unable to resist the lure of this new electronic deity, I eagerly jumped into the unknown world of Internet-based research.

It proved to be a disaster. Invited in 1985 to write an article for *Asian Survey* on recent developments in Chinese elite politics, I opened an account with the Palo Alto–based Dialog Information Services. In those days, noninstitutional subscribers had to pay stiff user fees to access Dialog, including per-minute connection charges plus surcharges for each hit generated by an online search. With data transfer speeds averaging only 1200 bits per second (1.2 Kbps), it could take several minutes to download a single journal article. If one hoped to cut down on wasted time and money, one's search strategy had to be carefully planned out in advance.

Because my article would focus on the impact of a series of high-level leadership changes in the CCP in 1985, I entered the following Boolean search terms into my trusty Kaypro II portable computer: "China *and* Party *and* leaders *and* Commun* *and* 1985" (the asterisk was a wild-card search term that would yield references to both "Communist" and "Communism"). Dialog accepted my input and spent precious minutes sifting through its various databases, consisting of hundreds of newspapers, magazines, and wire services, both foreign and domestic.

Suddenly the tiny screen on my Kaypro II lit up like a Las Vegas slot machine. I had expected my search to yield maybe 10 or 12 useful hits, since 1985 had been a pretty active year for CCP personnel changes. But I was not prepared for the avalanche of data that followed. Dialog informed me that my search had generated 287 hits, each one containing all five of my search terms. I was thrilled—a veritable gold mine of information was at hand. When Dialog asked me if I wanted to display the results in abbreviated bibliographic form or download the full text of all articles, I went for the full monty—a complete data dump.

Bad choice. As soon as the first article began to display on my screen, line by slow, agonizing line, I realized I had made a huge mistake. The item was from the society pages of the *Cincinnati Enquirer*. It detailed a lavish dinner *party* thrown in the spring of *1985* by a local *community leader* who served her guests using an exquisite set of Royal Albert *china*. I was in big trouble. I tried to terminate the data dump, but it was irreversible. The meter continued to tick as page after page of irrelevant text spilled onto my monitor with agonizing slowness. Of the 287 articles I downloaded that day—a process that took more than five hours—only 8 were relevant to my research. For those 8 good hits (plus 279 bad ones), I was charged $363, not a trivial price tag for an elementary lesson in my electronic church's golden rule: "Garbage in; garbage out." I did, however, learn a great deal about the manners and mores of high society in the great American Midwest!

UNDETERRED BY THIS early mishap, I continued to pursue my interest in the Internet as a tool for researching Chinese politics. In the early 1990s this interest led me to try something new and different. By then, e-mail was gaining popularity as a medium of communication among scholars. Within the university community Bitnet was the most popular network for connecting to the Internet. For those who traveled frequently or lacked a university-based Internet service provider (ISP), commercial services such as CompuServe offered dial-up modem access to the Internet in hundreds of U.S. cities and more than a dozen foreign countries.

In the winter of 1994 I moved to Yokohama, Japan, to direct a semester-long UC Education Abroad Program curriculum on peace and development studies at Meiji Gakuin University. Because all electronic communications in Japan were controlled by the government's telecom monopoly, Nippon Hōsō Kyōkai (NHK), Internet access was extremely expensive, and my CompuServe subscription was costing me a small fortune, more than $250 each month, in connection charges. Since I was in more or less regular e-mail contact with a number of other China scholars in various countries, I decided to economize on my online connection charges by periodically sending group e-mails on subjects relating to Chinese politics. My monthly telecom bills quickly dropped by 70 percent.

By the time I returned to Los Angeles in the late summer of 1994, there were twenty-one China watchers on my group e-mail list; by March 1995 the list had grown to thirty-one, including a handful of international journalists residing in China. At that point I decided to set up a dedicated online special interest group, or SIG, for specialists working on contemporary Chinese politics. The idea was to create an interactive electronic forum where scholars, journalists, diplomats, and other China experts could exchange information, ideas, and insights about current events and developments. I sent out a request to each of the thirty-one people on my group e-mail list, inviting them to take part in the new forum and asking them to provide the names and addresses of other China watchers who might be interested in participating. Needing an eight-letter alias for the group in order to conform to the standard DOS file-naming protocol, I called the group "Chinapol." Here is the letter I sent out:

Date: Wed, 15 Mar 95 08:45:00 PST
Subject: creating a Chinese politics forum

Dear friends and colleagues:

I would like to establish an on-line e-mail forum to facilitate rapid, informal communication among Internet-linked specialists in contemporary Chinese politics, economics, and related fields. Insofar as my personal list of e-mail addresses is rather limited, I would like to invite you to help me expand my mailing list. For the moment, I would like to limit the group (which I have called "Chinapol") to academics, Government analysts, and journalists who specialize in contemporary Chinese affairs. It may also be possible later to add a few advanced graduate students, people in the private sector, and others on an individual basis. . . .

The response was immediate and enthusiastic. By the end of 1995 more than 100 people had joined the group. Thereafter, membership in Chinapol grew slowly, leveling off at around 130 by 1999. Because a recipient list of that size was extremely awkward to manage, in the fall of that year I converted Chinapol to a private Web-based listserv, hosted by the UCLA International Institute. With the help of Richard Gunde, assistant director of UCLA's Center for Chinese Studies, I established a formal set of membership criteria as well as rules and regulations governing group communication and conduct. Membership quickly surged, passing the 200 mark by January 2001. In 2002 I added a fully searchable data archive, making it possible for subscribers to retrieve past postings from our restricted Web site by date, sender, or keyword. Membership continued to grow dramatically, as indicated in the following table:

DATE	MEMBERS
March 1995	31
March 1997	121
August 1999	136
January 2001	219
April 2003	431
August 2005	620
January 2007	743
September 2008	902

By the fall of 2008 Chinapol had more than 900 subscribers in twenty-five countries throughout the Americas, Europe, Asia, and Australasia, counting among its members 397 scholars, 262 journalists, 98 NGO and think tank analysts, 96 diplomats and government analysts, plus a scattering of independent consultants, international lawyers, and others.

FOR MORE THAN a decade Chinapol has been the primary information network linking the growing global community of China watchers. With its large multinational, multiprofessional, and multidisciplinary membership base, and its ethos of open information sharing and candid discussion of controversial issues, Chinapol has gained a unique reputation for promoting intellectual synergy, cross-fertilization, and critical analysis. Scholars in their offices can instantly communicate with colleagues in the field; journalists can gather background material and conduct timely interviews on breaking stories; diplomats and policy analysts can access expert opinion on issues affecting foreign policy decisions. Information about fast-breaking news stories—such as the March 2008 Tibetan unrest and subsequent Sichuan earthquake disaster—has often been made available first on Chinapol, forming the basis for timely reporting and analysis in the international media.

Chinapol has also, on occasion, contributed to the promotion of human rights in China. One such case involved a petition drive initiated by list members to protest the incarceration of a Chinese American research scholar, Song Yongyi. Song had been arrested in China in January 2000 while collecting research materials on the Cultural Revolution. He was charged with violating PRC "state secrets" laws, a vaguely defined but potentially serious criminal offense. Partly as a result of the Chinapol petition campaign and the attendant media publicity generated by group members, Song Yongyi was freed from captivity. Shortly after his release, he addressed an open letter to Chinapol:

> With tears in my eyes, I read the petition letter in support of me signed by you and 150 other distinguished senior scholars and colleagues. Some of them I know personally, others I don't, but you all came to my aid in times of crisis. . . .
>
> Without your petition letter, without the rescue efforts by . . . friends from all over the world, my academic career would have ended in a dark jail cell.
>
> No words in any dictionary can adequately express my gratitude. I will therefore give you a simple yet most sincere "Thank you!" from the bottom of my heart.

On another occasion, in October 2006, Chinese border guards in Tibet shot and killed two young Tibetan civilians who were attempting, along with a dozen or so others, to leave China on foot across a snow-covered Himalayan mountain pass. The Chinese government initially claimed that the Tibetans had attacked the guards, who had then fired in self-defense. But videotape footage taken by a member of a nearby Romanian mountain climbing expedition clearly showed that the two Tibetans had been shot at a distance by military snipers as the group peacefully trekked single file through the snow. A Chinapol member posted the video to the group within twenty-four hours, thereby alerting more than two hundred journalists to the story. The resulting storm of adverse international publicity forced the Chinese government to retract its claim of self-defense.

While the vast majority of Chinapol discussions focus on issues of immediate political or diplomatic concern, every so often a conversation will jump the tracks and become, well, downright surreal. Not long ago, a disagreement arose among several group members on the question of exactly what had—and had not—been decided during World War II at major Allied conferences held in Cairo, Potsdam, and Yalta with respect to the legal status of Taiwan. The conversation began innocently enough, when one member asserted that Taiwan had been recognized as an "inalienable part of China" at the Yalta Conference of March 1945. Then the fun began. (Be advised: The people quoted below are eminent China specialists; names have been withheld to protect their reputations.)

Professor A: By international treaty, at Yalta in March '45, Taiwan was recognized as an inalienable part of China. . . .

Professor B: Yalta did not discuss Taiwan. This was a three-way conference [Roosevelt, Churchill, Stalin] at which Chiang Kai-shek was not present. The Potsdam Declaration (where Chiang was present) said nothing about Taiwan's status. . . .

Journalist C: I am very sure Chiang Kai-shek was *not* in Potsdam, but he signed the Potsdam Declaration "by wire". . . .

Professor D: It does not seem so strange that Taiwan was not taken up in the declarations at Yalta and Potsdam. That was because it had been conclusively settled at the Cairo Conference, with the participation of Chiang Kai-shek.

Professor E: The view that Chiang Kai-shek was not present at Potsdam [has been] raised recently in Taiwan. . . . But the majority are still convinced of his presence there because of the famous photo that included the three leaders—Chiang, Stalin, and Roosevelt. . . . Could that photo have been doctored with the technology of sixty years ago?

Journalist C: The famous picture that you refer to must be the one of the Cairo meeting in 1943 of Roosevelt, Churchill, and Chiang. No Stalin! Chiang never met Stalin. . . . If there is a picture of Chiang and Stalin with Roosevelt in circulation . . . it must be a forgery. . . .

Professor F: And of course Roosevelt was dead by Potsdam.

Professor G: You are right that Chiang was not at Potsdam, and neither were Roosevelt (he was dead) nor Churchill (he lost the election). The meeting you are talking about was Cairo. Chiang was . . . at Cairo.

Professor H: Churchill WAS at Potsdam. The meeting at Potsdam . . . included Truman, Churchill, Stalin and others, but NOT Chiang. . . . [It] ended on 26 July with the Potsdam Declaration, to which Chiang assented by radio. Churchill resigned as British Prime Minister the same day. . . .

Professor I: Thank God none of our students can see how confused we are.

Thank God, indeed!

AS CHINAPOL'S SOLE list owner and moderator, one of my principal responsibilities, aside from vetting new applicants, is to keep the tone of conversation civil, collegial, and on point. With such a large subscriber base of articulate, well-informed people discussing issues that are often quite controversial, it is inevitable that disputes—and tempers—would flare from time to time, and over the years I have devised a system of yellow cards and red cards to deal with serious violations of the group norms.

While it is vital to allow for free expression of different viewpoints and shades of opinion on Chinapol, I strongly discourage partisan advocacy, polemical argumentation, and ad hominem attacks. Consequently, from time to time I run afoul of members who hold strong views about a particular subject (or about another member). At one point in 2003 my efforts to maintain an atmosphere of self-restraint in the midst of an intense debate over the ethics of the Beijing government led a small group of vocal critics of China's human rights policies to split off from Chinapol and form their own online discussion group, which they called Pangolinpol. (For the uninitiated, a pangolin is a large, scaly South African anteater.) Today Pangolinpol is the largest open-membership alternative to Chinapol.

In monitoring the tone and quality of Chinapol traffic, I have at times acted too quickly to terminate a thread (or conversation) that seemed to be veering off course. This happened most memorably in the winter of 2003, when I prematurely closed off debate on the subject of the newly emerging severe acute respiratory syndrome (SARS) epidemic in South China and Hong Kong. At the time, a number of unsubstantiated rumors were flying about in the media concerning the SARS mortality rate and a possible deliberate cover-up of the epidemic by the Chinese government. Hard facts, on the other hand, were extremely hard to come by. Under these circumstances, when the editor of a major East Asian newspaper (a Chinapol member) called for a total quarantine of China, I thought this was going too far, so I pulled the plug on the discussion, forcing it off-line. It was a questionable call on my part. The SARS epidemic turned out to be very serious, and the Chinese government was subsequently shown to have quite deliberately—and quite irresponsibly—suppressed timely disclosure of the rate and extent of infection.

As Chinapol membership increased, and the average flow of e-mail traffic swelled from three or four messages a day to more than thirty, displays of incivility and intolerance inevitably occurred, sometimes leading to the open exchange of epithets. At one point in 2005 a dispute flared among three or four members concerning allegations of paranoia on the part of certain U.S. China scholars. I tried to put an end to the name-calling quietly, through off-line persuasion. When repeated exhortations (and one yellow-card warning) failed to stanch the flow of insults, I posted a stern message to the group: "If you cannot stop yourselves from subjecting others to your personal peeves, polemics, and petty quarrels, I will do it for you. Chinapol is a serious forum for mature professionals, not a sandbox or a fraternity house. From now on I will shoot first and ask questions later."

That seemed to get people's attention, and the bickering soon subsided. For me personally, however, the most distressing incidents have been those in which I have had to red-card members who violated our rules of confidentiality and civility. Fortunately, this has happened only in a handful of cases. The most unpleasant of these involved a rather headstrong Beijing-based American journalist, whose intense views on the subject of the U.S. invasion of Iraq led him to post on Chinapol a blistering critique of George W. Bush's foreign policy. When I reminded him, off-line, that Chinapol was a forum for the discussion of China-related issues, he accused me of trying to suppress criticism of the Bush administration. This led to my issuing a cautionary yellow card, which, unhappily, failed to deter him from continuing his tirade. Finally, after repeated warnings, I red-carded him and removed him from the list. But it didn't end there. He logged on to a popular China-based blogsite, Danwei, where he went public with his complaints:

> Chinapol is not just another chat group; it is a hidden locus of power, influencing what you read in the media, what books teachers choose to teach in the classroom and what actionable advice is

being spoon-fed to Congress and various US agencies that in turn influences US foreign policy. . . .

As for moderator Rick Baum's legendary "discipline," he pokes fun at anyone he chooses, flaunting his status as moderator. . . .

[He] apparently keeps his commentator base happy with a velvet glove approach to US government agencies and right-wing media.

While I confess that I secretly find the idea of Chinapol as a "hidden locus of power" that influences U.S. foreign policy to be rather appealing, alas, it is not so, for Chinapol is nothing more nor less than the sum of its members' views, which range widely across the political and ideological spectrum.

A nonscientific survey conducted at the end of 2007 revealed that by a margin of roughly three to one, Chinapol members tend to be relatively optimistic about China's role as an emerging global power. When members were asked to choose between two op-ed articles, one presenting a positive assessment of recent trends in Chinese diplomatic behavior and the other a more critical assessment emphasizing China's use of its growing military might, 61 percent of the 352 respondents selected the positive article as most closely reflecting their own views, while 21 percent opted for the more pessimistic outlook. Among the 18 percent who abstained, the overwhelming majority volunteered that they could not choose between the two assessments, since each ostensibly reflected important—and more or less equally valid—aspects of China's international behavior. For reasons not entirely clear to me, Chinapol's journalists turned out to be somewhat more skeptical than its academics or diplomats of China's peaceful intentions.

Despite the occasional outburst of righteous indignation from an irate member, and despite periodic grumblings about the steadily increasing volume of Chinapol traffic, the forum functions smoothly most of the time, and many members regard it as an indispensable asset in their professional lives. Perhaps not surprisingly, China's increasingly active Internet police also seem to find it of some interest. I have been reliably informed that the Beijing authorities have been intercepting Chinapol messages flowing into and out of the e-mailboxes of some of our China-based members, who currently number more than 150. And every so often, perhaps as a reminder that Big Brother is (or could be) watching, Chinapol's UCLA administrator and I also receive strangely worded messages from nonexistent Chinapol members, hinting strongly at the presence of outside monitors. On one occasion a Beijing-based Chinapol member told me that a Chinese acquaintance of his, a mid-level government official, had, in the course of a personal conversation, casually revealed the contents of a recent, confidential Chinapol message.

My sense of being under official scrutiny was reinforced in the fall of 2005 when an old friend and Chinapol colleague, John Thomson, and I decided to organize a no-host banquet for our Beijing-based list members. Seventy-four members attended the event, held at the Louwailou Restaurant in Beijing's Chaoyang district, which was, by all accounts, a rousing success. More disconcerting, though, were the comically inept busboy and his walkie-talkie-toting colleague who hovered conspicuously around the edges of our soiree. As I observed their anomalous behavior, it occurred to me that they were almost certainly plainclothes security cops, flesh-and-blood cousins of Jing Jing and Cha Cha, China's anime-inspired cartoon Internet cops whose benign images appear as a pop-up warning to anyone logging onto certain Chinese Internet portals and Web sites. Evidently, the police had known in advance just when and where our banquet would be held. In my role as host for the evening, I invited our two *surveilleurs* to join the festivities, but they sheepishly demurred.

ALTHOUGH JING JING and Cha Cha are cute, cuddly icons, they are merely the visible tip of an enormous surveillance iceberg. Since 2000 the number of Internet users in China has gone up twentyfold, to more than 290 million, with 135 million individual Internet protocol addresses and almost 12 million registered Internet domain names. By the end of 2007 there were 1.5 million China-hosted Web sites. Although blogging is a relatively recent phenomenon, there are currently estimated to be more than 20 million active bloggers in China (up from only 2 million in 2005). On average, one new blog is posted in China *every half second*. By the time you read this, these statistics will already be badly out of date.

In an effort to keep pace with such dramatic growth, the Chinese authorities have hired tens of thousands of Internet police. Since 2001 the Beijing municipal government alone has recruited and trained more than four thousand of these cyber-cops, collectively referred to as Big Mama (*dama*). Police have cracked down heavily on unlicensed Internet cafés, shutting down more than 100,000 nationwide since 2002. And on college campuses around the country, thousands of student monitors—called "little sisters" (*xiaomei*) or "Internet nannies" (*wangbaomu*)—have been

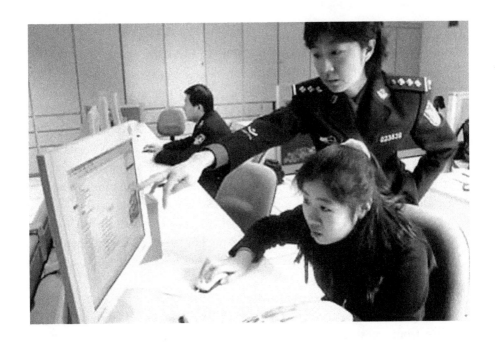

Cyber-police in Xicheng District, Beijing, scrutinize Internet Web sites for inappropriate content as part of a nationwide "Civilized Web" campaign, April 2006. In less than two weeks, almost two million "unhealthy" Web postings and photos were deleted from fourteen Chinese Internet portals, while six hundred Internet forums and chat rooms were shut down. Photo from Yesky.com.

hired to scrutinize postings in chat rooms, on bulletin boards, and at blogsites, to remind users to observe self-restraint in pursuit of the government's goal of creating a "civilized Web." When such local self-policing proves ineffective, the "little sisters" are expected to report offenders to local Internet cops. In addition, powerful software filters (some of them provided by Western suppliers such as Cisco Systems) have been installed by Chinese Web hosts and Internet portals to screen out undesirable ideas and even individual words. The government's extensive "nanny list" of proscribed phrases includes terms such as "Tiananmen incident," "June 4," "Dalai Lama," "Fang Lizhi," and "Chen Shui-bian." And many foreign news media periodically find their Web sites blocked in China, including the BBC and the *New York Times*.

In addition to routine self-monitoring, filtering, and police surveillance—which in one two-week period in the spring of 2006 resulted in the shutdown of six hundred Web forums and the removal of two million "unhealthy" (mostly pornographic) postings from fourteen Chinese Web portals—the authorities have periodically resorted to more heavy-handed tactics, sometimes referred to as "killing a chicken to scare the monkeys," to punish a few (and thereby deter many more) tech-savvy political dissidents who devise evasive techniques such as the use of proxy servers and encoded messages to circumvent the legendary Great Firewall of China.

Netizens who continue to openly criticize the CCP online can expect to receive the same type of treatment accorded the notorious Chinese blogger Liu Di. Better known by her pseudonym Stainless Steel Mouse, Liu was taken into police custody in 2002 and held for more than a year without formal charges being filed. Early in 2008 the human rights group Reporters without Borders noted that more than fifty Chinese cyber-dissidents remained under criminal detention.

Still, despite the use of Internet cops, "little sisters," and high-speed filtering technology, given the staggering (and ever increasing) volume of electronic messages flying into, out of, and around China at any given moment, total censorship and/or content control of the Internet is becoming increasingly impractical. When you add to this the extraordinary propagative capacity of the newest mass electronic medium to hit China, mobile phone–based text-messaging service, the task becomes virtually impossible. According to industry sources, there are currently more than 32 *billion* text messages being sent in China each month, an average of well over 700,000 per minute.

The aptly named "nail-house incident" of March 2007 provides a good illustration of the power of the new electronic media to thwart governmental intent. In this fascinating case, a middle-aged Chongqing couple, whose home was being forcibly appropriated by the municipal authorities to make way for a massive urban redevelopment project, refused to vacate their property without adequate financial compensation. In at least the past decade, such incidents, in which local governments pay only token compensation for seized properties, have become alarmingly widespread and have outraged many, many people. Still, until very recently, such seizures occurred in a virtual media vacuum, with little or no attendant publicity, and generally ended with the police physically removing the recalcitrant occupants. This time, however, something remarkable happened. Enlisting the support of local residents' groups and a generally sympathetic online community of Chinese bloggers and text-messaging cell phone users, the couple parlayed widespread public support, and the acute embarrassment this caused the Chongqing municipal government, into a nationwide media blitz portraying the couple's struggle as a heroic confrontation between citizen David and governmental Goliath. Hundreds of Web forums, chat rooms, and mobile phone networks all over China provided daily updates of the nail-house saga, complete with stunning photos of the small house perched atop a tiny spit of land at the center of a gigantic excavation pit. After *Southern Weekend* and a few other tabloid newspapers picked up the story in mid-March, the nail-house occupants received a generous financial settlement. Later, one popular tabloid newspaper hailed the "awesome nail-house event" as heralding the birth of "true citizen journalism." Such striking successes in mobilizing large numbers of electronically networked individuals to contest the power of the state, once almost inconceivable, have become more commonplace of late.

In some ways, the ongoing contest between China's expanding force of citizen techno-geeks and the state's equally dedicated army of authoritarian cyber-censors resembles a strategic arms race, in which one side's advances in techniques of evasion and deception spur the other side to develop new modes of deterrence and detection, and vice versa. With China's information wars continuing to ratchet ever upward, no clear winner is in sight. Yet there is mounting evidence to suggest that an expanding, increasingly noisy and contentious universe of instant electronic communications is subtly but irrevocably changing the nature of the Chinese government's calculus of political consent. This is true not merely because the rising flow of unfettered information is relentlessly eroding the dikes of Communist Party censorship but also because a more informed, attentive citizenry has begun to demand greater transparency, openness, and accountability in governance. Such long-term developments, though often difficult to detect in day-to-day experience, are worthy of close attention, for they will surely play an important role in shaping the future of the Chinese Communist party-state.

11

The Wild, Wild West

IN MY ROLE as Chinapol list moderator, I regularly scan various China-related Web sites, blogs, and listservs in search of useful information. In the early summer of 2001, I came across an intriguing advertisement posted on a popular e-mail discussion group for teachers of Asian history. Headed "English Teaching in the PRC," the ad was posted by an expat American, Kevin Stuart, who ran the highly regarded English Teaching Program (ETP) in Xining, capital of Qinghai in Northwest China. He was seeking summer volunteers to teach conversational English to ethnic-minority youngsters in a small rural township on the Tibetan Plateau.

Over the years scores of my UCLA students had taken two-week sightseeing trips to China, which generally included stops in Beijing, Shanghai, and Xi'an, and possibly one or two other major tourist destinations. The more serious students took six- or ten-week summer Chinese-language classes in Beijing or Shanghai, and a stalwart few enrolled in semester- or year-long language immersion programs at major Chinese universities. But only a small handful had ever experienced China's deep rural interior, and none at all had ever lived or worked among the impoverished, non-Han ethnic-minority peoples of the vast Northwest.

I reread the advertisement a few times. I was intrigued. Although Kevin was soliciting individual volunteers, it occurred to me that I might be able to recruit a substantial group of UCLA students. I was heading out to China in a few weeks anyway, so I decided to add Xining to my itinerary. I sent him an e-mail informing him of my arrival date.

RINGED ON THREE sides by the Tibetan Highlands, Qinghai, with an area slightly bigger than the state of Texas, is China's fourth-largest province (after Xinjiang, Tibet, and Inner Mongolia). Its capital city, Xining, lies near a confluence of medieval Silk Road routes at an altitude of 7,300 feet, near the meandering Yellow River. It is the largest city in the Amdo region of Greater Tibet, which came under Chinese control with the PLA's occupation of Tibet in 1950.

On Qinghai's northern plateau, at an altitude of 10,500 feet, lies the country's largest saltwater lake, Koko Nor. In the precipitous mountain gorges of the province's southern half are the headwaters of three of Asia's mightiest rivers: the Yangzi, the Yellow, and the Mekong. For this reason, many place-names in Qinghai contain the words *sanchuan*, meaning "three rivers."

Though impressive in size, Qinghai has a total population of only five million, slightly more than half of whom (54 percent) are Han. The remaining 46 percent comprise a variety of minority ethnic groups, including Tibetan, Hui, Salar, Mangghuer, and Mongol. In the 1950s and 1960s Qinghai acquired a reputation as China's Siberia, a vast, remote gulag where common criminals and political prisoners were exiled to serve out their sentences doing hard labor. Even today, on some of the roads approaching Xining, the alert traveler can spot road gangs in prison uniform working on suburban construction sites.

I arrived in Xining in late July 2001, at the height of the warm, dry Amdo summer. Not knowing what to expect, I was met at the airport by one of Kevin's students, a Tibetan youth named Xire Jiancuo. Xire, known to his teachers and classmates as Gregory, spoke clear, semifluent English. His brother owned a car, a Volkswagen Golf sedan, which was something of a rarity in this part of China. The three of us drove off to see Kevin.

Kevin's apartment in downtown Xining was a beehive of activity. Half a dozen teenage Tibetan youths were clustered around two desktop PCs in his living room, surfing the Web. A handful of others were in the bedroom, doing homework. All had come to Xining from widely separated villages in and around the Tibetan Plateau to study in Kevin's English program. All spoke intelligible, if imperfect English.

After offering me a strange-looking (and even stranger-smelling) brew consisting of caterpillar fungus and snow-lily buds immersed in a potent local highland barley liquor, Kevin talked about his program. A bearded giant of a man whose ample girth and scruffy appearance masked a gentle,

Kevin Stuart with Tibetan students in Xining, July 2001. Kevin's apartment was a beehive of activity for young Tibetans studying English and applying for community development grants on the Internet.

sensitive nature, he looked more like a southern Appalachian moonshiner than a dedicated educator. As he spoke, his students hovered around me, refreshing my drink from a large decanter. Glancing nervously at the unappetizing collection of flora lying at the bottom of the decanter (or were they fauna?), I silently prayed that none would find their way into my digestive tract.

Kevin had come to China in the mid-1980s to work as an English teacher with the United Nations Development Program in Inner Mongolia. Later he moved to Xining, where he started the English Teaching Program at Qinghai Teacher's College. By the late 1990s he was using the Internet to organize a social network of high school English teachers throughout the Amdo region, putting them in touch with one another and with international educators and philanthropic groups around the world. The advertisement he placed on the history teachers' listserv in the summer of 2001 was part of that outreach effort. It had been posted on behalf of a dynamic young rural Qinghai educator and community leader, Zhu Yongzhong.

Zhu Yongzhong teaches middle school and directs an English-language summer program for Mangghuer youngsters in Guanting township, about six hours (by rickety country bus) southeast of Xining. Mangghuers are an endangered ethnic minority with a total population of about 200,000, living in a handful of enclaves in Qinghai and Gansu. Of Mongol origin, they combine elements of Tibetan Yellow Hat (Gelugpa) Buddhism with various indigenous religious traditions, including shamanism and Daoism. Their language is primarily an archaic Mongol dialect. Rich in mythology and folklore, Mangghuer culture has been preserved in the modern era through a variety of seasonal festivals, shamanistic rituals, and elaborate traditions of singing, dancing, and storytelling. Over time, however, the five subgroups of Mangghuers, living in relative isolation from one another, have begun to absorb the cultural influences of their dominant neighbors, the Han, to the point that their long-term survival as a distinct culture has become problematic.

Zhu Yongzhong is a Mangghuer and has devoted his life to the advancement of the Mangghuer community and culture. In seeking to recruit native English speakers to teach in his summer program, Zhu's objective was to raise the educational standards of the Mangghuer and other ethnic-minority youngsters, giving them a level playing field on which to compete with the dominant Han. In Zhu's view, only by learning English could the minority children of Amdo gain sufficient traction in an increasingly globalized educational and economic marketplace, thus ensuring their competitiveness—and their ultimate cultural survival. It was a high-stakes gamble, and one the Mangghuers could ill afford to lose.

When I told Kevin that I might be able to bring a group of UCLA students to teach in Zhu's English program the following summer, he immediately suggested that I visit Guanting to observe the program firsthand, and he asked Gregory and his brother to escort me.

After a harrowing all-day journey in our VW Golf on narrow, potholed country roads, we reached Guanting. Located below a bend in the Yellow River, Guanting is a dusty backwater town of approximately two thousand residents, with one paved road and few modern amenities. There I met Zhu, who guided me on a tour of the local school facilities and introduced me to three foreign volunteers who, like me, had responded to Kevin's Internet advertisement. They had come to Guanting at their own expense from

Brooklyn, Hong Kong, and New Zealand. None was a professional English teacher, but all were eager to contribute. I arrived just as they were about to conclude their intensive two-week English-conversation classes. I sat in on the last two classes, held at Yongzhong's local headquarters, the Sanchuan Cultural Center, and was immediately impressed by the dedication of the teachers and by the intelligence and enthusiasm of their young charges. The closing ceremony that followed was an intercultural lovefest, featuring two hours of emotion-charged singing, dancing, skits, and speechifying. As I watched the forty excited, well-scrubbed Mangghuer youngsters, age twelve to seventeen, grinning proudly as they received their certificates of achievement, accompanied by their even prouder parents, I decided on the spot that I would be back the next year, come hell or high water.

After an overnight stay at Guanting's only hotel—a rundown, no-star inn with leaky plumbing, rock-hard beds, chipped plaster, cracked windowpanes, and no hot water in the guest rooms (the only available shower was in an outbuilding across an unpaved courtyard)—I set out with Zhu Yongzhong the next morning. We toured several local poverty-alleviation projects that he and his local community support group, the Sanchuan Development Association (SDA), had initiated in the area. Working with Kevin Stuart and his corps of English-speaking Tibetan students in Xining, members of the SDA had learned to surf the Internet in search of community development grants offered by international NGOs, philanthropic organizations, and foreign embassies in Beijing. By the time of my arrival in the summer of 2001 they had secured funding for more than two dozen projects throughout the greater Guanting area, including schoolhouses, greenhouses, wells, cisterns, and indoor latrines. They had also purchased hundreds of solar cookers—portable parabolic reflectors used to concentrate sunlight for heating water—for local residents, an extremely useful energy source in this severely deforested, fuel-scarce part of China. The SDA's good works represented an impressive synergy between local entrepreneurship and global networking via the Worldwide Web.

EN ROUTE FROM Guanting back to Xining, I accompanied Gregory and his brother on a memorable four-day journey to a number of remote townships, villages, mosques, and monasteries along the mountainous borders of the Tibetan steppe, where the Yellow River meanders between Qinghai and Gansu, carving out spectacular canyons and chasms in the rocky terrain of the Qilian Mountains. Our first destination was the famous Camel

Spring in Xunhua County, where the first Islamic travelers from Samarkand, forebears of today's Salars, settled in the thirteenth century. Legend has it that a rare white camel brought by these Central Asian nomads disappeared one night while they camped. The next day the camel was found near a spring, having been turned into stone, which the travelers took as a sign from God that this was an auspicious place to settle. The spring is still there, in the shape of a stone camel's head, though we had to crane our necks to view it over a locked gate. Today, there are fewer than 100,000 Salars remaining in China, with the largest concentration centered in Xunhua. Like the Mangghuers, the survival of the Salars as a distinctive ethnic community is very much in doubt. And like so many other places of religious worship in China, Xunhua's exquisitely designed, pagoda-style Camel Spring Mosque was completely destroyed by Red Guards in the Cultural Revolution; it was still under renovation at the time of our visit.

After an overnight stay in Xunhua, we set out to visit Tibetan Buddhist monasteries at Kumbum, Wutong, Longwu, and Wendu (the original home of the last Panchen Lama, who died in 1989). Today there are approximately 750,000 Tibetans living in Qinghai, the largest concentration anywhere outside of Tibet proper. Far off the beaten track, these oases of traditional Tibetan religion and culture are home to an ethnic minority that harbors deep distrust of the Chinese government and an intense reverence for the exiled Dalai Lama, whose photo was proudly (but surreptitiously) displayed everywhere we went. When anti-Chinese protests erupted throughout the Tibetan Plateau in March 2008, Qinghai's Buddhist communities were among the most active participants.

I received a bit of a surprise when we visited Gregory's hometown of Tongren (also known by its Tibetan name, Rebkong) for an overnight stay with his family. There I met the local Communist Party branch secretary, a Tibetan, who was presiding over the renovation of the village's Buddhist shrine. Like so many other places of worship, the shrine had been destroyed by Red Guards during the Cultural Revolution. Working with the SDA and its network of international donors, Gregory had raised sufficient funds to finance the shrine's renovation.

Over a cup of yak-butter tea (a dietary staple in northwest China), I chatted with the Party secretary. While we talked, I noticed that he was continuously fingering a string of Buddhist prayer beads. Since Communist Party members are required to renounce all religious belief as a condition of membership, I asked Gregory about this. He laughed and said that *all* local officials in this area were devout Buddhists. "If the Party wants atheists," he said, "they'll have to import them."

Like most poor rural hamlets on the Tibetan Plateau, Gregory's village had no indoor plumbing or other sanitary facilities. His family's home, more spacious and well appointed than most, was a traditional Tibetan U-shaped wooden courtyard structure, surrounded by an earthen wall fashioned from the local clay-like loess. An open compost pit in the garden at the back of the house, set against the outer wall, served as the family latrine. Running water was limited to a single cold-water tap in the court-yard. But on the roof, conspicuously displayed like some otherworldly totemic icon, was a *satellite dish*. At night Gregory's family would gather in front of their color TV to watch an eclectic mix of international program-ming—a Chinese variety show, a South Korean soap opera, a Hong Kong kung fu movie, and an American detective drama. The incongruity was striking. There I was, in an isolated rustic hamlet high up on the Tibetan Plateau, watching Detectives Dave Starsky and "Hutch" Hutchinson, their voices dubbed into Chinese, chase crooks across the metropolitan Bay City landscape. It boggled the mind.

More mind-boggling still was the journey we took the following day. After sharing with Gregory's family a traditional Tibetan breakfast of yak-butter tea, steamed bread, and *tsampa*—a thick, barley-based gruel mixed with yak butter and sugar—Gregory, his brother, and I said our good-byes and drove for a couple of hours to a dusty, nondescript town at the foot of a very steep mountain. There we parked our VW sedan and rented an ancient four-wheel-drive jeep for the two-hour ascent to our final destina-tion, Khaser village, a tiny Tibetan hamlet nestled high up in a remote mountain pass at an altitude of twelve thousand feet.

Without functioning shock absorbers to cushion the ride, our teeth, bones, and joints rattled continuously as the jeep climbed slowly upward along the unpaved, rock-strewn road, which was little more than a goat path. We crossed several streams, twice getting stuck in deep mud. About half an hour into the ascent, my back was aching badly and I was get-ting quite carsick. I begged Gregory to turn around and go back. He just laughed and said that it wasn't possible to do that, as the village chief was expecting us for dinner. So I closed my eyes, gritted my teeth, and aspired to stay alive long enough to see one more sunrise.

When we finally reached our destination, I was glad we hadn't turned back. The vista was stunning—a scene straight out of James Hilton's *Shan-*

Breakfast with Gregory's family consisted of yak-butter tea, *tsampa*, and steamed bread, Tongren, July 2001. From left: Gregory's father, the author, village Party secretary, and Gregory's brother.

gri-la. Jagged, snowcapped peaks on all sides surrounded a small hamlet at the edge of a lush green meadow, on the other side of which a family of yak grazed contentedly. It was spectacular. The village chief (who was a relative of one of Gregory's schoolmates) came out to greet us, motioning us toward a large, open tent that had been erected for the occasion in the center of the meadow. As soon as we sat down on wooden stools arranged around a long U-shaped table, we were served bowls of yak-butter tea, followed by glasses of *baijiu* (pronounced "bye joe"), an extremely potent, colorless barley-based liquor related to Maotai. The altitude evidently enhanced the alcohol's potency, for after the first few toasts the mountains seemed to be spinning around us.

There were more than twenty people under the tent—the chief's extended family and friends—and after we finished toasting, the main course was wheeled in, quite literally: an entire lamb, slaughtered, sliced open lengthwise, and slow roasted on a huge spit in honor of our visit. (I later learned that only a small handful of foreigners had ever visited Khaser village, and that Gregory's schoolmate had boasted to the village chief that I was an "important American professor.")

At twelve thousand feet the temperature drops rapidly when the sun begins to set, and I readily accepted the chief's offer of an oversized yak-skin coat for warmth. The mutton was amazingly good, and it kept coming, along with wheel after wheel of the best steamed bread I've ever tasted, made from fermented *maida*, a fine wheat flour used extensively throughout Southwest Asia. It was a feast fit for king, yet I felt uneasy, knowing that the people of this village were extremely poor and that the food and drink we were so eagerly consuming represented a substantial investment of village resources.

After dinner, the chief took me to see the new schoolhouse, which was a source of considerable local pride, as it was the first ever built in the village. Funded initially by a small international start-up grant secured by the SDA, the school was only half finished. The village had run out of funds before it could be completed. Suddenly it occurred to me that the evening's lavish fête may not have been entirely spontaneous. Was it perhaps an artful *guanxi* gambit—the unsolicited gift followed by the unstated obligation? *Ni bang wode mang, wo bang nide mang.* Was the 'important American professor' being subtly primed to donate to the school fund?

Unsure what to do, I discreetly checked my wallet and found that I had only two solitary ¥20 notes (less than $5), plus some pocket change. Too embarrassed to donate such a paltry sum, I left without making a contribution. Adding to my discomfort, the chief gave me the entire uneaten half of the lamb as a going-away present. My mortification was now complete. Wrapped in layers of slick, greasy newspaper, the lamb lay heavily across my lap as we bounced, bumped, and lurched our way back down the mountain, each jolt a fresh reminder of my embarrasing breach of etiquette. When we got back to Gregory's house, I happily gave the lamb to his parents, who accepted gratefully. Later, I mailed a check for $100 to the village chief, via Gregory's friend, but for some reason it was never cashed. To this day my guilt remains unassuaged.

At the end of an adventure-filled week in Qinghai, I decided to take advantage of my proximity to the Silk Road in nearby Gansu to visit the town of Dunhuang, site of the famous Mogao Caves of a Thousand Buddhas. Lying at the juncture of the northern and southern Silk Road routes, Dunhuang had, since early in the Christian era, been a major point of contact between China and the outer regions of Tibet, Central Asia, and the Middle East. Within Mogao's 492 individual grottoes, large and small, are housed some of the most extraordinary Buddhist murals, sculptures, and manuscripts of the ancient world. Although time—and Islamic rage—have wrought considerable damage to the iconic contents of the caves, many of the remaining frescoes, sutras, and statues (including a giant, thirty-three-meter bodhisattva in Cave No. 130) are simply stunning. Ostensibly for preservationist reasons (but also conveniently serving the goal of maximizing commercial revenues), local authorities carefully restrict tours of the Mogao caves, marketing them by the numbers. For the basic price of admission, ¥80 (about $10), ordinary tourists are assigned to small groups and permitted to visit just ten caves, selected by local guides. The ten caves designated for my group that day proved mildly disappointing and did not include any of the most famous, most elaborately decorated grottoes, including the so-called Kama Sutra Cave (Cave No. 465), with its fabled erotic art frescoes. Quite by accident, I overheard one tour guide telling another, in Chinese, that in the 1990s the same ¥80 admission fee had entitled visitors to see thirty caves of their own choosing. This knowledge did not help to elevate my spirits.

As I reluctantly exited the last of my ten assigned grottoes, grumbling to myself about the slim pickings on offer, I noticed a sign I hadn't seen before, informing visitors that for an additional fee of up to ¥200 *per cave*, they could visit a number of "special" (*teshude*) grottoes. Annoyed by such blatant price-gouging, I sussed out the approaches to a few of the high-cost caves. Spotting a large group of Japanese tourists moving toward the entrance of—yes, there it was!—Cave No. 465, I acted on impulse. Pulling my floppy-brimmed hat down low over my eyes, I walked quickly toward the outer edge of the Japanese group, stooping slightly as I did so, trying to blend in. As a six-foot, bearded Caucasian, I didn't think it would be easy, but I managed to insinuate myself into their midst without being noticed or challenged. Congratulating myself on my guile, I entered the dimly lit cave. As I pressed forward to make out the erotic detail on one of the Tantric frescoes, my luck ran out. I came face-to-face with an elderly Japanese woman who looked up at me and, with an expression of mixed shock and contempt, cried out in Japanese, "Gaijin!" (Foreigner!). This brought the local Chinese tour guide quickly to the scene, and after a brief interrogation I was escorted politely but firmly out of the cave. From that point until I exited Mogao's main gate several minutes later, I was followed, conspicuously, by a plainclothes security guard clutching a walkie-talkie. Exploring the "special" caves would have to await my next visit to Dunhuang.

My time in Qinghai having come to an end, I returned to Los Angeles, where I immediately began making plans for the following summer. Kevin and Yongzhong had eagerly accepted my offer to bring as many as a dozen UCLA students to Guanting to teach conversational English for three weeks. As it turned out, there was no shortage of volunteers. An initial e-mail solicitation to my students produced dozens of eager applicants. After winnowing the list down to twelve qualified, highly motivated candidates (one of whom subsequently dropped out for personal reasons), I enlisted the help of three faculty colleagues from the UCLA applied linguistics program, and the four of us cobbled together a preliminary English-teaching curriculum and held a two-day training workshop for the student volunteers.

By combining group-discounted air tickets to Beijing with an overnight "hard sleeper" train to Xining, we cut travel costs to a bare minimum, and with generous support from a small group of Friends of the UCLA Center for Chinese Studies, we partially subsidized the students' airfare. Once in Qinghai, room and board for the UCLA students would be provided by our local hosts, the SDA.

FOURTEEN OF US—EIGHT UCLA undergraduates, three graduate students, and three faculty members—set out for Qinghai in late July 2002. My faculty colleagues were Dr. Barbara Pillsbury, an anthropologist specializing in the minority cultures and religions of Northwest China, and Donna Brinton, a UCLA ESL (English as a second language) instructor. Donna was graciously standing in for Dr. Russell Campbell, director of the UCLA Language Resource Center. Russ, who had twice accompanied me on UCLA exchange visits to China, was forced to pull out of the Qinghai project at the last minute, due to a recurrence of colon cancer.

After an overnight stay in Beijing, where I had booked the group into an inexpensive hotel catering mainly to Chinese travelers, we got up early the next morning for an abbreviated sightseeing trip to the Forbidden City and Tiananmen Square. Our walking tour culminated with a visit to Mao's mausoleum, where a healthy-looking, pink-cheeked Mao double was still on display. From there, Barbara, Donna, and I escorted the students to Beijing's main train station, where we put them on an overnight train bound for Xining, 1,100 miles to the west. The two-tiered bunk beds were compact but fairly comfortable, with four berths to a compartment. Vendors with pushcarts made frequent trips down the aisles, selling all manner of fast food, from instant noodles to chicken's feet (a local delicacy). The students had random bunk assignments, and some found themselves sharing compartments with Chinese travelers. They were delighted to meet "real" Chinese, of course, though few of the UCLA undergraduates could converse in *putonghua*. Fortunately, our three graduate students all spoke Chinese fluently (two were PRC citizens). And two of the undergrads also knew a few basic conversational phrases in *putonghua*. But for the most part, the students had to make do with the familiar hand gestures, facial expressions, and voice inflections universally used at close quarters by travelers from different cultures. Further helping to break the ice was the fact that one of our undergraduates, Tapia Martinez-Russ, a gregarious, outgoing middle-aged woman who had been a lounge singer before returning to college, brought her guitar along and used it to good advantage wherever we went. Before we left Qinghai a month later, half the population of Guanting would be singing "Where Have All the Flowers Gone?"

Just before the train pulled out of the Beijing station, we instructed the students not to leave their valuables lying around near the door to their compartments, where professional pickpockets, known to frequent overnight trains, could get at them. With the students settled in expectantly for their great cross-country railroad adventure, Donna, Barbara, and I bade them good-bye and headed back to the hotel. Our plan was to spend the night in Beijing, then fly to Xining first thing next morning to prepare for the students' arrival. Notwithstanding the many joys of close-quarter intercultural contact, at my age I was not about to spend thirty-two hours in a cramped, smoke-filled sleeping car. Been there; done that.

After landing at the newly remodeled Xining airport around noon the next day, Barbara, Donna, and I were greeted at the baggage claim area by Gregory, who promptly escorted us to Kevin's apartment. There Kevin and I had a warm reunion, punctuated by glasses of cold beer and caterpillar-fungus liquor, diligently poured by his adoring Tibetan students. One of the students (all of whom were male) was flirting with Donna and appeared to be trying to get her drunk, though without notable success. After a pleasant and relaxed chat, we headed off to the train station to collect the UCLA students.

As they stepped off the train, the students were brimming with enthusiasm about their overnight adventure. Several had exchanged phone numbers and e-mail addresses with Chinese fellow travelers, and Tapia, our lady troubadour, had made a number of new friends with her music. Everyone was in an upbeat mood. It was almost dinner time, so at Kevin's suggestion we headed off en masse to the city's one and only all-you-can-eat Brazilian-style barbecue restaurant, where the students gorged themselves on mutton, beef, chicken, and pork. (The pork came as something of a surprise, as there is a substantial, pork-eschewing Muslim religious minority in Northwest China.) For the students it was a last supper of sorts. Over the next several weeks, they would be living among extremely poor people in widely scattered rural hamlets. Meat would be very scarce. Average per capita cash income in Guanting was equivalent to less than $100 per year.

After an overnight stay at a no-frills Xining guest house, we set out early the next morning for Guanting. The six-hour bus ride was made to seem much longer by the poorly paved roads and by the absence of a functioning suspension system in our rickety charter bus. But we finally made it, still in reasonably good spirits.

Long in advance of our arrival in Guanting, Zhu Yongzhong and his SDA colleagues had administered a series of English-language achievement tests and conducted oral interviews with middle-school students in more than a dozen mostly Mangghuer and Tibetan villages and hamlets within a two-hour radius of Guanting. More than five hundred youngsters turned up for these interviews, but there was room for only about two hundred in our program. Those who survived the competition were smart, ambitious, and eager to learn. Though they all had at least two years of prior English grammar and vocabulary instruction, their spoken English was rudimentary at best, and none had ever conversed with a native English speaker. Some had to travel on foot up to two hours each morning to attend classes.

As we got off the bus at the entrance to the Sanchuan Cultural Center, the Mangghuer children lined up to greet us, draping traditional Tibetan *khatags*, long white silk scarves, around our necks in a customary show of respect. This was followed by a spirited welcoming ceremony, featuring a good deal of singing and dancing by the local students and plentiful amounts of beer and *baijiu* for the honored American guests. After the ceremony was over, Barbara, Donna, and I divided the UCLA students into teams of two and dispatched them by taxi to six widely scattered villages, where they would live and teach for the next three weeks. The plan was to have them stay in the villages with their SDA host families during the week, teaching five hours each day. Then, on Friday afternoons, we'd send taxis to fetch them back to the "mother ship" in Guanting for the weekend.

Welcoming ceremony at the Sanchuan Cultural Center featured colorful native Mangghuer and Tibetan costumes and dances, ample supplies of food, and numerous cups of *baijiu*, August 2002.

Since several of the villages lacked indoor plumbing, electricity, and hot water for bathing, weekly showers and hot meals in town were deemed essential for maintaining troop morale.

In most of the village schools, simple educational materials such as textbooks, composition books, and even chalk were either nonexistent or in very short supply, and many students lacked such basic necessities as pencils and paper (not to mention, in some cases, shoes). Consequently, the UCLA volunteers frequently wound up purchasing school supplies for their students with their own pocket money.

During the first week of classes, Barbara, Donna, and I roamed from village to village, observing each class and dealing with emergent problems such as the limited supply of textbooks and the attempt by a number of eager local youngsters to crash the instructional program without invitation. Most important, the site visits gave us the opportunity to provide hands-on pedagogical guidance to the UCLA students, most of whom had never taught in a classroom before, let alone under such challenging conditions.

UCLA student Bill Golditch conducts an English lesson in a village classroom, August 2002. The message above the blackboard exhorts students to "Seek truth, be pragmatic, unite, and assist each other." Mao's portrait is still displayed in many schools and public offices in rural China.

After one of these early visits to a hilltop village classroom, the three of us were walking down the dirt road leading back to Guanting when we elected to take a shortcut across a nearby field. At the edge of the field, where it abutted a hillside, we came upon a large patch of mature cannabis plants growing wild, some as tall as six feet. After sniffing the narrow, jagged-edged leaves and crushing a few in our fingers, we satisfied ourselves that they were the real thing. Later that day I asked one of our SDA hosts in Guanting about the local cultivation and use of marijuana and was told that the plants were grown primarily for their hemp fiber, used in making clothes. With a shy smile, he also conceded that the recreational properties of cannabis were not entirely unknown in Amdo.

After some initial logistical confusion and inevitable stage fright, the UCLA students adapted quickly to the novel challenge of their teaching situation. Notwithstanding their inexperience or the austere living and working conditions, they turned out to be marvelously patient, intuitive instructors, adept at improvisation, while their young pupils made up for their lack of conversational experience with an excitement and an eagerness to learn that were inspirational.

By the end of the first week, things were going rather smoothly. There had been no major medical emergencies, no great personal crises, and no pedagogical disasters. A couple of the UCLA students experienced temporary culture shock when they discovered how little personal privacy or comfort they would have in their host families' homes, and a few suffered mild bouts of "Jiang Qing's revenge" as a result of the austere, mostly meatless diet, a condition rendered more troublesome by the extremely crude local latrine facilities. But these were well within the range of normal adaptation-and-adjustment issues, and the students' morale remained high.

With our students settled more or less comfortably into their daily routines, at the start of the second week Donna returned to Los Angeles so she could resume her teaching duties at UCLA. At this point Barbara and I found ourselves with a welcome stretch of free time. With backpacks, maps, and sunscreen in hand, we set off to explore some of Amdo's historic religious and cultural sites, cell phones at the ready in case we were needed back in Guanting. We boarded a bus at the Xining terminal and headed first for the famous Labrang Tibetan Buddhist Monastery, across the Yellow River in Xiahe City, Gansu. A small town unto itself, Labrang is situated at the eastern edge of the Tibetan Plateau, at an altitude of almost ten thousand feet. Within its outer walls are dozens of monumental structures with flat roofs and sloping walls, painted in the starkly contrasting traditional Tibetan colors of oxblood and white. Before 1959, Labrang, along with Kumbum, near Xining, was among the largest lamaseries in the Yellow Hat sect of Tibetan Buddhism. More than 3,600 monks lived and studied on its spacious grounds. After the Dalai Lama fled to India in the wake of the failed Tibetan uprising of 1959, however, all Tibetan lamaseries in China, including Labrang and Kumbum, were restricted by government decree to a maximum of 400 monks each.

At Labrang we spent several hours walking around the massive grounds of the monastery, observing various ceremonial rituals and chatting with friendly monks, nuns, and lay worshippers. After one such conversation, we were invited into the living quarters of two neophyte Gelugpa monks, where we shared with them a meal of *tsampa* and yak-butter tea. When our discussion turned to the subject of their relations with the Chinese government, the monks' distressed body language and careful verbal circumlo-

Tibetan neophyte monk poses for a photo with the author at the Labrang monastery in southeastern Gansu, August 2002. Despite the monk's warm smile, relations between Tibetan Buddhists and Chinese authorities continue to be tense.

cutions reminded me of the strained conversations I'd held with young Chinese scholars in Beijing after the Tiananmen crackdown. Their obvious discomfort spoke volumes about underlying tensions between the Chinese authorities and the Tibetan Buddhist community.

From Labrang, we boarded a rickety old country bus and headed for our next destination: Linxia, the cultural and spiritual center of China's 10 million Hui Muslims. The Hui are China's largest Islamic minority, followed by the 8.5 million Turkic-speaking Uighurs of Xinjiang. Culturally, Chinese Muslims display varying degrees of assimilation within Chinese society. At one end of the spectrum, the Hui are, at first glance, barely distinguishable from the Han. Widely distributed throughout China's western provinces, the Hui generally attend Chinese schools, speak *putonghua*, and often intermarry with the Han, though they differ from the latter in their religious practices and dietary requirements. Like other Muslims, the Hui follow halal food standards and do not eat pork or consume alcohol. At the other end of the spectrum are the more aloof, self-contained Turkic Uighurs, who generally live in their own ethnic enclaves, attend their own schools, speak their own language, and intermingle only sparingly with the Han. While members of all schools of Chinese Islam report varying degrees of intolerance, condescension, and discrimination at the hands of the Han, hostility toward the Chinese majority is generally highest among the more insular Uighurs.

The three-hour bus ride to Linxia was memorable for the intense scrutiny Barbara and I received as the only *laowai* in the vicinity. Wearing shorts and a T-shirt against the dry summer heat, I immediately became an object of mirth among the mostly elderly, mostly female Muslim bus passengers, who pointed to my hairy arms and legs and laughed unselfconsciously. Two men on the bus playfully rolled up their trousers to show me their hairless legs, a revelation immediately followed by a second round of laughter. Barbara's blonde hair was a further source of amusement to our fellow passengers. On a more serious note, the woman sitting next to Barbara confided that she was running away from her husband, who had attacked her with a knife and a pot of boiling water. Rolling up her sleeves, she showed us ugly red welts and slash marks on both arms. In response to our questions, the woman acknowledged that spousal abuse was a serious problem in this part of China and that female suicide was not uncommon. Her best friend, she said, had swallowed a fatal dose of pesticide.

Sometimes called the Mecca of Chinese Islam, Linxia is home to some of the most famous Muslim monuments in China, including the stately Nanguan Mosque, with its three distinctive, twenty-two-meter minarets. Sacked and burned by Red Guards during the Cultural Revolution, Nanguan was rebuilt in 1979 with state funds as part of a nationwide display of governmental benevolence toward China's five officially recognized religions—Daoism, Buddhism, Islam, Protestantism, and Catholicism (of the homespun, non-Papist variety). Apart from these five, however, the Chinese government was quite intolerant when it came to dealing with unauthorized religious groups, in particular foreign-affiliated bodies such as the Roman Catholic Church, underground Protestant sects, and self-organizing spiritual communities like the outlawed Falun Gong. Coercive repression of such groups was not uncommon.

Because our visit to Linxia took place less than a year after the September 11 attacks on the Twin Towers and the Pentagon, we were not sure how we would be received by the local Islamic community. In the aftermath of the October 2001 American invasion of Afghanistan, and subsequent U.S. support for China's crackdown on suspected Uighur terrorists in

Xinjiang, many Chinese Muslims harbored strong misgivings about America's motives and intentions. Under these circumstances, Barbara's deep knowledge of Islamic culture and tradition enabled us to break through the initial wall of suspicion and distrust. Outside the entrance to the Nanguan Mosque, which was our primary destination in Linxia, Barbara extracted a scarf from her backpack and put it on, modestly covering her head. Making sure that her arms and legs were also completely covered (though mine were not, reflecting the prevailing double standard of Islam), we entered the mosque's front gate. Barbara immediately began chatting with a group of Hui women, using a mixture of Arabic and Chinese. The women responded warmly, inviting us to meet the imam. As we were introduced, Barbara greeted the middle-aged cleric in Arabic with the customary salutation, "Peace upon you" (As-salāmu 'alaykum). I followed suit, crudely mimicking her speech and gestures. She then broke the ice with him by relating the story of her previous research among the Muslim minorities of Taiwan. His distrust allayed, the imam happily took us on a guided tour of the mosque, pausing to let us observe the madrassa, where a group of local young men were taking instruction in the Koran. Afterward, Barbara thanked him for receiving us in friendship—and for overlooking the fact that I was barbarically attired in shorts and a T-shirt.

After five days on the road, which included visits to a number of other local mosques as well as the stunning ancient Buddhist grottoes at Binglingsi and Maijishan, we returned to Guanting. Things were going very smoothly there—our cell phones had not rung once in five days—and the UCLA students were waxing enthusiastic about their experiences.

With just one week left in the teaching program, the SDA organized a field trip for our benefit, to attend the Nadun Harvest Festival, held annually by Mangghuers in this part of Amdo to celebrate the summer harvest and propitiate the local mountain gods. Attended by upwards of one thousand people from as far as one hundred miles away, it was a joyous occasion filled with singing, dancing, and traditional shamanistic rituals. Each local Mangghuer clan had its own distinctive ceremonial regalia. Since the men were normally responsible for tending and harvesting the crops, they alone were allowed to participate in the elaborate rituals of Nadun, which included a friendly competition among ornately costumed dancers from various clans.

While most of the UCLA students and teachers (including your faithful scribe) contented themselves with remaining on the sidelines as mere spectators, one of our more outgoing and adventurous male undergraduates, Bill Golditch, got caught up in the celebratory spirit of Nadun. Borrowing a costume from a surprised but delighted Mangghuer clansman, and accompanied by howls of laughter from everyone present, Bill did his own improvised version of a Mangghuer harvest dance. Looking less like a graceful terpsichorean than a crazed yak in heat (or was it intense pain?), he cavorted without inhibition for the appreciative audience. A tasteless display of Occidental chutzpah? Perhaps. But the rains came early to Amdo that autumn, and the crops flourished.

Our remaining time in Guanting passed very quickly. When the teaching program concluded at the end of August, we all gathered together at the Sanchuan Cultural Center one last time for a closing ceremony, held in our honor. The freshly scrubbed Mangghuer students, their parents, local teachers, and SDA members—close to four hundred people in all—converged on the center dressed in their Sunday best. Once again, as they had done upon our arrival, the children lined up to put *khatags* around our necks. Platters of fruit and cold drinks were passed around. Then the children, their parents, and teachers took turns performing skits and native songs and dances for us, and the *baijiu* flowed like, well, *baijiu*. Led by Zhu Yongzhong, the men of SDA performed a sweetly shy, lilting Mangghuer courtship song. When they finished, and much to the delight of our hosts, the UCLA students, some of whom were by this time rather well lubricated, responded to the musical challenge by performing several not-so-traditional American songs ("We Will Rock You," "Wild Thing," "The Night They Drove Old Dixie Down") and dances (Boogaloo, Funky Chicken). They also led the assembled masses in a spirited sing-along version of Guanting's current chart-topping hit single, "Where Have All the Flowers Gone?" It was a thoroughly memorable cross-cultural experience.

When it was time to take our final leave, something truly extraordinary happened. The Mangghuer youngsters, having bonded closely with their UCLA teachers, would not let them leave. As we began to move slowly out of the cultural center toward the bus, saying our sad good-byes, the children began to cry, softly at first, then more audibly. They surrounded their teachers and clung to them, clutching tightly onto arms, legs, and clothing. Gradually, the weeping grew louder and more intense. By this time, the UCLA students were crying too. Hugging and soothing their young charges, they sobbed along with them, promising to return someday as they sought to extricate themselves. I tried to videotape this remarkable

Zhu Yongzhong and the author say good-bye at the closing ceremony of our
teaching program, Sanchuan Cultural Center, August 2002.

scene, but my own tears kept getting in the way. The sound of mass moaning and wailing bordered on the surreal, and it took almost an hour to board our bus. When the bus doors finally closed, everyone on board was thoroughly shaken. No one spoke a word. There was nothing left to say.

I have never experienced anything remotely like that farewell scene, before or since. For two hundred Mangghuer youngsters, living in isolated mountain hamlets, our visit had brought a precious, real-time connection to an outside world they could only have imagined. And for the UCLA students, the bonds they formed with the eager, spirited youngsters of Guanting had provided a life-affirming reality check on the complacent materialism of middle-class American life. By any conceivable measure, it was a once-in-a-lifetime experience.

With our Guanting adventure at an end, Barbara and I put a tired but contented group of UCLA students on the train for the thirty-two-hour trip to Beijing. Waving to them from the platform, we watched the train pull out of Xining station. After a few moments of quiet reflection, we gath-

UCLA student Tapia Martinez-Russ bids a tearful farewell to her students at the conclusion of the Guanting summer English program, August 2002.

ered up our gear and headed for the airport. With two weeks left before the start of fall classes at UCLA, we were about to take off on another journey of discovery into China's wild, wild west. First stop: Chongqing.

DEEP IN THE interior of Sichuan, Chongqing, with an urban population of more than 14 million, is the largest Chinese city west of Shanghai. It also serves as a gateway to the scenic Three Gorges. Both Barbara and I wanted to take this storied journey one last time before construction on the world's largest hydroelectric power plant, the Three Gorges Dam, was completed. The project was scheduled to go into first-phase operation in the summer of 2003. Thereafter, the dam would gradually be filled, in measured increments over a six-year period, raising the water level in the upper reaches of the Yangzi River by a total of 575 feet and creating a 375-mile-long reservoir. In the process, the fabled gorges would be flooded, along with 135 cities and towns and 1,100 low-lying villages dotting the riverbank between Chongqing and Yichang, 400 miles downriver. Also scheduled for inundation were 1,300 archaeological excavations, 40,000 ancestral grave sites, and 178 major rubbish landfills.

Beginning in the mid-1990s, the Chinese government undertook to rebuild many of the affected cities and towns at new sites above the 575-foot level and to relocate more than 1.3 million people to higher ground. By any measure, the Three Gorges dam was a monumental undertaking, at an estimated total cost exceeding $25 billion.

On my one previous visit to the Three Gorges in 1993, dense fog and a heavy inversion layer had combined to reduce visibility severely. This time the weather gods cooperated, and the vistas were spectacular. En route downstream through the gorges, the cruise ship stopped at some of the cities and towns scheduled for inundation. The homes, shops, schools, and factories in these communities were being dismantled brick by brick, and we watched with fascination as the building materials were methodically sorted, stacked, and then carted off to higher ground, to be reused in new settlements.

We spoke with several local residents about their experiences with the government's relocation program. About half the people we talked to were pleased with the terms and conditions of their resettlement. For many, it meant they would have indoor plumbing for the first time in their lives. Others, however, seemed nervous and were reluctant to speak candidly to outsiders. Gradually we were able to piece together bits and pieces of information suggesting that a considerable amount of corruption had marred the resettlement effort. Local governments had been given large block grants from the central authorities, averaging ¥8,000–¥10,000 ($975–$1,300) per resident, with payouts varying according to location and economic circumstance. But by the time the funds reached (or rather trickled down to) those being resettled, most families received less than half their allotted entitlements. The remaining funds, we were told, were diverted by local officials to set up businesses, pay cadre staff salaries, retire existing debts, and build new houses and offices for friends and relatives. Moreover, many riverfront residents scheduled for mandatory relocation were offered substandard replacement housing in remote, inhospitable rural areas. Three years later, in 2005, a prize-winning documentary exposé by two Chinese filmmakers, *Before the Flood* (Yan mo), revealed the egregious misuse of government funds earmarked for the Three Gorges resettlement program. The film caused the Chinese government great embarrassment and triggered a detailed audit of the use (and misuse) of relocation funds.

In the course of that audit, which continued throughout 2007, hundreds of millions of yuan in corrupt transactions were discovered.

Yet despite problems in the Three Gorges relocation program, all along the upper reaches of the Yangzi River we saw evidence of the central government's massive new infrastructure investment program, known as Great Western Development *(xifang dakaifa)*. Initiated in 2000, the program was designed to shift billions of dollars in government revenues from China's thriving eastern seaboard to the remote interior provinces of the west, where the money would be used to build new highways, bridges, dams, tunnels, airports, railroads, and oil and natural gas pipelines. Along with billions of dollars in infrastructure investment would come substantial business opportunities for Chinese entrepreneurs and millions of new jobs for migrant workers seeking to improve their economic prospects by heading out to the wild, wild west. Though we could not see improvements in rural incomes and living standards in most parts of the western provinces at the time of our visit, an impressive amount of new construction was evident.

After a four-day, three-night downriver cruise, we disembarked at Yichang, where nine years earlier I had been shanghaied by a hypernationalistic pedicab driver. The city looked far more modern now—presumably due to its strategic location near the site of the Three Gorges dam. At least three new four-star tourist hotels had been built since my last visit, and this time I saw no pedicabs in the streets, only a brand-new fleet of Volkswagen taxis. At Yichang's gleaming new international airport, we boarded a flight for our next destination: Kunming, capital of southwest China's Yunnan province.

Yunnan shares borders with Vietnam, Laos, Burma, and Tibet and is home to twenty-four distinct ethnic minorities, the largest geographical concentration of diverse ethnic groups anywhere in China, and perhaps even the world. Our plan was to do a bit of local sightseeing in Kunming (including a visit to the ancestral home of the Hui minority's most famous historical figure, the Ming dynasty nautical explorer Zheng He), then fly to Zhongdian in the northwestern corner of the province. From there we would work our way back toward Kunming by bus, with intermediate stops at Lijiang and the famous Tiger Leaping Gorge (Hutiaoxia).

FAR OFF THE beaten track, Zhongdian is a mixed Tibetan-Han community with a large, active Yellow Hat Buddhist monastery, Songzanlin, and a small minority of Hui Muslims. Located on the southeastern edge of the Tibetan Plateau, not far from the sacred Meili Snow Mountain, Zhongdian had been a rest stop for Mao Zedong and the Red Army on their storied Long March; today a memorial shrine in Zhongdian's Old Town commemorates that 1935 visit.

Zhongdian County gained international notoriety in 1997 when its leaders petitioned the Beijing government to change its official name to Xi'ang-ge-li-la, "Shangri-la," the mythical mountaintop utopia made famous by James Hilton in his 1933 novel *Lost Horizon*. According to documents filed with the central authorities in Beijing, the mountain closest to Zhongdian's county seat was the real-life site of the plane crash described by Hilton. Stone tablets borrowed from a museum in nearby Lijiang were introduced to prove that Xi'ang-ge-li-la had been the name of a local village in ancient times. And photographs were submitted highlighting certain physical similarities between Zhongdian's mountaintop and the local World War II crash site of an airplane that resembled the one appearing in Frank Capra's Oscar-winning 1937 film version of Hilton's novel.

Not to be outdone, neighboring Deqin County filed a counterclaim seeking to establish that *its* mountain, the sacred Meili Snow Mountain, was the true site of the original Shangri-la plane crash. This bizarre naming competition dragged on for more than three years. The fact that Hilton's book was wholly fictional, or that he had never set foot in China, did not deter the applicants from vigorously pursuing their respective claims. Neither did the fact that the real plane crash took place a full decade *after* the publication of Hilton's novel and half a dozen years after Capra's film depicted the purported crash site. To outsiders, this surreal competition reeked of a calculated publicity stunt, a brazen attempt to lure unsuspecting tourists—and their wallets—to an economically depressed region of China.

Finally, toward the end of 2001, Zhongdian was officially awarded the right to change its name to Xi'ang-ge-li-la. A nearby airport, once all but abandoned, was quickly refurbished, its access road widened and paved, and the whole town was spruced up in anticipation of an influx of tourists. By the time we arrived in early September 2002, the reinvention of Zhongdian was well under way. Though the de rigueur oxblood and white paint was not yet dry on the "new" Shangri-la, a huge, half-finished five-star hotel vaguely shaped like Lhasa's famed Potala Palace had been plopped down in the center of the town. In keeping with the spirit of the mythical

Shangri-la, the town fathers had adopted a revised building code requiring all new construction to be in the traditional Tibetan style. Chinese street names and place-names were now translated into Tibetan, and shopkeepers were ordered to add Tibetan script to their storefront signs. This created some problems, since at least half the local shops were owned by Han or by Hui Muslims, who could not read or write Tibetan, while many of the Tibetan merchants were at best only semiliterate. Zhongdian's half dozen local sign painters were thus among the first indigenous beneficiaries of the town's makeover. A number of pseudo-chic specialty shops, catering to foreign tourists and trekkers, also opened for business, including the Living Buddha Internet Café and the Yakkety-Yak Snack Shack.

Other nearby communities also viewed Zhongdian's transformation into a cultural theme park as a potential source of tourist income. On a visit to Tiger Leaping Gorge, we discovered that the Muslim community there was seeking to cash in on the anticipated "Shangri-la fever." In one hillside village, the local mosque had been allowed to slide into decay and disrepair over the years. The imam had died, and no one in the village could read Arabic, the language of the Koran. When they heard about Zhongdian's transformation, however, the village elders decided to launch an Islamic revival. They spruced up their mosque, renamed it Xi'ang-ge-li-la, and dispatched a few of their most well-educated young men to a neighboring county to take instruction in the Koran at the local mosque. Though no paved roads led to their hillside village, which was accessible only on foot, the elders remained hopeful about the coming tourist boom. Not to be outdone, an even remoter village higher up on the same mountain dusted off its long-neglected Islamic identity and began to construct a brand-new mosque.

LYING ALONG THE bus route from Zhongdian to Lijiang, Tiger Leaping Gorge is a true natural wonder. A dazzling, ten-mile-long canyon carved between two mountains by the fast-flowing waters of the Jinsha River (an upstream feeder of the Yangzi), Tiger Leaping Gorge is a contender for the title of world's deepest river canyon. Its narrow breadth and treacherous rapids make it non-navigable, while its rugged cliffs and breathtaking vistas make it, to my eye, even more spectacular than the Three Gorges, several hundred miles downriver. Although motor vehicles are permitted limited access from either end of the canyon, Tiger Leaping Gorge is best traversed on foot. Scattered along its main hiking path (called the "high road") are a series of small but comfortable guesthouses, some operated by Western expatriates, catering to day-trippers and backpackers. At one such facility, Sean's Guesthouse, Barbara and I sipped ice-cold beer on the veranda as we gazed at the majesty of a mile-high sheer cliff directly opposite. Sean himself is a Tibetan, married to an Australian expat named Margo, who runs a small café at one end of the gorge, where she assists hikers and steers them toward her husband's inn.

By chance, the American manager of the Shanghai–General Motors Joint Venture auto plant was also staying overnight at Sean's, and we had an interesting conversation about the surging Chinese auto market. He told us that his plant was currently producing 150,000 Buicks a year yet was falling further and further behind the seemingly insatiable Chinese appetite for new cars. He just couldn't turn them out them fast enough. Consequently, GM was planning to double the plant's annual output to 300,000 vehicles within two years. At one point in the conversation, perhaps affected by the confluence of cold beer, high altitude, and a hot afternoon, I had a surreal vision, inspired no doubt by my Los Angeles upbringing, of the exquisitely tranquil Tiger Leaping Gorge choked with thousands of Buicks, stalled bumper to bumper at rush hour. More distressing than this idle fantasy, however, was Sean's subsequent disclosure that Tiger Leaping Gorge would soon go the way of the Three Gorges. A chain of eight dams for generating hydroelectric power was being planned for the Jinsha River. When the dams were completed, the river would submerge the gorge, irrevocably altering the region's ecology and forcing the relocation of eighty thousand people from dozens of villages upstream and downstream. Sean told us that he was joining with environmental groups to fight the dam proposal. We wished him luck. Even without a gorge-clogging horde of Buicks, the thought of losing this incredible natural wonder was deeply disturbing.

From Tiger Leaping Gorge we headed to our next destination, Lijiang, where we received another unwelcome surprise. Once renowned for its pristine, picture-book beauty and colorful Naxi ethnic-minority traditions, Lijiang's historic Old Town, at the center of a newer city of one million inhabitants, had been devastated by a magnitude 7.0 earthquake in 1996. Fully one-third of its buildings had collapsed. The subsequent reconstruction effort, intended to restore the unique architectural style and cozy small-town ambience of the original settlement, coincided with the dramatic takeoff of China's domestic tourism industry. Boosted by Lijiang's 1997 designation as a UNESCO World Heritage Site, the rebuilt town was now bursting at the seams with tourists, both Chinese and foreign. According to local officials, the number of visitors to Lijiang had exploded from ninety-eight thousand in 1990 to almost three million in 2002.

More disappointing than Lijiang's dense crowds was its profusion of kitschy, overpriced tourist attractions. For a pair of tickets to a performance by the famous Lijiang Naxi orchestra led by Dr. Xuan Ke, we paid ¥850, four times the monthly income of the average Yunnan farm family. But at least the Naxi performers were authentic. Other local attractions were more artificial and contrived. Altogether, there were more then 2,500 shops catering to tourists within the Old Town's 1.7 square miles.

Twenty minutes or so out of town, an impressive new cable-car concession, located inside the famous Jade Dragon Snow Mountain Scenic Area (admission fee, ¥60, or $7.50) charged tourists an additional ¥180 ($22) for a fifteen-minute ride up to scenic Glacier Park (Bingchuan Gongyuan). For another ¥60, visitors could ride a second cable car up to Yak Meadow, ten minutes further on. For ¥30 more, one could purchase a small container of oxygen, handy at such high altitudes. The mountain itself was beautiful, but its pricey venues and carnival-like atmosphere lent the place an air of unrestrained commercial excess.

All around Lijiang there were unmistakable signs of incipient Disneyfication. Perhaps the most striking example was an artificial Naxi village that had been erected on the outskirts of the city. Staffed by Naxi (at least some of whom looked suspiciously like Han) in ethnic costumes, the village was lined with fast-food stalls featuring faux Naxi cuisine and souvenir shops hawking overpriced faux Naxi artifacts, trinkets, and tchotchkes. Along with the overabundance of consumables, there were costumed "native" buskers who performed Naxi songs and dances for spare change. The overall effect was not unlike that of the traveling Wild West Show I had seen as a child, in which ersatz cowboys and Indians cavorted in full regalia before wide-eyed, cotton candy–eating crowds of city folk.

Inside the entrance to the Naxi village, a group of brightly costumed, pink-cheeked teenage girls performed a "traditional" Naxi courtship dance for the benefit of the tourists, who were mostly Han. To me, the performance smacked of ethnic condescension, since it implicitly contrasted the childlike innocence and naïveté of the Naxi with the more mature and worldly-wise Han. Over the years, I had witnessed many similar cultural performances in different parts of China, representing various ethnic minorities, and found most of them to be highly patronizing, if not down-right insulting. An official government Internet guide to China's ethnic minorities unintentionally captured the essence of such ethnic condescen-sion when it described the Uighurs (Weiwuer) of Xinjiang in the follow-ing terms: "*Weiwuer* love dancing, singing, and playing their own unique musical instruments. They are hospitable people. Visitors will be invited to taste sweet grapes, melons, and plums, drink tea, and join the lively dancing." That was it. Nothing more. Redolent of the simple labels that describe farm animals in a children's petting zoo, this description struck me as both banal and somewhat surprising in light of the Chinese govern-ment's palpable fear of Uighur separatists and terrorists.

Such childlike caricatures of the ethnic other were by no means unique or even unusual. Other non-Han minorities—including the Yi, Zhuang, Yao, Dai, and Bai—were described in similarly patronizing terms on the same government Web site. And in what can only be described as a stun-ning display of Han arrogance, the Communist Party chief of Tibet, Zhang Qingli, in a statement issued shortly before the outbreak of ethnic vio-lence in Tibet in the spring of 2008, described the Party's relationship with the Tibetan people thusly: "The Communist Party is like the parent to the Tibetan people, and it is always considerate about what the children need."

ON THE LONG flight home I let my mind wander through the journey just completed. Since leaving home six weeks earlier, we had crisscrossed five western provinces by air, train, boat, bus, taxi, and on foot. At times it seemed we had been moving backward through time, to another cen-tury. The vast, sparsely inhabited Tibetan Plateau was a world apart—poor, undeveloped, home to a variety of largely undisturbed ancient cultures and traditions. Yet all around the fringes of this vast western frontier, in scores of newly blossoming tourist oases and rebuilt cities and towns, there were clear signs of incipient economic awakening. In just a few short years, the government's Great Western Development program had sown the first visible seeds of progress. By the summer of 2002, a profusion of new infrastructure projects had sprung up from Yunnan to Xinjiang, herald-ing the rebirth of the ancient Silk Road. From what we could see, however, the main winners in this renaissance were Han entrepreneurs and their local governmental patrons and venture partners. Corruption had clearly tainted many new projects, a substantial number of which had yet to pro-duce tangible benefits for the indigenous peoples. To our eyes, not much new wealth or economic opportunity had yet trickled down to the local *laobaixing* in these areas. In 2002, according to official Chinese statistics, residents of China's four poorest western provinces (Qinghai, Gansu, Yunnan, and Tibet) had incomes eleven times lower, on average, than residents of Shanghai and Beijing. From the look of things, Great Western Development was going to be a long, tough slog.

12

Beijing Revisited

IN THE FALL of 2005 I was reunited with my old friend Jia Qingguo at Peking University. He and I had agreed to collaborate in teaching a class on the pros and cons of globalization. The class was the outgrowth of a pioneering agreement between Peking University and the University of California, establishing an experimental Joint Center for International Studies (JCIS) on the Beida campus. Since the early 1980s the University of California had been offering its students semester- and year-long Chinese-language instruction at Beida as part of its global Education Abroad Program. But we had never before incorporated substantive (i.e., non-language) classes, taught in English, into the EAP curriculum in China, nor had Chinese students ever been granted academic credit for enrolling in UC-accredited classes on their own campus.

JCIS was the brainchild of Professor Lynda Bell, of UC Riverside, and Peter Wollitzer, Asia Program director of EAP. Their idea was to bring a group of fifty UC undergraduates, majoring in various fields of international studies (but not necessarily Chinese studies), to Beijing and group them with a like number of Beida undergraduates in a series of courses constructed around the general theme of the challenges of globalization. Each course would be team-taught in English by a senior UC faculty member and a Beida faculty counterpart.

As director of UCLA's Center for Chinese Studies since 1999, I had been involved in the early planning and development of the JCIS, and it was my idea to invite Jia Qingguo—by this time one of China's best-known international relations specialists—to partner with me in teaching the program's first core course. In addition to our class, which we titled "Debating Globalization," other courses in the JCIS curriculum for the fall of 2005 included "The Economics of Development," "Sino-American Relations and the Rise of Asia," and "Cultural Representations of the Global: China and the West." For me personally, the most exciting aspects of the program were, first, the opportunity to build a bridge across the vast educational and philosophical gulf that has long separated the people of the United States and of China and, second, the challenge of bringing together one hundred of the best and brightest students from two distinguished universities to engage in collaborative studies of the costs, benefits, and unintended consequences of globalization, a subject barely in its infancy within China's traditionally Marxist-dominated educational establishment.

For the University of California there would be other benefits as well. On the pedagogical side, the program would help overcome geopolitical barriers to global information exchange while fostering educational outreach and intercultural understanding. At the same time, moving some instructional programs for UC students offshore also made good practical sense, since it costs less to house and train UC students in China than to build the facilities and hire the instructors and administrators needed to teach them at home. For its part, the foreign partnering institution would reap considerable benefit from exposing its students to world-class instruction and cutting-edge social science research while also deriving substantial revenues from the tuition and fees paid by UC students abroad. Worldwide, the EAP figures are impressive: in 2006–7, the University of California sent upwards of three thousand students to 150 universities in thirty-seven countries. Programs such as JCIS thus represent a rare win-win situation for all parties concerned, enabling the university to do well while doing good.

AS THE START of the 2005 fall semester approached, I was a bit apprehensive. I didn't know what to expect. To the best of my knowledge, nothing like this had been attempted in China since 1949, at least not in the social sciences. I had been given virtually free rein to design the globalization course—including selection of weekly lecture topics, textbooks, supplemental readings, audiovisual materials, and guest lecturers. Professor Jia then vetted my recommendations and made additional suggestions, which were incorporated into the final syllabus. Although he proposed a few minor changes involving a modest reduction in the amount of English-language reading required of Chinese students in the class, in the end the syllabus remained essentially as I had designed it. I wasn't sure if he agreed with all of my recommendations or if he was simply so busy juggling his many professional duties that he was relieved to let me do the heavy lifting of planning and designing the course. (In addition to being a full-time Beida professor and university administrator, Jia Qingguo is also prominent in local politics, serving on, among other things, the Standing Committee of the Beijing Municipal Political Consultative Committee.)

In a U.S. research university, our class would have been considered fairly mainstream and conventional, and would have raised few eyebrows. In a Chinese university, however, it was quite extraordinary. The syllabus encompassed such controversial topics as the global marketization of economic life, the social impact of the information revolution, the effects of rising global (and local) economic inequality, the relationship between economic growth and environmental degradation, globalization and the spread of political pluralism, and the putative "clash of civilizations," including the rise of global terrorism since 9/11. Required readings included works by Thomas Friedman, Jürgen Habermas, Samuel Huntington, Antonio Negri, Joseph Nye, George Soros, and Joseph Stiglitz, among others. I wasn't at all sure what to expect when China's brightest, most carefully cultivated young minds encountered such an eclectic mix of critical Western thinkers.

Happily, my anxieties proved unwarranted. In almost every respect, the teaching experience exceeded expectations. Compared to the undergraduates I had encountered at Beida during my previous, abbreviated tenure as a visiting scholar in 1993, the Chinese students I taught in the fall of 2005 were more open-minded, cosmopolitan, and knowledgeable about the outside world. They were also extremely bright and eager to learn. While they generally shared a heightened sense of national pride in a rising China, and while most were critical of U.S. unilateralism under President George W. Bush, they were neither particularly jingoistic nor notably xenophobic. Somewhat suspicious of the motives of the U.S. government, they displayed no hostility to the American people; without exception, they treated me and the other UC faculty members and students with consideration and respect.

Most of my Beida students appeared to have comfortably adapted to the new Chinese middle-class lifestyle. As the crème de la crème of Chinese university students (Beida's admission standards are even higher than

Harvard's), they tended to come from urban families where educational achievement was highly valued. A disproportionate number were the children of teachers. As aspiring young professionals, many (if not most) of them were well-informed, brand-conscious consumers. They dressed fashionably, and more than half owned laptop computers. Most were skilled Web surfers, and many had late-model, slim-line mobile phones, which they used incessantly to text message their friends. Most also appeared to have accepted, if only implicitly, the trade-off that Deng Xiaoping offered China's youth in 1992: the opportunity to satisfy their individual ambitions and raise their personal horizons in exchange for lowering their political expectations.

To be sure, my Chinese students expressed deep distress over the high levels of corruption among local Chinese government officials, and they clearly resented the government's intrusive attempts to propagandize and regiment their lives, for example, by trying to limit and control Internet content. Indeed, many of them were technically quite adept at evading obstacles to online information gathering thrown up by the Great Firewall of China. Yet aside from occasional participation in such relatively safe political activities as promoting heightened environmental awareness or protesting Japanese history textbooks (which continue to gloss over Japan's World War II brutality in China), they were not generally inclined toward political activism. Still less did they engage in outright defiance of the government. They were, in short, increasingly comfortable with their ascribed status as establishment elites-in-training. A few of them, including one of my Beida graduate teaching assistants, had joined the CCP in order to enhance their career prospects, but very few professed faith in the basic canons of Marxism-Leninism. Most were decidedly agnostic, both ideologically and spiritually. Notwithstanding their deeply ingrained reluctance to question authority, I found them generally quite likable, as well as teachable.

Although today's Beida students tend to be politically inert, they are nonetheless curious and inquisitive about the world around them. In our "Debating Globalization" class, Jia Qingguo and I touched on a number of controversial issues involving erstwhile Chinese ideological forbidden zones, including the emergence of the Falun Gong, the student protests of 1989, the widening prevalence of official corruption, and even the legacy of Mao Zedong. Such subjects had to be approached obliquely—generally by framing them in terms of the social consequences of marketization and the open policy, that is, as consequences of China's headlong, post-Mao encounter with the forces of globalization. Although most Chinese students in the class responded positively to my efforts to nudge them gently out of their accustomed intellectual comfort zones, a few displayed signs of cognitive anxiety and discomfort, while others experienced some difficulty with English comprehension. By the fourth week of the semester a dozen Beida students had bailed out of the class. But thirty-six of them stayed the course, along with fifty-four UC students.

For those Chinese students who sought additional information on controversial subjects, I offered an optional Wednesday afternoon salon, where they could informally discuss anything that interested them—anything at all. At first only one or two Beida students showed up, and they were quite shy about raising sensitive subjects, but as the semester wore on, they began to shed their inhibitions and to probe controversial political issues, including Internet censorship, the role of civil society in China's development, and the rising incidence of popular protests over illegal land seizures and industrial pollution. In addition, I spent one full salon session presenting a comprehensive, no-holds-barred account of the Beijing student movement of 1989, from the death of Hu Yaobang to the crackdown of June 4. Insofar as Beida students had heard only the Party's official line on Tiananmen since childhood, much of this information came as a revelation to them.

I also made available to a few of my students, upon request, my personal copy of a recent, highly controversial biography of Mao Zedong, *Mao: The Unknown Story*, by Jung Chang and Jon Halliday. Those who borrowed the book were taken aback by the authors' starkly negative, one-sided portrait of Mao as a treacherous, power-hungry tyrant who routinely betrayed friends, stabbed colleagues in the back, and cruelly mistreated the very peasants who carried him to power. While the book presented a good deal of important new factual material about Mao, its prevailing narrative tone was polemical and tendentious. Consequently, I had deeply ambivalent feelings about it. Of the five Beida students who borrowed the book, only one changed her view of Mao as a result. The others clung to their more comforting, officially sanitized truths. Their level of cognitive dissonance—measured by the vast gulf between what they had previously been told and what they now read—was simply too great.

Inside the classroom, I enjoyed an unexpected and thoroughly delightful degree of academic freedom. I regularly used the classroom's Internet-linked computer and related audiovisual equipment to access a variety of controversial Web-based materials and to project streaming videos from a number of "nanny-listed" Web sites; among these was a vivid BBC film clip that showed hundreds of farmers in Zhejiang being violently attacked by thugs who had been hired to break up a protest against a factory that was dumping toxic waste into their irrigation water. I also showed a number of politically sensitive films in class, including the PBS documentary *China in the Red*, which starkly depicts the dark side of China's dramatic economic surge of the late 1990s. Whenever I ran into a technical obstacle, such as a blocked Web site, my students expertly navigated around the problem. Jing Jing, Cha Cha, and their various "little sisters" would not have approved.

THROUGHOUT THE SEMESTER Qingguo and I invited a number of guest experts to speak to our class. The well-known American legal scholar Jerome Cohen lectured on the vital importance of building a rule-of-law society in China. Joshua Cooper Ramo, managing director of Kissinger Associates, spoke on the viability of the Beijing Consensus as a development model in the non-Western world. And the Canadian Broadcasting Corporation's Beijing correspondent Patrick Brown showed the class a remarkable documentary video about China's burgeoning HIV/AIDS epidemic. Photographed with the assistance of a young Chinese human rights activist named Hu Jia, who was later imprisoned for "endangering state security," Brown's video detailed how corrupt local officials in Henan had shut down a charitable home for fifty young AIDS orphans after the children's parents (along with tens of thousands of others in the province) had died from HIV/AIDS, contracted while selling their blood plasma at dozens of illegal rural blood collection centers. It was a chilling indictment of the entire political and public health establishment in Henan, from the provincial governor on down. The Chinese students appeared shocked but not particularly surprised at the revelation of official corruption on such a massive and destructive scale.

For many students, American and Chinese alike, the highlight of the semester was a guest appearance by Thomas L. Friedman, the *New York Times* columnist, who spoke to our class about his new book *The World Is Flat*. An entertaining speaker who trades in punchy personal anecdotes and breathless hyperbole, Friedman addressed an overflow crowd that included foreign media representatives and leading members of the

Beida academic establishment. Within five minutes of introducing his major thesis—that the spread of modern information technology has created a single, globally interconnected playing field on which those who embrace the high-speed world of digitized communications will prosper while those who ignore or reject it will be left behind—he had most people in the room eating out of the palm of his hand. In the process, he clearly demonstrated why he is widely regarded as the guru of globalization. On the other hand, his tendency to generalize and oversimplify for effect (for example, "Those who don't get on board the globalization train will be run over by it") got him into trouble with some of the UC students in the audience, one of whom, during the Q&A session, managed to get Friedman to concede that the global playing field isn't really level, that some countries, and some individuals, have enormous advantages over others, and that therefore the world isn't actually flat after all. Other UC students raised pointed questions about globalization's effects on labor rights, environmental quality, and human dignity. For the Beida students, who are not normally encouraged to freely analyze, let alone critique, the ideas of their academic instructors and political leaders, the Q&A session proved to be an extremely valuable lesson in critical thinking. Thereafter a number of my previously passive Chinese students began to ask questions in class discussions, with a bold few even daring to challenge their professors (imagine that!). Their metamorphosis—from inert recipients to active participants in the learning process—was particularly gratifying. For me, the opening of young minds has always provided the greatest rewards of my academic career, helping to rekindle my enthusiasm for teaching and preventing me from becoming cynical and complacent.

The students' research projects turned out to be both interesting and innovative. With the aid of two Beida graduate assistants, Qingguo and I divided the class of ninety students into six discussion sections, with roughly proportional numbers of American and Chinese students in each group. In addition to their weekly section meetings, each group was tasked with the following collective research problem: "Take any controversial issue or idea or hypothesis encountered in this class, devise a practical strategy for investigating it empirically, and then carry out a preliminary test at a Beijing field site (or sites) of your own choosing." We left the details to the students themselves, in consultation with their graduate teaching assistants. The only requirements we imposed were that each group had to systematically interview a substantial number of people at its chosen field

After delivering a guest lecture to the JCIS " Debating Globalization" class
at Peking University, author Thomas L. Friedman (center) pauses for a photo
with Professor Jia Qingguo and the author, November 2005.

site and then present its findings to the class at the end of the semester.

The results were impressive. One group decided to examine the attitudes of workers at a state-owned enterprise who faced layoffs or relocation as a result of Beijing's preparations for the 2008 Olympics. To carry out their research, they discreetly reconnoitered at the front gates of the gigantic Capital Iron and Steel complex in suburban Beijing, noting the daily human traffic patterns and peak flows. One day at lunchtime a group of them boldly walked through the factory gate, entered the workers' cafeteria, and conducted a dozen or so "guerrilla" interviews with workers before plant supervisors politely escorted them out. Another group of students interviewed executives from Chinese and Western banks in Beijing to elicit information about the anticipated costs and benefits of opening China's heavily protected financial services sector to foreign competition under the rules of the World Trade Organization. A third group interviewed foreign and domestic media executives in Beijing about their strategies for dealing with Chinese government censorship. For the most part, the projects were rudimentary, their methods weren't very scientifically rigorous, and their results were not statistically significant. But for the Beida students (and most of the UC students as well), it proved to be a valuable lesson in hands-on social science research.

ONE OF THE hottest topics of conversation on the Beida campus in 2005—indeed one of the hottest topics in the entire country—was the national talent competition to select China's Supergirl's Voice (Chaoji Nüsheng). Modeled along the lines of the hit U.S. TV show *American Idol*, the singing competition attracted 120,000 contestants from every part of China, ranging in age from four to eighty-nine. In the early rounds contestants gathered in five regional cities for preliminary judging. Each region selected one winner and several runners-up, and the regional winners then faced off in the national finals. What made the competition especially feverish was that, for the first time in Chinese history, viewers at home were encouraged to vote for their favorite contestants electronically, using the text messaging feature on their mobile phones. In the preliminary competition in Chengdu, more than 307,000 votes were cast via text messaging, which cost senders between ¥0.5 and ¥3 per vote, with the lion's share of revenues going to the show's sponsor, the Mongolian Cow Sour Yogurt Company. And when the finals were held in August 2005, the telecast attracted 400 million viewers—one of the largest Chinese TV audiences in history. In China's first nationwide exercise in electronic democracy, more than eight million e-votes were cast.

Not surprisingly, the experiment proved enormously popular with the general public, particularly among urban youths in the thirteen- to twenty-five-year age demographic. Also not surprisingly, the Communist Party's cultural watchdogs grew demonstrably nervous over the frenzy that accompanied the final round of voting, with some propaganda officials calling the show "vulgar" and "manipulative," and others claiming that it "embodied the perversions of an unprepared democracy." An intense intra-Party debate followed on the question of whether to pull the plug on the Supergirl's Voice competition in 2006. In the end, a groundswell of public support helped convince the authorities to allow the contest to be renewed for one more year.

The winner of the 2005 Supergirl's Voice competition, Li Yuchun of Sichuan, became an instant national celebrity, a veritable pop superstar. In October 2005, a weeklong computer fair was held on the Beida campus. For the first few days of the fair, student interest was lukewarm at best, and attendance was sparse. On the final day, however, billboards around the campus advertised a special promotional appearance by Li Yuchun, and suddenly the atmosphere changed. From my second-floor classroom window, I could see lines of students snaking for hundreds of yards around several university buildings, waiting for tickets to the University Exhibition Center. Never before had personal computing been so popular at Beida.

BEYOND THE GATES of Peking University, Beijing in the fall of 2005 was considerably more colorful, cosmopolitan, and comfortable than it had been twelve years earlier. My apartment in the Huaqing Jiayuan—a highrise housing complex near the Beida and Tsinghua campuses, adjacent to the Wudaokou light-rail station—was quite modern. It had a fully equipped kitchen with microwave oven, cable TV, heated floors, and a high-speed DSL Internet connection. Real estate offices abounded within the complex, and it did not take long to establish that a sizable majority of flat owners and occupants in the area were South Korean nationals—mainly businessmen, but with a substantial number of Korean university students as well. Because educational costs in China are considerably lower than in Korea (Beida's foreign student tuition was only $3,000 a year), South Koreans have increasingly opted for higher education in China. It's a crude indicator of their growing numbers that most restaurants in and around Beijing's major university campuses now have menus printed in both Chinese and Korean.

By Chinese standards rents were quite high in Beijing's Haidian district, where several leading universities are clustered. I paid ¥6,000 ($720) a month for a short-term lease on a fully furnished two-bedroom flat with floor space of 1,050 square feet. In 2005 the average monthly income of a Beijing family with two wage earners was about ¥3,900 ($470), which meant that an apartment like mine would have been well beyond the financial means of the vast majority of local residents.

Like urbanites elsewhere in China, Beijing's residents were flocking to buy their own apartments, combining liberal financial incentives offered by their work units with low-interest commercial mortgage loans to leverage first-time home ownership. By 2005 upwards of 60 percent of Beijing families owned at least a small flat, with an average floor space of about 450 square feet for a family of three. The market was definitely hot, and housing prices, particularly in modern, spacious apartment complexes like the Huaqing Jiayuan, were rising fast. In 2005 residential real estate in Beijing sold at an average price of almost $70 per square foot—up almost 20 percent over the previous year. In Shanghai and Shenzhen, prices were higher still. Many Chinese home buyers began referring to themselves as "mortgage slaves."

Much of the heat in the real estate market was the result of speculative buying and selling—multiple units purchased by a small number of affluent investors hoping to make a killing by holding onto their properties for a few years, riding the market up, then flipping them. Such behavior was facilitated by the absence of a capital gains tax on the sale of residential real estate. (A new tax law, designed to curb such speculation, was scheduled for introduction in August 2006.) In an attempt to block the government's efforts to stem the rising tide of speculative real estate investment, the owners of multiple residential properties—including my landlord at the Huaqing Jiayuan—often disguised the extent of their holdings by illegally registering their acquisitions in other people's names, usually family members or business associates. Thus, when I reported to the local police station to register as a resident alien, as required by law, my landlord's family choreographed an elaborate charade to mask the flat owner's true identity.

Along with an overheated property market, two other troublesome consequences of Beijing's rapid economic growth are massive traffic congestion and debilitating air pollution. Since 2000 the city's population has swelled from eleven million to seventeen million, and a dramatic surge in private car ownership has more than doubled the number of vehicles on Beijing's streets, to more than 3.3 million, with 1,200 new cars and trucks added, on average, each day. Beijing's nine million bicycles further contribute to the horrific congestion. Gridlock has become frequent on weekdays, and it is not uncommon for an eleven-mile cross-town taxi ride to take more than ninety minutes. On one occasion it took my taxi driver forty minutes to cross a single gridlocked intersection.

Heavy traffic has also brought with it some of the world's highest accident rates. According to the Beijing Traffic Management Bureau, in 2006 there were, on average, 1,038 collisions each day in the nation's capital. Nationwide more than 110,000 traffic fatalities occur annually, making this the leading cause of death for Chinese men and women ages eighteen to fifty-four.

The impact of rapid economic growth on air quality has been even more disturbing. Airborne pollutants have increased by 50 percent since

1995, and in 2005 Beijing was accorded the dubious distinction of having the world's highest airborne concentrations of lung-damaging nitrogen dioxide. In December 2006 Beijing's air contained, on average, six times the maximum pollution levels deemed safe by the World Health Organization. Nor is Beijing alone among Chinese cities in experiencing the profound environmental consequences of rapid growth. According to a World Bank survey, sixteen of the world's twenty most highly polluted cities are in China, and in 2007 the World Bank estimated that more than 650,000 premature deaths in China each year could be traced to air pollution.

In response to this growing crisis the Beijing municipal authorities have introduced a number of measures to mitigate pollution. Coal-burning stoves and power plants—major producers of the greenhouse gas sulfur dioxide—have been outlawed within city limits, with most of the affected firms and families shifting to cleaner-burning natural gas. Hundreds of Beijing's largest, most heavily polluting smokestack industries (including the gigantic Capital Iron and Steel Works, with its 135,000 workers) have been relocated to neighboring counties and provinces. Hundreds of thousands of trees have been planted within the Beijing city limits, urban sewage-treatment capacity has doubled, and all new cars sold in the capital city must meet stringent emission-control standards. Finally, five new municipal subway lines have been added in an effort to reduce the number of cars on the road, which produce 70 percent of Beijing's particulate air pollution. While such measures have surely slowed the process of environmental degradation, they have not yet produced a significant, palpable improvement in air quality, a crisis that has increasingly become the object of negative publicity in the world's media.

IF CHINA'S ACUTE urban growing pains have a silver lining, it is the growing public awareness of the need for concerted civic action to deal with them. With increasing boldness, ordinary citizens are banding together to protest such things as rising pollution, overheated real estate markets, adulterated food and pharmaceutical products, and bureaucratic corruption in local government. As a result, a more vigorous and assertive civil society appears to be emerging at the grassroots level in China. Voluntary associations are forming more frequently, independent of state sponsorship or control. Seeking to fill the void left by governmental programs and policies that are widely perceived as inadequate, inefficient, or inattentive to the real needs of society, these new grassroots NGOs have begun to grapple directly with some of China's most intractable developmental problems. Although the Chinese government has been distinctly cool toward the emergence of autonomous, self-organizing civil society associations, their numbers have nevertheless multiplied dramatically in recent years. By 2007 there were more than 317,000 registered NGOs in China, though no one can be certain of their precise number. More important, they are beginning to make their presence heard—and felt.

In October 2005 Peking University hosted an international conference, "Civil Society Development in Transitional China," on the role of NGOs in China's development. The conference was organized by Beida's new Center for Civil Society Studies, and a broad range of foreign scholars and representatives of global NGOs, such as the Ford Foundation and the Japan Foundation, attended, along with a substantial number of Chinese academics, think-tank members, and NGO activists from around the country. In the course of two intense days of plenary sessions and small-group discussions, participants presented thirty papers on topics ranging from "Citizen Engagement in Six Beijing Neighborhoods," to "The Struggle for Village Public Goods," to "The Development of Citizenship Rights in China," to "Political Participation of Chinese NGOs as Quasi-Interest Groups." Several of my JCIS students attended the conference as observers, and I was invited to present a paper on my experience with the Sanchuan Development Association in Qinghai.

During the conference I was struck by the high levels of professionalism, dedication, and enthusiasm displayed by the mostly youthful Chinese participants, by their courage in tackling controversial issues on the margins of political correctness, and, most of all, by their intense conviction that civil society organizations would eventually propel the country toward a more open and democratic future. Their idealism was both tangible and contagious—and was all the more impressive insofar as the Chinese government has not been at all supportive of grassroots efforts to mobilize Chinese citizens to participate actively in redesigning their own future or monitoring the state's regulatory performance.

Listening to the presentations at the conference, I was reminded of the courage of Beijing's Democracy Wall activists of 1978 and the dedication of the rural schoolteachers of the SDA. Clearly the spirit of civic activism was alive and well in China. As I left, I wished the young participants well. On the success of their mission to create a self-actualizing, self-organizing civil society rested the fate of the nation. If they failed, China would pay a heavy price.

BEFORE LEAVING BEIJING, I paid a visit to the new Olympic Stadium, under construction in the northern part of the city, just outside the Fourth Ring Road. Designed by the Swiss architectural firm of Herzog and de Meuron, with an assist from the renowned Chinese sculptor Ai Weiwei, the stadium had been under construction for more than two years, though its distinctive bird's-nest shape was not yet discernible at the time of my visit, in November 2005. Beijing's political elites had secured their winning Olympic bid four years earlier by committing themselves to a "green Olympics," an open media environment, and the promise of substantial progress toward human rights and democracy. As of 2005 it was difficult to detect much improvement in these areas. It was clear, however, that Beijing was undergoing an incredible pre-Olympic facelift. To make room for the sprawling new stadium complex—and dozens of other new Olympic venues and related urban development projects—more than 1.3 million Beijing residents were being uprooted, their residential neighborhoods demolished, and their households relocated to the suburbs. Budgeted at over $40 billion, Beijing's municipal makeover would cost almost twice as much as the central government's entire budget for health care in 2006.

Certain aspects of Beijing's full-bore Olympic preparations were rather disturbing. As the 2008 Games approached, the Chinese Olympic Organizing Committee promulgated a list of restrictions on the behavior of the half million foreign visitors expected to attend. Would-be spectators were told not to bring "anything detrimental" to China, including printed materials, banners, films, videos, photos, or audio recordings. Religious and political slogans were also proscribed, along with rallies, protest demonstrations, and marches, unless officially preauthorized. Coupled with previously imposed media restrictions that included prohibitions against mentioning in the press such controversial subjects as the 1937 Rape of Nanjing, the 1957 anti-rightist rectification campaign, the Cultural Revolution, official corruption, and media freedom, the Beijing Olympics promised to be a very tightly controlled, politically correct affair.

13

China Watching, Then and Now

AFTER COMPLETING THE JCIS program at Beida, I made a scheduled stopover in Shanghai. Invited to give a talk at Fudan University on the subject of China studies in the United States, I took advantage of the two-hour flight to reflect on the many subtle but important ways in which the vocation of China watching had changed since I entered the field in the early 1960s. As the sleek new China Eastern Airlines Boeing 737 ascended through Beijing's toxic yellow-gray inversion layer, I sat back, closed my eyes, and gathered my thoughts.

Alongside the stunning transformation of China itself, the study of Chinese politics has changed profoundly over the past half century. The founding fathers who made up the first generation of academic China watchers had widely diverse backgrounds. Some of them, affectionately known as Old China Hands (Zhongguotong), were raised in pre–World War II China by missionary parents. Deeply immersed in the language, culture, and politics of China, they included among their ranks such pioneering figures as Doak Barnett, Lucian Pye, and John Lindbeck. A second group, among them historians George Taylor and John K. Fairbank, first visited China as exchange students in the early 1930s, quickly finding themselves caught up in the swirling sociopolitical currents of the prewar era. A third cluster, including my own University of California mentors Arthur Steiner and Bob Scalapino, had been accidental Sinologists, first exposed to China as a result of compulsory military service in World War II. Finally, a few eminent political scientists, including Tang Tsou and Allen Whiting, migrated into Chinese studies from other academic specialties in the early years of the Cold War. Though they weren't always in agreement ideologically or politically, these pioneers collectively created the field of contemporary Chinese political studies. They lobbied for institutional funding (and professional autonomy) for graduate student research and training, they advised the U.S. government on policies toward the emerging People's Republic of China, and they mentored the first cohort of American social science–trained Sinologists, including Chalmers Johnson, Ezra Vogel, John Lewis, Richard Solomon, and James Townsend, among others. Under their tutelage in the 1960s and 1970s, my second-generation peers and I served our China-watching apprenticeships standing on the shoulders of giants.

Because Americans could not travel to China in those pre-normalization Cold War years, the study of Chinese politics involved, for us, a great deal of tedious library research, augmented by a generous helping of interpolation and inference. Our methodology consisted mainly of sitting in our offices (or university libraries), hunched over desks (or microfilm readers), attempting to make sense of recent events by assembling scattered shards of information gleaned from official Chinese media sources—newspapers, magazines, and radio broadcasts. Having to read these in the original Chinese slowed me down considerably, and the Chinese dictionary on my desk was well worn, its spine cracked from constant use. Luckily for me, some PRC media reports were available in English translation, courtesy of the U.S. government. The official PRC media were supplemented by a growing stream of confidential "internal" (*neibu*) CCP documents, such as the set of Four Cleanups directives I had purloined in Taiwan, along with a rather large number of propaganda-laced Taiwanese intelligence reports. These latter materials made a second Chinese dictionary necessary, since Taiwanese publications were always printed using *fantizi*, traditional full-form Chinese characters, whereas PRC media had switched to abbreviated *jiantizi*, or simplified characters. The entire mélange of polyglot source materials was then seasoned with a soupçon of refugee interviews and served up on a warm bed of speculation, conjecture, and just plain guesswork. It was certainly more art than science. The wonder of it is that although we Peking Toms operated at a distance from our subject matter, using dull, imprecise research instruments, sometimes screwing up pretty badly in the process, we actually got it right a lot of the time—at least in the big-picture sense. As the Harvard Sinologist Elizabeth Perry wrote many years later, "Under the circumstances, the quality of work produced by this newly-trained generation of American social scientists—with no first-hand knowledge of China—was actually quite remarkable. Relying almost exclusively upon official documents from the PRC (subsequently supplemented by Hong Kong interviews and the Red Guard press), their analyses of bureaucratic behavior and political mobilization have withstood the test of time surprisingly well."

As Perry noted, the hub of the China-watching universe in the '60s and '70s was Hong Kong. More specifically, there were five key institutions in Hong Kong that performed vital services for China watchers. First was the Universities Service Centre, which satisfied multiple needs of local researchers and visiting scholars alike—as library, copy center, office space, meeting place, and safe house. It was there that my career was launched in 1967–68.

Second was the U.S. Consulate-General on Garden Road, Hong Kong Central, where teams of researchers pored over key Mainland daily newspapers, magazines, and radio broadcasts, rendering them into English for publication in five major translation series: *Foreign Broadcast Information Service-China* (FBIS), *Survey of the China Mainland Press* (SCMP), *Selections from China Mainland Magazines* (SCMM), *Current Background* (CB), and *Joint Publications Research Service* (JPRS). Along with the BBC's *Summary of World Broadcasts*, these five publications were our Holy Scriptures, eagerly perused by China watchers everywhere in the English-speaking world.

Hong Kong's infamous rumor mill was the third vital source of information about Mainland China. Local Chinese-language tabloids such as *Ming Bao*, *Zhengming*, and the *Xingdao Daily News* provided a steady stream of fascinating, if frustratingly unsubstantiated "inside" information and gossip about key personalities, policies, and factional politics in Mainland China. One used such unverifiable sources at one's own risk, of course, and with extreme caution, but their appealing combination of titillating revelation and at least minimal plausibility made them extremely hard for scholars to resist.

Fourth was the Union Research Institute, a Hong Kong think tank founded in 1955 by a group of non-Communist Chinese intellectuals, with financial backing from the U.S.-based Asia Foundation. Devoted to gathering and analyzing political and economic intelligence from Mainland China, the research institute, with its annual *Communist China Yearbook*, its biographical *Who's Who in Communist China*, its hand-transcribed refugee interviews, and its up-to-date classified newspaper clipping files, played an important role in China-related research until its closure in the 1980s. Although never openly acknowledged, rumors of covert CIA funding followed the research institute throughout its existence. (Full disclosure: The Union Research Institute published my first book, *Bibliographic Guide to Kwangtung Communes*, in 1968. The book is a two-hundred-page annotated guide to the thousands of newspaper articles I had used in preparing my Four Cleanups monograph with Fred Teiwes.)

The fifth of Hong Kong's indispensable China-watching institutions was Father Laszlo LaDany, a Hungarian-born Jesuit priest who, until his death in 1990, was a one-man think tank. An indefatigable researcher, Father LaDany enjoyed extraordinary *guanxi* with the charitable groups that ran refugee camps on the Hong Kong side of the Chinese border, giving him unparalleled access to the very latest information from the Mainland, which he summarized and published in a biweekly digest, *China News Analysis*. According to Jim Lilley, who had a long and distinguished career in the CIA before becoming ambassador to China in 1989, Father LaDany's daily monitoring of Chinese radio broadcasts, his network of cross-border contacts, and his interviews with recent émigrés yielded the very best intelligence available to the United States in the decade prior to the normalization of U.S.-China relations.

On one occasion in the spring of 1968, Father LaDany invited me to his offices at Hong Kong University's Matteo Ricci Hall. Over tea, he introduced me to his small cadre of devoted translators and catalogers, who spent most of their waking hours monitoring and transcribing Chinese radio traffic and compiling a newspaper clipping file that was second to none in quality. When I asked him if I could have access to his files for my research, I was rewarded with a polite smile (of questionable warmth) and a firm, non-negotiable "I'm afraid not."

Because China's borders were tightly controlled in the pre-normalization era, few Chinese could legally travel to Hong Kong—or anywhere else. Illegal immigrants were more numerous, however, especially in the aftermath of the Great Famine of the early 1960s and again during the height of Red Guard violence in the Cultural Revolution, but since these illegals, some of whom had risked their lives to get across the border, faced mandatory deportation if apprehended by the British authorities, they usually kept a very low profile once they arrived in Hong Kong. Apart from Father

LaDany and his local *guanxi* network, only a tiny handful of Westerners enjoyed ready access to these illegal immigrants.

Periodically, Chinese refugees would find their way to the Universities Service Centre, attracted by the hourly rate of HK$20 (about US$4) for an interview with resident scholars, a rather generous sum by Chinese standards. Inevitably, the lure of easy pocket money in exchange for a bit of conversation attracted a number of imposters, who sometimes cooked up ingenious tales for the benefit of their credulous interviewers. On those rather infrequent occasions when an émigré proved both authentic and knowledgeable, the center's scholars would compete among themselves to hire him as a research assistant. Two particularly well-informed illegal aliens from Guangdong, given the sobriquets Xiao Yang (Little Yang) and Lao Yang (Old Yang) to shield their real identities, became more or less permanent fixtures at the Universities Service Centre in the late '60s. They were interviewed so frequently and so intensively by center-based scholars that it became a standing joke among us—told only half in jest—that the vast majority of scholarly books, articles, and Ph.D. dissertations written about China during the Cultural Revolution decade, 1966–76, were based on information provided by these two individuals. My own 1975 book on the Four Cleanups, *Prelude to Revolution*, is no exception.

Both Lao Yang and Xiao Yang made out rather well as a result of their Universities Service Centre connections. Lao Yang obtained a U.S. visa in 1976 and went to Ann Arbor, Michigan, where he worked for a few years as Mike Oksenberg's research assistant before moving to Florida, where rumor had it that he had opened a Chinese restaurant. At last sighting, Xiao Yang had changed his name to Saul and was a highly successful computer entrepreneur in Silicon Valley.

DURING THE CULTURAL Revolution decade in Hong Kong, a deep and at times bitter ideological schism opened among academic China watchers. As noted in chapter 3, a group of left-leaning young American scholars and graduate students, reacting to deepening U.S. involvement in the Vietnam War, declared themselves opposed to the war effort. Galvanized by the worldwide student movement of 1968, the rebels split off from the more establishment-oriented Association for Asian Studies, which had refused to take a position on the legitimacy of the war. Calling themselves the Committee of Concerned Asian Scholars (CCAS), the young dissidents began publishing their own journal, *Bulletin of Concerned Asian Scholars*, with the aim of providing a fresh outlet for "progressive" scholarship on Asia. In the pages of their journal, they subjected mainstream and "liberal" scholarship on Asia to critical scrutiny and propagated an alternative, neo-Marxist perspective on Asian Communism as humane, progressive, and anti-imperialist.

The anti-establishment outlook of the CCAS had a polarizing effect upon the field of Chinese studies. The young neo-leftists of the CCAS tended to embrace the visionary ideals of Maoism, though not necessarily its extreme methods or its excesses; more established scholars, in contrast, while often critical of U.S. involvement in Vietnam, were less inclined to suspend critical judgment of the nature and consequences of Maoism. Notwithstanding my own opposition to the war, I associated myself with the latter camp. I didn't feel comfortable with the CCAS's characterization of Asian Communism as progressive and liberating (I was still my father's son, after all).

I was also uncomfortable with CCAS allegations of clandestine U.S. governmental (and, in particular, CIA) manipulation of academic scholarship on contemporary China. While it was certainly true that the U.S. government played a significant role in stimulating the expansion of university-based Chinese studies beginning in the late 1950s (my own graduate training at Berkeley had been funded under a government-initiated program), and that a CIA front organization, the Congress of Cultural Freedom, provided behind-the-scenes funding for the flagship journal of contemporary Sinology, *The China Quarterly*, I had seen little or no evidence that the U.S. intelligence community was manipulating the research projects or findings of China scholars. Published at the School of Oriental and African Studies in London, *The China Quarterly* had an independent editorial board that maintained extremely high standards of scholarship, with the possible exception of its decision to publish Charlie Neuhauser's 1968 article misinterpreting the Four Cleanups. In almost all cases we China watchers defined our research projects based on our own individual tastes and preferences. If the U.S. government wanted to pay for them, so much the better.

The People's Republic's unofficial Hong Kong representatives at the *Ta Kung Po* and the *Wen Wei Po* thought otherwise, however, and they remained firmly convinced that the Universities Service Centre was a hotbed of foreign espionage, run by and for the benefit of British and U.S. intelligence. In point of fact, the center's most important patron in those days was not the CIA but the Ford Foundation, to the tune of approximately $100,000 per year. And to the best of my knowledge, neither the U.S. nor the U.K. government made any attempt to interfere in the center's operations, either directly or obliquely.

One incident stands out as emblematic of the strong emotions stirred up by the Vietnam War and by the CCAS's deep antagonism to it. In 1971 the former U.S. national security adviser McGeorge Bundy, who had earlier been one of the top Vietnam War planners under presidents John F. Kennedy and Lyndon B. Johnson, paid a visit to the Universities Service Centre. Upon learning that "McBundy," who was then president of the Ford Foundation, was coming to lunch, a group of about twenty CCAS-affiliated center researchers organized a symbolic protest against the war. When Bundy was introduced to the assembled scholars in the center's lunchroom, a CCAS spokesman, John Berninghausen, rose to his feet to read a prepared statement. Calling Bundy a "war criminal" with the "blood of innocents" on his hands, Berninghausen averred that it would be morally repugnant to break bread with such a person. Thereupon he and the other CCAS members silently and in unison turned over their lunch plates. Displayed on each overturned dish was the famous photo of a naked young Vietnamese girl who had been napalmed by U.S. forces.

Bundy was stunned, caught completely off guard. His face reddened, and he began breathing rapidly and unevenly. At this point, Mike Oksenberg, who was then in residence at the center, walked over to Bundy, helped him out of his chair, and led him away to another room, inviting those who disagreed with the CCAS protest to join them. A handful of young scholars followed, leaving the CCAS members in the lunchroom to continue their silent vigil.

After a very tense and awkward half hour of small talk in the lounge, during which Mike (who was no friend of the CCAS), along with one of Bundy's muscular young associates, David Finkelstein, considered the option of physically ejecting the CCAS protesters, reason prevailed and Bundy was escorted quietly out of the building. As he exited, still visibly in distress, he passed by the lunch table where the silent protesters continued to stare solemnly at the photo of the Vietnamese child on their overturned plates. Several of those present reported seeing Bundy wipe a tear from his eye.

In the days that followed, Mike continued to fume over the incident. At one point, he offered to personally contact the academic advisers of the CCAS members who had participated in the protest, to urge them to revoke the students' overseas study grants. The center's future director, John Dolfin, eventually talked him out of this. But the incident took its toll on scholarly collegiality, opening a deep wound that would heal only slowly. Not long afterward, the Ford Foundation terminated its funding of the Universities Service Centre.

Coinciding with the rise of intense antiwar sentiment, a cresting tide of "China fever" in the early 1970s spawned a spate of scholarly articles and monographs in defense of Mao's "great experiment." In Europe and the United States alike, many New Left scholars and CCAS members echoed the Maoist critique of "bourgeois powerholders" and bureaucrats, applauding the putative liberation of ordinary Chinese workers and peasants, and praising the efficacy of mass ideological campaigns in raising the Chinese people's political consciousness.

It wasn't until some time after Mao's death, in the late 1970s, that the scales began to fall from the eyes of the less doctrinaire members of the New Left. Stung by revelations of Red Guard brutality, economic paralysis, and incipient political chaos in China, many scholars who had been in thrall to varying degrees to the Maoist model of development began to rethink their positions. A young French scholar, Claudie Broyelle, who first visited China briefly in 1971 as a member of a women's delegation, made perhaps the most striking about-face. Under the watchful eye of the All-China Women's Federation, Broyelle's delegation conducted a brief investigation of the women's movement in China. When she returned to France a few weeks later, she wrote a glowing book, *Women's Liberation in China*, passionately praising the progress of Chinese feminism and uncritically repeating virtually everything she had been told by her well-prepped handlers from the Women's Federation.

Ardent converts to the Maoist cause, Broyelle and her husband returned to China a year or two after Mao's death, where they worked for three years at the Foreign Languages Press in Beijing. Witnessing at first hand the debunking of the Maoist mystique and the wholesale "reversal of verdicts" on the Cultural Revolution and its devastating consequences, they then produced a new book, *China: A Second Look*. In it, Broyelle wholly recanted her earlier, ardent endorsement of Mao's feminist utopia. Acknowledging her own gullibility and naïveté, she made a contrite self-criticism and issued a scathing indictment of China's Orwellian political system. Like so many others of this era, her thinking had ostensibly been "poisoned" by the Gang of Four.

Though Broyelle's was perhaps the most self-conscious, self-critical example, she was not alone in backing away from her earlier burst of irrational exuberance. Following the revelations of Cultural Revolution cruelty and brutality, many erstwhile admirers of the Chinese model began to acknowledge—sometimes grudgingly, sometimes not—the shortcomings of the Maoist experiment. To one degree or another, such well-known and respected China watchers as Orville Schell, Ross Terrill, Mark Selden, Jonathan Mirsky, Maurice Meisner, Marc Blecher, and my UCLA colleague Philip Huang, among others, swallowed their pride and readjusted their perspectives in the late 1970s. Even Mike Oksenberg found it necessary to change his tack after waxing enthusiastic about Maoist China in his 1973 essay "On Learning from China," in which he urged Americans to emulate the Maoists in their "dedication to building a more decent, just society."

Few scholars, however, were as openly contrite as Claudie Broyelle (in truth, few had as much to be contrite about), and some of them utterly refused to acknowledge their errant judgment. Sadly, a handful of New Left academics who had been badly wrong-footed by the post-Mao "reversal of verdicts" saw their promising careers brought to a screeching halt in the wake of the post-Mao backlash. Richard Pfeffer, Stephen and Phyllis Andors, Mitch Meisner, and Charles Cell were just a few of the younger American scholars who had staked their academic reputations on the success of the Maoist model— and then suffered the consequences when the model collapsed.

Along with a number of new-left Asian scholars, a handful of Hollywood celebrities also jumped on the Maoist bandwagon in the 1970s. One such proselyte was the actress Shirley MacLaine. At a National Committee–sponsored banquet I attended in Washington, D.C., in January 1979, honoring Deng Xiaoping and celebrating the normalization of U.S.-China relations, MacLaine was seated near the diminutive Deng. At dinner, she told him that she had been deeply impressed, on her visit to China a few years earlier, by a Chinese scientist whom she had met while touring a rural commune. The scientist told her that he had once been an ivory-tower intellectual, divorced from the masses, but under the guidance of Chairman Mao's thought he had seen the error of his ways. Sent to the countryside toward the end of the Cultural Revolution to redeem himself through farm labor, he told her how happy he was to be "serving the people" by growing cabbages. When she finished recounting her inspirational tale, Deng, ever the polite listener, looked her squarely in the eye and said earnestly, "He was lying."

Among those Americans who celebrated the virtues of Maoism in the 1970s, the most zealous by far were members of the Revolutionary Communist Party USA. Its leader, Bob Avakian, was a veteran of Berkeley's Free Speech Movement who had turned sharply leftward during the Vietnam War. Ironically his father, Spurgeon Avakian, was a popular Republican-appointed judge in the San Francisco Bay area. In the early 1970s Avakian *fils* served a jail term for desecrating the American flag during an antiwar rally, and by the mid-'70s he had become a radical Maoist.

In the spring of 1979, at a time when Deng was first introducing his economic reforms (and MacLaine was still enamored of her cabbage-patch scientist), I got a call from an associate of Bob Avakian, asking if I would be willing to let "Chairman Bob" (as he modestly called himself) speak to my Chinese politics class at UCLA. Aware of his reputation as an egoistic agitator and Maoist provocateur, I hesitated at first. But I ultimately decided it might be good for my students to hear from someone who believed passionately in the Maoist cause, so I agreed to let him speak.

Less than five minutes into Avakian's talk, or should I say rant, things began to get out of hand. He used the podium not to explain or defend Mao but to viciously attack Deng Xiaoping. Calling Deng a "half-pint pimp" and a "bourgeois backstabber," he hurled a bitter barrage of abuse at Deng and his reforms. Avakian defended the Gang of Four as innocent victims of Deng's "counterrevolutionary treachery," his face flushed with righteous indignation. After about fifteen minutes of theatrical bombast, I managed to cut him off, thanking him for his views and asking him to leave. I did not see any point in trying to reason with him, or hold a class discussion, while he was in such an agitated state. One of his associates obligingly escorted him from the lecture hall.

Not long after this incident, Avakian was served with an arrest warrant. It seems that one of the many protest demonstrations he organized against Deng Xiaoping had turned violent. Chanting "Mao Zedong did not fail; revolution will prevail," his zealous supporters had physically assaulted a group of taunting nonbelievers. Rather than face prosecution, Avakian jumped bail and fled to France, where he continues to live, three decades later, in self-styled political exile.

LACK OF DIRECT access to the People's Republic continued to disadvantage American China watchers until the late 1970s. Although a sprinkling of U.S. scholars managed to visit China before normalization—either as escorts accompanying cultural and scientific exchange delegations or as members of CCAS-organized "friendship groups"—it was not until January 1979 that the slow trickle of American academic visitors began to widen into a small stream. Thereafter, U.S. scholars and graduate student were permitted, for the first time, to conduct field research in China. While such opportunities were carefully controlled by the Chinese government, they served to open the door, however narrowly, for a new type of China scholarship, based on direct observation, local archival research, in-depth interviews, and on-the-ground fieldwork. For the first time since the wartorn 1940s, aspiring young American Sinologists could actually live and work inside China.

The 1980s undoubtedly would have spawned an even bigger breakthrough in fieldwork-based China studies had it not been for the misadventures of one particular graduate student researcher, Stanford University doctoral candidate Steven Mosher. Mosher was an early beneficiary of the post-normalization opening of China. While conducting anthropological fieldwork in a village in Guangdong in 1979–80, Mosher reportedly engaged in a series of deceptive and illegal acts, including bribing villagers with the "gift" of a Volkswagen van. He was expelled from China in 1981 and subsequently dismissed from Stanford University. After being kicked out of China, Mosher traveled to Taiwan, where he published a number of controversial photographs showing late-term abortions being performed on rural Guangdong women under highly unsanitary (and allegedly coercive) conditions. Thereafter, he became a zealous moral crusader against forced abortion in China. Reacting angrily to Mosher's unauthorized activities in China, and to his subsequent anti-abortion crusade, the Chinese government severely restricted fieldwork opportunities for all American scholars for several years.

Notwithstanding these restrictions, the normalization of U.S.-China relations attracted large numbers of American college students to the study of modern China. In the four years prior to Richard Nixon's 1972 China sojourn, my undergraduate Chinese politics and foreign relations classes at UCLA averaged 30–40 students each. Immediately after the Nixon visit, the numbers shot up—160 students in the fall of 1972, and more than 200 the following spring. Graduate school applications also rose substantially as a new generation of political scientists, sociologists, and anthropologists began gravitating toward Chinese studies. Across the country Chinese-language classes enjoyed a fourfold increase in student enrollments. The sudden surge of campus interest in China was the subject of a special, in-depth *Time* magazine profile in 1979.

A few major research universities led the way in the expanded training of graduate students in the 1980s, most notably Michigan, Columbia, Harvard, Stanford, and UC Berkeley. In political science, these and a handful of other major universities added a second (and in one or two cases, a third) China specialist to their faculties. With graduate enrollments accelerating, with faculty recruitment on the rise, and with new research funding made possible by a prolonged mid-1980s U.S. economic boom and stock market surge, China studies enjoyed an unprecedented growth spurt.

In this era of rapid growth, the University of Michigan stood out as the premier training ground for specialists in Chinese politics. With an exceptionally strong core of political scientists—including Allen Whiting, Mike Oksenberg, and Kenneth Lieberthal—plus an impressive group of China specialists in other disciplines (economics, philosophy, history, and sociology), Michigan became the foremost institution for studying contemporary China. From the mid-1970s until the early 1990s, no other university came close to the "Michigan mafia" in training outstanding Ph.D.s in Chinese politics. Mike was the principal driving force behind this success. He chaired at least two dozen Ph.D. committees in this period, far more than anyone else in the China field. (Doak Barnett, who had been Mike's mentor at Columbia, was a rather distant second, with more than a dozen Ph.D. advisees to his credit.) It is a testament to both Doak's and Mike's mentoring skills that their former students went on to dominate the academic marketplace in Chinese politics for more than two decades.

In addition to attracting more and better graduate students after normalization, the field of Chinese politics underwent significant methodological advances in the 1980s. For one thing, Chinese area studies—once virtually walled off from other fields within various social science disciplines—now came to be increasingly integrated within those disciplines. Political science departments across the country began to impose more stringent social science requirements on their Chinese politics graduate students, including courses on statistical methods, survey research, and comparative political economy, inter alia.

Members of the post-normalization generation were not only more rigorously trained in their own disciplines and associated research methodologies; they also acquired superior language skills. Whereas most students in my generation began studying Chinese only after entering graduate school, members of the post-1979 generation often completed two or three years of Chinese as undergraduates, enabling them to proceed to more advanced language training in graduate school. Consequently, when China eased entry barriers for U.S. graduate students in the 1980s, these young scholars were able to hit the ground running. By the mid-1980s the first few Chinese-language schools were opened to American students in China, including the University of California's Education Abroad Program in Beijing, which established language programs at both Beida and Beijing Normal University. With a linguistic head start and ready access to advanced Chinese-language training inside China, the post-normalization generation of China scholars attained levels of fluency in Chinese that scholars of my generation could only envy and admire.

The rush of language students to China beginning in the 1980s had one additional, unintended consequence: it served to weaken foreign demand for advanced language training in Taiwan. As the popularity of travel to Mainland China increased, foreign student enrollment in many Taiwanese language programs declined. Although the Stanford Center in Taipei, where I had studied Chinese in the 1960s, managed to sustain generally high enrollments, administrative pressures from within National Taiwan University, where the program was housed, resulted in its move in 1997 to Beijing's Tsinghua University, where it has continued to thrive.

Also in the 1980s Johns Hopkins University, in partnership with Nanjing University, inaugurated a program of academic studies in China. Located on the campus of Nanda, the Hopkins-Nanjing Center offered a rigorous master's degree program in international studies for both U.S. and Chinese graduate students, with faculty drawn from elite institutions in both countries. Recently celebrating its twentieth anniversary, the Hopkins-Nanjing Center, with more than one thousand alumni, has become a major focal point for academic interaction between Chinese and American graduate students.

THE WIDENING STREAM of American graduate students undergoing advanced training in China has been fully reciprocated—and then some. Beginning in the mid-1980s, a small number of China-born graduate students took advantage of relaxed U.S. entry barriers to enroll in American doctoral programs. Bringing with them a deep knowledge of Chinese society and culture as well as native fluency in the language, these overseas Chinese students enjoyed an initial advantage vis-à-vis their American-born academic counterparts. This advantage was offset, however, by two equally important educational deficits: for one thing, the earliest PRC postgrads in the United States lacked fluency in English, and for another, they were generally unfamiliar with the analytical methods of Western pedagogy. Raised and nurtured in a system that valued conformity, reverence for established authority, and rote memorization of educational texts, the first generation of Chinese graduate students encountered rough going in the United States. Many had only infrequently (if ever) conversed with native English speakers prior to arriving at their host universities, and their levels of oral comprehension and verbal fluency were generally low. To make matters worse, most had never before been exposed to the type of critical thinking and analysis that characterizes the American academic milieu. Unaccustomed to thinking outside the box, these early students often floundered—and sometimes failed—despite their high native intelligence and outstanding Chinese undergraduate dossiers.

My first PRC graduate student, whom I will call Cao, fit this general description. Recruited to UCLA in 1985 with a full academic fellowship (no Chinese students in those days could afford to pay American university tuition using their own resources), Cao struggled mightily for three years, taking a number of advanced political science and methodology classes that were clearly over his head, in terms of both English comprehension and analytical methods. But he worked night and day, never taking a holiday or a break. One semester, when I taught an early morning class twice a week, I would arrive on campus before 8:00 A M to find him asleep at his desk in the departmental library, a book open in front of him. Slender to begin with, he lost twenty pounds in those three years, almost suffering a nervous breakdown in the process. But he was determined to succeed. Carrying with him all his family's hopes and dreams for a better future, he literally could not afford to fail: the shame would have been unbearable. He memorized all his course texts and wrote his required seminar papers by stringing together loosely organized ideas and paraphrases drawn from published sources, interspersed with personal observations and comments. He spent any bits of spare time he had listening to English-language conversation tapes. He had no social life whatever.

Through sheer hard work and dogged determination, Cao narrowly squeaked through his Ph.D. preliminary examinations. Reading his exam papers, I noted some progress in his analytical abilities, and his English had improved considerably. But my satisfaction was short-lived, for he was simply not able to pass the next, and final, hurdle. When it came to writing a dissertation—his chosen subject was a comparative analysis of Chinese and Soviet foreign policy reforms in the 1980s—he could not manage the necessary originality of thought, analytical rigor, or fluidity of English prose. Over the next eighteen months he labored to produce three successive drafts of a three-hundred-page thesis. As his principal adviser, I spent countless hours—sometimes it seemed like weeks at a time—critiquing his work and editing his English. I was almost as exhausted as he was. After reading his third draft, which was nowhere close to being acceptable, I sensed that Cao was nearing the end of his tether—and I was reaching the end of mine.

After consulting with my department chair, I talked to Cao about alternative educational and employment possibilities. At first he balked, informing me in no uncertain terms that he could never go home without a Ph.D. degree. I replied that there were other routes to academic success and professional prestige, and that he needed to start thinking about career alternatives. He remained unconvinced. After our initial conversation, I called a friend who taught law at a private university in the Rocky Mountains. His law school was actively recruiting PRC students. In those early post-normalization years, Chinese students were an exotic academic rarity and were very much in demand on U.S. university campuses. So I described Cao to my friend, who seemed quite interested in him. I then had a second meeting with Cao, explaining to him the differences between the analytical methods of political science and the case-study technique used in law schools. The latter was, I told him, more precise, well defined, precedent driven, and by the book. He seemed somewhat relieved to hear this and reluctantly agreed to prepare for the Law School Aptitude Test.

Cao performed reasonably well on the test and was subsequently admitted to my friend's law school, with three full years of funding. Breathing a sigh of relief, I bade farewell to Cao, asking him to keep me informed of his progress. He wrote a few times the first year, indicating that he was working extremely hard (no surprise there) and had gotten reasonably good grades (to my great relief). Then there was a prolonged silence, which lasted for several years. The last I heard of him, in 1998, was that he was back in China practicing law—and presumably making his family proud.

By the end of the 1980s Chinese applicants to U.S. doctoral programs were far better prepared for the rigors of graduate study than Cao had been a mere half decade earlier. For one thing, top Chinese universities had begun to introduce Western-style analytical methods and textbooks into their core curricula. For another, the amount and quality of English-language training in Chinese public schools, K–12, had risen sharply in the intervening years. No longer did eager young Chinese students have to gather before dawn in front of foreigners' hotels to practice their English conversation while jogging with American tourists. The PRC government, moreover, had begun to fund substantial numbers of high-achieving graduate students who had gained admission to U.S. universities. Consequently, the flow of Chinese students to the United States increased dramatically, from a few hundred in the mid-'80s to tens of thousands in the early '90s. By then many Chinese graduate students could—and did—compete on a level playing field with native-born American students. Indeed, in the field of Chinese studies they enjoyed two critical advantages: native fluency in Chinese and easier access to Mainland Chinese field sites, research libraries, and documentary archives. After my painful experience with Cao, it was a great relief, over the next two decades, to serve as academic adviser to a number of extremely talented and well-trained Chinese graduate students at UCLA. As of this writing, eight of my Chinese students have completed their doctorates and gone on to hold academic positions in China, Hong Kong, and the United States.

According to U.S. government statistics, there were more than 62,500 Chinese graduate students enrolled in American universities in 2007, second in number only to Indian students; in the same year more than 8,000 Chinese nationals received U.S. doctorates, primarily in the fields of science and engineering. The number of social science Ph.D.s, while quite small in comparison with those holding science and engineering degrees (the ratio is approximately one to ten), has also increased significantly. By the early 2000s a small stream of Chinese undergraduate students, mostly funded by their own families, were also attending U.S. colleges and universities, a reflection of the rising affluence of the new urban middle classes along China's booming eastern seaboard.

The tumultuous Beijing Spring of 1989 exerted a powerful impact on the study of Chinese politics in the United States. In addition to generating a fresh wave of student interest in China on American college campuses (my classes at UCLA swelled substantially in the fall of 1989), the events of June 3–4 generated a dramatic upsurge in the number of PRC students applying to study abroad. A U.S. presidential decree signed by George H. W. Bush in April 1990 granted a four-year moratorium on the enforcement of U.S.

immigration laws to more than fifty thousand Chinese students and scholars residing in the United States, creating a fast track for them to obtain highly valued permanent resident status.

By the same token, however, the events of May–June 1989 produced an attitude of deepening suspicion on the part of the Chinese government toward the motives and intentions of Western scholars. One clear symptom was the visible tightening of Chinese scrutiny of foreign scholars' visa applications. Throughout the 1990s, and continuing into the 2000s, a number of eminent U.S. China scholars and journalists—including Perry Link, Jonathan Lipman, Jonathan Mirsky, Andrew Nathan, Peter Perdue, Gilbert Rozman, and Orville Schell—were denied visas on the grounds that they had allegedly engaged in "anti-China" activities during and after the Tiananmen disturbances. Making matters worse, several Chinese scholars living in the United States were arrested by PRC state security when they went back to China to conduct research on politically sensitive topics such as the Cultural Revolution, the Korean War, and China's nuclear weapons program. As noted earlier, one such scholar, Song Yongyi, obtained his release from captivity only after Chinapol members mounted a well-publicized online petition drive.

IN THEIR EFFORTS to comprehend the political and social consequences of China's rapidly changing developmental landscape, the post-Tiananmen generation of U.S. China scholars armed themselves with a broad array of new research techniques and methodologies. Game theory, rational-choice analysis, econometrics, statistical and formal modeling—most of them borrowed from the "dismal science" of economics—became the China watcher's essential tools of the trade. With field research opportunities in China expanding once again in the aftermath of Deng Xiaoping's globalization-embracing southern tour of early 1992, U.S. graduate students gained ready access to mountains of Chinese statistical data and to a wide variety of field research sites inside China, where they could test their theories, conduct in-depth interviews, and refine their analytical models in a relatively rigorous manner. Unlike the Peking Toms of my generation, who relied on library research, a handful of refugee informants of dubious reliability, and improvised, seat-of-the-pants research methods, China watchers of the current generation have at their fingertips a full and sophisticated arsenal of methodological weaponry. And the rapid development of the Internet has brought with it instant access to an extraordinary array of searchable information, including digitized links to the full texts of thousands of Chinese newspapers and journals.

The parallel revolutions in social science methodology and data storage and retrieval technology have undoubtedly served to raise both the quality and the empirical rigor of research on contemporary China. Graduate students today are far more capable of applying complex mathematical and game-theoretic models, and performing complex statistical analysis of large-N data sets, than I ever was. They are also more sensitively attuned to the need to study China within a comparative, cross-national institutional and political-economy framework. These are all important developments, representing significant progress in the field. But they have come at a cost.

Much has been written in recent years about the decline of area studies in American universities. Due in large measure to the increasing influence of deductive, rational-choice, and statistical-econometric models, graduate students interested in pursuing Chinese studies today appear to be investing less time and energy gaining deep cultural, social, and historical knowledge of their country or region of interest and proportionally more time studying formal modeling and quantitative techniques. Most leading political science departments, for example, now require all first-year students to undergo a rigorous sequence of statistics courses, and many departments (including my own) offer students the option of an additional year of advanced mathematics courses in lieu of a foreign-language requirement. When I completed my doctoral studies at Berkeley in the '60s, Ph.D. candidates in comparative politics and area studies were required to pass two foreign-language examinations at a high level of proficiency (at least one of which had to be French, German, or Russian). By contrast, today's Ph.D. candidates in international and comparative politics at many universities, including UCLA, need attain only moderate proficiency in a single foreign language, while students in other subfields need not demonstrate any language skills at all. I find this very troubling. Without the ability to communicate effectively with people from other cultures, one's worldview tends to be narrow and parochial.

Many graduate programs now offer "methodology" as a distinct subfield of political science, permitting students to substitute it for traditional fields such as international relations, political behavior, U.S. politics, or comparative politics. Increasingly, if almost imperceptibly, methodology has been elevated in importance from a useful set of research tools, or *means* used to study politics, to a self-contained object of study, that is, *an end in itself.* Broadly indicative of this trend, between 1968 and 1998, the proportion of articles in the *American Political Science Review* employing statistical and formal-deductive models of politics rose from 16 percent to 68 percent, while the proportion of articles principally using country-specific, qualitative analytical methods declined from 53 percent to 21 percent. Further reflecting this trend, most leading political science departments have de-emphasized area specialization in their recruitment of new faculty members, stressing instead the hiring of comparative generalists with substantial training in mathematics, econometrics, and/or formal modeling.

Lamenting the decline of area studies in U.S. universities, Chalmers Johnson in 1994 famously called the growing academic infatuation with deductive methods and rational-choice assumptions in political science "a disaster in the making." Speaking of the declining field of Japanese area studies, for example, Johnson bemoaned the "arrogant disregard" of area-specific expertise that increasingly characterized U.S. scholarship on Japanese politics, which, he claimed, "borders on malpractice."

Although Johnson is notoriously prone to indulge in dramatic hyperbole when driving home a point, there is more than a kernel of truth in his critique. In recent years several of my graduate students have displayed significant shifts in their primary research interests, moving away from *qualitative* research problems (guided by a relatively deep and intuitive understanding of China's history, institutions, culture, and language) toward a concentration on research problems that lend themselves more readily either to deductive modeling or to statistical analysis. In some cases, the problems selected for analysis appear to be chosen more for their modeling possibilities, or for the ready availability of complete sets of statistical data, than for their intrinsic importance or "puzzle power." Such research is reminiscent of the classic anecdote about the drunk who looked for his lost car keys under a street lamp. When asked why he was concentrating his search under the lamp, he answered, "Because that's where the light is."

The problem lies not with the techniques and methods of statistical and formal analysis themselves but rather with their tendency, when used in isolation from other, more traditional research methods and concepts, to facilitate the displacement of context-sensitive area knowledge by mere technical virtuosity. Two examples will help to illustrate the nature—and dangers—of such displacement. A few years ago I was asked to read a master's thesis that relied on the statistical technique of multiple-regression analysis to explain the unexpected victory of the pro-independence candidate Chen Shui-bian in the Taiwanese presidential election of March 2000. Armed with comprehensive demographic, socioeconomic, and party registration data for every county in Taiwan, the student set up a statistical model that included a rather large number of quantifiable variables (including age, gender, education, occupation, household income, party identification, and ethnic identity, inter alia). The student's statistical regressions revealed that Chen Shui-bian's victory—and the size of his margin of victory—were explained primarily by two variables: voter ethnicity and local unemployment rates. Each of these variables, when regressed against all others, displayed a "significance level" of <.03 (i.e., a probability of less than 3 percent that the results could be explained by pure coincidence). While this seemed reasonably conclusive on the face of it, in fact it was not. During the questioning that followed the student's oral presentation, I asked her if there were any other variables she could think of that might have influenced the outcome of the March 2000 election, factors she may not have considered. She thought for a bit and said, "No, I don't think so." I then asked if she had considered the possibility that Chen Shui-bian may have received a significant electoral boost, or "rally effect," as a result of an angry popular backlash against PRC military threats directed at Taiwan on the eve of the election. This seemed a distinct possibility insofar as public opinion polls had revealed that a substantial number of Taiwanese voters were deeply incensed over the Mainland's heavy-handed efforts to frighten them away from supporting Chen. The student looked at me blankly for a moment, then responded, "I never thought of that."

The second example of methodology gone awry concerns one of my graduate students who wished to write a paper on the political economy of corruption in post-reform China. He had just taken a course on formal modeling, and he enthusiastically set about trying to reveal the hidden logic that underlay the spread of corruption during the post-Mao era. He constructed an elaborate, multistage game-theoretic scenario involving a hypothetical local village cadre who had to decide, as a putatively "rational" actor, whether or not to solicit a bribe from a villager who was applying for a license to run a township enterprise. The villager, also assumed to be a rational actor, had to decide whether and at what stage to offer the bribe, and in what amount. The student first posited a set of basic assumptions (or parameters) that simplified the game by reducing the number of variables he would have to consider, including such things as the severity of the penalties for bribery and the probability of being caught. He next drew up an elaborate decision tree, posing a series of branching binary choices (i.e., solicit/not solicit; pay/not pay; small/large bribe) at successive decision points, covering every specific contingency facing both the cadre and the villager. The exercise required several pages of dense mathematical notation. At the end of this largely formalistic exercise the model conclusively demonstrated that, other things being equal, a rational cadre would be most likely to solicit a bribe—and a rational villager to offer it—if, and only if, the anticipated gains for each outweighed the perceived risks of being caught and punished. And the bigger the anticipated gains, the more likely the bribe was to be a large one. Eureka! Here was a case of a very complex modeling technique being employed to belabor a couple of rather simple and obvious points—an elephant gun used to obliterate the proverbial flea.

My purpose in raising these examples is not to disparage either econometrics or deductive modeling. Indeed, statistical methods, game theory, and rational-choice analysis have proved extremely valuable, for example, in exposing the operation of hidden institutional constraints on human behavior and in laying bare the underlying logic of apparently irrational and counterintuitive policy outcomes.[1] But such methods are best used in conjunction with other analytical tools and techniques—including case studies, documentary research, personal interviews, and direct observation. And they must be applied to real-world problems by analysts sensitive to the historical, sociocultural, and institutional characteristics and contexts of their empirical universe.

Notwithstanding my nagging concerns about recent methodological trends, there is reason for cautious optimism about the future of China

---

[1] Rational-choice theory seeks to explain how irrational collective outcomes may arise from the rational actions of individuals seeking to maximize their own immediate benefit. This theory has many relevant applications in modern China studies, including the failure of large-scale collective agriculture in the Maoist era due to "free riding" by individual farmers and the steady poisoning of the air and water by industrial polluters in the reform era, despite the obvious detrimental health effects and social costs. Similarly, a branch of deductive theory known as principal-agent relations has proved quite useful in explaining how and why local government officials (agents) in China often are able to ignore or subvert the policy preferences of higher-level authorities (principals).

watching. For one thing, the methodological pendulum may be start-ing to swing back in the direction of better balance between qualitative-inductive research techniques and quantitative-deductive ones. Such pendulum-like motions are not infrequent in academia, where popular new intellectual fads and fashions are subject to long-term modification and renormalization through trial and error. For another thing, the talent pool and academic preparedness of applicants for graduate schools appear to be improving over time, with Graduate Record Exam scores rising steadily. Finally, China's dramatic economic success has greatly increased the demand for Chinese area expertise in society at large. There are now far more employment opportunities than ever before for China specialists in nonacademic careers, professions, and economic sectors.

MY REVERIE ON the state of contemporary Sinology was interrupted by the flight attendant's announcement of our imminent arrival at Shanghai's gleaming new Pudong International Airport. Preparing to disembark, I felt reasonably upbeat: Notwithstanding the recent decline of area studies, the longer-term future of the China-watching enterprise seemed reason-ably assured.

14

The Gini in the Jar

NO SENSIBLE OBSERVER looking at China at the time of Mao's death in
1976 could have predicted the country's rapid emergence as an economic
powerhouse and potential peer competitor of the United States. In the mid-
1970s it was not even clear that the CCP would survive the devastation
wrought by Mao's Cultural Revolution. Now, thirty years on, few remnants
of Maoism are visible, yet the CCP remains deeply entrenched in power,
clinging tenaciously to its one-party political monopoly and the sovereign
perks flowing therefrom. With the vast majority of existing Communist
regimes, including the Bolshevik motherland, having collapsed in the Velvet Revolution of 1989–91, China's authoritarian leaders defied the odds
and survived this biggest of all political tsunamis.

How to explain the CCP's survival in an age of Leninist mass extinc-
tion? It isn't rocket science. It's the economy, stupid! The plain fact is that
most Chinese—in particular, most *urban* Chinese—have visibly benefited
from Maoism's demise, from Deng Xiaoping's market reforms, and from
China's full-bore global engagement. As Deng himself put it in 1992, "If
it hadn't been for the achievements of reform and opening up, we would
not have made it beyond June 4." Recent opinion surveys reveal that the
great majority of Chinese people, 71–86 percent (depending on the poll
cited), are currently satisfied with their country's "national condition," and
an only slightly smaller majority, 69–83 percent, are generally optimistic
about their own future prospects. Despite severe income disparities (indicated by China's steadily rising Gini coefficient) and an alarming prevalence of official corruption, and notwithstanding Beijing's dangerously

polluted air, horrific traffic jams, and an overheated property market, most Chinese are not itching to see the walls of Zhongnanhai come tumbling down.

The wellsprings of rising economic satisfaction are not hard to find. Along the heavily urbanized eastern seaboard, where most public opinion polling is concentrated, personal incomes have risen rapidly and life is getting better, at least for most. In 2006 Guangzhou became the first Chinese city to achieve an average per capita income of ¥62,000 ($7,500), with Shenzhen and Shanghai following close behind. By mid-2007, according to official statistics, just over 6 percent of Chinese families, roughly 80–100 million people, had attained middle-class status, with a median family income of ¥75,000 (around $9,000). According to various Chinese media sources, the typical middle-class family today is composed of an employed couple with one school-age child and no pets, living in a privately owned apartment with two mobile phones, a large-screen color TV with cable service, and an Internet-linked personal computer. Other common middle-class benchmarks include postsecondary education, white-collar employment, and—increasingly—a family car used mainly for weekend getaways. Not surprisingly, most members of China's emerging middle class live in and around big cities. Material markers of China's expanding urban middle class also include ubiquitous mobile phones (540 million at the end of 2008), Internet connectivity (310 million), private home ownership (65 percent), private automobiles (32 million, increasing at the rate of almost 10,000 per day), and foreign travel (34 million trips abroad annually). Also notable are the rising numbers of ATM machines (120,000), lawyers (165,000), postsecondary students (23 million), and KFC, McDonald's, and Starbucks fast-food outlets (3,000).

A SATISFIED, WELL-EDUCATED, upwardly mobile urban populace would not seem to provide particularly fertile breeding grounds for political unrest. But there is a troubling underside to this remarkable success story. A vast army of rural émigrés—members of the so-called floating population—lives and works on the margins of urban society. Freed from the oppressive household registration system that kept them moored to the land until the early 1980s, 150–200 million migrant workers—no one knows precisely how many—have poured into China's cities, where they have provided much of the manpower fueling the country's unprecedented development boom. Lacking effective minimum-wage protection and basic rights of urban citizenship such as police protection, access to public education, and affordable health care, however, they have become a marginalized underclass, severely underrepresented in census tallies and opinion surveys, and hence largely invisible. In early 2007 Shanghai was estimated to have 5.6 million migrants, Beijing 5.4 million, and Guangzhou 5 million. But the national leader in transient workers, with almost 7 million migrants, is the once sleepy border village of Shumchun, now the thriving metropolis of Shenzhen.

A forty-five-minute train ride from Hong Kong to Shenzhen in the late summer of 2006 confirmed the double-edged nature of that city's miraculous transformation. With annual economic growth averaging 28 percent over the past quarter century, Shenzhen is packed to the rafters with twelve million people, almost 60 percent of whom lack valid urban household registration. It is far and away the fastest-growing city in China—or anywhere else, for that matter. Because of its proximity to Hong Kong, and its status as one of four original Special Economic Zones designated by Deng Xiaoping in 1980, Shenzhen long enjoyed preferential foreign investment status and tax benefits from the central government. Today it has the world's fourth-largest container port, ranks first among Chinese cities in foreign direct investment and third (after Shanghai and Beijing) in the number of skyscrapers and star-rated hotels. Among the other impressive by-products of Shenzhen's rapid development are a large, well-educated middle class, a wide array of civil society associations, a vigorous mass media, and a relatively efficient and responsive municipal government.

Not surprisingly, there is also a Dickensian underside to this prosperity. Most of the city's seven million migrant workers are young women between the ages of sixteen and twenty-two. Few have marketable skills or local support networks. Shenzhen's labor market is rife with unscrupulous recruiters and miscellaneous hustlers and scammers seeking to prey upon the already powerless. Some migrant women wind up as prostitutes; others are kidnapped by human traffickers and sold elsewhere as wives or concubines. For those migrants lucky enough to find regular factory or construction work, the pay averages around $125 a month for a six-day workweek, which frequently involves long hours of mandatory, unpaid overtime. Migrants generally live in dingy, crowded dormitories and short-time hotels, and they are often locked down at night. By the time fees for room and board are deducted from their paychecks, little may be left to send home to their families—if they get paid at all. In many factories, employers routinely fall three or four months behind in paying their workers. Migrants who complain get sacked. Lacking municipal residency, they have no legal recourse. Recent labor laws promise to improve these grim conditions, but their effects have yet to be felt.

Street crime is also rampant in Shenzhen, and visitors are routinely advised not to carry purses, wallets, or other valuables that can be readily snatched. In just one of the city's six districts, Baoan, 18,000 robberies were reported in 2004 (by comparison, in all of Shanghai, a much larger city of eighteen million, there were only 2,200 robberies reported in the same year). Prostitution has flourished in Shenzhen's boomtown atmosphere, often becoming the employment of last resort for young migrant girls desperate to earn money to send back home. There are an estimated 120,000 sex workers in the city, mostly female, about 30 percent of whom are believed to carry sexually transmitted diseases. In one of the city's many red-light districts—a quarter-mile stretch of bars, dance halls, karaoke clubs, saunas, massage parlors, bathhouses, and venereal disease and abortion clinics known locally as Mistress Village—upwards of five hundred sex workers bring in more than ¥10 million annually, serving mainly cross-border day-tripping clientele from Hong Kong.

In an effort to clean up Shenzhen's thriving sex trade, municipal police in January 2006 raided 170 establishments in Mistress Village, citing violation of fire and building codes as a reason for shutting them down. In the old days such rousting-out tactics would have been effective. Fifty years earlier the Chinese government had ruthlessly stamped out prostitution and drug addiction within three years of the founding of the new regime. But in 2006 the sex workers of Mistress Village, together with their clients and community supporters, fought back. More than three thousand people gathered outside the Shenzhen municipal government offices the morning after the raid, carrying banners and shouting the slogan "Let us live; let us eat." Many of the women wore the racy costumes of massage parlor attendants. One thousand police were called in to break up the demonstration. They detained dozens of people before the crowd finally dispersed. Within a few weeks, however, most of the shuttered businesses had reopened, after reportedly paying hefty bribes—or fines—to municipal authorities.

But the story didn't end there. In November 2006 city officials struck again. This time police grabbed one hundred sex workers and their clients from the Futian red-light district and paraded them in yellow prisoners' uniforms through the streets of Shenzhen, using loudspeakers to read out their names and alleged misdeeds. The entire event was well photographed and reported by the press and was broadcast on television. But instead of having the intended effect of shaming and humiliating the women and their clients, the police came under a hail of criticism in newspapers, Internet chat rooms, and text messages. The All-China Women's Federation, China's principal protector of women's welfare, denounced the bizarre parade as an insult to the dignity of Chinese womanhood. And one lawyer wrote an open letter to the National People's Congress protesting that the parade was a flagrant violation of personal privacy and was illegal under current statutes. The women were reportedly back at work within a few weeks.

With Shenzhen having absorbed $35 billion in foreign direct investment since the early 1980s, an enormous amount of money has flowed through the city. The Shenzhen stock exchange—one of only two in China—is a beehive of activity, with more than 39 million investors, most of them small first-timers looking for a one-way ride up the wealth escalator. Since early 2007, however, share prices have fluctuated wildly, and a series of sharp market contractions in the second half of 2008 caused the Shenzhen composite stock index to drop by 65 percent, representing paper losses of approximately $1 trillion. (Investors in the even larger Shanghai stock exchange suffered paper losses of at least $2 trillion in the same period.) With many investors, small and large alike, leveraged up to their eyeballs, millions of punters took unaffordable hits. Ironically, just as the market was beginning to crash, a brand-new, modernistic steel-and-glass Shenzhen Stock Exchange Center, designed by the world-famous architect Rem Koolhaas, was rising majestically in downtown Shenzhen. When completed, it will have a trading floor of more than 150,000 square feet, roughly equivalent to two full-size soccer pitches (or three American football fields).

Along with its volatile stock market, Shenzhen's overheated property market has also felt the effects of the global recession of 2008–9. Prior to the onset of the recession, the combination of a booming local economy and an influx of speculative real estate investment, much of it coming from nearby Hong Kong, had caused the property market to soar by almost 30 percent annually since the early 2000s. By midyear 2006 the average cost of existing housing in Shenzhen was ¥975 ($120) per square foot, about 65 percent higher than in Beijing. More than one-third of Shenzhen's apartment owners spent 50 percent or more of their monthly incomes on mortgage payments. In the first half of 2008, however, real estate prices dropped sharply, leaving many recent Shenzhen home buyers with negative equity.

Shenzhen was one of the first cities in China to allow home owners to directly elect self-organizing committees to represent their interests. In recent years some of these committees have initiated lawsuits against local real estate developers and property management firms, whom they accused of colluding to artificially inflate housing prices. But they quickly ran up against a stone wall of bureaucratic obstruction from municipal housing authorities, who blocked their lawsuits. When one frustrated plaintiff decided to run for a seat on his neighborhood residents' committee, district officials sabotaged his campaign, first ruling him ineligible, then saying he could run only if he dropped his pending lawsuit. At around the same time, an angry Shenzhen home owner named Zou Tao used his personal Web site to call for a three-year boycott on all housing purchases, aimed at reining in skyrocketing real estate prices. His campaign, launched in the spring of 2006, gathered more than 100,000 signatures and generated sympathetic press coverage throughout China's coastal provinces. But it also drew the ire of local developers and municipal officials, and when Zou attempted to board a plane for Beijing to seek a personal audience with Premier Wen Jiabao, he was reportedly detained at the airport for several hours. Thereafter, municipal authorities confiscated his mobile phone, blocked his Web site, tapped his home phone, and banned local media from reporting on his boycott. When a mutual friend introduced me to Zou a few months later, in the summer of 2006, he remained optimistic. I asked him why he felt compelled to take on the local political establishment, and he replied that he was fed up with all the "money-grubbing [*jinqian chucaogende*] developers, brokers, speculators, and local officials." He continued, "The more they try to stifle people's outrage, the more people will protest."

ON THE TRAIN ride back to Hong Kong, I thought about the human costs of Shenzhen's phenomenal growth—and its rising commercial volatility. It seemed that Zou Tao's struggle against inflated housing prices was symptomatic of the acute urban growing pains being experienced up and down China's eastern seaboard. An awful lot of money and people have poured into places like Shenzhen, Guangzhou, and Shanghai. A massive influx of foreign direct investment—more than $700 billion since 1992—has been driving China's remarkable export boom, providing millions of low-end jobs for a vast army of unskilled migrants while generating high-end opportunities for China's emerging technical and managerial middle classes. What would happen, I wondered idly, if a prolonged contraction in global demand for Chinese exports should hit this high-powered, fast-paced industrial engine? Conceivably, the resultant shocks would reverberate throughout the entire Chinese economy, causing massive unemployment and sharply reduced gross domestic product (GDP) growth rates. Unable to calculate the sociopolitical consequences of such a chain of events, I pushed the thought out of my mind and enjoyed the passing scenery.

With the lion's share of investment targeted to industrial and commercial projects along the eastern seaboard, there has also been a pronounced geographical skewing of new wealth. Despite recent government initiatives like the Great Western Development program, provinces in China's vast interior have not fared nearly so well as those along the coast, and rural inhabitants have fallen well behind their urban counterparts. In the first half of 2006 China's overall Gini coefficient—the index used by economists to determine the relative skewing of income distribution—reached its highest post-1949 level ever, at .496, while the per capita urban-rural income gap grew to a post-1949 high of 3.3:1. According to recent statistics, the richest 20 percent of Chinese households now account for 58 percent of all personal income, while the poorest 20 percent account for only 3 percent, a top-to-bottom ratio of more than 18:1 (up from 6:1 in the late 1980s). By way of comparison, in 2005 the top 20 percent of U.S. households received 54 percent of all income, while the bottom 20 percent got just under 5 percent, a ratio of 11:1. Although more than 400 million Chinese have been lifted above the World Bank's benchmark poverty income threshold of $1 per day over the past two decades, in recent years there has been visible slippage in rural poverty alleviation, and in 2007 an estimated 400 million Chinese were still living on less than $2 per day.

Equally important, rising popular perceptions of inequity and injustice have increased the level of overall societal tension. In the decade between 1993 and 2003, the number of lawsuits filed annually by Chinese citizens against government officials increased from 27,000 to almost 100,000. In 2005, the All-China Federation of Trade Unions reported 314,000 labor disputes, up 20 percent from the previous year. Also in 2005, more than 30 million Chinese citizens submitted petitions to "letters and visits" offices around the country, seeking government intervention in a wide range of individual and collective grievances, marking a threefold increase over 2004.

When lawsuits and peaceful petitioning fail, direct action often ensues. Between 1993 and 2008 the number of annual "mass disturbances" in China (involving between fifteen and several thousand people) grew from 8,300 to more than 127,000, an average annual increase of 20 percent. In the past few years angry groups of home owners and farmers—sometimes numbering in the tens of thousands—have confronted local officials and property developers in dozens of Chinese cities and hundreds of rural townships to protest illegal land seizures and backdoor real estate development schemes. One recent estimate put the number of rural dwellers who have been victimized in fraudulent land deals at more than 50 million.

Although most analysts agree that both the frequency and the intensity of social protest and violence have risen sharply in the past decade, official statistics must be approached with caution. The meaning of particular categories such as "disturbances" or "incidents" is often highly ambiguous. To give but one recent example, in 2006 the Xinhua News Agency reported that in the preceding year more than 540,000 "public incidents" (*gonggong shijian*) occurred, resulting in 200,000 deaths and financial losses of ¥325 billion. But a close reading of the report suggests that the category "public incidents" may have included, in addition to purposive acts of collective social protest and violence, such involuntary acts as traffic accidents and industrial disasters. When it comes to reliance on official statistics, China watchers have learned to handle the data with extreme care.

Notwithstanding this occupational hazard, one clear by-product of the increase in social tension has been growing popular distrust in the integrity of government, especially *local* government. In 2004 the Central Party School in Beijing conducted a poll of five hundred Party and government cadres that confirms the existence—and severity—of this credibility gap:

OFFICIALS HAVING FULL TRUST
IN VARIOUS LEVELS OF GOVERNMENT

Central government	62.3%
Provincial government	30.3%
City government	14.9%
County government	8.9%
Township government	5.6%
Village government	3.7%

Although reliable survey data on certain politically sensitive issues are difficult to come by, a good deal of anecdotal evidence supports the conclusion that a major reason for lack of trust in local government is the widespread perception of rampant corruption, collusion, and thuggery among local law enforcement officials. In recent years there has been an epidemic of incidents involving angry crowds of township and village residents verbally confronting and even physically assaulting local police in response to egregious acts of police brutality, harassment, and wrongful detention.

Although the available data suggest that most Chinese people give the central government high marks on such conventional criteria of good governance as responsiveness, fairness, and "concern for people like me," the extremely high levels of distrust displayed toward subprovincial governments raise serious questions both for China and for those who would understand and explain China to the outside world: Just how unjust is the Chinese political system? Just how vulnerable is it to potential regime-threatening shocks? And what kinds of events could threaten its survival?

There are no easy answers. Even China's top leaders seem anxious and uncertain about the future. In September 2004 the CCP Central Committee frankly acknowledged the existence of a deepening crisis of legitimacy: "China's reform and development has reached a critical stage in which new problems are mushrooming. . . . The CCP's ruling status . . . will not last forever if the Party does nothing to safeguard it. . . . We must develop a stronger sense of crisis . . . and strengthen our ruling capacity in a more earnest and conscientious manner."

To deal with this crisis and raise flagging public trust, China's leaders have devised a number of high-profile policy initiatives. At the turn of the twenty-first century Jiang Zemin proposed an awkwardly labeled "theory of the three represents" (*sange daibiao lilun*), which aimed to create a more economically inclusive, socially diverse ruling party by, among other things, recruiting successful capitalists, entrepreneurs, and merchants into the CCP. Reversing almost five decades of deep doctrinal hostility to capitalism, Jiang opened the door to political legitimacy for China's newly affluent bourgeoisie. Since 2001 more than four million capitalists have responded to Jiang's ideological olive branch by joining the Communist Party. But with Party membership holding steady at just under 6 percent of the total population (73 million members in 2008), there are few indications that his policy has contributed materially to improving the quality of life for the vast majority of Chinese who occupy the lower rungs of the socioeconomic ladder, the *laobaixing*. Emblematic of the continuing hardships faced by those left out of China's economic boom, there has been an alarming increase in the number of suicides since the early 1990s, primarily among rural women, the elderly, and workers saddled with unpayable debts. According to the World Health Organization, China currently has the world's second-highest rate of female suicides, at 14.6 per 100,000, trailing only Sri Lanka in this category. On average, 280,000 Chinese commit suicide each year.

LIKE SO MANY other China watchers, I often rely on taxi drivers for information about what the "Chinese street" is thinking. In a wholly unscientific survey conducted between 2002 and 2004, I asked Chinese taxi drivers all over the country to talk about the theory of the three represents and comment on its significance. Most showed little or no understanding of the concept. A few took it seriously but were unable to explain it. A substantial number were indifferent or dismissive, with a handful displaying open contempt, including one Lanzhou cab driver who laughed as he told me, with heavy sarcasm, "When I get home from work at night, the first thing my wife and I do is discuss the three represents."

Even more cynical was a bit of irreverent doggerel that appeared as a text message on tens of thousands of Chinese mobile phones during the 2003 SARS epidemic. Lampooning Jiang Zemin's call for the CCP to "represent the demand for advanced productive forces, the development of advanced culture, and the fundamental interests of the broad masses," the text message's anonymous author sarcastically redefined the three represents:

THE "THREE REPRESENTS" OF SARS:
1. Represent the demand for development of special viruses;
2. Represent the development of the advanced culture of fear;
3. Represent the fundamental interests of the broad masses of wild animals.

They just don't make personality cults like they used to!

JIANG ZEMIN RETIRED in 2003, and his successor, Hu Jintao, tried to revive public confidence in governmental integrity with the promise of a kinder, gentler Communist party-state, coupled with an all-out war against corrupt officials and a commitment to sustainable, environmentally friendly development. Espousing the neo-Confucian value of building a "harmonious society" (*hexie shehui*), President Hu and Premier Wen Jiabao have sought to temper China's all-out pursuit of economic growth with greater attention to the fair and equitable distribution of income and opportunity. Pledging to end governmental inattention to the plight of those left behind in the rush to modernity—the rural poor, migrant laborers, ethnic minorities, the unemployed, and the unprotected elderly—the new leaders have begun to shift fiscal resources from the haves to the have-nots. The government abolished the agricultural tax in 2005 and capped permissible profits from land requisition a year later. In many provinces the minimum wage has gone up to an average of ¥450–¥550 per month ($57–$70), and the very poorest of China's urban poor receive modest cash subsidies, called "baseline guarantees" (*dibao*). Tens of billions of yuan in educational funds have been pledged for the development of rural schools, with the eventual aim of making rural education tuition free, and a national health insurance program was recently unveiled that will partially subsidize basic medical care and eventually provide hospital co-payment relief for up to 80 percent of China's rural dwellers. In some Chinese cities public schooling is available for the first time to children of migrant workers. Though welcome, these reforms are still in their infancy, and the funds actually allocated to augmented health, education, and welfare benefits have thus far been quite modest in relation to the magnitude of the need.

Notwithstanding its serious intent, Hu Jintao's harmonious society motif has been lampooned irreverently on the Chinese Internet, alongside Jiang Zemin's three represents theory. Substituting a slightly altered Chinese anagram for Jiang's original slogan, one group of waggish bloggers rechristened Jiang's theory "the theory of carrying three wristwatches" (*dai sange biao lilun*). Not to be outdone, another group of online netizens popularized a derogatory homophonic wordplay on Hu Jintao's "harmonious society" slogan, altering its meaning to "river-crab society." From there it was but a small step for an astute Chinese graphic artist to combine the two bowdlerized slogans into a single logo: a fat crab wearing three elegant Rolex wristwatches. This iconic image quickly spread throughout the Chinese blogosphere, where in the summer of 2007 it became a silent symbol of defiance against regime hypocrisy and Internet censorship. One intrepid blogger went so far as to suggest that the popular, Rolex-flaunting crab should be named the official mascot of the 2008 Beijing Olympics.

The government's commitment to green economic development has also met with considerable skepticism. In 2004 Hu Jintao pledged to make public the environmental costs of "brown" GDP (i.e., the yearly damage done to the environment and human health in each province), and a year later China's State Environmental Protection Agency (SEPA) was elevated to full ministerial status and promised additional resources and expanded authority to monitor, cite, penalize, and ultimately shut down chronic industrial polluters. By 2007, however, the green GDP initiative had quietly been shelved, reportedly at the insistence of angry provincial officials. With county and township governments throughout the country deeply dependent upon profits, tax revenues, and illicit, off-budget "gifts" collected from local industrial operators, collusive relationships between factory owners and local officials continue to impede effective environmental protection. To make matters worse, SEPA, the agency tasked with monitoring environmental quality and cracking down on polluters throughout the country, has not received the additional resources it was promised, rendering enforcement uneven at best.

Finally, the new leadership's declared war on corruption has also met with limited success. On the plus side, more than thirty thousand government officials were prosecuted for corruption in Chinese courts in 2005 alone, including 1,900 leading cadres at the county level and above. In the same year ¥7.4 billion ($925 million) in misappropriated funds were recovered by the government, up 62 percent from the previous year's haul. Yet no one has suggested that the problem is under control, and one gets the troubling impression of a gigantic iceberg whose visible tip bespeaks a vastly larger, submerged mass.

Few would question Hu Jintao's commitment to restoring integrity in government. But the obstacles are daunting, including, most notably, China's pervasive culture of institutionalized *guanxi*, in which officials routinely dine at the public trough, hire their cronies, solicit bribes from clients, and extract nonproductive rents, all while obligingly scratching one another's backs: *Ni bang wode mang; wo bang nide mang.* Tellingly, the corrosive impact of *guanxi* on opportunities for upward mobility— the routine expectation that people must give expensive gifts as a way to curry favor with their superiors—was the most frequent complaint raised by five hundred local Party and government officials interviewed in a 2004 survey, with 78 percent agreeing that a system of institutional checks and balances was needed to effectively combat the scourge of corruption. Yet today the CCP remains as resistant to the idea of limiting or sharing its power as it was at the height of the 1989 student demonstrations.

And here we come to the nub of what may be China's biggest problem: an insecure Communist Party leadership haunted by the recurring nightmare of being swept away in a rising tide of public unrest. Born of post-Tiananmen stress disorder and the shocking collapse of the Soviet Union, this fear has prevented the regime from taking what many people see as the necessary first steps toward overhauling its rigid, authoritarian political institutions. Without a free press to scrutinize the actions of state and Party officials, without a vigorous, pluralistic civil society to promote public policy awareness and civic participation, and without an independent judiciary to help level the playing field between the powerless and the powerful, the Chinese political system is not well equipped to cope effectively or proactively with the multiple stresses of a complex, rapidly developing, economically divided society.

A vigorous debate has raged on this question, both within China and among foreign observers. On one side are those who argue that through a combination of timely administrative adjustments, increased governmental commitment to the redistribution of wealth, and the wise exercise of state fiscal and regulatory authority—that is, through what we may term *enlightened techno-Confucian paternalism*—a one-party Chinese state can successfully deal with (if not wholly eliminate) the most pernicious effects of inequality, inequity, injustice, and perceived governmental indifference. Proponents of this approach frequently cite the example of Singapore as proof of the feasibility, if not the superiority, of a technocratic "soft-authoritarian" pathway to political and socioeconomic stability.

On the other side are those who hold that mere regulatory fixes and administrative palliatives, no matter how well intended, are insufficient to prevent even the most benevolent and technically adept neo-Confucian patriarchs from becoming corrupt, self-serving, and inattentive to the common weal. The basic problem, they suggest, was identified by Montesquieu some 250 years ago, on the eve of the French Revolution, namely, the fusion of powers: "When the legislative and executive powers are united in the same person or body," he observed, "there can be no liberty." The Greek philosopher Plato provided an even more succinct analysis some 2,000 years earlier, "Who will guard the guardians themselves?" later famously rendered in Latin as "Quis custodies ipsos custodes?" The only meaningful answer, say critics of China's one-party dictatorship, is a system of institutional checks and balances accompanied by pluralistic political competition, or *countervailing power.*

Who is right? Thus far no easy answer has presented itself. As attractive as the Singapore model might be, the analogy between China and Singapore is deeply flawed. For one thing, Singapore's successful modernization was underpinned by a historically unique constellation of economic, demographic, and institutional factors that are largely absent in China today. These include a robust rule of law and a professional, uncorrupt civil service, both of which were legacies of British colonial rule; high per capita income and education levels; and the absence of a vast, impoverished rural hinterland (Singapore split off from its larger, poorer rural sibling, Malaysia, in 1965). With a population of only 5 million, Singapore is, in fact, a city-state. On Transparency International's most recent global survey of perceived corruption, Singapore ranked as the fifth-most-upright country in the world (after Finland, Iceland, New Zealand, and Denmark), while China held down seventy-second place (behind Cuba, Brazil, and Croatia).

Moreover, despite Singapore's paternalistic, executive-dominated political institutions, despite its timid mass media and anemic civil-society associations, and despite the continued dominance of a single political party, the People's Action Party (PAP), the former British colony enjoys a degree of electoral competition that is wholly missing in China today. For all its nondemocratic instincts, the ruling party is required to compete regularly in free and open public elections, and this makes a difference, forcing government ministers to pay close attention to grassroots public opinion. Lacking even such rudimentary mechanisms of political accountability, China's prospects for emerging as the next Singapore should not be overstated.

On the other hand, there is little reason to expect regime collapse. While the Singapore model may be out of reach, China's strong economic growth—averaging close to 10 percent annually for more than two decades—has bought Party leaders a good bit of time to get their institutions right. Although the recent onset of global recession has arguably increased the urgency of political reform, thus far they have been content to tweak and fine-tune their existing institutions in an effort to make the organs of state power a bit more accessible, a bit more responsive, a bit more transparent, and a bit more equitable. On the positive side, they have introduced a system of controlled elections for village leaders in rural China and expanded the deliberative functions of people's congresses throughout the country. In an attempt to reach out to key non-Party groups and individuals in society, they have enlarged the consultative and advisory roles of traditional "united front" bodies such as the Chinese People's Political Consultative Conference and the eight officially recognized "democratic parties," remnants of China's brief democratic experiment of the late 1940s. And they have mandated the creation of electronic government—interactive public service Web sites in every province, county, and municipality, intended to promote timely dissemination of important local information and to solicit public input and feedback on governmental performance. None of these quintessentially techno-Confucian measures has involved the sharing of power or the toleration of political dissent, however; by the same token, none has raised popular expectations of imminent political liberalization.

Whether any or all of this will suffice to ensure China's long-term political stability is the $64,000 question. Those whose attention is focused primarily on China's thriving urban centers, especially along the eastern seaboard, generally incline toward accentuating the positive. And why not? It is there that the Singapore model seems most within reach. If, for example, we could envision Shanghai or Guangzhou or Shenzhen as independent, sovereign political entities, then a paternalistic, techno-Confucian future would be relatively easy to imagine and embrace. Some have even notionally defined a Greater China—comprising the most developed coastal areas of Guangdong and Fujian, together with Taiwan, Hong Kong, and Macau—as a single, virtually integrated regional entity. Such an entity, if it actually existed, would be an instant East Asian super-tiger, an economic and political powerhouse with virtually unlimited developmental potential. But Greater China does not exist in any meaningful political sense. What does exist is a vast, sprawling, diverse China, a China that is still mainly rural, mainly poor, mainly polluted by toxic waste, mainly unable to afford decent medical care, and mainly distrustful of corrupt government officials. Given the added problems imposed by a severe economic slowdown, this is not a China that inspires unreserved confidence in the future.

MUCH OF WHAT is right—and wrong—with China was on display during the 2008 Beijing Olympic Games. Marked by spectacular national pageantry, patriotic pride, and media hype, the Beijing Games commenced on August 8, 2008, or 8.08.08, a highly auspicious date on the Chinese calendar. Though I had originally planned to attend the Games, a surgical emergency forced me to remain in Los Angeles, where, after being relieved of a cancerous prostate gland, I watched the proceedings on television. Like millions (billions?) of others, I was blown away by the spectacularly colorful, well-choreographed display of human ingenuity, enterprise, and artistry that marked the opening ceremony. Though Steven Spielberg had resigned months earlier as an artistic consultant, citing China's continuing support for the murderous regime in Sudan, his absence was hardly noticed.

As for Beijing itself, the city looked—dare I say it?—exquisite, all dressed up in its gleaming new Olympic finery. The venues were simply breathtaking: Who can forget the dazzling design of the Bird's Nest, or the exquisite pastel luminosity of the Water Cube? And while attendance at many individual events was surprisingly sparse, the spirit of the Games was overwhelmingly festive and exuberant. Was it worth the $43 billion price tag? I think most Chinese would say, unequivocally, yes. It was their coming-out party, their moment in the sun, and they clearly relished it. Even the weather cooperated. Notwithstanding the many dire warnings of an environmental debacle, after two days of thick haze, Beijing's skies magically cleared. Alternating periods of bright sunshine and heavy rain kept airborne pollutants to tolerable levels, and for the first time in memory the city's pollution index dropped below that of Los Angeles, by a substantial margin. Even the traffic proved manageable, thanks to mandatory odd/even-day driving restrictions. It hardly mattered that the clean air was only temporary, a product of draconian industrial closures and one thousand silver iodide–tipped cloud-seeding missiles fired by the PLA on the eve of the opening ceremony. The Games were a spectator's delight, filled with color, pageantry, and human drama.

For me, one of the most enduring (and endearing) images of all—apart from the sight of Chinese President Hu Jintao uncomfortably biting his lip while rock guitarist Jimmy Page and pop diva Leona Lewis belted out a sanitized version of Led Zeppelin's racy 1970s hit "Whole Lotta Love"—was Chinese world-record-holding hurdler Liu Xiang kicking a wall in frustration, then crying out in anger after a foot injury forced him to withdraw from competition. It was an extraordinarily poignant moment.

There were, of course, a number of inevitable official foul-ups, foibles, and faux pas. In the government's desire to achieve a perfect display of Chinese progress and prowess, some troubling undersides were revealed: One young girl lost her moment of immortality when a censorious Politburo member decided that she wasn't pretty enough to appear onstage to sing her designated number at the opening ceremony; instead a more attractive substitute lip-synched the song. Visitors who traveled to Beijing from the provinces often found their access to public transport (and to the Olympic venues themselves) blocked by overly intrusive, dilatory security precautions; consequently, tens of thousands of ticket holders never made it to the Games, which helped contribute to the embarrassingly sparse attendance at a number of events. In many cases large numbers of colorfully attired office workers and schoolchildren were bused in at the last minute to fill half-empty arenas.

Of greater concern were the recurrent, visible traces of post-Tiananmen stress disorder. At least a dozen human rights activists—mostly foreign, and mostly decrying the lack of freedom in Tibet—were detained by police, while sixteen foreign journalists were roughed up while attempting to cover demonstrations of various sorts. Numerous international Web sites were locally blocked, and in Beijing intensive security at several four- and five-star hotels included the clandestine scanning of guests' computer hard drives. More disturbing still, dozens of law-abiding Chinese citizens who sought police permits to hold peaceful demonstrations at three officially approved "Hyde Park" sites around Beijing were subjected to extreme personal harassment when they sought to file their applications. By the second week of the Games, seventy-seven applications had been submitted to the Beijing municipal police. All but a handful were withdrawn under duress, while the rest were categorically rejected. Not a single permit was issued. And at least five applicants, including two women in their late seventies, were arrested and sentenced to extrajudicial "labor reeducation" simply because they applied for permits.

Most troubling of all, however, was the curtain of total media silence that was drawn over an emerging crisis involving contaminated Chinese milk products. Because of the government's overriding concern with managing its image, it systematically suppressed information about widespread melamine poisoning among Chinese children throughout the summer of 2008. As a result tens of thousands of children were poisoned before the alarm was finally sounded in mid-September. Such was the double-edged nature of Beijing's Olympic experience that while all was celebratory and harmonious on the outside, troubling residues of deeply ingrained authoritarian anxiety, insecurity, and overreaction lingered just beneath the surface.

LOOKING AT CHINA today, after more than forty years of almost continuous personal observation and interaction, my own feelings are thoroughly
mixed, a jumble of contradictory perceptions, impressions, and impulses.
Some days I wake up full of hope for this vast country and its incredibly
industrious, resilient people: The determined young men in Xian who got
up before dawn to jog alongside me, polishing their English-conversation
skills; the two young photographers in Tiananmen Square who showed
what a little individual initiative and enterprise could do; the Beijing university students of 1989 who thought—wrongly—that they could change
the world overnight; the Mangghuer youngsters who walked two hours
each morning to attend English classes in Guanting; the Chongqing "nail-
house" couple, who dared to challenge the government's right to seize
property without adequate compensation; even the old woman who poked
her finger in my chest at the Yellow Mountain as she railed against American bullying. These are all enduring, endearing images of a changing
China, a hopeful China, a China deserving of respect. And the enormous
nationwide outpouring of humanitarian aid and comfort that followed the
devastating Sichuan earthquake of May 2008 suggests the emergence of a
maturing, caring society.

Other days, however, I despair at the web of official arrogance, corruption, and self-aggrandizement that enmeshes local government, and
I shake my head at the CCP's near-pathological fear of unauthorized
political expression. In the months following the Sichuan earthquake,
which killed more than 86,000 people, including 5,300 schoolchildren,
two human rights activists were arrested, a half dozen journalists were
fired, three public interest lawyers had their licenses revoked, and dozens
of greiving parents were detained and harassed by local authorities. Their
offense? All had sought an official inquiry into the use of shoddy building materials in the construction of more than 7,000 school buildings that
collapsed in the quake. There is something profoundly disturbing about
a regime that arrests or intimidates citizens who demand inconvenient
rights, lawyers who represent inconvenient victims, journalists who ask
inconvenient questions, and intellectuals who tell inconvenient truths.
The long, dark shadow of post-Tiananmen stress disorder lingers in China,
casting a pall over the country's political life.

Nevertheless, in my more far-sighted moments I see a clear, if unsteady
light at the end of the tunnel. I see a civil society beginning to flourish; I
see students once again beginning to question authority, farmers stand-

ing up to corrupt officials, migrant workers demanding their legal rights, and an urban middle class experiencing the quotidian satisfactions of home ownership, mall shopping, and vacation travel. I even see some members of the next generation of Communist Party leaders speaking out—albeit timidly and tentatively—on the need for democratic pluralism and power sharing.

Social scientists have found that when authoritarian countries reach a per capita income threshold between $6,000 and $8,000 per year, there is a much higher statistical probability that they will introduce—and, more importantly, *sustain*—democratic institutions. Below that threshold, democratic transitions, while not uncommon, are almost never viable or stable. Taiwan reached the $6,000 threshold in the late 1980s, South Korea in the early 1990s. Assuming relative continuity in China's intermediate-term growth rates, the country should reach the $6,000 threshold (in constant dollars) within the next decade. Barring unforeseen catastrophes, given China's continued global engagement and market-friendly policies, and the demonstrated industriousness of the Chinese people, and notwithstanding the lingering political insecurities of CCP leaders, we may reasonably expect to see a somewhat more open and pluralistic China by the year 2020.

ASSUMING AT LEAST some movement in the direction of greater domestic political openness and liberalization, how will China behave in the international community? Will a more mature, developed, and self-confident China be a cooperative partner or a strategic adversary? For more than three decades, U.S. foreign policy has been predicated on the desirability of encouraging China's entry into the global community of nations, with the expectation (as articulated by Richard Nixon in a famous 1967 essay in *Foreign Affairs*) that a globally engaged China would be a less hostile, less dogmatic, and more "civilized" China.

How well has this optimistic prophecy fared to date? Opinion remains deeply divided. On the one hand, China's rise has been marked by a generally cautious, nonconfrontational approach to international relations. With the sole major exception of the Taiwan issue, on which PRC policy remains generally rigid and unyielding, China has acted flexibly and pragmatically in world politics since 1980. Among other things, it has:

- Become a responsible member of the World Trade Organization
- Exercised great restraint in using its veto power as a permanent member of the UN Security Council
- Supported international nuclear nonproliferation, antiterrorism, and anti–drug trafficking initiatives
- Actively participated, since the late 1990s, in twenty-two UN peacekeeping operations in such places as Cambodia, Haiti, East Timor, Lebanon, and Congo
- Taken the lead in organizing and hosting six-party talks on North Korean nuclear disarmament
- Become an active, cooperating partner of the Association of Southeast Asian Nations (ASEAN)
- Entered into negotiations to resolve long-standing territorial disputes with several of its neighbors, including Russia, Mongolia, Tajikistan, Kyrgyzstan, Kazakhstan, Vietnam, Nepal, and India

This is an impressive record of responsible behavior.

On the other hand, Beijing's relentless drive to reunify the "renegade province" of Taiwan, by force if necessary, appears to belie its leaders' oft-repeated claim of a "peaceful rise." With more than one thousand ballistic missiles aimed at Taiwan, and with a defense budget increasing at double-digit rates for almost two decades, Beijing's ultimate military intentions are a source of mounting international concern. Other causes for concern include an intermittently rising tide of virulent Chinese nationalism, aimed principally at Japan and the United States; a growing and seemingly insatiable Chinese appetite for natural resources and raw materials; a chronically undervalued Chinese yuan, which has enabled a vast surge of low-cost, labor-intensive Chinese exports to flood world markets; and Beijing's willingness to ignore egregious human rights violations in pursuit of its diplomatic and commercial interests in such chronic pariah states as Burma, Zimbabwe, and Sudan, not to mention its defiant rejection of all foreign criticism of its recent crackdown on popular protest in Tibet.

Such concerns are real and should not be discounted, yet they do not add up to an inevitable adversarial relationship between China and the West, as some have argued. For the past three decades a gradual, almost invisible process of international accommodation and convergence has been under way. For its part, China has totally abandoned its revolutionary Maoist credo, accepted the principles of a free-market economy, joined the prevailing Western finance and trade regime, and quietly undertaken to become a "responsible stakeholder" (in Robert Zoellick's felicitous phrase) in the international community. In each of these respects, China's behavioral adjustments have been real and substantial, adding up to a profound sea change in the Chinese Weltanschauung.

The fact that there remain significant differences of interest, orientation, and national priority between China and the West should hardly be surprising. Whenever a dynamic, rising power seeks a larger niche in a world dominated by a single, status quo–preserving superpower, a certain amount of friction is inevitable. Such friction—manifested in mounting competition for resources and raw materials, legislation designed to protect domestic products and jobs against low-cost foreign imports, differing strategic definitions of "vital" national interests, and a general tendency to view the other as a threat to one's own peace and security—need not be unduly alarming. The true art of positive diplomacy lies not in suppressing or denying divergent national needs, interests, and expectations but rather in learning to live with them, seeking common ground when possible, agreeing to disagree when not possible, and contesting when necessary.

A recent projection by Goldman Sachs suggests that the Chinese economy, measured in terms of total purchasing power, is likely to surpass the U.S. economy sometime before 2030, though per capita income and GDP will remain substantially lower in China throughout the present century. Militarily, the gap is expected to close somewhat faster. In 2004 the Pentagon estimated that Chinese military technology was about fifteen to twenty years behind that of the United States, with the U.S. lead gradually shrinking as China accelerates its selective acquisition of advanced weapons systems. More recent estimates of time to parity have been revised further downward, with some analysts now suggesting that between 2012 and 2015 the United States will lose its theater military superiority in the western Pacific, thus in effect rendering Taiwan indefensible. These are troubling projections. Yet, by focusing solely on China's rapidly growing economic and military *capacity*, we risk begging the vital question of China's ultimate *intentions*. Here the picture is more reassuring; for apart from the Taiwan case (which China continues to treat as a purely domestic matter), there is no empirical evidence to suggest that Beijing harbors aggressive designs on any other foreign country. On the contrary, Beijing has, since the early 1980s, behaved with considerable caution and restraint in exercising its growing diplomatic and military clout. Might China be biding its time, maintaining a low profile until it feels confident of its ability to confront U.S. military power? Conceivably, yes. But, again excepting the Taiwan case, there is no firm evidence to support such a conjecture. With few exceptions, China's behavior in world politics over the past quarter century has tended to converge with, rather than diverge from, conventional norms and standards of international diplomacy. To once again borrow Robert Zoellick's apt phrase, China has embarked on the road to becoming a responsible stakeholder in global affairs. Such a long-term trend should be reckoned as cause for cautious optimism about the future.

We should not, however, expect even a substantially cooperative, converging China to take a back seat indefinitely to unilateral American power, influence, and interests. As China continues to rise, it will inevitably be drawn to probe the limits of U.S. regional and global dominance and spread its wings as an independent force in world politics. As much as Americans may resist the idea of sharing the global stage with an energetic, self-confident Chinese peer competitor, such an accommodation will have to be made. The alternative is a new cold war—and the very real possibility of a hot war. In this respect it is the United States, rather than China, that faces the more daunting challenge, the challenge of gracefully accepting the eventual, inevitable diminution of its own unipolar global dominance.

In all this, considerable patience and understanding will be required. Demonizing China will prove counterproductive. For example, blaming China's undervalued yuan for our own ongoing national orgy of overconsumption and deficit spending does not help; neither does imposing punitive trade sanctions on China for "unfair competition" while we ourselves continue to protect and subsidize politically influential sectors of the U.S. economy. To be sure, China has engaged in unfair trade practices, its domestic record on human rights and political reform remains a sorry one, and Beijing's recurrent threats to reunify Taiwan by force have rightly been decried as bullying. But tectonic plates are shifting. Since 2005 China has revalued its currency by more than 20 percent, with additional adjustments anticipated.

Also, since the spring of 2005, Beijing has refrained from threatening military action against Taiwan, instead appealing to the common economic and cultural aspirations of the Chinese and Taiwanese people, and looking to Washington to restrain President Chen Shui-bian's more egregious attempts to push the envelope of Taiwanese independence. In this situation, the election of a new, reconciliation-minded Taiwanese president, Ma Ying-jeou, in March 2008, appeared to augur a period of greater cross-strait self-restraint and mutual accommodation.

Promoting further changes in the desired direction will take time and patience, along with a determination to regenerate the United States' severely eroded soft power, so that it may once again exercise moral leadership in a world beset by rising anxiety and insecurity. This will also take persistent international pressure, applied calmly and with sensitivity to Chinese national pride. We in the West would be well advised to identify ourselves with the forces of progress in China, rather than empowering the forces of reaction by vilifying China's every move. Nothing we can do will ultimately guarantee a peaceful, cooperative China. That is a job for future generations of Chinese themselves. The best we can do is help to make their task a bit easier.

15

Loose Ends

IN THE SPRING of 2006, while serving as a visiting scholar at Taiwan's National Chengchi University, I was invited to give a guest lecture at the Institute of International Relations, site of my 1967 Four Cleanups caper. As a prologue to my prepared remarks, I recounted to the assembled staff and scholars of the institute—most of whom were too young to have been around at the time—the full story of my audacious heist. It was the first time I had ever spoken in public about the incident, and I told my story with considerable trepidation. Adding to my anxiety was the presence in the audience of David Auw, the principal victim of my felony. I had asked my hosts to invite David specially for the occasion. I hadn't spoken with him in almost forty years, and seeing him in the audience was somewhat unnerving. How would he respond to my confession?

To my enormous relief both David and the rest of the audience, which included the institute's current director, responded to my tale with good-natured laughter. Afterward, over lunch, David, who is now comfortably retired, confirmed that he had not suffered any retribution for granting me unauthorized access to captured CCP documents. Evidently, the brief acknowledgment Jack Service inserted into the preface of my 1968 Berkeley monograph, effusively thanking the institute's director and staff for their generous support and cooperation, had satisfied both the institute's leaders and David's Defense Ministry employers, giving them substantial face and thereby exempting David from recrimination. Proposing a toast to David's health—and to Jack's savvy understanding of Chinese *guanxi* culture—I confessed to my luncheon companions that had it not been for the chance conjunction of David's desperately busy schedule and my own larcenous impulse on that fateful day in the spring of 1967, when I unthinkingly stuffed five top secret Socialist Education Campaign documents into my briefcase, my career would surely have taken a very different, and very likely less interesting, turn.

AFTER LEAVING CHINA in 1980, Sid and Yulin Rittenberg settled in North Carolina, not far from Sid's childhood home. There, in a contretemps rich in irony, they established Rittenberg Associates, a private consultancy advising major U.S. and international corporations on doing business in China. Sid, with whom I have remained good friends, has also tried his hand at teaching Chinese history, both at the University of North Carolina and at Pacific Lutheran University in Southern California. In 1993 he published a revealing personal memoir, *The Man Who Stayed Behind*. Now in his late eighties, Sid remains at a loss to adequately explain, to himself or to others, the intense revolutionary fervor that gripped him, and millions of ordinary Chinese, during the Cultural Revolution.

WANG GUANGMEI, LIU Shaoqi's elegant widow, whom Sid had publicly denounced in 1967, died of natural causes in October 2006, at the age of eighty-five. After her release from prison in 1980, she sold most of her family's possessions and dedicated her life to poverty alleviation in rural China, in memory of the thirty million people who perished during the Great Leap Forward. A brief obituary notice appearing in the Xinhua News Service stated that Wang was given a state funeral with full honors at Beijing's Babaoshan State Cemetery, the preferred place of interment for high-ranking government and Party leaders. Upon reading of her death, I took out my well-worn copy of the CCP's 1981 "Resolution on Certain Questions on the History of Our Party since the Founding of the People's Republic of China." Looking once more at her handwritten inscription on the flyleaf, it struck me that the symbolic honor of a state funeral could hardly compensate for the many long years of humiliation and abuse she and her family had suffered at the hands of Jiang Qing and the Gang of Four. Still, I think she would have been pleased by the remembrance.

DESPITE JIANG QING'S steadfast refusal either to confess or to apologize for her Cultural Revolution extremism, both she and Zhang Chunqiao (who ultimately did repent) had their death sentences commuted to

My reunion with David Auw (far right), Institute of International Relations, Taipei, March 2006. Also present, from left: Professors Chao Chien-min and Li Guoxiong of Taiwan's National Chengchi University.

life in prison in 1983. Suffering from cancer of the throat, Jiang reportedly hanged herself in 1991. Also suffering from cancer, Zhang Chunqiao was given a medical parole in 2002. He died three years later. Wang Hongwen died in prison in 1992, of liver cancer. Yao Wenyuan was released from prison in 1996 and died of diabetes in December 2005. Thus ended the inglorious saga of the Gang of Four.

ZHAO ZIYANG, THE purged former CCP general secretary who had tried unsuccessfully to negotiate with students occupying Tiananmen Square in 1989, remained in disgrace and out of public view from May of that year until his death in January 2005, at the age of eighty-five. For several years after he was deposed, the nature of Zhao's post-Tiananmen confinement was a hot topic of media speculation and conjecture. A profusion of wild rumors circulated concerning the state of his health and his prospects for rehabilitation. One report—later confirmed—had him living under armed guard on Beijing's Fuqiang Lane, in a modest dwelling once occupied by

Hu Yaobang. Another had him being admitted to a Beijing hospital in critical condition. A third claimed he had been released from house arrest, while a fourth denied that he had ever been placed under home detention. A fifth reported that Zhao had been charged with collaborating with the CIA; one variation on this theme held that Zhao had steadfastly refused to admit guilt, and another claimed that he had been cleared of all charges of criminal wrongdoing. A sixth reported a confirmed sighting of Zhao playing golf in Beijing. Yet a seventh had Zhao being instructed by Deng Xiaoping to resume administrative duties after a year of "investigation and research" in the provinces. Not since Mao's last years had such a variety of wildly contradictory rumors spread so quickly and so widely.

To assuage my own curiosity about Zhao, on a trip to Beijing in September 1991 I paid a visit to the gated residence at No. 6 Fuqiang Lane in the company of Dave Holley, Beijing bureau chief of the *Los Angeles Times*. Dave had been tipped off that this was the site of Zhao's confinement. Located on a quiet, tree-lined street behind the Peking Hotel, a few blocks west of Beijing's trendy Wangfujing shopping street, the house at No. 6 seemed quiet and unexceptional in every way. No one was visible either on the street or within the walled courtyard. Trying to look as casual and inconspicuous as two camera-toting foreigners on an obvious recon mission could look, Dave and I strolled slowly past the house, displaying no visible interest. After half a block or so we stopped, chatted idly for a moment, then turned back. This time we paused in front of No. 6, where Dave quickly snapped my photo. A small sign to the right of the metal gate read "Not open to public; visitors are respectfully forbidden." Seeing no signs of life, I sauntered casually over to the red metal gate, which had a small peephole in the center. Putting my eye to the hole, I saw a handful of uniformed security police relaxing in the courtyard, sitting on stools, smoking and chatting quietly. Before I could detect the presence of anyone inside the house itself, however, Dave, standing watch behind me, coughed loudly. I turned around to see the metal gates of the two houses on either side of No. 6 open to disgorge uniformed policemen, packing side arms and holding walkie-talkies. Having presumptively (but not definitively) confirmed Zhao's presence, we left the scene with all due haste. As we retreated, I swiveled around with my camera in an attempt to snap a parting shot of the entrance to No. 6, only to find two gendarmes following a short distance behind, with hands on holsters. Discretion being the better part of valor, I did not take the photo. Years later a close friend of the

Deposed CCP general secretary Zhao Ziyang's house of detention at No. 6, Fuqiang Lane, Beijing, September 1991. Sign at far left reads: "Not open to public; visitors are respectfully forbidden."

Zhao family confirmed that this was indeed Zhao's home—and his house of detention for sixteen years.

To date, Zhao remains in official disrepute, condemned in the authorized CCP history as a "splittist." Although he was quietly cremated and his ashes interred at the Babaoshan State Cemetery, his passing was virtually ignored by the Party-controlled media in China. On the day of his funeral dissidents were specifically warned against leaving their homes. A group of protesters nevertheless assembled outside the gates of Babaoshan, where they unfurled a hand-lettered banner that read "Ziyang's spirit lives forever; declare war on corruption."

THE MAN WHO preceded Zhao Ziyang both as China's premier and as Party general secretary, Hua Guofeng, died of natural causes in August 2008, at the age of eighty-seven. Although he had been widely reviled by Deng Xiaoping's supporters in the late 1970s for his slavish devotion to Mao's "two whatevers," and for his ill-fated economic policy of importing expensive state-of-the-art industrial plants from the West and Japan with little concern for their vital upstream linkages or downstream costs, today Hua is widely credited with having paved the way for a peaceful transition to the reform era. During his brief reign he spearheaded the arrest of the Gang of Four and permitted tens of thousands of "rightists," sentenced to hard labor in the countryside during the Mao era, to return to their urban homes and jobs. It was Hua who revived China's moribund system of higher education, reinstating the national college entrance examinations in 1977, and it was Hua, I recently discovered, who granted Sid Rittenberg his release from prison, also in 1977. As the first top CCP leader to be toppled without a violent purge, moreover, Hua set an important precedent for the peaceful transfer of power in China. After resigning from office, he remained a member of the Central Committee; as late as 2002 he was elected a delegate to the National Party Congress.

AFTER BEING PERMITTED to leave his U.S. Embassy refuge in Beijing in June 1990, Fang Lizhi, whose outspoken support for China's democracy movement in the late 1980s had indirectly contributed to Zhao Ziyang's downfall, emigrated to the United Kingdom with his wife, Li Shuxian. Six months later he accepted a temporary position at the Institute for Advanced Study in Princeton, New Jersey. Now in his seventies, Fang currently teaches astrophysics at the University of Arizona, where he has generally maintained a low political profile. In a rare interview granted after the death of Zhao Ziyang in January 2005, Fang was pessimistic about the prospects for an early reversal of the CCP's verdicts on Zhao Ziyang and the 1989 student movement, but he remained hopeful about the long-term future of political reform, expressing confidence that "In the end, China will walk on the path toward democracy and the rule of law."

THE STUDENT LEADERS of the 1989 Tiananmen protest have followed widely divergent career paths. After serving several years in a Chinese prison, Wang Dan was granted a medical parole in 1998. He emigrated to the United States, where he attended Harvard University. In 2005 he moved to Los Angeles, where he wrote his doctoral dissertation, "A Comparative Study of Political Terror in Taiwan in the 1950s." After escaping from China via Hong Kong in 1989, Wu'er Kaixi spent time in Palo Alto, California, before eventually emigrating to Taiwan, where he became a popular radio talk-show host. Other former student protest leaders, including Chai Ling and Li Lu, went on to become successful entrepreneurs in the United States. Wang Chaohua is finishing her Ph.D. dissertation in Chinese literature at UCLA.

In Hong Kong, Han Dongfang, now in his mid-forties, continues his tireless efforts on behalf of China's industrial workers. Against all odds, his organization, the China Labour Bulletin, has successfully sued a growing number of Chinese factory owners for recklessly endangering the health and safety of workers through exposure to debilitating occupational diseases such as silicosis (also known as Grinder's disease). Often described as China's Lech Wałesa, Han was presented with the prestigious Democracy Award by President Bill Clinton in 1993, on behalf of the National Endowment for Democracy. In 2005 he received the Gleitsman Foundation's International Activist Award, donating his $50,000 prize money to the China Labour Bulletin's Legal Defense Fund. That same year he was selected to give the prestigious Regents Lecture at UCLA, where it was my great pleasure to serve as his host.

Fu Yuehaua, the Democracy Wall activist, has not fared well since going to prison in 1979 for organizing a petitioners' march in Beijing. While in detention she had her gall bladder removed and has suffered from stomach ulcers ever since. After her release from prison in 1983, she became a street vendor and was subject to periodic police harassment and supervision. Sadly, Fu's mother recently died in the hospital when doctors turned off her ventilator machine because the family was unable to pay her medical bills, a tragic irony for a woman who had fought so long and so bravely on behalf of China's poor.

MORE THAN A decade has elapsed since the Hong Kong handover of 1997. In the interim China's leaders have adhered more or less conscientiously to the letter of the Basic Law, avoiding overt interference in the political, legal, economic, and social life of the Hong Kong Special Administrative Region. From time to time, however, Hong Kong has felt subtle political pressures from across the border. For example, several Hong Kong newspapers and magazines, reluctant to do anything that might offend the Beijing government, have indulged in conspicuous self-censorship in their coverage of events in Mainland China. There have also been recurrent reports of advertising boycotts orchestrated by pro-Beijing factions in Hong Kong against local publishers who habitually portray China in a negative light. A few independent publishers, such as Jimmy Lai of *Apple Daily*, have been forced to curtail their Hong Kong media operations. And the government-

owned broadcast conglomerate Radio Television Hong Kong, long a bas-
tion of media freedom in Hong Kong, has come under increasing pressure
to be more China-friendly. Finally, a number of Hong Kong academics
have complained of being pressured by their deans and department chairs
to refrain from being overly critical of China. Although such pressures are
both real and worrisome, Hong Kong today remains, for the most part, a
relatively open, pluralistic, and politically vibrant society, though not, by
any definition, a fully democratic one.

IN 2003 I paid a return visit to Yuanmingyuan, the Old Summer Palace
in Beijing. I had heard that major renovations were under way, but I was
unprepared for what I saw. I should have suspected something when my
taxi driver approached the site on a freshly paved multilane road lined
with a profusion of clear directional signs. Although it was not yet fully
open to the public, Yuanmingyuan was in major tourist-anticipation
mode. The overgrown fields and groves that had once encroached upon
its splendid ruins had been cleared away, and the monumental remnants
of long-neglected halls, pavilions, and courtyards were being restored to
their original eighteenth-century splendor. Also being rebuilt, based on
original landscape drawings, were the pristine lakes and gardens of the
palace grounds. It was all very fresh and new and clean—and, to my eye,
quite sterile. Equally distressing were the numerous souvenir kiosks and
pedal-boat rental concessions that now dotted the garden pathways surrounding the refurbished Lake of Blessings. Another shiny new cultural
theme park was under construction.

Walking toward the northeastern quadrant of Yuanmingyuan, where
its European-style palaces had been laid waste in 1860, I located the same
stone outcropping where, twenty-five years earlier, I had taught Bob
Dylan's songs to a group of young Chinese students. The gigantic stones
had been repositioned with scant attention to aesthetics. Hundreds of
marble columns, arches, stone animals, and tablets had been collected and
hauled to the edge of a restored eighteenth-century pond and deposited
alongside one another like so many random pieces of archaeological junk,
ill-fitting pieces of a monumental jigsaw puzzle. The site retained little of
its awesome pre-restoration majesty or tranquility. According to a large
plaque erected at the site by the state committee responsible for overseeing
the restoration project, the European palaces of Yuanmingyuan would not
be restored along with the rest but would remain in a state of almost total

destruction, thereby providing "irrefutable evidence of imperialist powers destroying human civilizations." The declared purpose was to retain "the dilapidated walls and pillars of the European Palace as a monument to national humiliation, encouraging the Chinese people to work harder to make the nation strong." I left the area feeling vaguely distressed.

NOT ALL THE environmental news was bad. A year after I visited Yunnan's dramatic Tiger Leaping Gorge in 2002, the movement to protect the gorge and its turbulent Jinsha River from a series of planned hydroelectric dams received a boost when the United Nations Educational, Scientific, and Cultural Organization declared the gorge a World Heritage Site. A year later, in October 2004, a loose coalition of nine environmental NGOs, in collaboration with international scholars, conservationists, and journalists, petitioned Premier Wen Jiabao to suspend the Tiger Leaping Gorge dam project, claiming that no serious environmental impact studies had been undertaken. After more than two years of official silence, Yunnan provincial authorities announced in May 2007 that there would be "absolutely" no new dam construction in the region of Yunnan's "three parallel rivers," including the Jinsha. For devotees of environmental protection, exquisite canyon views, and cold beer at Sean's Guesthouse, this came as welcome news indeed.

SINCE MY LAST visit to Xining in 2002 I have remained in regular contact with Kevin Stuart, Zhu Yongzhong, and a number of their former Qinghai English-language students. From them I learned that Guanting now has a brand-new two-star hotel, complete with in-room hot water and showers. My young Tibetan guide, Gregory, I am happy to report, received a full four-year scholarship to Reed College in Oregon, where he is currently studying anthropology. More than thirty other Tibetan graduates of Kevin's English Training Program have gone on to pursue higher education abroad, including eighteen in the Philippines, seven in the United States, four in Thailand, two in Germany, and one each in the Czech Republic, Norway, Chile, and Italy. Three of Kevin's Tibetan students have had their autobiographies published in English, both electronically and in hardcover, and a fourth has produced three independent documentary films.

As for Zhu Yongzhong and his Sanchuan Development Association colleagues in Guanting, since they initiated their English-conversation program in 2001, more than 280 of their Mangghuer middle-school graduates have matriculated to colleges and universities throughout China. Equally noteworthy, at last count Yongzhong and the SDA, with the assistance of Kevin's Internet-savvy, Web-surfing young Tibetan students, had raised more than ¥8 million ($1.1 million) in grants from international philanthropic organizations and foreign embassies to support 125 community development projects in Guanting and other nearby towns and villages. In recognition of his achievements, Yongzhong in 2006 was selected by the National Committee on U.S.-China Relations to participate in its prestigious Young Leaders' Forum in New York, honoring outstanding community leaders from across China. The coincidence was striking: Thirty years earlier the National Committee had sponsored my first visit to China; now it was sponsoring Zhu Yongzhong's first visit to the United States. En route to New York and Washington, D.C., Yongzhong stopped off in Los Angeles for a nostalgic reunion of the UCLA-Guanting class of 2002, held amid abundant tears, laughter, and, of course, ample supplies of *baijiu*.

ON A MORE unpleasant note, the long-smoldering tensions between Tibetans and the Han in China's far west erupted into open violence in the spring of 2008. What began as a series of peaceful demonstrations by Buddhist monks at monasteries in Lhasa, Labrang, Zhongdian, and elsewhere on the anniversary of the 1959 imposition of martial law in Tibet, gave way to a wave of physical assaults, burnings, and lootings by roving bands of angry Tibetan youths. The violence, which initially targeted Han merchants and migrants who had flooded into China's western provinces to reap the benefits of the government's Great Western Development program, spread quickly. In Xiahe, near Labrang, street fighting raged for two days and nights, and more than a dozen people were reported killed in Lhasa in a series of bloody encounters between Tibetan youths and Chinese police. In several towns and villages the Chinese national flag was hauled down and the Tibetan flag raised, and Gregory's hometown of Tongren suffered several days of violence after a Han street vendor refused to give a Tibetan child a refund on a malfunctioning helium balloon.

In response to the sudden epidemic of violence, China dispatched PLA combat units to occupy the main trouble spots, while other troops cordoned off major sections of the Tibetan plateau. With a clampdown on all unauthorized domestic media coverage and a total ban on foreign journalists, accurate information was extremely hard to come by. Rumors soon began to circulate—via text messaging, often accompanied by grainy cell-phone video clips and still photos—of Tibetan protesters being arrested, beaten, and killed throughout Tibet, Qinghai, Gansu, and Sichuan. As the crackdown progressed, there were few signs that Beijing was prepared to resolve long-standing Tibetan grievances. On the contrary, the man charged with restoring law and order in Tibet, Party first secretary Zhang Qingli—the same man who had referred to Tibetans as "children" in need of the CCP's "benevolent parenting"—took a very hard line, placing blame for the violence squarely on "the Dalai clique." It did not bode well for the future tranquility of the region.

In such a gloomy situation, my last direct communication from Kevin Stuart was an ominous one. In the repressive aftermath of the Tibetan unrest, I sent him an e-mail inquiring elliptically about his well-being and that of his Tibetan students. His response was terse and chilling: "So sad. Very hard times. Visa expires in mid-June."

AFTER BEING THE indisputable center of Western research on contemporary China for almost two decades, Hong Kong's Universities Service Centre suffered a gradual decline in the 1980s and 1990s. With Western scholars able to travel more or less freely to China, the center lost its cachet as the one indispensable place to conduct research on Mainland China. This decline coincided with its mounting financial difficulties, foreshadowed by the Ford Foundation's withdrawal as a major funding source after the 1971 incident with McGeorge Bundy. In 1988 the center was rescued from imminent bankruptcy by the Chinese University of Hong Kong, which assumed control of its operations and management. The center was relocated to the university's Shatin campus, and a new chief administrator replaced the longtime director of the center, John Dolfin. Interestingly, since the Hong Kong handover of 1997, the center's most frequent visitors are no longer Western scholars but rather Chinese researchers drawn from the other side of the border by the center's exceptional collection of Mainland journals and reference materials.

MY LONG-STANDING DISPUTE with my UCLA colleague Phil Huang continued to smolder for several years after it burst into the open during our televised PBS encounter in 1976, on the night of Mao's death. Like a number of other China scholars, Phil turned abruptly away from his earlier endorsement of the Cultural Revolution in the 1970s and became an outspoken critic of China's rigid system of bureaucratic authoritarianism. With his Maoist phase behind him, he went on to write several outstanding books about China's early modern development, and in 1986 he became the founding director of the UCLA Center for Chinese Studies, a post I later filled from 1999 to 2005. At one point in the late 1980s our UCLA colleagues Perry Link and Ben Elman tried to patch up the quarrel between Phil and me by getting the two of us to join them on a tennis court for a game of doubles, under the familiar Sino-American slogan "friendship first, competition second." By design, Phil and I were partnered in the first set, but we played poorly together and lost, 6–3. We then switched partners, whereupon Perry and I lost to Phil and Ben, 6–4. As it happened, however, the game score was less important than the symbolic contest, in which competition handily trounced friendship. Afterward, Phil and I sat down over a cold beer and warily discussed an armistice: We might not like each other, but we agreed to work together for the good of Chinese studies at UCLA. Though we never again quarreled openly, I breathed a deep sigh of relief when Phil retired from UCLA in 2005.

IT SADDENS ME to report that the Joint Center for International Studies' Globalization Studies program at Peking University was discontinued after its successful inaugural run in the fall of 2005. Despite (or perhaps because of) its exciting aura of intellectual innovation and exploration, the JCIS encountered a series of administrative hurdles in its first year of operation. Reportedly, some Beida Party and administrative officials were uneasy about the program's unusually high degree of academic freedom and autonomy. In any event, the institutional resources needed to ensure the program's continued smooth operation at Peking University were not forthcoming. Reluctantly, the UC's Education Abroad Program decided to transfer the JCIS program from Beida to Shanghai's Fudan University, where it enjoyed a successful relaunch in the fall of 2006.

CAROLYN AND I separated in 1989, divorcing three years later. She subsequently completed a Ph.D. in psychoanalysis and opened a private practice in Los Angeles. Proving that some apples fall close to the tree, Matthew, having earned a Ph.D. in political science from UC San Diego, was granted tenure in 2004 in the UCLA political science department. As far as I know, we were the only père-and-fils faculty tandem in the same department within the entire ten-campus, 15,000-faculty University of California system. Most recently Matt left UCLA for a full professorship at Harvard's Kennedy School of Government. He and his wife, Jeeyang, who also teaches political science at the Kennedy School, made me a proud grandpa in 2001.

After graduating from UC Berkeley with a B.A. in music, Kristen earned a master of fine arts degree from the Peabody Conservatory in Baltimore, where she developed her considerable talents as a classical guitarist. Kristen is also a certified Feldenkrais Method physical therapist, a technique she learned while undergoing treatment for acute tendonitis brought on by long hours of practicing her musical art in graduate school. She and her architect husband, Jan, live in San Diego, where they had their first child in 2009.

MY FATHER and H. Arthur Steiner passed away within a few months of each other in 1994. Right up to the end my dad seemed utterly incapable of offering me a straightforward compliment or expressing pride in my accomplishments. Nor could he ever concede that I had been right about the differences between Mao and Stalin. Still, I knew by the gleam in his eye that he loved and respected me, and that is what mattered most. As for Arthur Steiner, my debt to him is substantial. He fired my passion for learning and gave focus to my intellectual curiosity. In a touch of supreme irony, I was delivering a lecture on the Great Leap Forward to Professor Steiner's former class at UCLA, Poli. Sci. 159, when I was notified of his death. As I absorbed the news, relayed by a departmental administrator, I looked out into the sea of bright, earnest student faces, wondering how many had stumbled into my course by accident, or because of a mere scheduling convenience. Would any of them be touched, as I had been three decades earlier, by something—an idea, an anecdote, a book, or a professorial challenge—first encountered in this classroom?

MIKE OKSENBERG DIED from a recurrence of melanoma in February 2001, at the age of sixty-two. Happily, he and I had reconciled several years earlier. At a 1997 Hong Kong reunion dinner for scholars who had worked at the Universities Service Centre in the 1960s and 1970s, Mike pulled me aside to apologize for his vindictive attack at the 1981 Toronto Asian Studies convention, saying it was "the worst thing I have ever done." When I asked if his apology extended to the perverse pleasure he appeared to derive from humiliating me after our Camp David encounter in February 1989, he smiled and said, "Nahhh. You *deserved* that one."

At a conference held in Mike's honor at Stanford University during the terminal stages of his illness in October 2000, his friends and associates roasted him affectionately. Weakened by disease and by a strenuous chemotherapy regime, Mike nonetheless relished the roast. Various speakers, including Condoleezza Rice, directed good-natured jibes at him, and I recited my 1975 poem "For a Peking Tom." This time Mike grinned from ear to ear. Afterward we hugged, and our eyes teared up. He even promised to change my grade on the poem from C+ to A–. Mike sent me a last e-mail two months later, shortly before his death. In it, he playfully recalled our 1970 Banff conference hoax—and suggested that we do it again: "I've been trying to reach you by phone to cook up a joke. I think the time has come for one. The field is getting far too serious."

Requiescat in pace!

ON A CLEAR, balmy spring weekend not long ago, I returned to UC Berkeley, site of my graduate student apprenticeship. There I spent a nostalgic afternoon reminiscing with Bob Scalapino at his home high in the Berkeley Hills. We chatted about the old days—Berkeley in the '60s, the Cultural Revolution, the Free Speech and anti–Vietnam War movements, the polarization of campus politics—and about the many changes that China and we ourselves had undergone in the intervening decades. Though he displayed visible distress over the declining international stature of the United States in recent years, Bob was cautiously optimistic, as always, about China's developmental trajectory and the prospects for long-term stability in U.S.-China relations.

Bob had recently lost his loving wife and life partner of sixty-three years, Dee, and his emotions were close to the surface as we retraced his life and career from his time as a budding young graduate student at Harvard on the eve of World War II, to his service as a Japanese-language officer in the U.S. Navy, to a doctorate awarded in Chinese studies at Harvard in 1948 under the tutelage of the late John K. Fairbank. Bob had been teaching at Berkeley since 1949, the same year the Chinese Communists marched triumphantly into Beijing, and though he retired from teaching in 1990, he never lost his unquenchable curiosity about or enthusiasm for China. His proudest moment, he told me, was his authorship of the China/Taiwan section of the famous "Conlon Report" on U.S. foreign policy in Asia, prepared for the U.S. Congress in 1959. In it, Bob flatly challenged existing U.S. policy toward Chiang Kai-shek, arguing that Taiwan's ruling

Nationalist Party was autocratic, corrupt, unpopular, and undeserving of the label "Free China." Chiang's frequent talk of "recovering the Mainland" was mere hollow cant, he noted, and had little or no chance of ever being realized. Under these circumstances, the United States should, he argued, sponsor the creation of a separate "Republic of Taiwan," which would make no claim to governing, or even being a province of, Mainland China. Roundly denounced as a "two China" solution by the reunification-minded leaders of both the People's Republic and Taiwan, Bob's proposal strongly foreshadowed the growing movement for Taiwanese independence under Lee Teng-hui and Chen Shui-bian some forty years later. When I left Bob's house, the sun was setting over San Francisco Bay. As we parted, I told him how very fortunate I was to have had him as a friend and mentor.

BLESSED WITH AN inquisitive nature, outstanding role models, rich opportunities, and abundant good fortune, as a young man I became powerfully drawn to the lure of contemporary China. Almost from my first classroom encounter with Arthur Steiner, China has been my passion, my calling, my own personal Shangri-la and Chimera rolled into one. Although three decades of economic reform and global engagement have made China's political and social reality far more accessible—and far less bizarre—than they were in Mao's time, the People's Republic remains for me a profound puzzle. Ever changing, ever fascinating, and ever frustrating, it compels my attention even as it stubbornly defies comprehension. I cannot look away.

Epilogue

THE ONSET OF global recession in the second half of 2008 brought a good deal of uncertainty and stress to the Chinese economy. With foreign demand for Chinese manufactured goods dropping sharply toward the end of the year, tens of thousands of factories along China's eastern seaboard were shuttered, leaving upwards of twenty million workers, most of them rural emigrants, unemployed and without an adequate social safety net. In many cases, factory owners simply padlocked their gates and skipped town without notice, leaving their workers unpaid and angry. In Dongguan, a major coastal production center near Guangzhou, almost half of the city's 3,800 toy manufacturers went out of business in the winter of 2009. By spring, unofficial estimates placed China's urban unemployment rate at close to 8 percent—twice the government's official figure. Meanwhile, projections of China's GDP growth for 2009 slid downward, from 12 percent to 8 percent.

For years the conventional wisdom among political economists has held that given China's extreme polarization of wealth, inadequate welfare net, and oversupply of unskilled labor, a GDP growth rate of less than 8 percent annually would produce a sharp increase in the likelihood of social unrest. PRC leaders have not been oblivious to this risk. In an effort to jump-start China's ailing economy, the central government in December 2008 announced a new ¥4 trillion ($600 billion) stimulus package designed to increase public spending on infrastructure projects and social welfare. To put more money into circulation, central bank regulators lowered interest rates and instructed local branch managers to lend more money to thousands of firms struggling to survive in the face of reduced exports. At the same time, local governments in some areas handed out cash vouchers to new car shoppers and first-time home buyers. And in January 2009, Beijing unveiled a three-year, ¥850 billion ($123 billion) program to build a network of rural hospitals and clinics and to provide rudimentary national health insurance.

By the fall of 2009, the massive surge in government spending, together with sharply relaxed controls on credit and lending, succeeded in halting, if not totally reversing, China's economic slide. Employment in the construction industry rose; padlocked export firms began reopening their doors, using preferential loans secured at below-market interest rates; and housing and new car sales recovered to near pre-recession levels. Third-quarter economic growth was estimated at 8.9 percent—a substantial recovery from the worrisome first-quarter figure of 6.1 percent. Notwithstanding such apparently healthy numbers, however, economists were divided on the structural soundness of the recovery. Some worried that the lion's share of stimulus money was flowing not to households in need, but to "crony capitalists" with close ties to government officials. Others were concerned that too little was being done to reorient the Chinese economy away from an over-dependence on export growth toward greater emphasis on stimulating domestic consumption.

Though expert opinion was divided on the costs and gains of China's Keynesian stimulus, the potential for social unrest remained worrisome. Early in 2009, government spokesmen bluntly warned that the country was entering a period of increased hazard. "Without doubt," said one official, commenting in the January issue of the authoritative Outlook magazine, "Chinese society in 2009 will face even more conflicts and clashes that will test the ruling capacity of the Party and government at all levels." To guard against spreading unrest, Chinese leaders stepped up their security precautions. Tibet was sealed off to tourists and journalists, and a fresh clampdown on liberal bloggers, investigative reporters, political dissidents, and civil society activists was vigorously—and at times violently—enforced.

Adding to the political stress was the conjunction in 2009 of several important political anniversaries, including the sixtieth anniversary of the PRC's founding, the fiftieth anniversary of the 1959 Tibetan rebellion, the twentieth anniversary of the Tiananmen crackdown, and the tenth anniversary of the suppression of the Falun Gong. In China, political anniversaries have often been focal points for organized protest, and the authorities were leaving nothing to chance. In anticipation of rising turbulence, the CCP early in 2009 created an elite national task force to oversee security preparations during the anniversary year. To underline the task force's importance, it was placed under the overall command of Vice President Xi Jinping, widely regarded as the presumptive heir apparent to Hu Jintao.

Despite such added precautions, ethnic violence erupted in Xinjiang in the summer of 2009. In early July, reports reached the Uighur community in Urumqi of the fatal beating of two Uighur migrant workers in a Guangdong factory. Demanding punishment of the perpetrators, hundreds of angry Uighur students took to the streets of Urumqi, confronting Chinese shopkeepers and bystanders alike. Though there were conflicting accounts of who initiated the violence, and who bore responsibility for escalating it, the outcome was disastrous. A virtual carbon copy of the ethnic rioting in Tibet a year earlier, the violence in Urumqi resulted in the deaths of 46 Uighurs and 137 Han Chinese. In the aftermath of the bloodshed, Chinese authorities launched a "strike hard" campaign in Xinjiang, aimed at disrupting Uighur "terrorist cells" and "rooting out the places where criminals breed." At the same time, strict new media controls were imposed on journalists seeking to report from Xinjiang.

The Chinese government's unremitting, reflexive efforts to paint ethnic unrest in Xinjiang and Tibet as the work of criminals, terrorists, and (in the case of Tibet) agents of the "traitorous Dalai clique," reveal a deep-seated flaw in the political culture of Chinese Communism. Although few would gainsay the efforts of Hu Jintao and Wen Jiabao to smooth the harsh edges of authoritarian rule by adding a rhetorical veneer of neo-Confucian paternalism, benevolence, and social harmony, at least one essential component of the Confucian canon has been conspicuously absent from China's official political discourse: the "rectification of names" (*zhengming*). In a key section of the Confucian *Analects* dealing with the requisites of good governance (Book XIII.3), Confucius enters into a dialogue with two of his disciples. The disciples ask the Master about the essence of upright rulership, and the Sage responds that the most important thing is to attach accurate names to things. The greater the discrepancy between the essence of things and the names affixed to them, warns Confucius, the more precarious is the authority of the state:

If names be not correct, language is not in accordance with the truth of things. If language be not in accordance with the truth of things, affairs cannot be conducted successfully. When affairs cannot be conducted successfully, propriety will not flourish. When propriety does not flourish, punishments will not be properly meted out. When punishments are not properly meted out, the people will not know how to comport themselves.

I have suggested throughout this book that the continued existence of a profound chasm between rhetoric and reality may be taken as a crude measure of political fragility. The harder a regime must work to spin political reality and impose its own labels on things, the more insecure it reveals itself to be.

The need for a thoroughgoing rectification of names in China was brought home to me yet again on the twentieth anniversary of Hu Yaobang's death, April 15, 2009. On that date, I received a lengthy e-mail message from one of the Chinese students who had taken my fall 2005 "Debating Globalization" class at Beida. One of the more reticent and withdrawn students in the class, she had never once questioned her government's position on key political issues. Now a practicing lawyer, she told me that after taking my class she had started using proxy servers to read banned Internet materials about the events of 1989. She was ashamed, she said, at how naive she had been back then. "They treated us like children," she admitted, "and we accepted it." She was writing now to tell me that on the previous day, April 14, she and a friend had made a pilgrimage to Gongqing City in Jiangxi, where Hu Yaobang's ashes are interred. They had been intending to pay their respects, but two plainclothes police officers had intercepted them at the entrance to the cemetery, urging them to leave. "For the first time in my life," she wrote, "I defied the authority of the Chinese Communist Party." And she confessed that this modest act of personal rebellion had evoked in her ambivalent feelings of anxiety as well as empowerment. She then reminded me of an informal talk I had given to a small group of Beida students during one of my Wednesday afternoon salons in the fall of 2005, on the subject of distortions in Communist Party political labels. "Your words stayed with me," she said. "I could no longer accept the government's designation of

Hu Yaobang as a 'bourgeois liberal.' He was a great and tragic hero." She thanked me for stimulating her curiosity and closed with the hope that someday all misleading labels would be appropriately rectified in China. I thanked her for her note, wished her well, and added a brief postscript to the effect that I could not agree more.

LES MICHELS
Provence
October 2009

Author's Notes

2

PAGE 13 My interest in the "red" versus "expert" controversy in China grew out of my master's thesis, completed in 1963. The thesis centered on the origins and implications of Mao's "voluntarism," his trademark insistence that the "human factor"—volition, leadership, organization, and esprit de corps—rather than impersonal economic forces or material technology ultimately determine the course of human history. At the suggestion of my thesis advisor, Chalmers Johnson, I submitted a section of my 120-page thesis to UC Berkeley's in-house journal of Asian affairs. The article, my first academic publication, appeared in the September 1964 issue of *Asian Survey*, under the title "Red and Expert: Politico-Ideological Foundations of China's Great Leap Forward."

PAGES 34-35 My Ph.D. dissertation was eventually published in two parts. The latter half appeared first as a Rand Corporation monograph, "The Cultural Revolution in the Countryside: Anatomy of a Limited Rebellion," in Thomas W. Robinson, ed., *The Cultural Revolution in China* (Berkeley: University of California Press, 1971). The first half, on the Four Cleanups, was published a few years later, as *Prelude to Revolution: Mao, the Party, and the Peasant Question, 1962-66* (New York: Columbia University Press, 1975). By the time it finally appeared in print, I had developed a rather strong aversion to anything having to do with the Four Cleanups, a classic example of post-dissertation stress response. And in the three decades since *Prelude to Revolution* was published, I have never been tempted to revisit that particular part of my life's work. Fortunately, the research that Fred Teiwes and I did on the Four Cleanups has largely withstood the test of time, and has not—at least, not yet—been superseded or rendered obsolete.

3

PAGES 39–41 Although the original CCP verdict on the Lin Biao affair has never been altered, more than thirty-five years later the known facts of Lin's alleged coup attempt continue to belie the official version of events. In their recent book *The End of the Maoist Era: Chinese Politics during the Twilight of the Cultural Revolution, 1972–76* (Armonk, NY: M. E. Sharpe, 2007), Fred Teiwes and Warren Sun call the official story of Lin's demise "the worst fabrication ever concocted by CCP historiography." The gripping family drama of the Lin Biao affair is revealed in Jin Qiu, *The Culture of Power: The Lin Biao Incident in the Cultural Revolution* (Stanford, CA: Stanford University Press, 1999).

PAGE 46 Jiang Qing's precipitous downfall brought with it an equally sudden reversal of fortune for one of her most prominent Western biographers, my former Berkeley classmate Roxane Witke. In the early 1970s, when Jiang Qing was still riding high, Witke, then teaching at the State University of New York, was granted a series of exclusive interviews—sixty hours in all—with Mme. Mao in her sumptuous private villa in Guangzhou. In Witke's subsequent book, *Comrade Chiang Ch'ing* (Boston: Little, Brown, 1977), she painted a generally sympathetic portrait of Jiang as a militant feminist whose career had been blocked (and her downfall later secured) owing to the seething resentment of male chauvinists within the CCP leadership. Mao was reported to be very angry at Jiang for inviting Witke to conduct these interviews without his permission. After Jiang Qing was arrested and her reputation discredited, Witke's objectivity as a scholar was sharply questioned in some reviews of her book. A few years later the Australian journalist Ross Terrill published a thoroughly negative biography of Jiang Qing, *The White-Boned Demon: A Biography of Madame Mao Zedong* (New York: Morrow, 1984), which had the effect of driving the final nail into Jiang's reputational coffin. Sadly, Witke's career never fully recovered from the blow to her credibility.

PAGES 52–54 The 1970 Banff conference, scene of the "Kunming incident" hoax recounted here, resulted in the publication of a volume edited by Bob Scalapino, *Elites in the People's Republic of China* (Seattle: University of Washington Press, 1972). The book includes June Dreyer's sensitive analysis of ethnic minorities in the Cultural Revolution, though her chapter contained no mention either of the Kunming incident or of the notorious feuding Tibetan warlord brothers, Ma Dapu and Ma Dafu. How quickly they forget!

PAGES 58–60 The 1981 Toronto AAS paper that occasioned such a harsh response from Mike Oksensberg turned out to be rather well regarded in the academic community. Three different versions of it were eventually published. The original monograph was issued as *Scientism and Bureaucratism in Chinese Thought: Cultural Limits of the "Four Modernizations"* (Lund University, Research Policy Institute, Discussion Paper No. 145, April 1981). Shortly afterward, an abridged version—surgically shorn of much of its dense academic jargon (thanks, Mike!)—appeared as "Science and Culture in Contemporary China: The Roots of Retarded Modernization," *Asian Survey*, December 1982. A third, even more highly condensed version was published in *The Wilson Quarterly*, Spring 1983.

4

PAGES 69–71 Behind the benign facade of the slogan "Friendship first, competition second," the world of state-supported athletics in Mao's China was a high-pressure, ultra-competitive one. Recently one of my former undergraduate students—a six-foot-eight-inch professional Chinese basketball player, Kai Chen, who toured with the PRC national team in the 1970s—wrote a book exposing the culture of ritualized conformity, intense personal and political rivalry, backbiting, and betrayal that characterized the cloistered world of professional athletics in China. See Kai Chen, *One in a Billion: The Story of a Pro Basketball Player in China* (Bloomington, IN: AuthorHouse Books, 2007).

5

PAGE 92 Zhou Enlai initially formulated the Four Modernizations—accelerated development of Chinese industry, agriculture, science and technology, and national defense—in 1974. After the deaths of Zhou and Mao, the slogan was revived as the centerpiece of Hua Guofeng's plan to rapidly close the technology gap between China and the West by importing large numbers of complete "turnkey" plants from advanced capitalist countries, to be paid for with massive exports of Chinese energy resources. The program proved wildly expensive and impractical, and the government abandoned it by 1980. Its failure contributed to Hua's downfall by giving his critics added ammunition in their efforts to discredit him.

PAGES 92–93 China's initial opening to the outside world in 1978–79 brought with it the establishment of several foreign news bureaus in Beijing, along with the assignment of additional diplomatic personnel to foreign embassies there. Consequently, a large number of Western journalists and diplomats were on hand to record the first tentative stirrings of post-Mao Chinese society. These early awakenings, both positive and negative, were captured in a number of excellent books, including Roger Garside, *Coming Alive: China after Mao* (New York: Mentor Books, 1981); John Fraser, *The Chinese: Portrait of a People* (New York: Summit Books, 1981); Fox Butterfield, *China: Alive in the Bitter Sea* (New York: Bantam Books, 1982); and Jay Mathews and Linda Mathews, *One Billion: A China Chronicle* (New York: Ballantine, 1983).

PAGES 98–99 The arrest and imprisonment of human rights activists Fu Yuehua and Wei Jingsheng in 1979 set in motion a cyclical pattern marked by oscillating phases of political relaxation and constriction. Recurring at more or less regular intervals of twelve to eighteen months, this pattern repeated itself for more than a dozen years. The cycles generally followed the Newtonian principle of action-reaction. A cautious initiative by liberal Party reformers— say, a proposal to introduce limited local elections—would trigger a wave of heightened popular expectations and demands for further reform. Worried that such demands would get out of hand ("Give them an inch and they'll take a mile"), Party conservatives would attack "bourgeois liberalization" and demand "unity and stability" (code words for tightened political and ideological control). Caught between two conflicting wings of his own party, Deng Xiaoping played the role of balancer throughout the 1980s and early 1990s, tacking first one way and then the other in an effort to satisfy both the liberal and traditionalist wings of his reform coalition. The resulting cycles of reform and reaction are examined in my book, *Burying Mao: Chinese Politics in the Age of Deng Xiaoping*, enlarged paperback ed. (Princeton, NJ: Princeton University Press, 1996).

6

PAGE 100 Although Deng is justly famous for his "white cat, black cat" aphorism, what he actually said in July 1962 was "No matter whether it is a yellow cat or a black cat, whatever method works to serve the restoration of agricultural production, we should use that method." Later the quote was modified to express a generic preference for practical results over ideological prescriptions.

PAGES 100–102 Mao's Memorial Hall at the south end of Tiananmen Square first opened to the public in May 1977. According to Dr. Li Zhisui, the embalming technique Chinese state morticians used to preserve the Chairman's remains had been developed in the Soviet Union and was later introduced into China from Vietnam, where it had been used to preserve the corpse of Ho Chi Minh.

PAGES 116–117 Although the student demonstrations of November–December 1986 ended more or less peacefully, with students voluntarily vacating Tiananmen Square, Deng Xiaoping's anger at the sheer insolence of their behavior was clear. In a speech to a closed-door meeting of senior party leaders at the end of December, Deng said: "We cannot allow people who turn right and wrong around . . . to do as they please." Praising Poland's government for its handling of street demonstrations in 1981, Deng said the Polish leaders had showed "cool and level-headed judgment. Their attitude was firm. . . . They resorted to martial law to bring the situation under control." And he went on to say that there would be no backing down in the face of student demands: "If we do not take appropriate measures, we will be unable to control this type of incident; if we pull back, we will encounter even more trouble later on." In retrospect, Deng's hard-line warning proved to be a chilling precursor of the Tiananmen crackdown of May–June 1989.

7

PAGES 124–125 Because of his role as Fang Lizhi's escort to the presidential banquet in Beijing, Perry Link became persona non grata in China. Since 1989 he has been unable to secure a visa to travel there.

PAGES 125–126 On the conflict between the White House and Ambassador Lord over the Fang Lizhi affair, see Patrick Tyler, *A Great Wall: Six Presidents and China* (New York: PublicAffairs, 1999), pp. 346–47.

PAGES 127–134 A thinly fictionalized account of the origins, development, and dynamics of the Tiananmen Square student demonstrations and subsequent military suppression can be found in Ma Jian's extraordinary novel *Beijing Coma*, translated by Flora Drew (New York: Farrar, Straus and Giroux, 2008).

See also Richard Baum, *Burying Mao: Chinese Politics in the Age of Deng Xiaoping* (Princeton, NJ: Princeton University Press, 1996), chapter 11.

8

PAGE 148 For an analysis of the sources, extent, and impact of drug abuse in post-reform China, see Niklas Swandström and Yin He, "China's War on Narcotics: Two Perspectives" (Silk Road Studies Program, Central Asia–Caucasus Institute, Johns Hopkins School of Advanced International Studies, December 2006).

PAGE 149 The drama of the Tank Man, discussed here, was explored in detail in a television documentary of the same title, produced in 2005 by Antony Thomas. The film is referenced at http://www.pbs.org/wgbh/pages/frontline/tankman/view/.

PAGES 152–153 The Chinese government's classification of foreigners based on their degree of friendship (or enmity) is detailed in remarks made by a Chinese diplomatic defector, Zhou Liming, to the UC Berkeley China Forum, July 13, 1990.

PAGE 153 Some of the young Fudan University scholars I met on this occasion went on to have distinguished political careers. Wang Huning, for example, became a principal political adviser to President Jiang Zemin, while Zhou Mingwei became deputy minister of China's Taiwan Affairs Office. Whatever personal feelings and doubts these men may have harbored concerning the events of the spring of 1989 have never been expressed in public.

PAGE 155 As of the autumn of 2009, there were no indications that the CCP intended to undertake a reappraisal of its original verdict on the Tiananmen "turmoil" anytime soon. When pressed, Party and government officials respond obliquely that "history will decide."

9

PAGES 156–157 Throughout the 1980s and early 1990s the veteran CCP ideologue Deng Liqun spearheaded the conservative assault on Deng Xiaoping's economic reforms. On his efforts to derail the reform program, see my article

"Deng Liqun and the Struggle against Bourgeois Liberalization, 1979–1993," *China Information*, Spring 1995.

PAGE 158 For more on the resurgence of Chinese nationalism in the 1990s, see my chapter "Present Nationalism and Communist Power," in David Arase, ed., *The Challenge of Change: East Asia in the New Millennium* (Berkeley: University of California, East Asia Institute, 2003).

PAGES 166–170 The politics of the Hong Kong handover are analyzed in two articles I wrote during my 1997 residency in Hong Kong: "Enter the Dragon: China's Courtship of Hong Kong, 1982–1997," *Communist and Post-Communist Studies*, December 1999; and "Britain's Betrayal of Hong Kong: A Second Look," *Journal of Contemporary China*, Winter 1999.

PAGE 171 Although the quote here attributed to Napoleon concerning the "sleeping giant" is merely legendary, Rudyard Kipling issued a similar but very real caveat in 1889: "What will happen when China really wakes up, runs a line from Shanghai to Lhasa . . . and controls her own gun-factories and arsenals?" What indeed!?

10

PAGES 173–174 Although I was a member of the first U.S. computer science delegation to visit China after the Cultural Revolution, my initial attempt to analyze its emerging computer revolution came many years later and was published as "*DOS ex Machina:* The Micro-Electronic Ghost in China's Modernization Machine," in Denis Simon and Merle Goldman, eds., *Science and Technology in Post-Mao China* (Cambridge, MA: Harvard University Press, 1989).

PAGES 175–176 Chastened by my botched attempt to analyze Chinese leadership changes using materials accessed via the Dialog online database, I started over, using conventional documentary sources to write the piece. The results were published as "China in 1985: The Greening of the Revolution," *Asian Survey*, January 1986.

PAGE 179 The role of Chinapol member-journalists in exposing the truth about the 2006 slaying of two Tibetan refugees is documented in the *Christian Science Monitor*, October 25, 2006.

PAGES 181–182 At the peak of the SARS epidemic, in the late spring and early summer of 2003, the death toll in China reached 350 (out of more than 2,000 people believed infected). Globally, the death toll topped 800 (out of more than 8,000 suspected infections). Thereafter the epidemic subsided rapidly, for unknown reasons. After initially blocking efforts by the media and the World Health Organization to assess the extent of the epidemic, Chinese authorities reversed themselves, firing the minister of public health and vowing to be more transparent, a pledge that has been honored only episodically.

PAGES 182–183 The complete text of this diatribe against Chinapol (and against me personally), together with various readers' responses, is at the Danwei blogsite (June 28, 2006), under the title "Chinapol Has an America Problem," http://www.danwei.org/internet/kicked_out_of_chinapol.php.

PAGES 186–187 The saga of the Chongqing "nail house" is recounted in Howard French, "A Couple's Small Victory Is a Big Step for China," *International Herald Tribune*, April 6, 2007. For an analysis of the problem of Internet censorship and mass media control in China, see my article "The Political Impact of China's Information Revolution: The Media, the Minders, and Their Message," in Cheng Li, ed., *China's Changing Political Landscape* (Washington, DC: Brookings Institution, 2008).

11

PAGE 189 Greater Tibet is a premodern geocultural entity encompassing the widely scattered Tibetan Buddhist populations of five western Chinese provinces. In addition to Amdo in the northeast (encompassing Qinghai, southwestern Gansu, and northwestern Sichuan), the other major regions of Greater Tibet are Kham (including northeastern Yunnan and southwestern Sichuan) and Ü-Tsang (Tibet proper). The present provincial boundaries were established by the PRC government in 1951.

PAGES 196–197 A modern writer's odyssey through China's far western frontier regions is beautifully presented in Vikram Seth, *Heaven Lake: Travels through Xinjiang and Tibet* (New York: Vintage Books, 1987). An excellent introduction to the Mogao caves at Dunhuang is Robert Whitfield et al., *Cave Temples of Mogao: Art and History on the Silk Road* (Los Angeles: Getty Trust Publications, 2000).

PAGES 206–207 While living in Guanting, I initiated a research project in collaboration with one of my UCLA graduate student volunteers, Xin Zhang. In it, we examined the history, organization, and local impact of the Sanchuan Development Association. Our findings were published in "Civil Society Revisited: The Anatomy of a Rural People's NGO," *The China Journal*, July 2004. A more intensive study of Qinghai's emerging civil society, titled *The Other China*, is under preparation by Anne Thurston of Johns Hopkins University.

PAGES 209–211 The Three Gorges dam is the subject of a critical study by Chinese environmental activist Dai Qing, *The River Dragon Has Come!: The Three Gorges Dam and the Fate of China's Yangtze River and Its People* (Armonk, NY: M. E. Sharpe, 1998). For a fascinating look at life along the Yangzi on the eve of the opening of the Three Gorges dam, see Peter Hessler, *River Town: Two Years on the Yangtze* (New York: HarperCollins, 2001).

PAGE 216 The same Chinese government Web site that describes the Uighurs in childlike terms goes on to describe the six million Yi people of Southwest China as follows: "Yi live on farming and animal husbandry. Their traditional painting, sculpture, and silversmith are beautiful. Fire Festival in June is a big day for Yi. Just like other minority groups, they are good in folk dancing and singing." See "China's Ethnic Minorities" at http://www.index-china.com/minority/minority-english.htm.

12

PAGES 226–227 On the phenomenal success of reality-TV shows in post-Mao China, see Hui Xiao, "Narrating a Happy China through a Crying Game: A Case Study of Post-Mao Reality Shows," *China Media Research* 2, no. 3 (2006), at www.chinamediaresearch.net/vol2no3/060307_Hui_Xiao_done_CO.pdf.

PAGES 228–229 Post-Mao China's dramatically worsening environmental problems are examined in Elizabeth Economy, *The River Runs Black* (New York: Council on Foreign Relations, 2004).

PAGE 230 For an excellent collection of essays on the emergence of civil society groups and NGOs in post-Mao China, see Jonathan Unger, ed., *Associations and the Chinese State: Contested Spaces* (Armonk, NY: M. E. Sharpe, 2008).

13

PAGES 232ff My Fudan University presentation "China Watching in the United States" was published in Robert Ash, David Shambaugh, and Seiichiro Takagi, eds., *China Watching: Perspectives from Europe, Japan and the United States* (New York: Routledge, 2007).

PAGE 236 The experiences of "Xiao Yang" in the Cultural Revolution are documented in Gordon Bennett and Ronald N. Montaperto, *Red Guard: The Political Biography of Dai Hsiao-ai* (Garden City, NY: Doubleday, 1971).

PAGES 239–240 One book that contributed mightily to the post-1976 demystification of Mao and the Cultural Revolution is Simon Leys, *Chinese Shadows* (New York: Viking Press, 1977). In it, the pseudonymous author (real name, Pierre Ryckmans), a onetime cultural attaché at the Belgian Embassy in Beijing, scathingly exposes the recent rash of shameless pandering to Chinese leaders by sycophantic foreigners, as well as the appalling disregard (or, even worse, cover-up) of Cultural Revolution atrocities by people who ought to have known better. A useful review of the United States' curious epidemic of China fever in the 1970s is provided by Harry Harding, "From China with Disdain: New Trends in the Study of China," *Asian Survey*, October 1982.

PAGE 242 Steven Mosher's egregious violation of the anthropologists' golden rule—"Leave no footprints!"—led the American Anthropological Association to reexamine its norms and standards for the conduct of anthropological fieldwork. Mosher's actions also resulted in more stringent ethical standards being written into the Human Subjects Protocols that guide behavioral research at major U.S. universities. Among Mosher's most provocative writings are *Broken Earth* (New York: Free Press, 1983) and *Journey to the Forbidden China* (New York: Free Press, 1985), both of which present blistering indictments of the CCP's policies toward China's rural population.

14

PAGES 254–255 The accuracy and validity of Chinese public opinion polls are matters of controversy for two main reasons. First, polling organizations often "soften" the questions asked in such surveys in order to hedge politically sensitive issues and avoid presenting respondents with negative inferences about sociopolitical conditions or government policies; second, polling samples are often selected without rigorous attention to demographic variables or the scientific requirements of random sampling. For example, since city dwellers are easier to interview than rural folk, there is often an undisclosed urban bias in the data. This bias is further compounded by the frequent practice of excluding migrant workers from opinion surveys, which leads to systematic underrepresentation of some of the most disadvantaged, aggrieved groups in Chinese society. For typical recent survey results, see "China's Optimism: Prosperity Brings Satisfaction—and Hope," *Pew Global Attitudes Survey*, November 16, 2005, at http://pewglobal.org/reports/display.php?ReportID=249.

PAGE 255 On the nature and composition of China's middle class, see "Dissecting China's Middle Class," *China Daily*, October 27, 2004, at http://www.chinadaily.com.cn/english/doc/2004-10/27/content_386060.htm.

PAGES 255–266 On the plight of China's migrant workers, see Dorothy Solinger, *Contesting Citizenship in Urban China: Peasants, Migrants, the State and the Logic of the Market* (Berkeley: University of California Press, 1999).

PAGES 257–258 The illicit commercial trafficking of large numbers of young women for sex, concubinage, and marriage in contemporary China is an unintended consequence of the country's one-child policy, introduced in the 1970s. With male children in substantially higher demand than females, this policy has engendered the widespread (albeit illegal) practice of sex-preferential abortion, leading to a severe shortage of reproductive-age females. The current ratio of Chinese males to females in the fifteen- to thirty-year age bracket is approximately 115:100; and when sex ratio at birth is considered, the disparity becomes even greater—120:100 in the year 2005—thus indicating that the shortage of females is getting worse. See Susan Greenhalgh, *Just One Child: Science and Policy in Deng's China* (Berkeley: University of California Press, 2007).

PAGE 262 The Party's acknowledgment of the urgent need to "strengthen ruling capacity" appears in "Resolution of the CCP Central Committee on Building the Ruling Capacity of the Party" (September 19, 2004). A partial English text is at http://www.chinadaily.com.cn/english/doc/2004-09/27/content_378161.htm.

PAGES 262–263 At the Party's Sixteenth National Party Congress in 2002, Jiang Zemin's colleagues gave him a lavish retirement gift, embedding his "Theory of the Three Represents" in the Party's constitution, alongside "Mao Zedong

Thought" and "Deng Xiaoping Theory," as one of the ideological cornerstones of Chinese Communism.

PAGES 266–268 In a number of articles and essays written over the past half dozen years, I have advanced the argument that given the continued absence of critical feedback and input institutions—including a free press, self-organizing civil society associations, autonomous interest groups, and an independent judiciary—China is unlikely to achieve long-term, sustainable political equilibrium and stability. See, for example, "Systemic Stresses and Political Choices: The Road Ahead," in Yun-han Chu et al., eds., *The New Chinese Leadership: Challenges and Opportunities after the 16th Party Congress* (Cambridge: Cambridge University Press, 2004); and "The Limits of Consultative Leninism," in Mark Mohr, ed., *China and Democracy: A Contradiction in Terms?* (Washington, DC: Woodrow Wilson International Center for Scholars, Asia Program Special Report #131, June 2006).

PAGES 272–276 The question of whether (and when) China is likely to emerge as a threat to vital Western and U.S. interests has been the subject of a virtual avalanche of books since the mid-1990s. The case for an increasingly hostile, adversarial China is argued in Ross Munro and Richard Bernstein, *The Coming Conflict with China* (New York: Alfred A. Knopf, 1997). The alternative case, for a globally engaged, potentially cooperative China, is presented in Bates Gill, *Rising Star: China's New Security Diplomacy* (Washington, DC: Brookings Institution Press, 2007). Ironically, today's pitched battles between China bashers and "panda huggers" often tend to mirror the theoretical lines of contention in the ongoing debate over whether interests or values drive the behavior of nations in the international arena—the very same debate that drove me away from the field of international relations more than forty years ago. The best recent book detailing trends in U.S.-China relations is Robert L. Suettinger, *Beyond Tiananmen: The Politics of U.S.-China Relations* (Washington, DC: Brookings Institution Press, 2003).

15

PAGES 286–287 After a prolonged period of electronic silence in the aftermath of the Tibetan riots of 2008, Kevin Stuart sent me a note informing me that he had been forced to leave China. Following a brief sojourn in Hawaii, he attempted to return to China in the spring of 2009, but was asked to leave once again. He is currently teaching ESL in the Philippines.

Suggestions for Further Reading

In addition to the books and articles cited in the preceding section, an excellent resource for the general reader seeking to understand the broad sweep of modern Chinese history, society, and politics is Jonathan Spence's magisterial *The Gate of Heavenly Peace: The Chinese and Their Revolution* (New York: Viking, 1981). For a fascinating firsthand account of one family's efforts to cope with the turmoil and tragedy of the Chinese revolution and its tumultuous Maoist aftermath, see Jung Chang, *Wild Swans: Three Daughters of China* (New York: Simon and Schuster, 2003). A sensible, well-balanced overview of Communism's impact on modern China is provided by Jonathan Fenby, *Modern China: The Fall and Rise of a Great Power* (New York: Harper-Collins, 2008).

A number of excellent biographies of Mao Zedong are currently available. The most riveting of these is a memoir covering the last two decades of Mao's life, written by his personal physician, Dr. Li Zhisui, *The Private Life of Chairman Mao* (New York: Random House, 1996). As indicated in chapter 12, I am rather skeptical of the objectivity of the more recent and deeply critical biography, *Mao: The Unknown Story*, by Jung Chang and Jon Halliday (London: Random House, 2005).

Two engrossing personal memoirs of the madness that gripped China during the Cultural Revolution are Gao Yuan, *Born Red: A Chronicle of the Cultural Revolution* (Stanford, CA: Stanford University Press, 1987); and Carolyn Wakeman and Yue Daiyun, *To the Storm: The Odyssey of a Revolutionary Chinese Woman* (Berkeley: University of California Press, 1987). Orville Schell's *Discos and Democracy: China in the Throes of Reform* (New York: Pantheon Books, 1988) vividly captures both the manic excitement and creeping disillusionment that marked the first decade of reform in post-Mao China.

The complex, enigmatic modern history of Tibet is made readily accessible in Patrick French's lively narrative, *Tibet, Tibet: A Personal History of a Lost Land* (New York: Alfred A. Knopf, 2003).

Finally, five recent books by China-based journalists provide deep insight into the struggles of ordinary Chinese attempting to deal with a rapidly changing socio-economic and political environment in post-reform China: Seth Faison, *South of the Clouds: Exploring the Hidden Realms of China* (New York: St. Martin's Press, 2004); Ian Johnson, *Wild Grass: Three Stories of Change in Modern China* (New York: Pantheon Books, 2004); John Pomfret, *Chinese Lessons: Five Classmates and the Story of New China* (New York: Henry Holt, 2006); and Philip Pan, *Out of Mao's Shadow: The Struggle for the Soul of a New China* (New York: Simon & Schuster, 2008); and Rob Gifford, *China Road* (New York: Random House, 2007).

For those interested in more intensive scholarly analyses of the dynamics of Chinese society and politics under Communism, I also recommend the following works (in alphabetical order):

Esherick, Joseph W., Paul Pickowicz, and Andrew Walder, eds. 2006. *China's Cultural Revolution as History.* Stanford, CA: Stanford University Press.
   Based on newly available research materials, this superb collection of essays on the dynamics of Mao's Last Revolution sheds fresh light on the traumatic imprint of the Cultural Revolution on the lives of ordinary Chinese.
Fewsmith, Joseph. 2008. *China since Tiananmen: The Politics of Transition.* 2nd ed. Cambridge and New York: Cambridge University Press.
   A lucid analysis of the complex economic and political crosscurrents of post-Tiananmen China. The reign of Jiang Zemin and Hu Jintao is examined against a backdrop marked by the erosion of Communist ideology and the regime's efforts to adapt to the constraints of modernization and globalization.
Friedman, Edward, Paul Pickowicz, and Mark Selden. 1991. *Chinese Village, Socialist State.* New Haven, CT: Yale University Press.
———. 2005. *Revolution, Resistance, and Reform in Village China.* New Haven, CT: Yale University Press.
   Based on collaborative fieldwork in a North China village over a span of two decades, these two volumes present a vivid, peasant's-eye view of Communism's impact on the Chinese countryside, from the onset of land reform, agricultural collectivization, and the Great Leap Forward in the 1950s to

the Cultural Revolution and the post-Mao market reforms of the 1980s and 1990s.

Goldman, Merle. 2005. *From Comrade to Citizen: The Struggle for Political Rights in China*. Cambridge, MA: Harvard University Press.

A sensitive analysis of the uphill struggle faced by China's intellectuals in their effort to secure an autonomous political voice and the rights of full political citizenship.

Lieberthal, Kenneth. 2003. *Governing China: Revolution through Reform*. 2nd edition. New York: W. W. Norton.

A comprehensive textbook filled with vital information about Chinese government, politics, and the Chinese Communist Party.

MacFarquhar, Roderick. 1983. *The Origins of the Cultural Revolution*. Volume 1, *Contradictions among the People, 1956–57*. New York: Columbia University Press.

———. 1987. *The Origins of the Cultural Revolution*. Volume 2, *The Great Leap Forward, 1958–60*. New York: Columbia University Press.

———. 1997. *The Origins of the Cultural Revolution*. Volume 3, *The Coming of the Cataclysm, 1961–66*. New York: Columbia University Press.

This comprehensive three-volume study of Chinese "high politics" in the trauma-filled decade from the advent of the Hundred Flowers Movement in 1957 to the onset of the Cultural Revolution in 1966 is likely to remain the definitive work on the subject for years to come.

Nathan, Andrew, and Perry Link, eds. 2001. *The Tiananmen Papers*. Compiled by Zhang Liang. New York: PublicAffairs.

Reportedly leaked to the editors by a pseudonymous mole within the CCP bureaucracy, the confidential documents in this collection provide a unique inside look at the Chinese leadership's deepest fears, and the political calculus that underlay their decision to crack down on protesting students in Tiananmen Square in 1989.

Naughton, Barry. 2007. *The Chinese Economy: Transitions and Growth*. Cambridge, MA: MIT Press.

A clearly written, comprehensive guide to Chinese economic policy and performance from 1949 to the present, with special attention to patterns of demographic growth, rural economic performance, the technological transformation of industry, and problems of environmental quality and sustainable development, inter alia.

Peerenboom, Randall. 2002. *China's Long March to the Rule of Law*. Cambridge: Cambridge University Press.

A comprehensive review and analysis of the institutional progress and problems displayed by China's legal system in the post-Mao reform era. Employing a comparative perspective, the author generally sees the glass of China's emerging legal order as half full.

Pei, Minxin. 2006. *China's Trapped Transition: The Limits of Developmental Autocracy.* Cambridge, MA: Harvard University Press.
Viewing Chinese reformers' efforts at political-institutional adaptation with a critical eye, Pei argues that in the absence of institutionalized checks on CCP power, China's post-Mao regime is doomed to founder due to inherent structural contradictions between a semi-open, marketized economy and a closed, deeply corrupted one-party state.

Saich, Tony. 2001. *Governance and Politics of China.* New York: Palgrave.
A complement to Lieberthal's 2003 textbook, Saich provides a rich and detailed assessment of the fabric of local governmental processes and state-society relations in post-reform China.

Tsai, Kellee. 2007. *Capitalism without Democracy: The Private Sector in Contemporary China.* Ithaca, NY: Cornell University Press.
Based on an extensive survey of China's "new class" of successful private entrepreneurs, the author persuasively argues that China's emerging capitalists show little inclination to promote democratic political ideas, demands, or values.

Yang, Dali. 2004. *Remaking the Chinese Leviathan: Market Transition and the Politics of Governance in China.* Stanford, CA: Stanford University Press.
Countering pessimistic predictions of an emerging legitimacy crisis in Chinese politics, Yang argues that there has emerged in China since 1989 a more sensitive, responsive, and adaptive form of authoritarianism, one that has successfully employed technocratic rather than democratic remedies to address problems of inequality and injustice, thereby bolstering the regime's political legitimacy.

Index

A

AAS (Association for Asian Studies), 58–60, 236, 289, 299
abortion, 242, 307
academic exchange programs, establishment, 85–86, 87–88, 89*f. See also* Peking University; UCLA
air pollution, 228–29, 269
Akers, Michelle, 163
All-China Women's Federation, 258
Alley, Rewi, 94–95
American Anthropological Association, 306
American Political Science Review, 250
Andors, Phyllis, 240
Andors, Stephen, 240
anti-Americanism, 158–63
Antonioni, Michelangelo, 71
Apple, R. W., Jr., 125–26
Apple Daily, 283
area studies, decline, 249–50
artists, Yuanmingyuan, 85
Asia Foundation, 234
Asian Survey, 297
Association for Asian Studies (AAS), 58–60, 236, 289, 299
automobiles, 189, 214, 228, 242, 255
Auw, David, 22–23, 26, 28, 277–78, 279*f*
Avakian, Bob, 241

B

Babaoshan State Cemetery, 278, 280
Baker, James, 118–19, 121
Banff conference, 52–54, 290, 298–99
banking activity, 225, 292–93
Baptist University, Hong Kong, 168
Barnett, A. Doak, 52–54, 232, 243
basketball, 16–17, 61–62, 70–71, 299
Baum, Carolyn, 4, 11, 14–16, 30, 34, 35, 36, 47, 54–55, 118, 288
Baum, Jeeyang, 289
Baum, Kristen, 36, 54, 118, 289
Baum, Matthew, 11, 14–16, 30, 34, 47, 54, 118, 288–89
BBC World Service, 165
Before the Flood (film), 210
Beida. *See* Peking University

U

V

W

CPSIA information can be obtained
at www.ICGtesting.com
Printed in the USA
BVHW07s0459241018
530958BV00002B/11/P